D0966723

Theism
in the Discourse
of Jonathan Edwards

Theism
in the Discourse
of Jonathan Edwards

R. C. De Prospo

Newark: University of Delaware Press
London and Toronto: Associated University Presses

©1985 by Associated University Presses, Inc.

Associated University Presses
440 Forsgate Drive
Cranbury, NJ 08512

Associated University Presses
25 Sicilian Avenue
London WC1A 2QH, England

Associated University Presses
2133 Royal Windsor Drive
Unit 1
Mississauga, Ontario
Canada L5J 1K5

The paper used in this publication meets the minimum requirements of the American National Standard for Permanence of Paper for Printed Library Materials Z39.48-1984.

Library of Congress Cataloging in Publication Data

De Prospo, R. C., 1949–
   Theism in the discourse of Jonathan Edwards.

   Bibliography: p.
   Includes index.
   1. Theism—History of doctrines—18th century.
2. Edwards, Jonathan, 1703–1758.   I. Title.
BT100.E32D4   1985   230'.58'0924   84-40406
ISBN 0-87413-281-9 (alk. paper)

Printed in the United States of America

CONTENTS

Theism
in the Discourse
of Jonathan Edwards

Indeed, some of these new writers, at the same time that they have represented the doctrines of these ancient and eminent divines as in the highest degree ridiculous, and contrary to common sense, in an ostentation of a very generous charity, have allowed that they were honest, well-meaning men; yea, it may be, some of them, as though it were in great condescension and compassion to them, have allowed that they did pretty well for the day in which they lived, and considering the great disadvantages they labored under; when at the same time, their manner of speaking has naturally and plainly suggested to the minds of their readers, that they were persons, who, through the lowness of their genius, and greatness of the bigotry with which their minds were shackled and thoughts confined, living in the gloomy caves of superstition, fondly embraced and demurely and zealously taught the most absurd, silly, and monstrous opinions, worthy of the greatest contempt of gentlemen possessed of that noble and generous freedom of thought, which happily prevails in this age of light and inquiry.

Edwards, *Freedom of the Will*

1
THE PHENOMENON OF JONATHAN EDWARDS

> Our cause is indeed extremely unhappy, if we have such a
> book to be our grand and only rule, our light and directory,
> that is so exceeding perplexed, dark, paradoxical and hid-
> den, everywhere in the manner of expression, as the scrip-
> tures must be, to make them consistent with Arminian
> opinions; by whatever means this has come to pass,
> whether through the distance of ages, diversity of customs,
> or by any other cause.
> —Edwards, "Miscellaneous Remarks"

1. Introduction

It can hardly be that the modern scholars of Jonathan Edwards are all
wrong; it can hardly be that Haroutunian, Winslow, Miller, Faust, and
Johnson, and later Heimert, Holbrook, Shea, and Delattre, and most recently Tracy and Fiering, and others, miss even a single important insight
about the Edwards who for all of them, to varying degrees, is produced by
Puritan and Enlightened traditions, or that additional study of Edwards as
a product of these traditions can do more than refine or qualify, or add
support to an established position in an established scholarly controversy,
or test established views against new materials, some of the as-yet-
unpublished manuscripts by Edwards that continue slowly to trickle out of
the Beinecke Library at Yale. About Edwards as the child of early American
culture there is clearly very little left to say.

It may be, however, that virtually everything is still to be said about the
modernism of the modern American scholarship of Edward's writings, and
maybe of American literature generally, because it may be that in their very
concentration on Edwards and other American writers, modern scholars
fail to perceive themselves or their method. What remains to be done is not
to supplement interpretations of Edwards as the scion of Puritanism or of

the Enlightenment or of Lockean idealism or of the eighteenth-century Connecticut River Valley, but to locate his provenance differently, in none of these supposed nurseries of modern culture in America but in modern interpretations themselves. So to define the phenomenon of Edwards is in effect to change the subject, which in effect opens a field that awaits not another study of Edwards but the first one. The following reading will be an attempt to interpret the interpretations that do more than just explain but create Edwards, an attempt to interpret phenomenologically not only his writings but the modern readings of his writings that collectively, equally, comprise the current text of his works.

Because a phenomenology of Edwards must comprehend so much, even those modern commentaries which appear only distantly related, such as modern commentaries on Puritanism, it will seem a long time getting to the point, and digressive after getting there—at least to a perspective that defines the point as just Edwards's writings; or, more generously, just Edwards's writings and other, apposite eighteenth-century American writings; or, most generously, these plus the modern scholarship of Edwards. It may also appear unusually contentious in striving continually to expose unacknowledged implications in the work of modern scholars. It will almost certainly appear stylistically dense, and perhaps overly ambitious substantively as well, trying as it will to remain continuously and explicitly cognizant both of its method, even while in the act of interpreting, and of its ultimate goal to remodel the whole corpus of American literature, even while scrutinizing details that may seem relevant only to Edwards's writings.

But because the background of the current text of Edwards's writings is identified phenomenologically as modernism, a phenomenology that opens with an interpretation of modern American cultural historiography and that refers continually to this historiography begins precisely at the beginning and keeps precisely to the point. Although so expansive a definition of the subject is rare in modern American literary studies, it is rather common in phenomenological studies of other than American writers, even in some by American scholars, such as, for example, Geoffrey Hartman's of Wordsworth or J. Hillis Miller's of Thomas Hardy, and has even been applied to American writers, though generally by foreign-born critics who specialize in foreign literatures, such as in Shoshana Felman's recent analysis of Henry James; two American critics of American literature who are attempting currently to deconstruct the modernism of American literature, along with that of the modern criticism of American literature, are John Carlos Rowe and Paul Armstrong. The contentiousness of this reading is admittedly more than simply apparent, although the subject here does differ significantly from that of other modern studies of Edwards and thus confronts them only obliquely, and although the final effect of this reading may be to further the ambition of modern American cultural historiography to incorporate all American culture within some coherent whole, a reconciliation that will be speculated upon more fully at the end of this chapter. But a lack of theoretical sophistication is notorious in literary studies, is especially acute in American scholarship, and is becoming apparent even to some modern American intellectual historians, those who conclude—as recently reported in a different context by Lawrence Veysey—that at least the earliest modern American cultural historians must now be demoted from guides to "fascinating primary sources, reflecting, often poignantly, the beliefs and attitudes of some early twentieth-century American academics." In referring, repeatedly, critically, and at length, to many early modern scholars of American culture who are seldom mentioned any more in contemporary scholarship, this reading will assume, first, that they are, indeed, "primary sources" and thus not at all negligible (which seems to be Veysey's point) but worthy of the same special attention usually reserved only for the "primary sources" of imaginative literature or of "raw data," and, second, that the lack of reference to them in contemporary scholarship signifies not a maturity that can confidently take the founders for granted, but an unself-consciousness that fails to recognize continuing indebtedness to the founders. As for stylistic difficulties, phenomenological analyses have always put unusual strains on common usage because they aspire to make manifest modernist assumptions that hide not only in the large structures of whole arguments and philosophies but also in the small structures of diction and phrasing. Heidegger feels obliged in the introduction to *Being and Time* to apologize for the "awkwardness and 'inelegance' of expression" necessitated by the task of doing more than just speaking "about *entitities*"—the task of grasping "entities in their *Being*." Derrida more recently and more brazenly announces that deconstruction is expressed in a "simultaneously faithful and violent circulation between the inside and the outside" of modern discourse, a kind of criticism that is inevitably "interested in itself" while criticizing modern discourse, and that produces in this self-reference a "certain textual work that gives great pleasure." The present reading of Edwards's writings will try, more modestly, to maintain reflexiveness without the use of too much specialized terminology, which is particularly incongruous to the relatively plain style of most American literary studies, although such restraint will tend to lengthen exposition, specialized terminology being, after all, a technique of compression[1]

Finally, the tendency to expand from Edwards's writings to the corpus of American literature is an entirely conventional technique, being merely the scholarly application of the romantic figure of synecdoche, which is really only a species of symbolism, used commonly not only in phenomenological criticism, such as in Derrida's finding—in addition to "something irreducibly Rousseauist" in Rousseau's writings—"a yet quite unformed mass of roots, soil, and sediments of all sorts" that connects Rousseau to a whole pattern of discourse; as in Michael Riffaterre's accomplishing a whole theory of textuality from the close readings of several lyric poems; as in Tzvetan Todorov's letting the modernism of a particular national literature stand for that of the entire Western World; and as in Northrop Frye's wholly practical reminder that given the limitation to a single lifetime "if we wait for a truly qualified critic to tackle" broad subjects with a commensurately broad reading "we shall wait a long time." But the synecdochic technique occurs also in many, less theoretical modern American studies of individual American writers that find in them the makings of representative men. Some of the best examples of these are of course modern studies of Jonathan Edwards; although the technique of studying Edwards rhetorically to comprehend a great deal more than just Edwards may be common, the technique will be practiced with unusual self-consciousness in this reading, and the whole that the part is seen to embody will differ structurally from that commonly extrapolated by modern American cultural historians.[2]

What may be most forbidding about this reading is the appearance of being yet another terrorist attack undertaken on behalf of "structuralism" or "poststructuralism" or "deconstructionism." Although there are fields today in which a large number of scholars will automatically applaud such measures as performed on behalf of methodological liberation, as emanating from some literary-critical equivalent of Protestant Geneva (today it may actually be Paris), modern American cultural historiography is certainly not such a field. Modern American cultural historians are much more likely automatically to condemn such measures as planned in some literary-critical equivalent of Moscow or Havana, or maybe even Tehran—to condemn, that is, if they can trace the origin of such measures at all.

References to Heidegger and Derrida *et al.* are therefore made to achieve clarity, not certification, at least not of any kind of status that modern American cultural historiography considers worth having. As Husserl writes in a letter, only some inner compulsion can lead to the practice of phenomenology in the German University of the turn of the century, "the things themselves [having] gained such power over me that I could not do otherwise." So, eighty-odd years later, a phenomenology of Edwards is no appeal for preferment or approval within modern American cultural historiography, which has still to reach that maturity evaluated by Heidegger according to "how far [a field] is capable of a crisis in its basic concepts."[3]

2. Theism

Theism will be defined in this reading as a discursive pattern that is based on the ultimate duality between Creator and Creation and that continues indefinitely to generate hierarchical duplicities. The duality of theist discourse is fatal, capable of merging into unity at no time, in no place, according to no perspective; the otherness of God and the differences between Him and His creatures are within theist discourse, neither apparent nor provisional but absolutely true. They are not only fundamental and irrevocable but glorious and consolatory; they are not a regrettable diminution of man's understanding and enjoyment of God but a discursive foundation of theology and an emotional basis for worship, a condition that makes religious discourse, as well as discourse of other kinds, possible. Divinity and humanity, spirit and flesh, virtue and sin—all are upheld by theism not transiently, until the Fall and the defects of fallen consciousness can be overcome, but forever. They are to be considered statements of the eternal truth applied to various parts of Creation.

The central problem of theism is not that reality is divided, but that men have to live in a world with a perception that cannot be relied upon to indicate the divisions. This is a problem that is not, even ideally, solved by fusion, which in theist discourse is both impious and incredible. It is solved instead by final, unmistakable segregation of the two sides, the glimpse of which is the visionary delight of saints in this life, the full knowledge of which will be their reward in the next, the final manifestation of which will be the end of the world. Defined in this way, theist discourse may be said to constitute Christian writing from the early Church Fathers to American Puritans, uniting them in expressions of the dualism of truth and experience which vary so insignificantly that Augustine speaks for Edwards when lamenting that truth and experience will remain "entangled together in this world, and intermixed until the judgment effect their separation."[4]

But theism can be said to be broader still, including Puritanism and Protestantism, and Christianity, and "free"-thinking—even the most "enlightened" and agnostic—and even the atheism of a discursive pattern that differs from the humanist one, first articulated in romantic writings, in which Creator and Creation are joined in what is now spoken of as nature. Taken thus to be the condition of all discourse that is not humanist, the presence of theism in the writings of Jonathan Edwards is peculiar neither to them nor to their immediate, or even their extended, circumstantial, chronological, or cultural environs. It is well and consistently expressed in them, and it has accordingly come to be misread, in the necessary and creative sense of *misprision*, with unusual thoroughness and subtlety in humanist interpretation, which is why Edwards's writings have here been chosen as the particular oeuvre through which to expose it. What in the context of theist discourse like Edwards's is an arrangement of absolute duplicities is, in that of humanist discourse, a series of dialectical contradictions; what functions within theism as the bedrock of divine sovereignty becomes within humanism the unstable ground from which man rises, the site from which grows a modern discourse simply unutterable within theism. The reading that follows will be of Edwards's writings as a particularly revealing phenomenon of this transformation.[5]

The word *theism* is chosen because it is—relatively—at least in current literary studies and especially in American literary studies—"terminologically unspent" in Husserl's phrase, having relatively little familiar denotative content, like Heidegger's coinages from the Greek, approaching the hypothetically perfect unequivocalness of the pure seme that has been called by more recent phenomenological linguists "degree zero." Philology shows *theism* actually to have been overspent, having been (ab)used so freely as to possess the stigma (or the distinction)—rare in diction but, interestingly, rather less so in religious terminology—of being its own antonym. For certain seventeenth- and eighteenth-century writers *theism* denotes, both negatively and positively, avant-garde tendencies toward natural religion: Descartes is called a "mechanic theist" by a commentator at the end of the seventeenth century; Rousseau celebrates theism as the equivalent of deism; and Kant identifies it similarly as a more reasonable (in the higher, Kantian sense of reason) corrective to obscurantist theolatry. But for other writers, at these times and later, *theism* denotes precisely the opposite, the belief in revelation and the rejection of polytheism, pantheism, and deism. In modern theology and modern histories of religion *theism* tends simply to be contrasted with atheism and other rejections of monotheism throughout all religious history. But this superfluity of significations, especially of antonymous ones, can be seen to be self-annihilating, too many overdeterminations becoming ultimately an absence of determination, so that *theism* seems at last more available a signifier than other, better-known terms like *Puritanism* or *classicism* or *medievalism*. In order to specialize the use of *theism* in this reading, the term's use must be distinguished only from the usage common among modern theologians. Notwithstanding a recent title, there is no possibility for such a phenomenon as "the new theism," or even "current theism," in humanist discourse, and to specify a separate, premodern category of theism as "classical" or "traditional," as recent studies have done, represents an unwitting pleonasm. *Theism* as defined here is systemically other than modern.[6]

The discursive pattern—theist, humanist, or whatever its center—is meant to categorize discourse in the way that various phenomenological units have categorized various groupings of semiotic phenomena. Its status is entirely heuristic and conventional, and its value is measured by no criterion other than its ability to organize literary phenomena. The discursive pattern hereby acquires a privilege, one that is as controversial in modernism generally as the method that produces it, and one that might seem extravagant in the narrow realm of modern American literary studies. The privilege may be stated as that of extending itself as far as the coherence and abstractness of its structure permits; it does not weaken incrementally by extending over more discourse and more time but remains strong as long as it restricts its claim to manifesting only phenomenological, rather than "factual" or "objective" regularities. Conversely, no discursive pattern is necessarily strongest when joining writings that happen to share "factual" or "objective" affinities, such as chronological or cultural or intentional ones, which are irrelevant to discursive identity and which often obscure discursive difference. The discursive pattern is thus theoretically shielded from the sort of empiricist skepticism that so often meets generalizations, especially those which propose the existence of intellectual phenomena—"isms," pejoratively— and which are so widespread in modern American cultural historiography that even scholars who concentrate exclusively on literature—Perry Miller, for example, or, currently, Sacvan Bercovitch—are defensive and guarded and a little apologetic when stating the names of such entities as "Puritanism," whose reality is more than necessary to their studies, but which constitutes the very character of their retrospect. There will be no concessions to extraliterary factors or their partisans in this reading, no parenthetical eclecticism. Regularities among documents produced in different eras—such as those of Augustine and Edwards; and in different nations, such as those of Edwards and of Milton and Pope; and for different purposes, such as those of Edwards and of Franklin and Jefferson; and by intellectual opponents, such as those of Edwards and of the "Arminians"—are as plausible as any *gestalt* and as powerful as they can be made to appear structurally consistent.[7]

That such generalizations are essential has up to now only been implied in American literary studies, their statement characteristically being hedged, or occasional, or tentative. See, for example, Bercovitch's heavily qualified insistence in the opening of *The American Jeremiad* that there must finally be some such entity as Puritanism, and, later in that book, more powerfully but still not generally enough, that a "figural frame of mind" becomes so pervasive in nineteenth-century American discourse that it converts dissent into "variations on a theme" and exacts "unmatched ideological consensus." Or see Ernest Lowrie's similar, hesitant claim, in the opening of *The Shape of the Puritan Mind, The Thought of Samuel Willard* (1974), that sufficient consensus exists at least among sixteenth- and seventeenth-century radical Protestants to make his title meaningful. Or see Norman Fiering's cautious conclusion in *Jonathan Edwards's Moral Thought and Its British Context* (1981) that intellectual agreement exists at least among those major seventeenth- and eighteenth-century thinkers who are aware of one another's work. Or see James Davidson's fleeting surmise in the opening of *The Logic of Millennial Thought* (1977) that eighteenth-century New England might be closer religiously to first-century Asia Minor than it is to twentieth-century America. The English religious

historian John Coolidge's introductory comment on the reality of international Puritanism in *The Pauline Renaissance* (1970) is more confident, asserting that the Bible has come to seem to the latest biblical scholars much
more consistent than to some modern American scholars of Puritanism,
such as Herbert Schneider, to whom the Bible is so protean as to "sanction
anything at all," and also asserting that Puritanism follows the Bible almost
as closely as Puritans hope, hinting that some single phenomenon might
comprehend even more than just sixteenth- and seventeenth-century Protestant discourse. Modern phenomenological studies are of course polemical in the devising of large categories for the documents of the past, the
late Michel Foucault's *epistemes* having become famous, or infamous,
enough to be provoking some discussion among American intellectual
historians, which is acknowledged by David Hollinger's essay in the recent
collection, *New Directions in American Intellectual History* (1979), as have the
mentalités of the French *annales* historians, and the paradigms of T. S. Kuhn,
and even, though to a lesser extent, the metasemiotic units devised by
Derrida to collect whole archives of texts, which he calls the systems or
patterns of language, and whose primary example is *logocentrism.* Less well
known but analogous categories are Ferdinand De Saussure's hypothetically synchronic *"state"* of a language in the ideal condition of perfect stabil-
ity; the *"topos"* proposed by Ernst Robert Curtius as a stylistic constant that
unifies texts beyond the ability of texts to explicate; and what Lucien Goldman has recently distinguished from both the conscious and unconscious
as the *implicit* or the *nonconscious* that achieves the deep self-determination
of texts, the character and agency of which texts are necessarily unable to
declare. *Discursive pattern* is another name for this basic unit of
phenomenological analysis. In concentrating entirely on identifying a
theist discursive pattern in American literature this reading risks offending
not just modernism in general, which is accustomed by now to the irritant
of phenomenology, but modern American literary scholarship in particular,
which is as yet hardened only to modest, unself-conscious versions of
phenomenological classification.[8]

This risk is more than a liability incurred after the existence of theism has
been proposed; it inheres in the origin of the proposition and must be run
repeatedly in order to keep the proposition alive. The discursive pattern is
not the one "thing" that, lying, sleeping, hidden, or otherwise unknown in
Edwards's writings or anywhere else, escapes phenomenological analysis.
Nor is it descended positivistically from phenomenological analyses like
those acknowledged above. Its being depends entirely, from within the
context of modern American literary studies, on its difference from other
categories produced by another type of analysis that must, at least potentially, be as coherent as the one being described here. The reality of the
latter and of all its applications depends symbiotically on the reality of the
former, to which it must continually refer in order to define itself. Thus is

theism no new "thing" stumbled upon while perusing disinterestedly and empirically the record of early American culture, no "discovery" according to modern usage; nor has the "real" Edwards, whose existence has already been doubted by one of his modern scholars, been discriminated from among the many false ones begotten either by his own vagaries of those of his critics. Thus is a phenomenology of theist discourse no restoration of an original anachronism, nor is a phenomenology of Edwards's writings a "factual" rebuttal to modernist error or distortion. The current phenomena of early American literature and of Edwards are not just empirically contested by collecting the original documents and those acknowledged explicitly by them as antecedents, since even such apparently minimal arranging of the record reconstitutes the record according to the interests implicit in the arrangement.[9]

Readings are accomplished through the application of techniques that are discursively partial, through the asking of the only kinds of questions that can be posed—the only questions possible, within a particular discursive pattern, that are answerable ones, ones liable or even destined to be answered. And readings only pretend, as a rhetorical disguise for their partiality, to be neutral or "objective." So to say that the early American literature of today and that the Edwards of today are the creations of modern scholarship represents only a reminder. This reading will try to be mindful of this partiality, and of its own, and thus to revise the past, which revision requires the frequent and explicit positing of an other vision, and thus to create its own Edwards, which incarnation requires the frequent and explicit positing of another Edwards. Claiming only the impure motive to subject Edwards to another form of modernist imperialism, fighting openly on its own, not Edwards's, behalf, it will refer negatively to modern American cultural historiography almost as often as it refers positively to Edwards's writings. A purely methodological version of the "protestantism *à outrance*," the intrinsic difference that Emerson ascribes to Thoreau, is accepted—for better or worse, Emerson's eulogy containing both about equally—as a motto of this reading: "he did not feel himself except in opposition. He wanted a fallacy to expose, a blunder to pillory . . . ."[10]

3. The Genealogy of "America"

Edwards's place in the history of American religion is a matter of interest even before his death in 1758, and it remains one throughout the nineteenth century for segments of the Protestant intellectual and religious communities. The early Edwardseans try hard to acclimate their mentor's theology to the religious controversies that arise in the late eighteenth and early nineteenth centuries. Nineteenth-century American romantics, of various calibers and vocations, hail the parts of Edwards's life and works that they feel can be reconciled with their own. William Ellery Channing believes Edwards to be a mystic beneath his Calvinist bibliolatry and calls Edwards's personal narrative "one of the most pathetic and beautiful sketches ever given of the deeper workings of the soul," reputedly with tears in his eyes. George Bancroft comments that as a historian Edwards, despite being inhibited by "perverting and cramping theological forms," anticipates the humanist emphasis of later romantic historians like himself. Harriet Beecher Stowe praises Edwards for having helped to instill a "climate of questioning" that bears fruit in the liberated speculations of Emerson and Theodore Parker. Early romantic opinion establishes the criteria according to which Edwards is evaluated by modern scholarship. His thought seems to contain both antiquated and forward-looking aspects. The debate is, and continues to be, over which is more significant to his thinking.[11]

An apparently fatigued commentator on Edwards recently begins an essay by stipulating that Edwards's modernity is a "dead issue." This might be welcome, but it is not true, not just because the ingenuity and ambition of modern scholars will continue to revive the issue, but because modernity, whether wholly, partly, or nowhere present in Edwards's writings, has become essential to the positioning of Edwards in American cultural history. The very lack of consensus, the very interminability of the debate, is what shows the vitality, indeed, the necessity, of the issue, which, far from having become irrelevant, has become indistinguishable from Edwards's identity. The continuing interest of modern scholars in Edwards has a continually modernizing effect, whose impact becomes broader and simpler as the interest filters down to the perennial anthologizing of about the same medley of short works and excerpts from long ones—namely, "Sinners in the Hand of an Angry God," a large part or all of the "personal narrative," perhaps a few entries from Miller's selection from Edwards's notebooks, *Images or Shadows of Divine Things*, and, in the longer anthologies, perhaps excerpts from the *Treatise on Religious Affections* and *The Nature of True Virtue*, all chosen to demonstrate together the coexistence of themes of general, which is to say, modern, interest with those of only antiquarian interest, which are of course less fully represented, the curious and marked contrast between which is invariably a topic of any introduction to a selection from Edwards's writings. No matter how variously or complexly defined or evaluated, inconsistency, measured against some specific or general standard of modernism, is, to every level of modern hindsight, from the most to the least sophisticated, the condition of Edwards's writings.[12]

The presence of such unanimity in the modern perception of Edwards (or of anything else) constitutes a single phenomenon, the phenomenology of which analyzes not the "object" but the process of perception. This process does not derive from, but imposes upon Edwards's writings to create the phenomenon of Edwards, who in none other than the least examined, neoromantic, genealogies is the author of his own image. A phenomenological reading of Edwards must begin, therefore, certainly not with the writings of Edwards, nor even with those of Edwards's modern scholars, whose writings represent only a narrow application of a discursive pattern, nor with those of modern American cultural historians of early America, who are also, a bit more generally, practicing a discourse on a particular subject, but with the origins of the modern discursive pattern itself. This origin is to be found not even in the United States but abroad, in the first romantic writings in Europe and in the earliest neoromantic commentaries on them. To back up and away so far may seem like a parody of the conventional "review of the literature." Phenomenologically, it is not the preface but the subject proper. The phenomenon of Edwards cannot be understood prior to an understanding of that of modernism.

"America" is not born in Puritan New England, nor in Cavalier Virginia, nor in Revolutionary Pennsylvania, nor in Protestant England or Renaissance Europe, and neither are these cultures born in the eighteenth, seventeenth, sixteenth, or fifteenth centuries—unless, to put an end to this phenomenological reduction, chronology itself is understood as a phenomenon of retrospect. All originate in modern historiography, which originates in romantic discourse and which includes as belated applications of the modern discursive pattern the writings of Tyler, Rourke, Parrington, Miller, Van Doren, Curti, and all the other first modern scholars of early American culture. To seek the origin of "America" as an "objective" reality deeply imbedded in the past is to be comprehended by modern American cultural historiography. To study early American culture as a product of modernism is to practice a phenomenology that can comprehend both.

Much of the latest scholarship of early American culture prides itself on having gone beyond, even having rejected, the simplifications of "consensus" social history or what David Hollinger has called the "myth and symbol" school of cultural history. In a recent review essay in *American Quarterly* Daniel Howe comments that Bercovitch's *The American Jeremiad* "is an unfashionable book. It reminds one of those writings of the 1950's that undertook to capture the essence of the American Experience by looking carefully at selected literary sources, without always specifying clearly the social reference of those sources. During the 1960's and 1970's this approach came under severe criticism." Here is the kind of environmentalist criticism that American literary and intellectual historians take to heart and that makes them so insecure and inconsistent. Howe's review accurately summarizes the program of the 1950s, although it is shortsighted in implying that the program originates in the 1950s; the effort of professional scholars to generalize an "American Experience," whether belletristically or in interdisciplinary ways, dates back at least to the 1920s, and the conception that there can be such a phenomenon as a national experience occurs earlier, in the earliest romantic historiography, in Emerson and Bancroft and Parkman in the United States and in Hume and Gibbon and Hegel and Tocqueville in Europe. Howe's review also accurately reflects the scholarly climate of the 1960s and the generally patronizing way that many contemporary scholars view the Americanists of what seems to them a less exacting and less advanced period in American scholarship.[13]

But Howe is wrong about the currency of Bercovitch's book because he seems unconscious of the underlying, and still virtually invisible connection between the founders of modern American cultural historiography and the most apparently independent scholars among their descendants. What makes Bercovitch's book exceptional is not its unusual backwardness but its unusual acknowledgment of a theoretical foundation that continues to support modern American cultural historiography, the more firmly and pervasively for being seldom noticed or admitted. Bercovitch is unfashionably cognizant of and explicit about the ubiquity of ideology in American culture, including American scholarly culture, and so he threatens empiricists like Howe with exposure as secret, or, worse, unwitting ideologues. To suppose that modern American cultural historiography, especially that of the early culture, is highly evolved—as do such prominent scholars as Sidney Ahlstrom and Edmund Morgan, and, most recently, Emory Elliott, to whom "the historiography of early New England has in the past forty years reached a level of sophistication unmatched in the study of any other part of American history"—is an extremely vulnerable position from the phenomenological perspective, to which the field seems methodologically very primitive.[14]

This deficiency might be represented by two recent books, both of which are ambitious, well-funded, and favorably reviewed. One of them practices a pansexual caricature of psychohistoriography according to which oedipal rage accounts, directly, for the belligerence of early American evangelicals on the one hand and, indirectly, for the pacifism of early American Quakers on the other—just the kind of promiscuous explanation that enemies of psychohistoriographical methods have to fabricate when not lucky enough to find a real example like this one. The other conceives of literary influence as the organic propagation of ideas through reading, a neopositivism that may be forgivable when practiced by Parrington in the 1920s but that is a subject of derision for Roland Barthes in the 1960s. Roman Ingarden and other early phenomenologists of reading have been replacing this neopositivism with much more complex transactions between readers and texts even before the 1960s, and J. L. Austin, Wolfgang Iser, Norman Holland, Stanley Fish, and a host of modern theorists of reading have been busy deconstructing it for the past twenty years. Contemporary theorists like Harold Bloom and the late Paul de Man hardly even bother mentioning it any longer.[15]

What modern American cultural historians can genuinely take pride in is not the maturity but rather the cohesiveness of the field, although the establishment is shrewdly self-effacing. To suppose that no position in American scholarship is powerful enough to provoke a coherent opposition (as a scholar friendly to phenomenological methods recently and somewhat wistfully has) is to be taken in by the apparent disorganization of scholarship in the United States. That the potency of an American ideology may paradoxically be attributable to the seeming nonentity of any unified American ideology is suspected by Bercovitch, although he has not yet quite identified the cause of his unease nor yet quite freed himself sufficiently to deconstruct American ideology. The paranoia that scholars are so apt to feel for hidden powers outside the academy, or inside only in the administrations of academies, might profitably be redirected at conspiracies closer to home.[16]

What is the genealogy of "America"? and why might this question be a critical one—that is, neither too easily answered to be worth asking, nor too simplistic, in supposing that there is a single genealogy, to be answerable? The question alludes of course to Nietszche, and implies that there might be something as unsavory in the beginnings of "America" as the etymological fraud claimed by Nietszche in the development of morals, and implies that the phenomenology of "America" might well be as intricately paradoxical as that traced by Nietszche in Western ethics. Modernism according to Nietszche's philology transforms medieval caste distinctions into modern ethical ones, wealth into nobility, and poverty into wickedness. Certainly modern American cultural historiography can similarly be revealed as having transformed the strange distinctions of early American discourse into inchoate forms of familiar, modern ones, and as having condescended to early American culture as to a backward, feeble, parent, thus legitimizing the hegemony of modernism by the subtle means of absorbing, with apparent deference, an alien culture. The child, according to the philosophical pedophilia that romanticism bequeathes to all modern etiologies, is thus made father to the man.

That unanimous suppositions are by definition unself-conscious, that they appear, when they appear at all, in the disguise of one (and usually not a prominent one) among a variety of positions, is an insight that occurs throughout phenomenological analyses. Nietszche's *Genealogy of Morals* begins by stating that "we *must* mistake ourselves" as the necessary, paradoxical condition of remaining ascendent as arbiters of right and truth. Heidegger states the paradox similarly, if a great deal more technically, in *Being and Time*, and also at the outset; the "self-evidence" with which what Heidegger calls *Dasein*, in this context no more than modern consciousness, takes itself to be descended from "tradition" constitutes a self-delusion whose pretense is necessarily "covered up" by modern consciousness in the very process of tracing its descent. The lesser-known phenomenologist Adolph Reinach phrases the paradox more simply as the irony according to which what is taken to be "self-explanatory" is rather what "has passed a thousand times and is just passing for the thousand and first time," inexplicably.[17]

In our own time and country Kuhn determines that a criterion for the strength of scientific paradigms is their capacity to conceal their tendentiousness, especially from themselves, and John O. Lyons's phenomenology of the self contends that the persistence of the conception of the individual in modern culture depends for the most part on silencing the revolutionary *éclat* with which the self is invented. Among contemporary literary theorists, Derrida says that modern histories continue to be written only due to a sustained "dissimulation" or "motivated repression" through which history manages to hide itself from itself; Todorov recalls Bertrand Russell's observation that one way a whole pattern of thinking can disguise its breadth is by pretending to itself to be a mere part of itself; and de Man notes that a discursive pattern can maintain its hold through "the curious privilege of rendering itself invisible."[18]

That "America" is a single phenomenon created by modern American cultural historiography rather than an "object" with all the potential variety of the uncomprehended world, and that modern American cultural history is being written in necessary ignorance of the assumptions that permit the writing of it, and, most controversially, that such a simple phenomenon as modern American cultural historiography exists at all, rather than a profusion of individual and collective approaches too various to be comprehended meaningfully by one name, are commonplace propositions phenomenologically. That they will probably seem incredible to most modern American cultural historians testifies phenomenologically only to the power of the paradigm, or the *episteme*, or the *topos*, or the *gestalt* that controls the field. Modern American cultural historiography can afford to confess unanimity only by becoming willing to abandon unanimity, which confession otherwise amounts to methodological suicide. No very successful modern American cultural historian should risk it.

Supposing the age of discovery for "America" to be the romantic one, and the Founding Fathers to be the romantic writers of the late eighteenth and early nineteenth centuries, the origin of "America" is correctly to be sought in a past that is not very distant temporally and not at all distant discursively, but that is not situated geographically in the English colonies, nor in the United States, nor even just in the English-speaking world. In Kant's *Critique of Pure Reason*, to take an example from one of the earliest, foreign romantic phenomenologies, the definition of thought as a continuous effort of unification states the condition necessary to the formation of "America" by modern American cultural historiography. Searching for a unitary phenomenon underlying the apparently disordered randomness of experience, thought as described by Kant succeeds—he gives as one example the consolidation of "earths" in early modern chemistry into the binary phenomenon acid and alkali, and predicts that this division will be further consolidated, as of course it is in the conception of *ph*—up to the point of conceding the possible existence of unknowable "things as such" (things-in-themselves) that escape comprehension. "America" is comparable to Kant's premonition of the conception of chemical acidity, is the product of the identical unifying labor, and is compounded by modern American cultural historians who, even more than Kant, concede the possible existence of "objects"—the "land," the "frontier"— that may affect or determine experience in ways that thought cannot precisely know, or—if reluctant to admit this limitation, as is predominantly the case in modern American cultural historiography for reasons that will be speculated upon more fully later in this chapter—that thought can pretend to know through various methodological sublimations of self-denial, such as "naturalism" or "environmentalism." The historiographical counterpart of unity is continuity, which is equally essential to the formation of "America" and equally foreign to the time, place, and discursive pattern of colonial or early national culture in North America. In Hegel's phenomenology of history, to take another early, foreign example from a romantic Founding Father, thought unifies time through the conception of the dialectic, according to which no "thing," not error, not failure, not even death, escapes the systemic whole of *Geist's* development, but contributes as "determinate negation" to "the transition . . . by which the progress through the complete succession of forms comes about of itself," to pick one of a hundred expressions of dialectical unity from *The Phenomenology of Mind.* Hegel's intention is to make continuous all culture, from the chemical restlessness that produces the first living creatures (the beginning of the *Phenomenology* can be said to preview the conception of protean "soup" devised by post-Darwinian evolutionist visionaries, which is less a sign of Hegel's prescience than of the neoromanticism of later evolutionist theory) to the political restlessness that produces Napoleon, and his quest is continued past the first decade of the nineteenth century by such successors as Husserl, whose professed disregard for Hegel does not prevent him from sharing the similar, if more modest, assumption that thought "has followed from the Renaissance up to the present an essentially unitary line of development." The ambitions of modern American cultural historians are even more modest, but similarly Hegelian. Just as ontological disparaties are resolved into the unity "America," so are temporal disparaties resolved into the continuity "America."[19]

The evidence that modern American cultural historiography is neoromantic can be made to look quite massive. Citing it is worth doing, not to convince modern American cultural historians disinclined, with good reason, to accept their kinship—phenomenologically, their position is not genuinely induced and so not susceptible to empirical refutation, since,

~~phenomenologically,~~ "fact"- or "instance"-finding or citing does not dictate but rather is dictated by the holding of positions. This evidence is made important, is in truth created, by the intent to deconstruct the field. Polemics might claim some morbidity to be festering beneath the apparent good health of modern American cultural historiography. The only legitimate claim is that a sameness begins to exist as phenomenological analysis is performed. The "discovery" of modern American cultural historiography is no more a mere finding of current research than the "discovery" of "America" is a mere finding of fifteenth-century exploration.[20]

Modern scholars of American literature are dedicated to establishing American literary independence before Norman Foerster calls them to arms in the introduction to *The Reinterpretation of American Literature;* they fight for more than a generation afterward to promote American literary nationalism, and a remarkable number continue to fight the same battle today. The commonness of this cause is evident when it is implicit—as when Matthiessen feels in *American Renaissance* that he can take nationalism for granted and concentrate on the finer point of stylistic excellence— or when it is qualified—as when Parrington insists upon, and Miller and Feidelson concede the importance of foreign "influences," and even when it is contested in such defensive minority opinions as those of Howard Mumford Jones. The persistence of the urge to define the Americanness of American literature has become not only a symptom of parochialism to scholars who pride themselves on their cosmopolitanism—see, for example, William Spengemann's work on American autobiography, and especially his scornful comment in a recent review that "American scholars have done practically nothing for the last thirty years *but* concoct autonomous traditions for our literature," and Norman Fiering's work on the international contexts for a variety of seventeenth- and eighteenth-century American writers and traditions—but an irresistible, and somewhat embarrassing reflex even to those scholars who are self-conscious enough to admit still to be governed by it—see, for example, Joseph Lynen's confession in the opening of *The Design of the Present* that "the student of American literature is more than slightly handicapped by his commitment to give greater emphasis to matters of nationality than they probably deserve, for he must somehow distinguish American writings from the English tradition," and also R. W. B. Lewis's complaint, in a review of Fidelson's *Symbolism and American Literature,* appearing at virtually the same time as Lewis's own *The American Adam,* that too much emphasis is placed by American scholars, not excluding himself, on the "big idea" that somehow gathers in all that is worthwhile and characteristically American in American cultural history.[21]

The burden of proving American cultural independence curiously persists as an obligation even into the latest scholarship. In the seventeenth and eighteenth centuries American cultural backwardness is undeniable, apologized for and exhorted against by every major early national leader, a chorus of which is collected by Constance Rourke in the beginning of "The Roots of American Culture," and in the nineteenth and early twentieth centuries American cultural backwardness remains plausible. But few circumstances since 1950 can be cited to justify the continuation of any major anxiety over this, certainly not in a significant number of professional students of American culture who have been paying attention to cultural developments since World War II. Whatever is prolonging nationalistic tendencies in modern American cultural historiography must be much more powerful than mere "facts," according to any but the most myopic view of which the tendencies seem atavistic, and not a little bit dangerous.[22]

The chronic nationalism of modern American cultural historiography need not be attributed to foreign threats or domestic insecurities; it need not be understood as historically "caused" at all, but as a fortuitous shape appropriated from the happenstance of American history by a conservatism much more fundamental than that dedicated to protecting a specific homeland from a specific danger. It can be understood as structurally consistent with the modern discursive pattern that expresses unity even through such exclusionary forms as chauvinism and the many other modernist prejudices, including racism. If circumstances were prior to discourse, the precariousness of the Revolution and fledgling nationhood would have articulated an indigenous culture. That none is articulated, certainly not in the estimation of Revolutionary and early national writers, and not even in that of modern American cultural historians, to none of whom is nationalism fully articulate in early American culture, suggests another filiation for "America." That an indigenous culture begins fully to be articulated only in the mid-nineteenth century, according to a virtual consensus of both nineteenth-century American writers and their twentieth-century American commentators, suggests both the character of this other filiation and with what other phenomena "America" ought to be associated. Although American nationalism benefits from the convenience of being able to distinguish a single, unitary culture from those of Europe, it does not seem capable in its earliest form of summoning such a culture into existence. It might therefore be said to represent one of the discourses of modernism that begins in romantic writings and continues to this day. Its durability in modern American cultural historiography is remarkable primarily for revealing the origin and continuing affiliation both of scholarly and of popular modern American discourse.[23]

So the sense that has become common that American nationalism originates in the Revolutionary period, if not earlier, is not to be trusted. American nationalism does not exist, in the modern definition, in the writings produced during this time, an independent culture being expressed not by Revolutionary and early national writers but rather by participants in a later, more profound revolution than the one in 1776. Any measure of the early hopes for the future of the United States shows the preponderance to foresee only a variant, an improved one in the opinion of Patriots, of the culture of the Old World; because the realization of such an ideal depends on imported values, neither hopes for the New World nor criticism of the Old can suppose the United States headed for genuine cultural independence.

Early calls for the achievement of American literary excellence such as those collected by Rourke are voiced according to a discursive pattern that continuously resists Rourke's intent to discover an inchoate nationalistic urge, the "roots" of modern American culture, in early American writings. They define literary achievement as the refinement, according to universally accepted aesthetic principles, of the raw materials of American life, which definition precludes the possibility that American life can inspire a revolution in aesthetic principles. The many appeals during early national times for an American Shakespeare or Milton do not provide any seminal role for nationality in literary excellence; both Shakespeare and his anticipated American counterpart are primarily men of genius, secondarily men of particular countries. When faced with the likelihood that the young United States would not soon contain many gifted men of letters, early national leaders blame the immaturity of the American economy, excusing American literary aridity for the reason that the United States has yet to produce sufficient wealth to support a leisure class of poets and readers of poetry. This excuse for the actual failure to reach literary prominence reflects the same aesthetic ideal that anticipates potential success. Literary productivity in each instance is assumed to be only superficially related to place. An American Shakespeare would differ from the original only to the degree that his artistry would be exercised on a different national experience; the subjects of his art would be American, but the value of his art would be determined, again, by universal aesthetic principles. The absence of American Shakespeares reveals to patriotic eighteenth- and early nineteenth-century American writers not that American genius differs fundamentally from European, nor that American culture is fundamentally second-rate, but that the American economy cannot yet afford to sponsor for a critical mass of people the insulation from want necessary for the growth of *beaux arts* and *belles lettres*. What is ironic only to a modern retrospect is that the principles by which art is originally judged in the United States, and the conditions under which art is originally produced here, neglect the one factor that will come to be considered the most original to American culture.[24]

What is unusual about the preceding review of early American literature is not its characterization of other-than-modern attributes, which has been made many times before and which must be made at least in passing by even those modern American literary scholars who study the early literature for its proto-modern aspects, nor its emphasis on these other-than-modern characteristics, whose significance has to be reckoned (although again often only in passing) as at least quantitatively large, even by those modern scholars least interested in them. The unusualness lies rather in the review's attempt to appreciate early American literature without the condescension according to which "the Colonial Period might be dismissed entirely, so far as its actual literary product is concerned, but it must be studied nevertheless with minuteness since it was the crucible in which was evolved the America we know." Expressed thus a long time ago by Frederick Lewis Pattee, patronizing attitudes toward early American literature are not yet so dated as they might be expected to be. The novelty will be to consider that the spectacle of early American writers lamenting their failure to be original while in closest proximity to the purest form of what is supposed by modern American cultural historiography to be the very origin of indigenous American culture is produced not by any contradiction inherent in early American literature but by the difference between humanist and theist discursive patterns. The land is not that which early American discourse ironically overlooks, but that which modern American discourse secretly injects, the land having a so much lower status in the theist discursive pattern that the land can be said, comparatively, not to exist there at all.[25]

Cults of the land or of the environment are hard to distinguish from American literary nationalism, and are as persistent as nationalism in modern American cultural historiography. The two are interdependent; nationalism, seeking a force that is capable of determining a culture and that is undeniably native to America, settles on the land, some determining residue of which is preserved in both the literary and material culture after the wilderness is settled and the frontier is civilized. Although physically overrun and degraded, the land pervades the culture forever, a positive equivalent of genuine or imagined threats to nationhood and able more substantively to unify the culture of the United States as "America." But the constancy of environmentalism throughout modern American cultural historiography is no more persuasively attributable just to historical circumstances than is that of nationalism. Again, as is the case with nationalism, the conception is historically tardy, simultaneous not with the height of the environment's physical power, which must be presumed again to occur in Colonial and early national culture, but with the rise in the nineteenth century of the modern discursive pattern.

The environmentalism of modern American cultural historiography can be seen to represent a basic orientation that contains, but is not restricted to or initiated by the self-conscious method whose invention is conventionally ascribed to Frederick Jackson Turner and associated with such orthodox advocates as Walter Prescott Webb and such later "myth and symbol" theorists as Henry Nash Smith. Environmentalism of the type applied to American culture and made popular by Turner is widespread in earlier romantic historiography, both in the United States and abroad; Bancroft says that "even [Pilgrim] children caught the spirit of the place" in the Cape Cod wilderness, and that early Virginians "unaided by an active press . . . learned from nature what others caught from philosophy." Francis Parkman later notes a similarly naturalizing effect of what is to him and, later, to Webb and numerous American environmentalists of the nineteenth and twentieth centuries, the prototypically American environment of the nineteenth century, the prairie, twice anticipating Turner's surmise that in encounters with the frontier mankind reverts to his original, precivilized state. And Tocqueville expresses throughout *Democracy in America* the presence of a causal link between the land and the American people, in one passage adumbrating the "frontier hypothesis" in prophesying that although the east is "the cradle of the English colonies" and will remain for a time the "center of power . . . to the west of it the true elements of the great people to whom the future control of the continent belongs are gathering together almost in secrecy." Van Wyck Brooks is no doctrinaire environmentalist, is, rather, methodically eclectic, but his anti-intellectualism does not prevent him from dignifying American letters as a form of *"heimatkunst"* inspired directly by the homeland. Perry Miller has the reputation of concentrating exclusively on the intellect in early American culture, but he is continually respectful of the influence of the environment, as has been pointed out in several recent revaluations of his scholarship. Miller conceives American Puritanism as an interplay between ideology and circumstance, as for example in his central conception of the peculiarly American character of the jeremiad, and of the peculiarly American character of Puritanism as a whole, which Miller concludes late in his career to have been created not so much by ideology as by circumstance, "the wilderness [taking] over the task of defining the objective of the Puritan errand." Matthiessen's belletrism is frequently punctuated by environmentalist commentaries, such as that the profusion of exotic "things" encountered in a life at sea causes Melville to take heart and to an extreme the advice of a seventeenth-century English rhetorician to "find symbols everywhere," and, similarly, that American gothicism characteristically reifies European predecessors: "The notable thing about the American marvelling at the weird was that it was not the manufactured Gothic article of a 'Monk' Lewis, but something indigenous, something inescapably there." Smith, although he begins *Virgin Land* with the assertion that the myth of the land is precisely what is not to be taken for granted, immediately afterward and continually throughout the book takes the land for granted; in the prologue, a page after criticizing the mythology of the West, he begins practicing it, promising to "trace the impact of the West, the vacant continent beyond the frontier, on the consciousness of Americans," a hypostatizing of the land as "objective" and prior to consciousness that is indistinguishable from Turner's.[26]

Leo Marx, after tracing at length in the beginning of *The Machine in the Garden* the ancient cultural origins of the pastoral myth and its infraliterary development, proposes that the "reality" of the new world makes the myth over in the image of the American environment. Floyd Stovall, although in concentrating on literary criticism in the United States has for his subject texts one stage farther removed from the American environment than fiction or poetry or popular literature, nevertheless promises at the outset of *The Development of American Literary Criticism* that criticism written in the United States "is genuinely American" and "that it has come to be what it is through a process of growth sustained, in part at least, by the absorption of native materials." Bercovitch, contrary to the charge of "unfashionable" intellectualism, grants the environment at least as much significance as Miller does, even more significance, since in *The American Jeremiad* Bercovitch defines the jeremiad as even more open to environmental influence than Miller contends, capable in Bercovitch's account of being Americanized by mere anticipation of encounters with the land, as (according to Bercovitch) happens to the first American jeremiad, Winthrop's "A Model of Christian Charity," written while Winthrop is still on board the *Arbella*.[27]

Leslie Fiedler's absorption with the psychosexual maladjustments of the American fictional imagination is founded on the unquestioned assumption that the American novel is formed as a European genre is refashioned by "America's world of alien experience." Spengemann's internationalist perspective does not preclude the conclusion that "America creates Americans." David Laurence's appreciation of Fiering's having "set to one side the question of 'American-ness' and 'Americanization' that became so obsessive and tiresome in the 'old' intellectual history of early New England" does not prevent Laurence's intuiting nonetheless that there is, "vaguely, a common New England frame of reference easy to intuit but maddeningly difficult to give an account of without making a fool of oneself." And Richard Slotkin's very current and still very fashionable work contains a Lawrentian, mystical respect for the "mythopoeic consciousness," indistinguishable from D. H. Lawrence's "blood consciousness," which ideally just absorbs the nature of the American environment, indistinguishable in Slotkin from Lawrence's famous American "IT," and merely transcribes the experience in the few American narratives that, luckily, survive in a primitive, unretouched state. Titles resembling "The Significance of the Frontier" and "Nature's Nation" continue to emanate from major and not so major University Presses everywhere: "The Lay of the Land" (1975), "Prophetic Waters" (1977), "In The Presence of Nature" (1978), "New World, New Earth" (1979), "Discoveries, Explorers, Settlers" (1979), "The City of Nature" (1980), "Nature and Religious Imagination" (1980).[28]

Environmentalism is so thoroughly disseminated throughout modern American cultural historiography that its presence is almost impossible not to detect. It is still practiced at times with almost the freshness of a romantic historian and at times with almost Webb's epigone zealousness: "[for early Americans] natural history was patriotic in that it called attention to the unique 'productions' of the new world; the distinctive plants, animals, fossils, and minerals of the United States were a rich resource for American 'nationalism'" (1976); "[for early Americans] nature was central, and they wrote *natural* history and *natural* philosophy which challenged traditional beliefs" (1978); an early American landscape description "seems to grow in the observer's mind as he stands viewing the landscape. . . . It springs up on the spot, the urgent discovery of a traveler" (1979); no nineteenth-century American, one can "take for granted," can "escape some influence of the frontier" (1980). Environmentalism is endorsed offhand, as a gratuity paid to conventional wisdom: "In Samuel Danforth's compelling metaphor, the Puritans ran an errand into the wilderness, but the wilderness claimed them, even as they tamed it, and redefined the errand in distinctively American terms" (1976; this is not, remarkably, a quotation from Miller, but an approving summary of his work). And environmentalism is insinuated, whether deliberately or not, in what might seem unlikely contexts, such as a recent discussion of Jonathan Edwards's pastorate in which the depletion of free land around Northampton is estimated, without any explicit reference to Turner, a miniature closing of the frontier, an environmental crisis that leads, so the subtle application of Turnerian theory goes, to sufficient restlessness among young men in Northampton to make them vulnerable to the religious enthusiasm of the Great Awakening.[29]

But although the prominence of environmentalism in a variety of forms in modern American cultural historiography is immediately manifest, that environmentalism is exclusively a modernist discourse, and is not to be found in early American literature, is not at all apparent, since modern studies have been striving to indicate not only that "the wilderness masters the colonist," in Turner's phrase, or that the wilderness forces colonists "to remake their values," in Slotkin's, but also that the colonists are at least dimly aware of their conversion, are proto-environmentalists themselves. By now probably all of the passages from colonial writings and narratives of exploration that seem to reflect a recognition of nature's power to transform individuals and cultures have been collected to show that environmentalism can be found in the earliest American culture and that it increases more or less regularly forever afterward. This is Parrington's position when in the introduction to *Main Currents in American Thought* he cites Crèvecoeur's metaphor of transplantation in order not only to describe the naturalizing of European emigrants by the American environment but also to argue that one literate eighteenth-century European emigrant glimpses the process, and it is Kenneth Murdock's position when he claims that John Smith is not only democratized by the Virginia wilderness but is semi-conscious of his reformation. Further, it is Leo Marx's position in arguing that seventeenth- and eighteenth-century pastoralists are ready to add "topographical realism" to their mythmaking in light of new information about the New World, and Spengemann's when arguing that educated eighteenth-century Americans possess a conception of "Lockean environmentalism," and, most recently, Patricia Caldwell's in detecting a "marked difference in tone or feel" in American Puritan conversion narratives because the "American version of deliverance is imaginatively mediated and substantially affected by a real geographical place," to cite five examples spanning more than half a century and including scholars who cannot be identified as orthodox environmentalists in order to suggest the prevalence of the assumption not just that the environment gradually naturalizes Americans but also that environmentalism evolves in American culture concurrently.[30]

In making this claim, that its own environmentalism derives from the very beginnings of American culture, from the original progenitor, the ur-environment "America" that speaks through it and to which it gives voice, modern American cultural historiography comes closest to revealing itself, and becomes most vulnerable to a deconstruction of its genealogy that shows "America" on the contrary to be descended from it. Here modern American cultural historiography performs the maneuver for which phenomenology is most vigilant—the inadvertent, inevitable undermining of the pretense, common to all modern discourse that is not fully self-conscious, of finding an authorization external to itself. The discursive foundation of environmentalism in early American literature, on which the claim for an "objective" foundation ("America") of American culture must for the most part be based, appears to virtually any perspective not interested in finding one to be remarkably, scandalously weak. The evidence is simply not "there," or at least is so little present in the early documents themselves that the evidence of environmentalism that modernist retrospect so insists on perceiving must be sought elsewhere. This suspicion is fostered not only by the anomalousness of early documents or large parts of early documents that modern American cultural historiography chooses to ignore, but also by the anomalousness even of those that it selects.

Crèvecoeur's metaphor of transplantation can be interpreted, for example, differently from and more precisely than Parrington's reading as connoting only superficial change between European and American culture, since transplantation alters only the situation and not the genetic identity of a plant. This interpretation is not only botanically correct (according to eighteenth-century botanical standards and to modern botany as well, as long as transplantation is neither confused with nor taken as a metonymy for evolution), but is consistent with everything else Crèvecoeur says about

American culture in the rest of "What is an American?", the "letter" in which the metaphor appears, and in the rest of his *Letters from an American Farmer* (1782), which can be seen consistently to subordinate the environment as raw and formless material that negatively places limits on, but cannot determine the morphology of human culture.[31]

Such a discourse of nature is wholly alien to environmentalism. It is not a refutation, since controversy indirectly confirms the existence of the opponent. Nor is it confusion or misstatement, since error implies the latency of truth. It is another discourse entirely, one that relegates the environment expressly and at length to a status that differs from and is inferior to the central status the environment occupies in the modern discursive pattern. The subordination of nature is qualified by very little intrinsic to the corpus of early American literature, which contains countless passages describing the environment as contributing only passively and incidentally to the formation of consciousness, and so to the identity of a culture.

That the New World alters only superficially the character of man is continually declared in early secular writings that describe the land as the fallow ground to which the traditional principles of human culture might be moved, not the source of new ones. This is also declared in early religious writings that describe the land as a desert that the universal principles of Christianity might fill, not a paradise from which some natural religion might grow. When Crèvecoeur, and later Jefferson and Freneau, cite the beneficial effects of an uncultivated environment on the American yeoman, their claims are explicitly based on a belief that the fertile, as yet unimproved potential of the land discourages vice by demanding continual labor, and not—at least not explicitly—that the land actively communicates virtue. An American represents to them an example of human being fortunately situated so as to help govern man's worst instincts, a discourse of place that is hard to distinguish from that of Virgil's *Georgics*. The leaders of early Pilgrim and Puritan communities also consistently base their hopes for the New World on the environment's passive characteristics, when, infrequently, they cite the environment at all in these hopes. They consider the absence of civilized temptations in the wilderness to be the major environmental contribution to the welfare of the church.

Support for these conclusions need not be sought beyond the early American writers and documents most often included in modern anthologies: Freneau's identification in "The Rising Glory of America" and other early poems of American culture as an improved version of European culture; Jefferson's dedication, in *Notes on the State of Virginia*, to meticulous surveys of the Virginia landscape, including some of what would seem Virginia's unprecedented features, such as the "Natural Bridge," which find universal averages connecting the New World geographically and topographically to the old; Bradford's interpretation of the New World (both before and after his arrival there) as a waste place containing only hardships that would test whatever Christian resolution the Pilgrims bring with them; Winthrop's similar view that the American environment is peripheral to the realization of Providence in the Puritan venture in Massachusetts Bay; Cotton Mather's disdain for "natural histories" of the world because according to him neither the founding nor the survival of Christian communities is attributable primarily to natural causes. An enormous number of both secular and religious estimations of the environment in seventeenth- and eighteenth-century American literature agree that human nature is given, that individuals vary within known, relatively inflexible limits, and that no circumstance, no matter how unusual, can produce an original human being. The New World is revolutionary primarily to modernist retrospect; in the theist discourse of the original explorers and colonizers, the New World is more accurately called an undiscovered part of the old, which contains many examples of "howling wilderness," and the moral counterpart of "howling wilderness," in medieval times—"as late as 1386, when Grand Duke Jagello proclaimed Lithuania a Christian land . . . his more conservative subjects retreated into the forests to worship holly"—and several remained as late as the seventeenth and even the eighteenth century—"John Dury, who traveled beyond the utmost northern skirts to Sweden in 1636, wrote home to England about the colonization of North America. 'Is not there more hope to do good to Christianity in building up the waste places here and hereabout in Europe than in laying new foundations without settled ground?' he asked a New World-minded friend. Dury had good reason to wonder. Well into the eighteenth century, people in the Scandanavian Alps worshipped the Norse god Thor and honored Thursday as a holy day." The ideals of the pastoral society and of the city on the hill can, without any very strenuous interpretation, be shown to share a discursive reliance on the authority of universal laws and a subsequent discursive indifference toward the indigenous experience of the early American environment. To assert otherwise, as modern American cultural historiography continually and ingeniously maintains, is to be, in Derrida's words, "contradictorily coherent. And, as always, coherence in contradiction expresses the force of a desire."[32]

American cultural independence cannot be established nor even wished for without a basic revaluation of the environment, and this does not come until American culture is governed by the revolutionary appreciation of nature expressed in romantic discourse. Expectations of the inauguration of a national cultural tradition are thus not so old as the Colonial inclination for freedom from England, nor are they frustrated during a period of slow national growth, but are promptly fulfilled once the wish is clearly and widely articulated. Romanticism is thus a great deal more than just one among several episodes in the cultural history of the United States. It provides a discursive basis for the very existence of "America," and is (phrased, ironically, according to its own genealogical discourse) the par-

ent of "America." Without romanticism American artists can never discover inherent beauties and truths in native materials and never achieve
stature that is more than incidentally American. The leaders of American
culture in the mid-nineteenth century base their belief that high artistic and
philosophical endeavor can evolve from an unrefined environment on romantic naturalism; they produce a literature whose themes are based on
romantic humanism and whose styles and forms reflect romantic aesthetics; and they identify their achievement as an organic part of the cultural
development of all mankind according to romantic historiography. The
American "renaissance" phenomenologically springs from nothing—not
the land, not the people, not some combination of the two. Such a birth
does not occur at all, not even immaculately, and certainly does not recur,
but is the dissimulation according to which the American brand of romanticism feigns descent. Nothing other than modernism replaces a theist
discourse of an American province that might, after cultivation, afford a
leisure class of belletrists, with the modern one of an American heartland
nourishing artists and philosophers directly from the soil.[33]

Complicity between romanticism and an indigenous American culture
confers tremendous power on the unitary model in modern American
cultural historiography. Unity is an ideal of romanticism and unitary
theories of history are only one of its many expressions in romantic discourse. Modernist theories of American culture are discursively akin to the
romantic histories of Hegel and Tocqueville and Bancroft and Parkman,
and so to the essays of Emerson and Thoreau that proclaim the unity of
time, and to the romances of Hawthorne that intimate it, and the poetry of
Whitman that incants it. Depending on nothing so fragile as the conscious
respect of modern theorists for romantic predecessors, unity endures as
one of the regularities of the modern discursive pattern. A semi-explicit
romantic kinship is present, for example, in what is still considered the
most influential study of American romanticism. Matthiessen accepts the
romantics' claim to universal nativity, their identification with the blossom-
ing of the human spirit they believe to recur cyclically throughout the ages,
and agrees with their aesthetics, implicitly by devoting all of his long study
to the artistic merits of their writings, and explicitly by prefacing the study
with a profession of belief in their belonging to a literary continuum, the
culmination of the past and prelude of the future. Matthiessen's scholarship echoes the romantic discourse that tells how literary sophistication
arises from no literature and no sophistication, but from the environment,
from "America." That this mystical genealogy is accepted and that the
implication that American romanticism is spontaneously generated goes
unnoticed betray the peculiar, vestigial romanticism of modern American
cultural historiography. What most distinguishes culture in the United
States from culture elsewhere is not Americanness but a dogged, neoromantic persistence in attesting to Americanness. The phenomenology of

"America" exposes the odd, sometimes comedic efforts of modern American discourse to pass off narcissism as ancestor-worship thus to hide from the ultimately inescapable truth of being self-begotten.[34]

4. The Puritan Annex

Such skepticism about the reality of "objects" upon whose "objectivity" modern American cultural historiography relies can be shown to be inherent in it; that is, deconstruction of modern discourse occurs from deeply within modern discourse, and cannot profess to be applied from without. The pure manifesting of the implicit must be substantiated, however, by divesting particular phenomena of their apparent objectivity, or, even more practically, by deconstructing a phenomenon whose apparent objectivity is particularly cherished by modern American cultural historiography and is crucial to its mission. The former will be attempted only as the conclusion of this reading, in the final section of the last chapter, in which a few celebrated texts of American romanticism and one of American modernism will be shown themselves to undermine the discourses of "America" and of "Americans" while in the very process of articulating them. The latter will comprise the body of this reading, which concentrates on the writings of Jonathan Edwards because they have been worked over with unusual rigor and persistence by modern American cultural historiography to make them conform to the unitary model of American culture. This effort suggests that Edwards's writings are somehow both unusually tempting and unusually resistant to modernist interpretation, that they represent more than just the theology and ecclesiology and sermons of even so gifted and prolific an eighteenth-century New England minister. (Cotton Mather is probably as smart and even more prolific and not much more tedious and yet he has attracted less, though similar, modernist attention.)

Edwards's writings have been made into a microcosm of early American literature, containing conveniently within a single writer's work all the poverty and riches, all the backwardness and precocity, with which early American literature as a whole confronts a modern retrospect eager to absorb it as a predecessor. Edwards is, unlike Mather, neither quite a Puritan (a name he abjures), nor is he quite enlightened, unlike, say, Franklin in the secular realm or, say, John Woolman in the religious, and so he stands Janus-like in between past and future as potentially the link between— possibly a very incarnation of continuity. So once more, and again neither perversely nor pedantically, discussion of Edwards's works or even of the modern scholarship of them must be delayed. Because the modern phenomenon of Edwards is but an instance of the modern phenomenon of Puritanism, and, even more generally, of all preromantic discourse, a phenomenology of Edwards will continue now by attempting at least in brief to deconstruct the general program of modern American cultural historiography to annex Puritanism to the present. Working inevitably, but self-consciously, from within the modern perspective, this reading will accept Edwards's representative status, but with the subversive interest of using him to undermine the unitary model and to embody the possibility of substituting a different one.

The agreement among major modern theorists that American culture is somehow unified is almost as remarkable as their failure to notice, or—perhaps more likely—to call attention to their agreement. The very lack of notice is a sign of unanimity so profound that superficial controversies and superficially various theories that are made possible by underlying agreement are taken for granted to signify the robust, contentious heterogeneity of the field. Take, for example, Parrington's and Miller's famously antagonistic positions on American Puritanism: to Parrington Puritanism is the most provincial element of early American culture that contributes hardly anything to America's liberal destiny; to Miller Puritanism contains potentials that lead to the emergence out of the medieval mind of the modern one and thus represents the foundation of American cultural growth. Both Parrington and Miller, however, depict a cultural evolution that makes sense only if American culture is assumed to be organically whole; the standard of political liberalism against which Parrington measures Puritanism is narrower than the one of inchoate humanism used by Miller, but each supposes American cultural history to be an organism whose development can be gauged normatively. Their opposition is merely partisan, Parrington counting only statements of liberal principles as advancing American culture, whereas Miller considers more subtle, implicit, even unconscious sympathy for humanity to be progressive. Their purpose is identical, which is the discovery of a fundamental unity, the stream of American thought or the mind of New England, according to which goal Miller's scholarship is more valuable. By incorporating Puritanism Miller unifies more of American culture, and captures what is by any estimate a major, and fugitive portion of American culture, and thus better serves the cause of unity.[35]

Or take several of the definitive modern works on American culture that seem too idiosyncratic or methodologically disparate to be joined under any single heading, much less what may seem the simplistic one of unitary theory. The subjects of Matthiessen's *American Renaissance* and Smith's *Virgin Land* may seem on the surface to have virtually nothing in common. Matthiessen concentrates on a handful of great works of nineteenth-century American literature written in less than a decade by five of the greatest writers of American literature. Smith pays attention to subliterary as well as to great works, includes over two hundred years of American cultural history, and defines an American myth democratically, as having been formed by popular writers as well as by bellelettrists and as having been absorbed by common people as well as by intellectuals. But the structure of American culture assumed by both is essentially the same. Matthiessen argues that the achievement of the 1850's represents the acquisition by American writers of universal aesthetic principles that date from the English Renaissance and that continue to guide the best American literature even through the twentieth century. Smith argues that concerns for the American environment characterize every stage of American mythopoeia, from the promotional literature of the early national period through Turner's frontier thesis. Both of these arguments assume continuity and imply support for a unitary model of American culture. Although more easily recognized in Smith's book, the breadth of which itself suggests discovery of a unifying theme, this can be seen also in Matthiessen's more sparing reference to the artistic continuum uniting the heritage and legacy of the climacteric of American cultural excellence he celebrates.[36]

The theoretical resemblance between the early work of R. W. B. Lewis and of Leo Marx ought to be obvious. In *The American Adam* Lewis depicts the transformation of the Adamic myth from a European religious abstraction into an American cultural reality. In *The Machine in the Garden* Marx shows the similarly reifying effect of the American environment on the Greek pastoral ideal. Their studies differ not methodologically, but only thematically in choosing to identify the dominant mythology of American culture differently, with Lewis analyzing the debate in the U.S. over whether Adam stands for human perfectibility or human limitation, and with Marx analyzing how American advocates of the pastoral garden inadvertently guarantee the destruction of the garden by the machine. The pattern of cultural evolution in both studies is the same: a myth emerges into the real world of popular creeds after having languished for centuries in the moribund realm of ancient ideals and is reconstituted in ways that can be called uniquely American. Both books show how American culture coheres around a single centripetal idea.

These three pairs of cultural historians are representative, the first, of the founders of modern American cultural historiography among professional scholars, and the second two, of later generations of important theorists. To them can be added several more analogous pairs: Carl Van Doren's studies of Franklin resemble Parrington's broader ones in praising the liberality of Franklin's thought and tracing its descent in Revolutionary and later times, and he also anticipates Miller's studies of Edwards and of Puritanism in seeing intimations of nineteenth-century humanism in Edwards's writings; Rourke pioneers the study of nonimaginative literature and material culture to show the presence of a genuine aesthetic value in the popular and practical arts of early American culture and to reveal that in the seventeenth and eighteenth centuries can be found the roots of its nineteenth-century flowering. Feidelson's study of symbolism resembles Matthiessen's stylistic analysis in identifying American literature with the (supposed) improvement upon earlier figuration (supposedly) achieved by modernism; Russel Nye's cultural history resembles both Miller's and Parrington's in discovering the very essence of early American culture in a tendency to assume the perfectibility of man. Daniel Boorstin's study of Jeffersonian idealism begins by assuming that American philosophy is identified by anti-contemplative tendencies necessitated by the settlement of the wilderness and continues by arguing that a Jeffersonian equation of God with nature represents the origin of the pragmatic concentration of the visible world that runs throughout the most characteristically American thought; Richard Chase restricts himself to American novels and finds in them a unity that distinguishes an American genre from its English counterpart, and he ascribes this unity to the unusual concern of all American novelists in all times for their environment. Alan Heimert links American Puritanism to later democratic reforms, thus integrating Puritanism with modern American politics much as Miller joins Puritanism to modern American philosophy and literature, and Richard Poirier discovers in nearly all American literature, from the novels of Cooper to the poetry of Gertrude Stein, a stylistic signature as indelible as the generic one found by Chase.[37]

The unitary model continues to govern the work of more recent scholars, including those who seem least respectful of "classic" theory or theorists. A number of well-known studies published in the 1960s and 70s decry various scandals in American cultural history. Fieldler's speculations are notorious; Slotkin, Bercovitch, John Cawelti, and Richard Drinnon, among others, condemn hidden pathologies in American tradition. Their attacks may reflect political dissent, but they conform as much structurally to the unitary model as do more conventionally impartial or complimentary appraisals. The charge that aggressive and imperialistic tendencies encouraged by colonization and settlement have endured long past their origins in American culture to incite unproductive and redundant violence supplies American culture with a unifying stigma. A culture organized by viciousness is structurally identical to one organized by liberalism, or a concern for the land, or innocence.[38]

The only criteria that fail to note the ubiquity of assertions of continuity in modern American cultural historiography are those generated by the field, which oversight insures that the proliferation of these assertions—that span periods from the seventeenth century or earlier to at least the nineteenth century, joining writers and traditions separated by over three centuries in often no more than a sentence or phrase—will be explosive. A few continuities are proclaimed in the first romantic histories—Tocqueville sees Puritans as proto-democrats long before Miller or Heimert do; Bancroft sees the Constitution rooted not only in early American culture but in Jewish antiquity; Emerson sees his early avatar in Montaigne before Miller proposes one for him in Edwards; Thoreau glimpses his own image in old texts by overlooking evidences in them of superstitious piety.[39]

A great many more continuities are proclaimed in the early professional scholarship of American culture: Parrington sees an embryo of Emerson in Roger Williams, Miller sees it in Edwards, sees an inchoate Theodore Parker in Solomon Stoddard, and quotes Stephen Whicher with approval on the continuity between Puritanism and the American Renaissance. Robert Spiller has just recently reiterated his program for the scholarship of early American literature, which is "to move toward a better understanding of our complex but nonetheless distinctive American character." And in the most recent studies assertions of continuity are legion and still growing. Among only the most recent and ambitious are: that a curiosity about unexplored territory unites Columbus with Thoreau (Franklin, *Discoverers, Explorers, Settlers*), unites Columbus with a spirit of adventure that grows continuously from the 1500s and that blossoms in nineteenth-century American culture (Spengemann, *The Adventurous Muse*), unites seventeenth- and eighteeenth-century American explorers with twentieth-century American vacationers (Wilson, *In the Presence of Nature*); that a search for the "design" of nature joins Winthrop, Bradford, Fitzgerald, and Emerson, in that order (David L. Minter, *The Interpreted Design as a Structural Principle in American Prose*), that Edward Taylor's "symbolism" is an emergent variety of that of *Song of Myself* and of the *Four Quartets* and that Ann Bradstreet's supposed subjectivism in "Contemplations" is a lesser version of Whitman's in "When Lilacs Last in the Dooryard Bloom'd" (Lynen, *The Design of the Present*), that Cotton and Nathaniel Mather so spiritualize quotidian experience as to "establish a base from which lines extend through American literary history, to Jonathan Edwards, Benjamin Franklin, Emerson, Hawthorne, and even Whitman" and that the *Magnalia* "deserves a place beside the best histories of George Bancroft, William A. Prescott, Francis Parkman, and Henry Adams . . . and deserves to stand near (if necessarily below) the shelf of expansive works that include *Moby-Dick* and the novels of Yoknapatawpha County" (David Levin, *Cotton Mather*); that a nationalistic sense of American destiny joins the Puritan errand with that of Martin Luther King (Bercovitch, "The Puritan Errand Reassessed"), that the stylistic signature of Puritanism remains evident through the writings of Joel Barlowe to those of Whitman (Mason Lowance, *The Language of Canaan*), that "such characters of our later literature as Captain Ahab, Hank Morgan, or Jay Gatsby reflect the persistence of certain ideals and impulses which are rooted in American Puritanism" (Emory Elliott, introduction to *Puritan Influences in American Literature*). The length of this list is determined only by limitations of space and energy, and witholds all but one reference to Edwards's precocity, citations of which represent by far the largest single category of unitary assertion. In his review of *Puritan Influences in American Literature* Spengemann contemplates charging the editor and publisher with false advertising, since so few of the essays in the collection deal explicitly with Puritan influences. What Spengemann discovers, however, is not so much chicanery—although there may be that, too, in the shrewd estimate that continuity sells—as a *gestalt,* a presupposition so profound that continuity can credibly be asserted as the discovery even of scholars who neither consciously seek nor consciously realize that they have found continuity, and a presupposition to which a university press and several fairly prominent scholars of early American culture adhere so docilely that they are about as embarrassed by Spengemann as the emperor and his courtiers are by the child in Andersen's famous parable.[40]

Theorists like Parrington and Miller, Matthiessen and Smith, and Lewis and Marx all help to establish and to preserve the unitary model in modern American cultural historiography. Others take part, but few contribute a substantialy different way of organizing the culture and none who might do so is nearly so successful. That Fiedler and other professing jeremiahs support the historiographical establishment even while rebelling against the social or political one suggests the power of the model, which can be seen to underlie the scholarship of rebels, and also of critics who conceive American culture as the competition among multiple factions, and of critics who fancy themselves hostile to historiographical generalizations of any sort, and of critics who are dismissive of the significance of the early culture in general, and of critics who seem indifferent, either overtly or implicitly, because of their narrow foci, to theoretical issues of any kind. The unitary model is not yet manifest enough within modern American cultural historiography to be opposed or even ignored effectively, and its indeterminacy within the field prevents significant exception to it to be taken.

What might appear to be the most striking departures from theoretical unanimity—the preponderance of modern theories that suppose American culture to be made up of interactions among multiple forces—can be seen as the best evidence of theoretical agreement, and of a widespread neoromanticism. In the modern discursive pattern, multiplicity reveals, and is made possible by what modernism takes to be the inexhaustible plenum of "life." Differentials are therefore relative, stemming from a single node whose singleness is confirmed by the very diversity with which it realizes itself, just as differentiation among species confirms the existence of a biosphere and as differentiation among functions confirms the existence of an organism. Even the most dramatic differences, conflicts, especially the bitter ones, fratricidally confirm the original fraternity among the opponents. Varieties and antagonisms depart from sameness and amity only as their signifiers, and this apparently equivocal semiosis is never more certain that when an absent unity is made to seem most impossible to restore, when diversity is made to seem infinite and imponderable, since the greater the abundance of signification, the greater the "signs of life"— the more evident the existence of *ens entium*, or *Geist*, or Absolute, or Over-Soul. Modern American cultural historiography never shows its discursive tie to romanticism more clearly than when proposing that "America" evolves into multiplicities, which proposals represent a continuation of the romantic discourse of immanence.

The simplest applications of this discourse are those which see American culture growing through struggles among opposing or tangential contenders for the American "mind," a variation of the unitary model that continues to be common. Perhaps the most obvious early example is Parrington's binary division pitting various forms of liberalism against various forms of illiberalism, the process tending toward unification as liberalism triumphs and its opponent retreats into historical exile. Another, and very recent example is Spengemann's contention in *The Adventurous Muse* that indigenous venturesomeness tends finally to predominate over imported domesticity in American narrative. Somewhat more complex versions that are somewhat more valuable to modern American cultural historiography because they can comprehend more of American culture and rescue at least some parts of apparently retrograde traditions like Puritanism, which Parrington and others condemn wholesale, are those which conceive American culture as ongoing tensions among two or more opponents (arrangements in threes seem actually to be the most popular)—tensions that persist throughout American history, thus unifying the culture through more syncretic or dynamic structures. An example of a two-contender conflict is the "court-country" opposition cited by Gordon Wood and others. Tripartite conflicts are represented by the three-party system of Memory, Hope, and Irony, devised by Lewis in *The American Adam*; the three psychological types, evangelical, moderate, and genteel, more recently devised by Philip Greven in *The Protestant Temperament*; and the three relations to the American environment devised even more recently by Franklin in *Discoverers, Explorers, Settlers*.[41]

The most complex and effective application of the romantic discourse of immanence is the one that least simplifies this discourse, which is dialectical analysis. Here differentiation is accounted the very means through which unity gradually emerges. This analysis is applied most often, predictably, to that part of American culture that appears to modernism most different and thus in need of the strongest conciliatory method. The studies of Puritanism or of the early culture generally that have come to dominate modern American cultural historiography are thus invariably dialectical, which indicates both that the early culture is the greatest potential anomaly to the unitary model, and also that specialization, area study such as that of Puritanism, in narrowing focus does not exclude but rather magnifies the theoretical interests of the field. Far from an exception, Puritan scholarship is an epitome of unitary theory and is the area that unitary theory is most ambitious, and pressed hardest, to contain.

The dialectical analysis of Puritanism, as well as of earlier biblical and classical traditions, extends far beyond modern American cultural historiography to include all modern historiography that is not phenomenological in its methods, and even some that is. For example, Arthur Lovejoy's seminal presentation of early Western ontology detects in classical philosophies as early as Plato's a dialectical opposition between realism and idealism, traces its descent in that between pure hierarchism and a latent organicism in the conception of the "great chain," and sees a climax in the destined advent of modern monistic ontology as the great chain "broke down of its own weight," a collapse viewed with "instructive irony" by modern dialectical hindsight. Similarly, if less expansively, modern religious historiography consistently views radical Protestantism as implicated dialectically in the provenance of modern philosophies and religions that reject radical Protestantism, dialectical analyses being applied to both European and American religious history in various forms and with varying degrees of theoretical self-consciousness. One of the first and still an influential dialectical interpretation is Max Weber's analysis of the economics of Protestantism, holding in essence that the dual commerce with both flesh and spirit encouraged by Protestantism results in concentration on the former, a consequent prosperity, and an eventual decline in piety.[42]

Dialectical interpretations dominate the later twentieth-century scholarship of Protestantism in both Europe and the United States: Herbert Schneider, to whom the Bible sanctions anything, sees convenient biblical permission for the American colonies to tame the "howling wilderness," whose exploitation enriches Puritan life while simultaneously impoverishing Puritan religion; Ola Winslow mentions in her biography of Edwards that by the eighteenth century "life had grown less solemn" in New England "as it had become less precarious, inevitably"; Edwin Gaustad comments in his study of New England's first Great Awakening that "pietism, for good or ill, rests most comfortably on those who are least comfortable"; and Edmund Morgan sums up this Puritan dilemma as the incredibly difficult task of "living in this world without taking the mind off God."[43]

The dialectical sublation of Puritanism seems to other modern scholars an ironic consequence not just of its economic, but of its evangelical success: William Haller notes that the evangelical mannerisms of the most effective Puritan preachers in England implicitly contradict the piety of their message, that these evangelists strive so to "drive home the application to the individual life of the theory of predestination, election, and sanctification" that their congregations begin inevitably to confuse the driving force of preachers with the dispensations of God; the evangelical contradiction of Puritanism is variously named by other modern scholars as one between piety and moralism, the vision of God and the kingdom of God, the invisible and visible churches.[44]

A more purely intellectual secularism is also seen by some modern scholars as the dialectical fate of Puritanism: Gaustad argues that the provisional endorsement granted by Puritanism to reason and observation constitutes a weakness exploited by the Englightenment in the championship of the human mind; Morgan agrees that rationalism is always a potential of Puritanism, the eventual dominance of rationalism representing only the "carrying [of] an accepted Puritan principle farther than other Puritans"; and Heimert goes still farther by stating that because "one of the classic assumptions of the Puritan mind was that the will of God was to be discerned in nature as well as in revelation," Puritanism is incapable of contesting the enlightened claims, becoming more insistent in the American colonies in the late seventeenth and early eighteeenth centuries, that God's will is "best derived, not from His word, but from His works," and that this pliancy, among others, justifies calling Puritanism not a "retrograde philosophy" but one that "provided pre-Revolutionary America with a radical, even democratic social and political ideology . . . and inspired a thrust toward American nationalism."[45]

If there is a single modern scholar who most influences the current understanding of Puritanism he is Perry Miller, and Miller is undoubtedly the most skillful dialectician among modern American historians of Puritanism. He holds in *The Seventeenth Century*, the second volume of *The New England Mind*, that anthropocentric tendencies begin to undermine Puritan piety as early as the seventeenth century, and finds them in increasing allowances made by American Puritans for the temporal welfare, especially the psychology, of human beings; his method is to conclude relations of the letter of Puritan orthodoxy with revelations of its latent contradictory spirit. In other works he argues that the vulnerability of Puritanism to dialectical change can be recognized in the half-way covenant of 1662 and in Solomon Stoddard's further liberalization, both of which Miller interprets as compromises with a new spirit of democracy, and in the kind of Puritan homily, which begins to spread in the early eighteenth century, that draws "tedious" analogies between spiritual truths and everyday facts of life, which Miller interprets as concessions to the new science. And his most intricate ironies trace the process through which Puritan piety is transformed, without the addition of any extraneous influence, into forms of humanism, dialectical analyses that are virtual, though unacknowledged quotations of Hegel's dialectic of master and slave, through which the Puritan-slave learns the art of omnipotence-mastery in the very helplessness of his servitude. See, for example, Miller's clever descriptions of how the inwardness encouraged by Puritanism, and made especially intense and communal among American Puritans after

Cromwell's revolution, turns into psychologizing in "Errand Into the Wilderness," or how polemic defenses of the Puritan faith in the seventeenth century lead inevitably and imperceptibly to the interjection into divinity of the humanity of divinity's defenders in "The Marrow of Puritan Divinity," or in that same essay how the covenant inevitably tends to raise man to the level of God no matter how relentlessly covenant theologians strive to keep man down.[46]

Like Miller, modern American cultural historians conclude generally that the transition from Puritanism to more humanistic ways of thinking amounts, to use Clarence Faust's pyrotechnic image, to the self-detonation of "explosives" planted in Puritanism at its birth and carried about with increasing carelessness through the years. Faust links this instability to ambiguities in Puritan portrayals of God as lawgiver, craftsman, and divine first principle with extremist factions growing up around each of the three to form a trinity of theological divisions (another three-party system) into which Puritanism splits. God the lawgiver is worshiped by churches that emphasize religious duties and ceremonies, wherein lies idolatry, Episcopacy, Popery; God the craftsman is served through various forms of natural religion, Deism, rationalism; and God the divine first principle is invoked by enthusiasts, separatists, Quakers. More recent scholars detect similar mitoses of Puritanism into immanence, which is considered intrinsic to Puritanism, and transcendence, into symbolic and nonsymbolic epistemologies, into "chronometrical" and "horological" conceptions of time. According to these organic interpretations Puritanism seems never to be stable, in no theology, in no church, not even for an instant of time.[47]

Specialization within modern American cultural historiography—at least in the area of Puritanism—that might be considered most likely to foster doubts about unity because Puritanism seems to differ most, if only superficially, from modernism, does not presuppose fundamental diversity within the field. There are to be sure plenty of scholars who contest Puritanism's relevance to the modern world, but they do so marginally, either in asides to studies that are understandably inclined to concentrate on other periods or movements in American culture, or as brief factual corrections of theorists like Miller, accusing them of partial readings of the evidence. Challenges made in the name of accuracy sometimes come from opposing unitary theorists, as in Miller's refuting Parrington over Thomas Hooker and the Mathers, which of course represents no departure from the unitary model, or are made on behalf of "objectivity" alone, which still fail to imply theoretical alternatives since they constitute a precise negation, a mirror image that depends no less on the precedence of unitary theory than does the filiopietism of the ephebī of unitary theorists. An early example of the latter is Howard Mumford Jones's denial that "there is anything in seventeenth-century American literature to prophesy that

American letters should take just this shape," but that change occurs non-systematically in unpredictable and incomprehensible fits and starts.[48]

That dissent over Puritanism is restricted to such purely negative rejoinders indicates once again the power of the unitary model, which in all cases confines opposition to the terms of unity; of course no modern literary scholar makes a career and no book-length study of Puritan literature is published contending that Puritanism manages successfully to cling to superstitions about God. Both scholarly controversy and specialization are genetically conservative, both depending for their existence on the priority of the unitary model. This dependence is direct, and thus a bit more obvious, in the case of specialization, which is guided to the study of minor figures and obscure institutions by the suggestions of unitary theory that these hitherto unstudied parts of the culture can be fit organically into the cultural whole. What is most remarkable about specialization in modern American studies of the early literature is that no matter how many potential anomalies are found, and these multiply automatically as more early discourse is read by an ever-increasing number of specialists, no truly alternative theories arise to accommodate them. Rather than organizing new findings into new theories, specialists tend to avoid theoretical comment as perhaps inappropriate to studies of modest scope, or to ascribe anomalies to the influence of magnification alone, as if what were evident to a close view need not be so to a long one, or just explicitly to withold theoretical judgment until more "evidence" is accumulated; in one particularly striking example of specialists' ambivalence, a recent study of Samuel Willard, after having shown at length, if only implicitly, the irreconcilable differences between Puritan theology and modern discourse, concludes nonetheless with a syncretic flourish linking Willard through Edwards and Franklin to "the life of the mind in America."[49]

Personal loyalty to the unitary theorists, or their students, who more often than not trained them, is not necessary to prevent specialists from deliberately contesting the unitary model. The structure of specialization is, like that of the practical sciences described by Kuhn, virtually closed to theoretical controversy. As modern American cultural historiography gets older and extends over more of the early literature, it increasingly resists theoretical change as no more than a hindrance to the work it must get done. Kuhn argues that practical science advances—for a significant period of time and a significant proportion of scientists—through acceptance of a paradigm. Although modern American cultural historiography lacks the formal organization of a practical science, and although Kuhn himself warns against transferring his analysis to social sciences and humanities, the unitary model seems by now to have acquired the inertia of one of Kuhn's paradigms, remaining ummoved in scholarly controversy and in area studies like that of Puritanism, and in the narrower ones of a single discourse like covenant theology, or of a single movement like the Great Awakening, or of a single genre like the jeremiad. And the model is never more firmly in place than in the study of an individual Puritan writer like Jonathan Edwards.[50]

The establishment of Edwards's precocity is central to the annexation of Puritanism by modern American cultural historiography and represents an important victory of the campaign. All of the various applications of and apparent exceptions to unitary theory that appear generally in the scholarship of the early literature reappear in the scholarship of Edwards, which does not just sample the field but constitutes a more accessible, more easily presented and understood miniature. The phenomenon of Edwards, which begins here for the first time to be examined, is, like all phenomena, the product of an entire system of perceiving, and like them is organized in ways that reflect primarily the structure of the system. There is nothing fundamentally singular about Edwards, nothing that differentiates him fundamentally from other early American writers who have been subjected to modernist retrospect, nothing that colors or alters this retrospect in any more than superficial ways. Because the phenomenon of Edwards is determined by modern discourse, a phenomenology of Edwards reads the modernism of the study of Edwards. Its penultimate reach is now the scholarship of Edwards in particular; its ultimate one will be Edwards's writings themselves. Such an ordering is indirect or digressive only to the modernist idolatry of "objects"—the "man," his "works," his "life"—that is particularly common in American culture, including American scholarly culture, probably due to no more than a near coincidence between the advent of modernism and the advent of the United States as an independent nation. Phenomenologically, such an order is a mimesis of the only act that discourse, regardless of genre, directly represents, which is the act of reading. Edwards's writings are thus not the starting point but the goal of a phenomenology. Edwards the "man" is no subject for phenomenology at all.

Edwards has been made into the paragon of the basic contradiction that modernist retrospect sees as both intrinsic and fatal to Puritanism, and this is wholly the condition of Edwards's prominence in the modern canon of American literature. To become typical of a unified American culture, Edwards has first to be redeemed from the doctrinaire Calvinist that he can so easily appear, a redemption that not only need not but must not be entire, since an Edwards who is uniformly modern is as useless to the interest of establishing continuity between past and present as one who is uniformly medieval, which is the real theoretical motive behind what appears to be the simple scholarly discretion that insists repeatedly, in even the most modernist of interpretations of Edwards, that he is not after all merely Emerson or Channing in disguise. There is some inconsequential dispute among modern American cultural historians over whether Edwards is to be hailed as protohumanist or dismissed as a medieval scholastic, an entirely evidentiary dispute in which the question is not whether a Puritan can anticipate modernism (which possibility all modern cultural historians at all interested in Puritanism assume) but whether evidence of modernism is present in Edwards's case, whose outcome is foreordained in favor of Edwards's precocity because the inclusion of so apparently orthodox a Puritan by the unitary model is much more valuable as a tribute to its inclusiveness than his exclusion would be a safeguard of its consistency.[51]

For example, the disagreement between Parrington and Miller over Puritanism takes place in little over the writings of Edwards. Parrington discounts Edwards as a historical anachronism seeking to reestablish an illiberal doctrine long after the time for illiberal doctrines has passed. Evaluated according to Parrington's historical norm, Edwards seems eccentric, a misguided enthusiast swimming futilely against the main current of American thought. Parrington offers no real explanation of Edwards's thinking, no more than he does of Puritanism generally, but merely brands them as deviating from American culture for reasons that need not overly concern a modern American cultural historian. Parrington has no theory of Edwards's writings, nor of the Puritanism they espouse; rather, he has a theory that excludes them. This negative response to Edwards and to Puritanism remains the primary form of objection to theories finding protoromantic and protomodern features in both. The response is no genuine alternative and its statements have accordingly been brief and few. The modern scholarship of Edwards contains several articles that attempt to deny his precocity by recalling evidence of his resistance to cultural change. The view that he is left behind by the progress of American cultural history is contained also in brief discussions of Edwards in larger contexts. Not one of the many book-length studies of Edwards is devoted to this position.[52]

Miller's interpretation of Edwards is a local application of his interpretation of Puritanism, and he influences the modern scholarship of Edwards much more than Parrington or any other of Edwards's detractors among modern American cultural historians. Miller's advantage is again that in the absence of a positive accounting he provides one by joining Edwards theoretically to modern American culture. Miller is not just the originator of a certain approach to Edwards; he is mainly responsible for identifying Edwards in a way that makes Edwards memorable to modern posterity. Again, it only pays tribute to the power of Miller's scholarship to say that the modern phenomenon of Edwards is in large part his invention.

What Miller helps to create is predictably divided into two dialectically conflicting parts. On the one hand there is the Puritan with a firm, conscious, even beleaguered grip on his entire heritage; Miller never underestimates the depth either of Edwards's understanding of God's sovereignty or of his voluntary submission to it. On the other there is the protohumanist budding not just alongside the pietist in Edwards's mind but on some of the very same branches that support pietism. Thus where piety sanctions a regard for the visible world as the "second book" of God there could grow a special attentiveness to nature, stimulated by Edwards's inherent curiosity and his acquired knowledge of Enlightened science, which heads toward the natural science of a later age. Or where a concern for religious affections is permitted there can arise, because of Edwards's inherent compassion and perhaps also his familiarity with Locke's sensational epistemology, a fascination with the heart that looks forward to the emotionalism that modern humanism will encourage with incomparably fewer and weaker restraints than those with which Edwards says feeling should be shackled. Although Miller finds several of the limbs of Edwards's thought to be from his point of view sterile, he discovers enough humanity to interest modern scholarship and to gain the privilege to teach modern scholarship how and where to search. Those modern studies that follow Miller's lead are not only numerically predominant; they amount to the entire field of major study of Edwards's thinking. Whether Miller "actually" fathers them is unimportant; the truth is that Miller's interpretation, presented in several books and articles appearing over two decades, is a thorough, widely publicized, successful identification of Edwards with modernity, and that the vast majority of subsequent modern studies are prompted by similar insights.

Miller is not the first to discover conflicts in Edwards's thought; Leslie Stephen calls Edwards "a kind of Spinoza-Mather" combining "the logical keenness of the great metaphysician with the puerile superstitions of the New England Divine" as early as 1876. I. Woodbridge Riley sees in Edwards a miscegenation "of mingled English and Welsh blood" leading to "conflicting logical and imaginative powers," and several more of Edwards's earliest students see similar divisions, a list of whom is compiled by Holbrook. Nor is Miller the first to call one of the contenders in Edwards's psychomachia an intimation of modernism; both Stephen and Riley imply as much, Parrington says so, and Van Doren says so too, and even earlier than Parrington, in the early 1920s. But more than any of these commentators Miller interprets the division in Edwards's thought as the dialectical contradiction that is advancing American intellectual history, of which to Miller Edwards's mind is representative. And unlike Parrington or Van Doren, who never doubt that the handful of lyrically protoromantic effusions among Edwards's writings are overwhelmed by volumes that speak of "forgotten issues in a forgotten dialect," Miller decides that the essence of Edwards's thought anticipates modernism.[53]

The reason Miller never defends systematically his belief in Edwards's historical precocity is that he never has to; he is shrewd in contenting himself and his readers with no more than strong implication, prefacing several chapters in his biography of Edwards with lengthy quotations from such later philosophers as Nietszche and Bergson, and mentioning in pass-ing, in that work and elsewhere, Edwards's affinities with the great roman-tic writers of the United States and England. This casualness suggests an expectation that modern American cultural historiography is likely to con-cur, which turns out to be largely correct. When pressed into answering the accusation that he overstates the case, Miller responds only once directly, and then parenthetically, in the introduction to the reprinting of "From Edwards to Emerson" in *Errand into the Wilderness,* saying that his critics overstate his stake in the claim of Edwards's modernity; but he simply lets stand the contention in the essay that Edwards is so frightened by his naturally pantheistic tendencies that he constrains them with an unnatur-ally pious style. Other evidence of Miller's belief in Edwards's modernity includes his explicit agreement with Channing's statement that Edwards's radical monotheism is but a step away from pantheism and his assertion that entries he finds in Edwards's unpublished notebooks are to Edwards "what the *Prelude* was to Wordsworth, a secret and sustained effort to work out a new sense of the divinity of nature and the naturalness of divinity." Miller continues in the introduction to his publication of these entries in *Images or Shadows of Divine Things* to note "startling parallels" between Edwards and Wordsworth.[54]

The list of modern scholars who present similar opinions is a very long one. The labor of compilation is, again, Sisyphean, and again a very large part will have to stand for the immense whole. Because the Edwardsean division of modern American cultural historiography is itself so large as to require subdivision, begin just with dialectical interpretations. An early essay by Frederick Carpenter resembles Van Doren's in arguing that Ed-wards is a protoromantic thinker struggling to put off an "ill-fitting cloak of Calvinism"; Winslow, whose biography of Edwards precedes Miller's, anti-cipates Miller's likening Edwards to Wordsworth by comparing Edwards's boyhood in East Windsor to the "fair seed time" of the *Prelude,* and sees Edwards's later thinking to have been driven ahead by a dialectical opposi-tion between a progressive philosophy and an antiquated theology. A bit later Rufus Suter discerns a similar dialectic, except to him the precocious opponent is Neoplatonism, followed by Alfred O. Aldridge (a theoretically cordial religion versus a practically heartless one), followed by Sidney Ahl-strom (Enlightenment versus piety), followed by Edward Davidson (a youthful joy in sensation versus a mature callousness). A bit later Peter Gay sees a foreward-looking mind opposed by a reactionary historicism, Richard L. Bushman sees an introspection prescient of Oedipal urges, secreted in the journals, of course, opposed by a public utterance loud in support of traditional theocentricity, a psychologism also suggested much earlier and in a larger context by Miller, who sees a "subjective mood" underlying and ultimately superseding Puritan theology in *The Seventeenth Century,* and Daniel Shea who, like Davidson, sees a young naturalism

opposed by a grown-up abstraction. Contemporary expressions of the Edwardsean dialectic include Mason Lowance's conflict between epistemologically timid and epistemologically daring "typologies," Tracy's
between personal misgiving and evangelical zeal, which is strikingly similar to Bushman's, and also to Miller's expressions of Edwards's
psychomachia, like that mentioned at the end of Miller's "The End of the
World" between the simplified piety of Edwards's sermons and the "secret
meditations" in which the very existence, let alone the divinity of God is
supposedly doubted, and, finally, Fiering's between new-fashioned post-
Cartesian intellectualism and old-fashioned pietism, or between the
philosophical richness of "naturalistic ethics" and the "intellectual poverty" of the conception of human depravity, an opposition that to Fiering is
severe enough to cause Edwards to write with "brilliance" at one moment
and with "sophistry and evasiveness" the next. One can sympathize with
William Scheick's conclusion that in the face of such apparent diversity
"efforts to systematize Edwards's thought will, it would appear, not comprise a major trend in future studies." But Scheick fails to consider the
possibility that in proposals of such dialectical complexity inheres a single
theoretical foundation, and that these proposals systematize in the very
multiplication of contraries.[55]

Another type of argument for Edwards's modernity, one, not surprisingly, that is typical of literary studies, is that his writings are on significant
occasions stylistically precocious. The connection between these arguments and the modernism of the modern literary criticism of early texts in
general is particularly apparent, since they rely conspicuously on the unexamined assumption that symbolism is a type of figuration not invented but
only perfected by modern writing, that symbols exist in varying numbers
throughout literature, with a general tendency toward growth, which sort
of modernist imperialism has captured many another early writer than
Edwards and many another early tradition than American Puritanism.
Here again Miller's commentary can be taken as exemplary when, for
example, he says in his biography of Edwards that Edwards's "originality
was not substantial but primarily verbal—which justifies calling him an
artist—although his innovations in language portended an ultimate revolution in substance," assuming not only that originality, which Miller
identifies primarily, as he goes on to specify, as symbolic technique, inheres somehow in language but also that this inherence is so distinct from
the "substance" of language as to be capable of revolutionizing language
from within, which is of course yet another, stylistic extension of the
dialectic. Only a few years after the appearance of Miller's biography of
Edwards Feidelson comments in passing, as if this can already be taken for
granted, that "theology aside, Edwards anticipated the symbolic consciousness of Emerson," and concurrence among contemporary critics is
broad, including Davidson's calling Edwards "America's first symbolist,"

Shea's crediting him with having produced "the first organic metaphor, perhaps in our literature," Robert Daly's corrective expansion of such too-modest claims—he is responding in particular to Miller's and Ursula Brumm's supposed short-sightedness regarding the origin of symbolism—to include not only Edwards among early symbolists but also medieval writers and seventeenth-century Puritans, a claim that reveals with special clarity that Edwards's linguistic gift, no matter how great, alone has little to do with claims for his stylistic modernity, Lowance's taking for granted at the outset of his study that "continuities between Edwards, Emerson, and Thoreau" are evident in the "great debt" owned by nineteenth- and even twentieth-century American literature to the "symbolic language of New England Puritanism," and Cherry's concluding with a flourish at the end of his that "Edwards was decidedly symbolic in his approach to physical nature." The sensibleness of such claims is as yet so robustly common in modern American literary scholarship that it remains totally unaware of itself as a claim, and thus totally impervious to doubts about the universal paternity of symbolism that are conventional elsewhere, for example in the phenomenological aesthetics of Todorov, who reports as an already standard insight that in "the notion of the symbol . . . is concentrated the whole, or at least the major tendencies, of the romantic aesthetic."[56]

But by far most common are arguments that Edwards adumbrates various aspects of modern philosophy, so common that here even further subdivision is necessary to present this type of argument in any orderly way. A general protoromanticism is discovered in Edwards over a century ago by Bancroft, whose famous quartet of Edwards, Kant, Rousseau, and Reid is probably the first of numerous, rather casual connections of Edwards with a variety of romantic and modern luminaries, including Emerson and Hawthorne (Miller in *The Seventeenth Century*), Wordsworth (Miller, and later Clarence Faust and Thomas Johnson), Shaftesbury (who is considered in this context as philosophically a progenitor of romanticism), Rousseau again, and Thoreau (Fiering), Cooper (Robert Milden), Coleridge (Sang Hyun Lee), Whitman (David Scofield Wilson), and, more ambitiously, Melville and the Marquis de Sade (Fiering), Kierkegaard (Miller and later Carse), Stephen Crane, Emerson, Melville, Henry James (Shea), Pearce (Lee), Freud and the *Gestaltists* (Lynen), Whitehead (Roland Delattre), and, most ambitiously, T. S. Eliot (Lynen), Picasso (Carse), Saul Bellow (Shea), and, what must be the record for modernist reach, De Saussure and Derrida (Wayner Lesser).[57]

The protoromanticism in particular of Edwards's ontology is the focus of many of his modernist scholars, including Miller; Douglass Elwood (who generates a book out of what amounts to a qualification of Miller's suggestion of Edwards's pantheism, calling it instead a "pan*en*theism" that compromises by placing God deeply within nature without identifying Him precisely with nature, a fine distinction Colacurcio has lately endorsed);

Faust and Johnson, to whom Edwards's personal narrative is "more pantheistical than its author was perhaps aware"; Roland Delattre, who adds to pantheism an aesthetic dimension according to which God is "immediately related to everything that has a finite existence" and immediately "present to his creature in the manner in which beauty is present"; William Clebsch, who says that Edwards "brought together the noumenal and the phenomenal" to the degree that spiritual things "manifested themselves palpably and nature mirrored God"; and Lowance, who agrees with Heimert that Edwards's ontology represents "denial of the possibility that the universe is devoid of meaning."[58]

Another version of the argument for Edwards's philosophical precocity interprets his "post-Millennial" eschatology as somehow anticipating a utopian commingling of Providence and history; another interprets his ecclesiology as anticipating either modern evangelical techniques, which sometimes praises Edwards for making communion more widely available and sometimes damns him for inciting religious hysteria, one recent study even insinuating that Edwards might be suspected to have been a protocult leader, or as anticipating modern political suffrage; another interprets his conception of human depravity as anticipating modern misanthropy and his piety as anticipating modern pessimism or fatalism. Finally, there are those who would make Edwards into a postmodern, a protophenomenologist at last.[59]

To continue would be to give modern empiricism a surfeit of its own, satirically to imply that evidence does not materialize and levitate to support or attack theoretical positions. Neither these compilations nor the longer ones that might be amassed prove the unanimity of the field to modern American cultural historians or scholars of Edwards, who will remain convinced that they know perfectly well what they are about, and that they are certainly not about the obedient, or, worse, the unconscious, paying of fealty to a reigning paradigm. Let the lists stand, then, as evidence only that empiricism is nothing other than a form of rhetoric and that rhetoric, as used to be common knowledge, is for hire. A case can be made, according to a method that modern American cultural historiography itself deems one of the most persuasive, that a single modern identity of Edwards pervades modern American cultural historiography, at its beginnings as a profession in the 1920s, in its latest scholarship, continuously throughout the nearly two generations since Edwards becomes a favorite of modernism in the United States, and not only in specialized studies but in textbooks of American literature and culture, that this is the Edwards accepted and published by university presses in this country and abroad, that this is the Edwards who is being taught at all levels of American education, and, perhaps most important empirically, that this is the Edwards accepted as canonical by that bible of American literature, Spiller's *Literary History*, in which Johnson describes Edwards's conception of nature as identical to nineteenth-century theories of correspondence: "All that he witnessed as manifestations of the sensible world became shadows of divine truths. The concrete image henceforth was to be the symbolic fact. From now on, nature was analogy, as it had been felt by mystics from the beginning of time. Among American men of letters in the next century, Bryant came to expand it in his own way; and Emerson most articulately of all.[60]

The modern phenomenon of Edwards cannot be separated from that of Puritanism in general. Neither has priority; rather, both are interdependent, both contributing to the maintenance of the unitary model, the keeper of which is modern American cultural historiography, which is but one discourse of the whole humanist discursive pattern. This network is not easily broken. The removal of Edwards is especially difficult because his inclusion requires a large investment and is representative of the entire program of unifying American culture; he will be guarded jealously. But investment incurs risk. To include Edwards the unitary model is at least fully extended, because of the explicit strangeness of Edwards's theism, because of the interpretive daring required of modern studies to make Edwards's theism seem familiar. In reaching for Edwards modern American cultural historiography may have gone beyond the limit of its elasticity; its hold may be not just tight but strained. A break here might start the disintegration of the entire structure. If Edwards's writings can be seized, they might become a cornerstone for a new model of American literature. One reason that this reading begins by ranging so freely beyond Edwards's writings is to prepare for so general a deconstruction. The phenomenology of Edwards will be designed to aid in the substitution of a different model of American literature for the unitary one that the modern phenomenon of Edwards serves so well. To refer once again, in conclusion, to Nietzsche, "the raising of an altar requires the breaking of an altar," and, to quote the even more iconoclastic improvement on Nietzsche's phrase by the contemporary Nietzschean Foucault, the breaking of an altar requires that somebody "take a hammer to it."[61]

In the passage from Edwards's notebooks that appears on the title page of this chapter Edwards makes one of his very rare attempts at humor, noting with heavy irony that the Bible that supports the theology of his "Arminian" opponents becomes a very conflicted and ambiguous thing after having been interpreted to serve their own, to him unscriptural purposes. The attitude in the passage toward the "Arminians" resembles the attitude of this reading of Edwards's writings toward modern interpretations. Modern scholarship creates an extremely complex text of Edwards's writings, whose complexities, which include deletions, reflect the effort to make a text that anticipates modernism. Thus, somewhat as Edwards dedicates himself to correcting what he considers misreadings of the Bible, so will this reading try to call attention to the partialities of the modern text of

Edwards. But the resemblance is significantly inexact. The Bible is to Edwards both more and less than a text; it is more in containing the mark of what is according to the dualistic epistemology of theist discourse a real object, no matter how difficult this mark may be to read, a somehow genuine signification of otherness, the signifier of the ultimate signified that, in theist discourse, need not be put in quotation marks, originally the word of God and only subsequently a palimpsest overwritten by the defacements of human interpretation; it is less than a text in lacking the polysemy that according to phenomenologies of humanist discourse is the property especially of semiotic phenomena (are there any other kinds of phenomena?) which permits new texts to form whenever new acts of reading occur, according to which readings neither obscure nor enhance but constitute texts. Edwards's task is to cleanse the Word of a film of obfuscation. This reading can neither defer so piously to an other, which in humanist discourse is superstitious, nor strive so piously for disinterest, which in humanist discourse is either naive or hypocritical. Just as certainly as there is a superhuman signification transcending the words of the Bible according to theist hermeneutics, so certainly is there conversely no quintessential Edwards hiding beneath layers of modernist criticism according to phenomenological semiotics. No Edwards can be distilled from his modern commentators because all have dissolved into the humanity that, notwithstanding the occasional knocking on wood or cautionary platitude that can be provoked by reign on a treacherous eminence, is the whole substance of modern discourse and the cynosure of all the sciences of man. Modern commentaries do not corrupt, but are the genesis of Edwards's identity. An Edwards untouched by modern readings is more than difficult to recover. There is simply no such "thing."

This is not to say that Edwards's interpretive task is easier—he takes for granted and converts to discursive stimulation what might, and does, bring on pious aphasia, that God can be neither written nor read—nor does this say that the difficulties of phenomenological interpretation must strike one dumb, since the nonentity of an "objective" Edwards allows for the production of other, phenomenal ones. But the theism of Edwards's exegesis is not the same as the humanism of this reading of his writings, and it will be the method of this reading continuously to evidence that, and it will be the ultimate goal of this reading thereby to manifest both theism and humanism as joined by what is the only indissoluble bond, no mere historical, diachronic connection, but the synchronic, semiotic one of difference. As parts of a metasemiosis, theism and humanism are mutually dependent, generating one another; singly, they do not exist at all. The relationship between them is no happenstance, no accident or coincidence that can be counteracted or contested by subsequent happenstance or the citation of counterinstances, but is the systemic difference that constitutes intelligibility. Their interdependence is necessitated by consciousness.

The strength of this reading is not to be measured quantitatively by the amount of discourse, either in Edwards's oeuvre or in early American literature generally, that it rescues from anachronism, although the quantity will be considerable; the unitary model is capacious only for modern literature and intimations of modern literature. The unitary model is extremely selective otherwise, excluding a large proportion of the record of early American literature, both voluminous and important to the judgment of those early Americans who gather and arrange for the preservation of this record, an exclusion that applies especially to Edwards's writings, the major treatises that he obviously considers his theological legacy being represented piecemeal in his modern text, in new contexts either obliquely related or unrelated to their original ones, while the journals and personal writings he considers less worthy of publication are elevated to central positions. Nor is the strength of this reading to be measured by the related criterion of service to the field, although again this might not be inconsiderable. Now that studies of early American literature are numerous, exclusions from the record of the early culture are becoming inhibiting, the supply of early documents that can believably be called protomodern being about exhausted while the rest, the majority, remain ineligible for serious scholarly attention until a new model is advanced that makes their theism interesting and meaningful.

This reading is strong, rather, primarily in the relatively greater clarity of its recognization of the modernism that escapes the notice of modern American cultural historiography. This cognizance will subject Edwards's writings to a more self-conscious, and thus more formidable kind of modern patronage, and in so patronizing his writings it will suggest ways to annex more of early American discourse more firmly than is possible under the unitary model. A phenomenology of early American literature fulfills the program of modernism to comprehend the past. One of its advantages over the current unitary model is the same as Miller's over Parrington, which is that it turns more of the documents of early American culture into parts of a whole—a differential and dipartite whole, but a whole nonetheless.

This chapter converses at length with modern humanism. The next three chapters of this reading, which deal primarily just with Edwards's writings, will continue to do so not only in frequent direct references, but also structurally, first, by replacing the dialectic of Edwards's writings with a consistency based on the assumption that theism is not their superficial or intermittent profession but their voice, sounded not just in apostrophes to God but in the murmur of personal writings and philosophical speculations; second, by replacing with the topics and order of the next three chapters, on Edwards's discourses of Creation, of Providence, and of Grace, the modern trivium of science, history, and psychology. Edwards's difference can thus be displayed through continuous implicit allusion to the appearance of his likeness, an impression not only of learned modern specialists in early American culture or students of Edwards, but of everyone reading the record of the early culture today. The final chapter will once again more directly oppose modern interpretations, first by comparing Edwards and Franklin to propose the utility of establishing theism as another discourse whose pattern both would associate early American writers, such as these two, who have been either superficially divorced or superficially joined, and would integrate documents of early American culture that fall outside the unitary model, next by contrasting Edwards with Emerson to recommend conversely the same remodeling of American culture to distinguish between theism and humanism, and finally by speculating on what might lie beyond the current enthnocentrism of modern American cultural historiography.

Such vigilance might seem to reflect a quixotic urge to free Edwards from his modern servitude. It actually serves the purpose of supplanting the modern metaphysics of American culture with a phenomenology, deconstruction that will begin now to attempt to wrest from unity the writings of Jonathan Edwards and that will continue ultimately to attempt to gather around them a theist discourse that clearly stands apart.

2

CREATION

The spirit of God may act so, that his actions may be agreeable to his nature, and yet may not at all communicate himself in his proper nature, in the effect of that action. Thus, for instance, the Spirit of God moved upon the face of the waters, and there was nothing disagreeable to his nature in that action, but yet he did not at all communicate himself in that action; there was nothing of the proper nature of the Holy Spirit in the motion of the waters.

—Edwards, *Religious Affections*

1. Introduction

The topics of this and the next two chapters are not ones chosen by Edwards to structure his work. The treatise whose topic most closely resembles that of this chapter he calls *A Dissertation Concerning the Chief End for which God Created the World;* although his last published work, the *Dissertation* contains neither all, hardly even most, of his thinking on this topic, nor the most finished version. The reason for this is that as a theologian his main concern is for Divinity, to which the topic of Creation is subordinate, only one of several areas in which Divinity is expressed, and of them not the most expressive. As the title of the *Dissertation* conveys, even that work is interested in the world only to the degree that the world reflects divine motives. Thus both the priority and the constitution of this chapter represent a decision to begin with a topic that Edwards not only does not consider of primary importance but does not consider sufficiently meaningful as a context to restrict any one of his works to it, and to collect passages that are scatted among various works on various subjects written at different times.

The text of Edwards's writings that will be constructed in the three central chapters of this reading refers unavoidably to humanist discourse. To begin with nature is to prepare for man a field on which to exercise his will; to continue with history is to record the experience of this exercise; to conclude with personality is to arrive at the study of man himself. The logic of this order depends on the assumption of human primacy. In the context of theist discourse it is a solecism; it would be mistaken as mere error by Edwards and deplored by him as the product of either or both a bad heart and bad reason. It does not exist as a positive, substantial discourse in the theist discursive pattern at all. The initial purpose of this transposition is to preserve in modern discourse the alienness of the theism of Edwards's writings. Doing so requires more than the archaic capitalization of words; Creation, Providence, and Grace no longer have even the look of translit-erations now that modern usage has assigned a lower-case meaning to each. But the familiar understanding of them can be exploited to convince a modern readership of the strangeness of a theist discourse that assumes their reality as uncritically as nature, history, and man are assumed to be real by natural science, the social sciences, and the humanities. The an-thropocentricity of modern discourse cannot be annihilated, but can serve as a background against which the difference of a discourse otherwise arranged might appear in greater relief. This phenomenology of Edwards's writings will strive to stay aware of the disparities between the two discur-sive patterns, and the final purpose will be to create a different phenome-non of Edwards's writings that reflects simultaneously on the integrity of each.

Edwards says that the meaning of nature lies exclusively in its status as a creation of God. Striving to turn all intellectual pursuits into a form of religious devotion, he studies the natural world only to the degree that he thinks it manifests the design of its Creator. His earliest empirical writings may, as is often claimed, show a fascination with material things, but this interest is soon subordinated to theology. Edwards is not a scientist, not-withstanding the claims of his earliest editor, Sereno Dwight, and one of his modern critics, David Scofield Wilson. He lacks Newton's ability to focus continuously on particular phenomena, and thus cannot suspend the desire to discover large metaphysical truths long enough to find local physical laws. Nor does he share Locke's willingness to concentrate on developing a natural philosophy of the mind, but rather devotes himself to speculating on what lies beyond the mind's ken. Natural man and his natural environment seldom interest Edwards intrinsically. Nature com-mands his attention only insofar as it reveals its divine origin, a theocen-tricity that arguably characterizes both Newton's and Locke's epistemology as well, that explains such apparent anachronisms as Newton's belief in the supernatural character of gravity, Newton's eschatological obsession later in his career, and Locke's continual pious references to a sovereign God, and that casts doubt on whether even Newton is properly to be identified as a scientist or whether even Locke is properly to be identified as a psychologist in the modern sense.[1]

To Edwards, the primary goal of all theology is to define the original relationship between the Creator and all of His works, and Edwards pursues this goal no less in controversial works than in ontological studies of the universe and lyric celebrations of the beauties of nature. To isolate Edwards's discourse of Creation requires not only that the *Dissertation* be combined with related notebook entries, but that excerpts be taken as well from other works, *Religious Affections, Original Sin, Freedom of the Will,* and *The Nature of True Virtue* in particular. Together these comprise Edwards's discourse of Creation. The consistency of this discourse, the very existence of this text is denied by arguments for Edwards's modernity, which try to expose contradictions between his theological principles and philosophical method on the subject of nature as well as on other subjects. It is said, for instance, that the limitations of created intellect that Edwards stresses when discussing man's subordinate position in Creation are implicitly transcended by the knack for solving divine mysteries displayed by the intellectual, Jonathan Edwards; or that the relative worthlessness of material things that he cites as a norm of the hierarchy of being is transcended by his joy at perceiving "images or shadows of divine things" in nature. That Edwards often preaches a humble acceptance of the imperfections of the natural world cannot be contested; a presumed glorious practice of periodically transgressing this rule has been the central perception of most modern scholarship.

Both Edwards's pious admissions of the limitations of created being and several of the passages in which he seems to modern scholarship to be going beyond them will be included in his discourse of Creation. Its coherence depends on the reconciliation of all of these passages according to a dualism that is more supple than modern interpretations admit, and that allows Edwards to see enough of the Creator in His works to share the empirical sensitivity of the most advanced eighteenth-century science without becoming so close to Him as to write in ways not structurally consistent with the theist discursive pattern. This reading practices the "philosophical semantics" recommended by Lovejoy as particularly necessary for a genuine understanding of "the word 'nature,'" a practice that Lovejoy himself does not follow consistently enough, and one that modern American cultural historiography is particularly loath to apply to the "naturalism" of such early American writers as Edwards.[2]

2. Reason and Revelation

Edwards's *summa* is supposed to have been a history of the work of redemption, a comprehensive theodicy that, according to Miller, "would have reached religious conclusions that would have transcended the Age of Reason and anticipated Kierkegaard." Edwards does not live to finish it.

He dies in 1758 just as he is to begin a new career as president of Princeton. His last completed work turns out to be the *Dissertation*, published posthumously, in which he gives formal expression to the discourse of Creation that is implied in all his previous explanations of how the histories and characteristics of particular creatures answer God's purposes. There are a few scholarly estimates that consider the *Dissertation* "as his most important work"; there are a great many more that like Miller's virtually ignore the *Dissertation* while paying enormous attention to the projected "history" of the work of redemption. But the *Dissertation* is full of the apparent contradictions between rationality and piety that appeal to modern interpretations as evidence of Edwards's unconscious sympathy for the Enlightenment and discomfort with Puritan restraints on the intellect, and so might deserve a more prominent place in his modern text.[3]

Edwards seems uncertain in the opening pages whether reason or revelation should be his guide. He begins with a logical discussion of the relationship between motives and actions that seems to imply the facility with which reason can analyze behavior to find the disposition of the will. Edwards first divides motives into three categories. Least important is the "subordinate end," pursued "not at all upon its own account, but wholly on the account of a *further* end" that Edwards calls "ultimate." An ultimate end, though valued "for its own sake," may be of either chief or inferior importance. Any number of ultimate ends may be pursued, but all are inferior to a single chief end, which is "most valued, and therefore most sought after." Edwards proceeds to show how each type of end can contribute to the motivation of even the simplest action: Suppose a man "goes on a journey to obtain a medicine to restore his health"; the man's desire to get the medicine is subordinate to the end of curing himself; this latter end is "ultimate," valued "for its own sake," but it might be either chief or inferior depending on whether health were "most sought after."[4]

Edwards uses classical logic in the beginning of the *Dissertation* in order simply to define the terms with which he intends to analyze God's ends in Creation. A man making a trip to the apothecary resembles God creating the universe; the latter act, no matter how much greater and more mysterious, is similarly explicable through rational inquiry. The assumption that the Creator is something like, though infinitely greater than His creatures is not precocious; it is stated for example in the writings of Aquinas centuries before Edwards implies it here. Such comparisons do not diminish God so long as the incommensurability between their items is not forgotten, and Edwards is never reluctant to envision divine attributes as human ones in which limitations and "changeableness and other imperfections" are imaginatively removed. But although there is no necessary impiety in approximating divine motives from the knowledge of human ones, to imply that they are equally accessible to reason, as Edwards's analysis in the beginning of the *Dissertation* might, would encourage the notion that man's natural faculties are sufficient to know God, and this no truly pious theologian can allow.[5]

Perhaps anticipating this possibility, Edwards insists, when confronting the mystery of Creation itself in the first chapter of the *Dissertation*, that reason must seek the cognitive assistance of revelation: "Indeed," he admonishes in the first expository paragraph of chapter 1, "this affair seems properly to be an affair of divine revelation. In order to determine what was designed, in the creating of the astonishing fabric of the universe we behold, it becomes us to attend to, and rely on, what he has told us, who was the architect. He best knows his own heart, and what his own ends and designs were in the wonderful works he has wrought. Nor is it to be supposed that mankind—who, while destitute of revelation, by the utmost improvements in their own reason, and advances in science and philosophy, could come to no clear and established determination of who the *author* of the world was—would ever have obtained any tolerable settled judgment of the *end* which the author of it proposed to himself in so vast, complicated, and wonderful a work of his hands." The classical philosophy on which Edwards's logic in the introduction to the *Dissertation* is based fails to acknowledge the Christian God as Creator of the universe, even after studying the universe for centuries. This ought to teach all Christians that a rational analysis of actions, based on man's experience of his own, cannot alone be trusted to explain the actions of God. Only the heeding of divine decrees will discover the meaning of the world to man. Piety, Edwards goes on to say, does not so much assist as supersede reason; although revelation "has been the occasion of great improvement" in reason and has "taught man how to use" his rational faculties, yet revelation must remain "the principle [*sic*] guide" for the inquiry.[6]

These two, nearly contiguous passages from the beginning of the *Dissertation* can easily be interpreted as dialectically opposed. Pondering a subject somewhat removed from God, Edwards displays how an enlightened mind can use logical argument and concrete example to dispel confusion arising from what Locke terms "mixed modes"—ideas, in this case about the will, that have become divorced from experience. A few pages later, in contemplation of a divine mystery Edwards seems to revert to an irrational piety. This is the pattern found by modern critics who, like Miller, see a dialectic in Edwards's thought between an original thinker and a servant of Puritanism, between the rationalist and the pietist, between the modern and medieval mind.

Even more interesting to modern dialectical interpretations would be the impression that the rationalist in the *Dissertation* is ultimately more conspicuous. After turning quickly from reason to revelation in the first chapter, Edwards shifts as rapidly back to listing the "things that appear to be the dictates of reason," and follows the dictation of his own mind throughout the work, though pausing periodically to take divine instruction. Because of its seeming irrelevance to the logical method that directs most of the *Dissertation*, Edwards's piety might be dismissed as a religious posture; maybe he fears that his intellect aspires too high, that he is venturing dangerously close to a definition of what his faith teaches is undefinable. If this is the case, expressions of what a modern critic calls the "mind-set" of Edwards's age might properly be ignored in favor of those parts of the *Dissertation* which seem to demonstrate an unselfconscious ability to comprehend eternal things.[7]

But a very different structure can be discovered in the same passages. Those that in the *Dissertation* analyze behavior in the abstract certainly differ, in their choice of evidence, in their method of inquiry, even in their style, from others that quote Scripture. But Edwards intersperses them because he takes for granted a consistency that today must be made explicit. The consistency becomes apparent when the three types of ends Edwards deduces are recognized as complicating the relationship between motives and actions, a complication that is manifest when, in his notebooks, Edwards applies the hierarchy of ends to a similar illustration in which the morality of an act of healing is in question.

Discussing sincerity in entry no. 1153, Edwards imagines "a man that is kind to his neighbor's wife that is sick and languishing and is very helpful to her case, and makes a show of desiring her restoration to health and vigor, and not only makes a show, but there is a reality in his pretence—he does heartily and earnestly desire her restoration and uses his true and utmost endeavors for it." One of these "true and utmost endeavors" might be a trip to the apothecary, and the action can be noted as one sign of sincerity. If the man in Edwards's illustration goes on this errand, then his ultimate end, valued "for its own sake," would be the curing of his neighbor's wife. But the action can not itself communicate that motive. Trips to the apothecary look similar whatever their cause; and although close investigation of this one might find some clues, more information is needed to determine the ultimate end.

Suppose then that knowledge of the man's behavior is extended to previous and subsequent actions, which Edwards's illustration from the notebooks provides. Observation of the man nursing his neighbor's sick wife or otherwise demonstrating his solicitude would indicate that the trip is motivated by the sincere desire to restore the woman's health, and the ultimate end would thereby be discovered. But the man's chief end remains unknown. Perhaps that "which is most valued, and therefore most sought after" by him is truly virtuous, which for Edwards would be the welfare of being in general, to which the health of even a single ailing Christian contributes somewhat, and which therefore deserves some attention. The chief end might, however, be wholly vicious, consisting, as Edwards reveals at the conclusion of the illustration from the notebooks, in "no other than a vile and scandalous lust, he having secretly maintained a criminal intercourse and lived in adultery with her and earnestly wishes for her restored health and vigor that he may return to his criminal pleasures." Edwards ends his story with this disclosure to emphasize that apparent sincerity is no proof of internal morality. Although the man's ardent solicitude does serve his chief end, it is superficially misleading.[8]

Although knowledge of a particular action fails to reveal the chief end of an agent, knowledge of all of his acts might appear sufficient to determine it. The omniscience that Edwards assumes in the case of the adulterous couple uncovers their secret, the chief end that is not apparent in the man's medical attentions alone. But although characters can be transparent hypothetically, they are hardly so in Puritan congregations, Edwards having uncovered more than one wolf hidden among his flock at Northampton. The "external behavior" of an errant Puritan, he knows, occurs largely "in secret, and hid from the eye of the world." Many of the actions that reflect a man's chief end are known by God alone.[9]

But even if all "external behavior" can be observed, behavior still fails to reveal a chief end according to Edwards's analysis of the will, since the complexity of ends makes impossible the inference of disposition from activity; Edwards doubts whether any action whatsoever can signify a chief end. Actions that manifest subordinate, least important ends will seldom be mistaken to reveal chief ones; that anyone would go to the apothecary for the pure joy of the trip is unlikely (though not impossible). But others, like earnest efforts to restore the health of a neighbor's wife, are more likely to be considered direct manifestations of the will, and the acceptance of this kind of behavior as self-revelatory is what Edwards's distinction between merely ultimate and truly chief ends discourages. Because even the most passionate action may reveal only an ultimate end, behavior, no matter how thoroughly observed and acutely interpreted, can never surely evidence a chief end.

Thus in the case of the adulterous couple Edwards can only pretend to know, for the purpose of showing how ultimate ends differ from chief ends, the true disposition of the man's will. Edwards cannot determine it, however, even by witnessing the couple making love, since passionate love-making need not reveal a chief end any more reliably than passionate medical care. The man's philandering might not, Edwards must be willing to suppose, indicate a paramount lust, but only another ultimate end. Possibly, not even very improbably, the man remains essentially virtuous despite this momentary lapse into sin; for, as Edwards notes in *Religious Affections*, "those sins to which a man by his natural constitution was most inclined before his conversion, he may be apt to fall into still," since "grace does not rule out an evil natural temper." One reason why Edwards would so qualify the efficacy of Grace is that he consistently suspects any necessary connection between "external behavior" and the true disposition of the will, which uncertain relationship allows, finally, for a man's chief end never to be acted upon in life. In the notebook entry in which the illustration of the adulterous couple appears, Edwards distinguishes between "acts of the will" and acts of the body, cautioning that "although the motions of the body follow the acts of the will by the law of nature which the Creator has established, yet that don't make the motions of the body the acts of the soul." Edwards stresses the distinction here in order to stress that God requires a spiritual obedience rather than good works. But the distinction again reveals an epistemology that concedes an agent's will may never be known through observation of his actions. Although the chief end of the man in the illustration may truly be adultery, he may never act to consummate his lust. This chief end may exist forever in secret, but, according to Edwards's analysis, it can remain nonetheless superior to all conflicting motives that actually restrain it, such as the desire to protect himself and his good name. "Whosoever looketh on a woman to lust after her," Christ warns, "hath committed adultery with her already in his heart" (Matt. 5: 28). Edwards is no existentialist. He must presume to know more than all of a man's behavior in order to state his chief end; determination of it depends on a pretended access to an extraordinary and direct revelation of his heart.[10]

What may seem no more than an atypically prurient little illustration can be seen to have a wide discursive significance. It joins Edwards's epistemology with that of the Bible, as expressed not only in Matthew but in many scriptural separations of the soul from the body in both testaments, such as the psalmodic caution that "the inward mind and heart of man are deep!" (Psalms 64:6). It also joins Edwards's epistemology with that of Augustine, who concedes behavior that even more obviously than adultery violates the Law, such as suicide, may nonetheless be ordered by "Him whose commandments we may not neglect" and so manifest a gracious disposition that no observor can possibly detect, and with that of Cotton Mather, whose reluctance to execute accused witches purely on the basis of "spectral evidence" derives not from a humane squeamishness over capital punishment, as some of Mather's humanist apologists claim, but from the epistemological discretion that agrees with his father Increase's agreement with Lactantius, according to whom "devils so work that things which are not appear to men as if they were real," which possibility gives "spectral evidence" the uncertain status of oxymoron. Perhaps a more surprising epistemological agreement can be found in Newton, whose faith in observation is explicitly qualified by the reminder that "in bodies, we see only their outward figures and colors . . . but their inward substances are not to be known by our sense, or by any reflex act of our minds."[11]

Perhaps more surprising still is the discovery of virtually identical disclaimers in what are usually considered the equally or more enlightened contexts of Alexander Hamilton's warnings in "Federalist #1" against the motives of anti-Federalist opponents—there might be a "dangerous ambition" that "lurks behind the specious zeal for the rights of the people"— and against even his own motives, which admittedly "must remain in the depository of my own breast." There is also Thomas Jefferson's admission in *Notes on the State of Virginia* that the characters of slaves, who are to Jefferson so much simpler and more frequently exposed than those of their superior and more restrained masters, remain nonetheless essentially invisible and subject only to inexact speculation. Emerson's proclamations that "all external life declares interior life" and that "all form is an effect of character" and that "the soul makes the body" represent in the context of theist discourse no visionary confidence in the potential wholeness of being or in the potential omniscience of knowing, but mere imprudent error. When James Carse in his recent study says that "morality for Edwards is totally visible," he is reading Emerson, not Edwards.[12]

If Edwards cannot identify the chief end behind a man's activity without extraordinary assistance, he has reason to seek a divine revelation of the "chief end for which God created the world." As Edwards defines it, reason does not compete with revelation, but rather arrives at the boundary past which only revelation can lead. The mind need not be chastened by irrational piety, but recognizes limitations in the very course of reasoning. The analogy between human and divine behavior is pious because the mystery of God's chief end is suggested by the mysterious relationship between the actions and motives of men. Using none but rational means, Edwards implies that the "astonishing fabric of the universe" can hardly be taken as a transparent expression of Divinity.

The agreement between reason and revelation signifies more than a local coherence in Edwards's writing. It conflicts fundamentally with modern interpretations because it demonstrates employment of a dualistic epistemology that exists only in the theist discursive pattern. In distinguishing always between the will and manifestations of the will, Edwards shows a distrust of appearances that is fundamental to theism and marginal to humanism, according to which latter discourse the deceptiveness of appearances can always—ideally if not actually—be clarified.

Edwards's distrust of what can be understood as the theist equivalent of modern phenomena is evident throughout *Religious Affections,* the work most directly concerned with explaining how the state of the soul might be verified. According to "the laws of union which the Creator fixed between soul and body," the affections, which Edwards defines as "the more vigorous and sensible exercises of the inclination and will," register on the body through "motion of the blood and animal spirits." The affections, however, are themselves insensible; the reactions of the body are only sensible consequences of affections, and Edwards takes pains to distinguish between the invisible cause and visible effect: "Nor are these motions and animal spirits and fluids of the body any thing properly belonging to the nature of the affections, though they always accompany them in the present state; but are only effects or concomitants of affections, that are entirely distinct from affections themselves, and no way essential to them." These statements are not merely prolix. Edwards multiplies prepositions in order increasingly to distance affections from their manifestation, and he continually anticipates the careless identification of feeling with the show of feeling in order emphatically to refute the connection.[13]

He denies himself any sure means of determining the will from actions, conceding in the introduction to *Religious Affections* that he is ill-equipped "to distinguish between true and false religion, between *saving affections* and experiences, and those manifold fair shows and glistering appearances by which they are counterfeited." The treatise is devoted mainly to acknowledging that truly religious affections are impossible to confirm. This failure often leads to "inexpressibly dreadful circumstances," especially for a New England pastor during the awakenings of the early eighteenth century. But whatever earnest wish and practical need Edwards has to correlate appearances and reality, his epistemology forbids a solution. The body, the sole "medium of communication" in this world, registers the intensity, but not the object of desire. It can be observed, both by the person aroused and by others, manifesting a strong inclination, but it cannot itself express the quality, or morality, of the inclination. A sincere and passionate love of God can therefore feel and look the same as a sincere and passionate love of the self, or of a woman, as is the case in the illustration from the notebooks. Actions of men are to Edwards as "the leaves of a tree" in Scripture, "which though the tree ought not to be without them, yet are no where given as an evidence of the goodness of the tree." Revelation teaches, and Edwards's reason agrees, that the body gives unreliable evidence of the soul.[14]

In limiting what he can know with certainty, Edwards restates an injunction at least as old as Christianity and central to Puritanism. Augustine distinguishes between appearance and reality in both human and divine contexts: "For as the sound which communicates the thought conceived in the silence of the mind is not the thought itself, so the form by which God, invisible in His own nature, became visible, was not God Himself." Calvin mentions the distinction in a principle of church government, warning in his *Institutes* that no sure sign of spiritual election can be perceived in the demeanor of any professing Christian. But modern interpretations of Edwards propose that, at least when gripped by those infrequent, heightened affections he hopes are gracious, Edwards senses a union between the visible and invisible that contradicts dualistic epistemology and anticipates romantic visionary experience, and this despite unmistakable evidence that when Edwards contemplates these emotions, both his own and those of others, in the tranquility of his theological writings, the dualism of his understanding is pronounced, leading him to question feeling in ways that seem precisely to differentiate him both from later romantic visionaries and from supposedly protoromantic contemporaries.[15]

The cult of sensibility and the related literary movements of the Gothic and the sublime are growing in England in Edwards's time, and they win a number of American adherents not long after his death. These movements are often viewed as anticipating romanticism, in part because all three celebrate feeling; whether in the form of excessive joy and sorrow in sentimental novels by Sterne and MacKenzie, terror in Gothic tales, or awe in sublime landscape poetry, the cultivation of intense feeling for its own sake is becoming common in late eighteenth-century English literature. This emotionalism is seen to anticipate the emphasis on feeling as an avenue of spiritual transcendence that characterizes later romantic writings. Edwards is deeply involved in the roughly contemporaneous emotional upheavals of the American Great Awakening but in *Religious Affections* Edwards is highly and continuously suspicious of extravagant religious feeling. Although agreeing that a person under the influence of grace may react strongly, he agrees with Calvin that "no external manifestations and outward appearances whatsoever, that are visible to the world, are infallible evidences of grace." Religious enthusiasts, as devoted to emotion as the literary cultists of sensibility, trouble Edwards throughout his career, both because they threaten to infect congregations with false affections and because their excesses discourage less uninhibited Christians from opening themselves to what might be authentic awakenings.[16]

In order to associate Edwards with such sentimentalists, and with the later romantic writers who assert that a powerful attraction to earthly things, such as a landscape or a lover or one's fellow man in general, can itself become religious, Edward's definition of genuine holiness, stated repeatedly in *Religious Affections* and elsewhere, must somehow be elided. Some excuse must be found for his frequent and explicit warnings that, although rapture for God may look and feel like rapture for creatures, holiness grows not out of natural affections but in spite of them: "One that has the power of godliness in his heart, has his inclination and heart exercised towards God and divine things, with such strength and vigor, that these holy exercises do prevail in him, above all carnal or natural affections, and are effectual to overcome them; for every true disciple of Christ loves him above father or mother, wife and children, brethren and sisters, houses and lands; yea than his own life." This is not a pious platitude. Edwards is not speaking against exciting insights to the contrary. Although such insights may be expressed a little less than a century later in the United States, to Edwards there are no alternatives save perverse blasphemy and dull confusion. Here a dualistic epistemology, supported by both Scripture and reason as Edwards understands them, is applied to the experience of life in a way that seems most intelligent, and is most intelligible, in the context of a theist discourse.[17]

Distinctions between holy and natural affections, as well as those between chief and ultimate ends, are applied by Edwards also in his analysis
of the divine motive for Creation. If the expression of any agent, man or
God, is never identical to his inner self, then the theologian, even more
than the moralist, can never presume to know his subject; thus Edwards
inevitably emphasizes the supremacy of revelation over the empirical
study of nature in seeking God's chief end. His acceptance of this epistemology may seem disappointing, the truths it finds ordained, about as
disappointing and foreordained as Newton's theological extension of his
epistemological aporetics, which is that "much less" than is the essence of
things accessible to observation "have we any idea of the substance of
God." But this epistemology proves flexible in Edwards's service, answering many questions that today seem insoluble without transcending
its dualistic restrictions. Perhaps the greatest lesson of Edwards's thought
will come from a current understanding of how he is inspired not despite
admitting the inexpressiveness of the visible world, but through this admission, how although God is not present to him, as deity is to later
romantic writers for whom the real and ideal are united, Edwards's God
can generate a several-thousand-page discourse of Divinity.[18]

3. The Logic of Creation

In analyzing the relationship between the will and action of an agent in
the *Dissertation*, Edwards deduces the necessity of a chief end that neither
reason nor observation can identify. This chief end is the equivalent in
Edwards's analysis of the will to a first cause in his analysis of being, and
just as the laws of behavior require for him the existence of a mysterious
chief end, so does the logic of Creation imply a mysterious first cause.

Reason is to Edwards an instinctive tendency of the mind. So fundamental does it seem to him that in his early notebooks he even supposes, in
what may be a deliberate catachresis of Locke's terminology, that it is "an
innate principle . . . that the soul is born with—a necessary, fatal propensity." That Edwards might so explicitly defy Locke, even in private, suggests the importance to him of establishing reason as a universal attribute
ordained directly by God. Reason must be an innate propensity because it
will be convinced of the necessary existence of God in deducing the logic of
creation.

The most prominent characteristic of reason to Edwards is its demand
for linear causality: "All our reasoning," he observes later in the same
notebook entry, "depends on that natural, unavoidable, and invariable
disposition of the mind, when it sees a thing begin to be, to conclude
certainly, that there is a *cause* of it; or if it sees a thing to be in a very orderly,
regular, and exact manner, to conclude that some *Design* regulated and

disposed it." This assumption is more significant than it may appear. It informs all of Edwards's controversial works, it is central to all theist theology, providing for example foundation for the first of Aquinas's five "ways" of proving the existence of God, and it appears unimportant only in the context of the humanist discursive pattern, in which linear causality becomes either a specialized or a philosophically naive etiology because of its implicit, but profound, inconsistency with the centrality of man.[19]

Throughout *Freedom of the Will*, Edwards accuses "Arminian" opponents of forgetting that causality is linear. As the editor of the Yale edition of *Freedom of the Will* points out, Edwards does not once in the volume feel the need to attack his opponents on moral grounds, but rather restricts himself to a purely logical refutation of the contention that the will of man might be meaningfully free. Edwards has remarkable confidence in his ability to establish God's sovereignty in logical terms, since he is of course aware of the theological and moral stakes involved in the question of predetermination; in *The Great Doctrine of Original Sin Defended*, a work less reluctant to accuse opponents of impiety, Edwards says that in defending man's free will "Arminians" erect "as strong a fortress" for Deists and other atheistic and unscriptural thinkers. Edwards's virtuosity in *Freedom of the Will* lies in his ability to ground his faith in what he considers common sense, much as in the *Dissertation* he shows how the logical analysis of human motives ought to lead all reasonable men to the Bible to discover the ends of God.[20]

The logical absurdity of "Arminianism" exposed by Edwards in *Freedom of the Will* is that "Arminianism" is based on the assumption that "a thing that begins to be should make itself." This contradicts linear causality, which requires an extrinsic, or prior cause for everything. A truly rational mind will never, according to Edwards's definition of reason, accept an effect as originating "freely," which to him means uncaused; thus to seek such an effect, a "free" act of the will, is to drive the mind "back *in infinitum*," through an unending series of antecedent causes, "and that is to drive it out of the world." This infinite regression shows more than the discovery of a logical mistake. The absurdity of defending free will Edwards reveals by the logical deduction that only through what to him is a manifestly impossible endless chain of prior acts could the will determine itself. The heresy of the "Arminians'" argument, which he does not bother to condemn explicitly in *Freedom of the Will*, lies in their implying that the divine attribute of self-determination can belong to man. That the rational mind cannot conceive of self-creation is to Edwards indirect proof of the Divinity of self-creation, for he writes in a passage from his *Notebooks* that is discursively indistinguishable from Thomist Metaphysics, or even from Aristotelian metaphysics, "if something has been from eternity, 'tis either an endless succession of causes and effects, as for instance an endless succession of fathers and sons or something equivalent; but this supposition is attended with manifold apparent contradictions, as there must have been some external, self-existent being, having the reason of his existence within himself—i.e., he must have existed from eternity without any reason for his existence—both which are inconceivable." The "manifold apparent contradiction" of thinking of eternal being as an infinite series of antecedent causes is that logic demands the existence of some unfathered first cause to begin the series by the same rule of linear causality that denies the possibility of any such thing existing in nature. This logical quandary, which ought to arise whenever man ponders the origin of something, does, indeed, drive the mind "out of the world," and in so doing not only refutes the notion of freedom of the will but demonstrates the necessity of a first cause existing outside the logic of cause and effect. This is God Himself. In *Freedom of the Will*, Edwards restricts himself to a purely rational analysis that demonstrates how theist reason is consistent with theist religious belief.[21]

The logic of Creation is thus shown to agree with the revelation of the Bible. God fashions man's natural faculties so as to reveal both the necessity of His existence and His sovereignty. Because the presumption that a thing can exist "without any determining cause is contrary to all use and custom," man deduces rationally that the world must have an antecedent cause. Perceiving "the astonishing fabric of the universe," man concludes that it must be made by a Being both apart from and superior to it: "We first ascend, and prove a posteriori, or *from effects*, that there must be an eternal cause; and then secondly, prove *by argumentation* . . . that this being must be necessarily existent; and then thirdly, from the proved necessity of his existence, we may descend and prove many of his perfections a priori." Reason must concede the existence of a mysterious first cause because, given linear logic and the existence of the Universe, "there is no other way." God is real not only to the Christian heart through belief in revelation, but to the rational mind, which has "nothing else to make a supposition of." Such so-called theistic proofs seem unimpressive, seem merely ingenious or clever, to humanist hindsight, because in the context of humanist discourse they amount to a sort of punning, the transposition of a marginal etiology to the exalted status of a proof of the existence of God. Within theist discourse there is no tension between linear causality and divine sovereignty, so to connect the two requires no rhetorical wit. When Edwards connects them he simply recalls that within theist discourse there can be only one logical answer to the question of origin, which is posed as a means of making reason chasten itself throughout theist discourse, from the Bible, "Has the rain a father, or who has begotten the drops of dew? / From whose womb did the ice come forth, and Who has given birth to the hoarfrost of heaven?" (Job. 38:28.), through the poems of Edward Taylor, "Upon what Base was fixt the Lath, wherein / He turn'd this Globe, and riggalld it so trim?" to Edwards's own prosaic admonishments.[22]

The insistence with which Edwards attacks any idea of self-generation as a violation of common sense shows his belief in its effectiveness as a polemic technique. It is directed not just at eighteenth-century Puritans; it appeals to the common sense of all theists, and is based on a logic that originates in classical antiquity and that remains undisturbed by the scientific and philosophical developments of the Enlightenment. Locke, in a passage that Edwards mentions in his notebooks, satirizes the attempt to discover a first cause in nature with the story of an Indian philosopher "who, when asked what the world stood upon, answered, it stood upon an elephant: and when asked what the elephant stood upon, he replied, on a broad-backed turtle," and so on, *in infinitum*. One of the great practitioners of "enlightened" science, Joseph Priestley, cites the linearness of natural generation to refute the partisans of spontaneous generation: "Completely organized bodies, of specific kinds, are maintained [by champions of spontaneous generation] to be produced from substances that could not have any natural connexion with them. . . . And this I assert is nothing less than the production of an affect without any adequate cause. If the organic particle from which an oak is produced be not precisely an acorn, the production of it from any other thing is as much a miracle, and out of the course of nature, as if it had come from a bean, or a pea, or absolutely from nothing at all." And Priestley's American friend and correspondent Thomas Jefferson confirms the rational necessity of a Creator who has logical priority over the world, reasoning that if one "suppose the earth a created existence," one "must suppose a creator then; and that he possessed power and wisdom to a great degree." Lovejoy attests to the unanimity with which the "principle of sufficient reason" is accepted throughout the seventeenth and eighteenth centuries, and he is undoubtedly too cautious in restricting the unanimity to just those two centuries. The principle is employed in both classical and Christian antiquity, and continues to be articulated, although sometimes in decadent forms, in the early nineteenth century, at least in the United States. Poe, who declares utter belief in the logical necessity of the priority of a Creator in *Eureka*— "that Nature and the God of Nature are distinct, no thinking being can long doubt"—dramatizes, or melodramatizes, the impossibility of finding a first cause in nature in exposing as suidical and homicidal and liable to the discovery not of profundities but of abysmal depths the curiosity that insists on getting to the bottom of things, such as the essence of love in "Ligeia" or of friendship in "The Fall of the House of Usher" or of being, itself, in the *Narrative of A. Gordon Pym* or "Descent Into the Maelstrom" or "Manuscript Found in a Bottle." Edwards, Locke, Priestley, Jefferson, Augustine, the poet of Job, or Heraclitus, who warns that "you could not in your going find the ends of the soul, though you traveled the whole way: so deep is its Law," would all recognize as an expression of the futility of trying to regress along an infinite series of antecedent causes to discover the first one an image that appears in Poe's "The Conqueror Worm," which is supposed to be written by Ligeia and commanded by her to be read to her on her deathbed, in which the frustration of such searches is lyricized as a spiraling "that ever returneth in / To the selfsame spot." Only the style and genre of Edwards' theist epistemology are changed in Poe's "Letter to B." when he warns that "as regard the great truths, men oftener err in seeking them at the bottom than at the top; the depth lies in the huge abysses where wisdom is sought—not in the palpable places where she is found. The ancients were not always right in hiding the goddess in a well."[23]

That Edwards can be placed in such secularly prominent and theologically unorthodox company in the eighteenth and nineteenth centuries reveals a likeness that neither he nor "enlightened" thinkers would claim. However, discourses like this one about the structure of causality are universal in the theist discursive pattern, and they are supple enough to withstand intellectual disputes. They remain uncontested in controversies and can be seen to reveal a discursive affinity joining writings in which opinions seem most widely to differ. Underlying disparities in intention, temperament, and belief, such discourses can be understood to show discursive regularity. The acceptance of linear causality bridges whatever gap may seem to exist between Puritans and eighteenth-century philosophers, and demonstrates how in the eighteenth century a writer can without inconsistency be both pious and "enlightened."

Thus can apparently unimportant expressions, such as those of linear causality, be seen to contain far-reaching discursive significance. The impression that linear etiology is trivial is founded not on an absence of empirical evidence of its prevalence; on the contrary, not only can it be seen to support Edwards's entire discourse of Creation and, what is the theological crux of this discourse, the rational proof of the existence of a transcendent God, but also to underlie the much larger archive of "occasionalist theory," which contains writings from the Patristic tradition through the Enlightenment, and to which Edwards's discourse of Creation corresponds. Linear causality is unremarkable, rather, only in the context of humanist discourse, which, having derived varieties of dialectical causality as the etiology fundamentally consistent with radical humanism, either exiles linear causality to the province of applied sciences, such as pathology or epidemiology, or tolerates it as a harmless superstition of theoretically naive scholarship, such as positivistic studies of reading or "influence" studies. Peripheral to modernist retrospect, linear causality is central to theism.[24]

The discursive fecundity of linear causality within theism extends beyond the theology and the quasi-theological natural philosophy of the Enlightenment, reaching even into the belletristic writings of the Gothic tradition, as is the case in Poe's fiction, poetry, and even his criticism. The absurdity of seeking a first cause in nature that Edwards analyzes and that

Poe dramatizes is reified generally in the characteristic predicaments of all Gothic protoganists, whose search for the solutions to Gothic plots so often requires plunging into some unfathomable abyss. Examples of this include the profusion of secret underground passageways in the novels of Brockden Brown, especially in *Edgar Huntly,* in the pit, the maelstrom, and the secret Antarctic caves of Poe's fiction, and even the suberannean network of rivers suspected to exist beneath Florida's treacherous landscape by William Bartram in his nonfiction but nonetheless Gothic *Travels.* All Gothic topography might therefore be interpreted as a hyperbole of nature's imperfection, structured after nothing more "real" than the discourse of the radical distinction between cause and effect. Gothic terror might similarly be interpreted as a melodrama of idolatry, structured after nothing other than the moral corollary of this distinction. The implications of linear causality in theist discourse are far from obvious or uninteresting. They suggest that theism may comprehend an archive containing writings from classical and Christian antiquity not just through those of Edwards but through those of Poe, whose gothicism might be seen to represent a belletristic form of that cautionary motto from Deuteronomy that Edwards improves upon so notoriously at Enfield, and they suggest also how modernism disguises through seeming indifference both the power of the discursive pattern from which modernism departs and the power required of modernism to achieve a separation. Ishmael plays with "Descartian vortices" as a philosophical conceit and pulls his foot back. For Edwards, and for Poe as well, falling is the natural state of man that can be altered, or postponed, only by the miraculous intervention of God.[25]

A final discursive significance of the assumption that Creation is ruled by linear causality is that the discourse of nature with which linear causality is consistent differs radically from that of the humanist discursive pattern. The logic by which Edwards and other theists distinguish cause from effect is rejected in favor of various forms of organic, or dialectical causality by Hegel and other German romantic philosophers, and subsequently by modern artists and philosophers throughout the Western world. One of the most revolutionary and distinctive aspects of Hegel's thought is that he believes, unlike Edwards, that "a thing that begins to be" can, indeed "make itself," or at least develop according to the dialectic between opposing elements intrinsic to it. All phenomena are interpreted in romantic discourse as containing in some way both the energy and the genetic potential to turn themselves into something else, and usually something better. Thus Emerson asserts in a passage from the late essay "Fate," which concludes with an outline of his own version of the Hegelian dialectic, that within the violent turmoil of natural change, within "the whole circle of animal life—tooth against tooth, devouring war, war for food, a yelp of pain and a grunt of triumph," inhere the seeds of a higher form of being, and that "the whole chemical mass" is thereby being "mellowed and refined for higher use." The existence of the universe does not argue the creativity of an extrinsic agent to the romantics; to them, nature, even in its simplest features, is self-generative and self-improving in precisely the manner that to Edwards is unthinkable. The enormity of the stakes involved in substituting a dialectical for a linear causality is recognized by the etiological revolutionaries, themselves, as when Hegel mentions, with apparent casualness, after having rejected "occasionalist theory" and "theistic proofs" as based on an incorrect and unexamined assumption of absolute difference between subject and object, that he would prefer "to avoid the name, 'God,' because this word is not in its primary use a conception as well, but the special name of an underlying subject, its fixed resting place," thus implying in the *Phenomenology* in what seems almost a sly premonition of Nietzsche's famous slogan, the death of the creative God of theist discourse. From the perspective of Hegel, and Kant, and after them of Husserl, linear causality represents no more than a convention, and not a very advanced convention, of consciousness—"we can extract clear concepts [of cause and effect] from experience, only because we have put them into experience"; "In this cosmological argument [that the existence and priority of a creative God are proved by the very existence of the universe] there are combined so many pseudo-rational principles that speculative reason seems in this case to have brought to bear all the resources of its dialectical skill to produce the greatest possible transcendental illusion." Linear causality can become a phenomenon of consciousness only in the discourse of modern phenomenology, however; in that of theist logic and metaphysics, linear causality is one of the many objective proofs of the objective existence of a Creator.[26]

Just as the logic of behavior proves to Edwards that the will of an agent is not necessarily shown in his action, so does the logic of Creation distance the Creator from His works. Edwards's analysis is governed by an assumption of linear causality in both cases, and it can be seen in both to fit a theist discourse that distinguishes God hierarchically from Creation. The dialectical causality of later romantic writers is, in this light, a crucial innovation. Another assumption about the origin of nature is necessary to support another discourse that claims God, or the Absolute, or Over-Soul, to be embedded deeply within nature rather than situated distantly above nature. The new romantic logic combines the cause of creativity with the result, such that "everything real is self existent" in Emerson's phrase, and thus makes immanent deity thinkable. Had he ever read it in its fully developed form, Edwards would have considered this proposition no more than illogical and impious. Edwards's inability to conceive an identity between Creator and Creation does not blind him to the subtle resemblance between them, however. Although he holds lesser expectations about the experience of nature than do romantic writers, Edwards perceives a likeness between natural beauties and divine excellency sufficient to inspire a religious enjoyment of the wilderness of eighteenth-century New England.[27]

This enjoyment is one of Edwards's attributes that most intrigues modern critics. Remove Edwards's discussion of the logic of Creation, remove also the many qualifications he attaches to his idea of the visibility of divine beauty, and the resulting text, though short, resembles romantic discourse. The restoration of the former passages will require a careful examination of precisely those disclaimers taken lightly by modern interpretations with the aim of demonstrating a consistency between the theoretical piety of Edwards's epistemology and the actual sensations of his personal experience.

4. Analogy

The view of Edwards that is most productive of modern scholarship is the one that locates his proto-modernism in stylistic precocities. Miller clearly has symbolism in mind when, in the long introductory essay to *Images or Shadows of Divine Things*, he suggests that Edwards extends typological interpretation of the Bible to a typological interpretation of nature, implying that to Edwards nature is at least as clear a sign of divinity to Christian experience as the Bible is to Christian exegesis. Delattre argues similarly in his later study that the "family resemblance" that Edwards recognizes between God and nature is close enough to permit the apprehension of divinity "through experience of an encounter with definite, concrete, substantial being and not in and through the abstract, ethereal, incommunicable, or untouchable." Similar views are held by Carse, Shea, Lowance, and others.[28]

In order for these descriptions to be correct, Edwards must at times contradict the dualistic epistemology he follows in the logical analyses of the *Dissertation* and other works, which can be said precisely to define God as "ethereal, incommunicable, and untouchable." But like his rationalism in the *Dissertation*, Edwards's sensationalism can be shown never to be even unconsciously revolutionary. The way in which he sees natural "images or shadows of divine things" to relate to the things themselves is expressed in a discourse of analogy that is perfectly consistent with his discourse of causality, and another expression of the theist discursive pattern.

It is evident from the illustration with which Edwards begins the *Dissertation* that he believes in the existence of analogies between human and divine behavior; it is evident also that this type of analogy is designed to prevent the confusion of God with His creatures. Edwards several times points out that analogy must never be mistaken for identity, that although God is not wholly different from man in kind, He is infinitely greater than man in degree. In a notebook entry that echoes Aquinas, Edwards concludes that "the difference between the nature of the deity and created spirits . . . is no contrariety, but what results from His greatness and nothing else. . . . So that, if we should suppose the faculties of a created spirit to be enlarged infinitely, there would be the deity to all intents and purposes." To see the Creator in the creature necessitates an imaginative leap that the imagination cannot span, multiplication to the *n*th power that emphasizes the subordination of man and the supremacy of God in the very act of attempting to liken one to the Other. The analogy between God and man is as much like identity as the analogy between the creating of the universe and making a trip to the apothecary.[29]

Because the priority of God is not challenged by Edwards's discourse of analogy, His separateness from Creation is preserved. Although "there is some analogy," Edwards points out in his *Treatise on the Nature of True Virtue,* between "secondary" or natural beauty and the "spiritual and virtuous beauty" of God, it holds "only so far as material things can have analogy to things spiritual, of which they can have no more than a shadow." The earthly shadow is distinguished invidiously from the truth that the shadow merely outlines. Material things are therefore the lower analogues of truths, indicating them in but a vague and inarticulate way. To specify analogues as "lower" is necessary only in the context of humanist discourse. According to the definition of analogy in the theist discursive pattern, such modification is redundant, "lower analogue" amounting in theist discourse to a pleonasm. Although Aquinas's typology of analogies is torturously complex, Aquinas defines all types as joining hierarchically differentiated beings, especially those analogies joining creature and Creator: "Thus there is a proportion between the creature and God as an effect to its cause and as a knower to the object known. However, because the Creator infinitely exceeds the creature, the creature is not so proportioned to its Creator that it receives His causal influence in its perfection, nor that it knows Him perfectly." Such "proportion," which according to modern usage is more accurately termed disproportion, applies throughout theist ontology. "Nothing is more striking" according to a twentieth-century critic of Shakespeare "in serious sixteenth-century literature than the universal use of analogy," and nothing is more striking than the consistency with which renaissance and other theist writers define analogy as a slight resemblance between unequal entities.[30]

The pejorative meaning of shadow and the dualistic meaning of analogy that supports it hold not only when Edwards is comparing divine attributes to human ones, as is the case in both *The Nature of True Virtue* and the introduction to the *Dissertation,* but also when he compares the material creations of the world, even the most impressive ones, with God's glory. In his notebooks Edwards remarks that although the "greatness, distance, and motion, etc. of this great universe has almost an omnipotent power

upon the imagination," yet the "greatness of vast expanse, immense dis-
tances, prodigious bulk, and rapid motion is but a little, trivial, and childish greatness in comparison of the noble, refined, exalted, divine spiritual
greatness. Yea, those are but the shadows of greatness and are worthless
except as they conduce to true and real greatness and excellency, and
manifest the power and wisdom of God." Nature, much like reason, must
bow to God at the point at which nature seems most independent; a sublime landscape for Edwards connotes the capacity of nature to embody not
God, but His shadow, thus revealing nature's pathetic inferiority to the
Creator.[31]

Analogy, and the shady status it confers on nature, are positively to be
associated with the epistemological and ontological strictures that control
theist discourse, including that of the bible, such as in proscriptions against
idolatry, "ye saw no manner of similitude on that day, . . . lest ye corrupt
yourselves, and make you a graven image, the similitude of any figure"
(Deuteronomy 4:15–16), and in the consistently negative connotation of the
figurative use of "shadow": "our days on earth are as a shadow, and there
is none abiding" (1 Chronicles 29:15). These strictures generate an enor-
mously complex series of discriminations meant to express as finely as
possible the elusive status of resemblances that are not identities, communications imperfectly conveyed, adjacencies that do not overlap, the
panoply of which Foucault has with appropriate archaism named "conve-
nientia" and with appropriate complexity defined as an "immense, taut,
and vibrating chain, this rope of 'conveneince'" in which "at each point of
contact there begins and ends a link that resembles the one before it and
the one after it; and from circle to circle, these similitudes continue, holding the extremes apart yet bringing them together in such a way that the
will of the Almighty may penetrate into the most unawakened corners."[32]

This description of the theist definition of analogy shows it to be more
intricate and more difficult to apply, and perhaps even more interesting
than the humanist redefinition, according to which analogy becomes identity ontologically and symbolism stylistically, and "shadow" accordingly
becomes potentially indistinguishable from substance. According to Emerson in that early compendium of romantic discourse in the United States,
Nature, the "analogical import" of "trivial facts" is based upon a fusion
between mind and matter that "is not fancied by some poet, but stands in
the will of God," a redefinition that is applied with eternal retroactivity by
Johnson when in Spiller's *Literary History* he declares that "nature was
analogy, as it had been felt by mystics since the beginning of time." In
Nature Emerson says that nature is a "great shadow pointing always to the
sun behind us" that hardly diminishes the original radiance, which small
lack can be compensated for by visionary perception.[33]

Only an unexamined acceptance of this humanist ontology and its corresponding aesthetics will condemn theist figuration, in which figures are

genuinely divided into tenors and vehicles whose separateness is essential, and theist generics, the epitome of which is the allegory in which meaning and narrative are as genuinely divided and whose separateness is equally essential. The latter is the "mere allegory" or "hideous and intolerable allegory" that Thoreau and Melville, and virtually every romantic writer who bothers to comment on theist rhetoric condemns. And only an unexamined modernism delivers the conversely patronizing faint praise that theist rhetoric adumbrates humanist rhetoric. Consider Carse, to whom "morality for Edwards is totally visible," and Cherry, to whom "an image or a shadow was not a token for things absent in space and time" but "a representation of a visible object which opened up invisible truths within that object." Cherry is (mis)reading Edwards through the misprision of Emerson and other revisionist romantic aestheticians.[34]

Although to Edwards "the creation of the world is but a shadow" of God's glory, the beauties of nature, which Edwards usually associates with biological and physical symmetries, obviously have theological import to him. Infinite amplification of natural felicities approximate divine perfection in the same way that raising human attributes to the nth power does, and "the adaptness of a variety of things to promote one intended effect, in which all conspire, as the various parts of an ingenious complicated machine," can be cited accordingly as evidence of the perfectly harmonious character of the Creator. The integration of apparently disparate elements in nature is remarked by Edwards as connoting an aesthetic standard of *concordia discors:* "That sort of beauty which is called Natural, as of vines, plants, trees, etc., consists of a very complicated harmony; and all the natural motions, and tendencies, and figures of bodies in the Universe are done according to proportion, and therein is their beauty. Particular disproportions sometimes greatly add to the general beauty, and must necessarily be, in order to a more universal proportion."[35]

The existence of a wonderfully complex structure in the universe is not interpreted by Edwards as evidence of the divinity of nature. Matter as he speaks of it does not so organize itself. Rather, Edwards says in another notebook entry, it tends toward chaotic asymmetry: "For if there be no such internal cause or power belonging to the nature of these bodies themselves that should, as it were, incline 'em to such a figure rather than any other, then it would be a strange thing if any two of them should happen to be of the same figure; for in themselves, they must be supposed indifferent to all kinds of possible figures, which are infinite, and therefore are as likely to be in one of all these infinite figures as another." The structure of the universe is miraculous to Edwards because it reveals the artistry of God in overcoming the formlessness of His raw material. To him, the order of the universe reveals extrinsic regulation. So nature does not manifest God intrinsically, nature's intrinsic character being chaotic, but in submission to divine artifice. That nature has form is in effect unnatural, or at least improbable; form in nature signifies a principle of order both superior and opposed to matter. The universe may be perceived as the poem of God, but a poem conforming to an Aristotelian aesthetic in which abstract form is imposed upon actual formlessness, such that the coherence "that there is in the bodies of all animals and plants and in the different parts of inanimate creation" indicates a continuous omnipotent governance of fugitive atoms. The symmetries of nature reveal the power rather than the essence of God.[36]

Understood as the conquest of natural disorder, *concordia discors* can be taken to reflect the agency of God. It does so, however, no more directly than the existence of nature itself, since just "as bodies are shadows of being, so their proportions are shadows of proportion." The formal symmetries of nature are no more to be identified with genuine beauty than natural things are to be with genuine being. Edwards can agree with only a modest version of the argument from design: "We may descend and prove many of [God's] perfections *a priori*," that is, from the discovery of many complex proportions in the universe. Edwards is very harsh on theological opponents who exaggerate, he thinks, the proximity of the manifest glories of Creation to the invisible glory of God. God is, indeed, related to Creation, but not immediately and therefore not such that His image is readily discovered. The relationship rather is explicitly and exactly a mediate one, consistent with a dualistic epistemology, ultimately one more expression of theism.[37]

Edwards's deduction in *The Great Doctrine of Original Sin Defended* that Creation must be continuous does not, as may appear to a modern retrospect unfamiliar with Aristotelian and Thomist etiology, vitiate the distinction between God and His works. Rather, it extends, in a perfectly logical and consistent way, the conclusion in *Freedom of the Will* that nature requires a supernatural first cause. Edwards bases his theory of continuous creation entirely on this extension, which he states initially in his notebooks: "The reason why it is so exceedingly natural to man, to suppose that some latent *Substance*, or something that is altogether hid, that upholds the properties of bodies, is, because all see at first sight that the properties of bodies are such as need some [external] cause, that shall every moment have influence to their continuance, as well as a cause of their first existence."

Just as miraculous intervention is required by reason to originate nature, so is the continuation of this force necessary to preserve nature. The "properties of bodies" that Edwards mentions here are their obedience to physical laws that are not only beautiful, but economical as well, functioning to perpetuate the entire universe. The interdependence of all material things does not convince Edwards that the universe is self-contained, as some neo-Newtonian utilitarians and materialists come to believe. Rather, interdependence convinces him that the world at every moment requires an external cause. He sees matter in the same entry as intrinsically self-destructive no less than formless: "Here is something in these parts of space, that of itself produces effects, without previously being acted upon, for that Being that lays an arrest on bodies in motion, and immediately stops them when they come to such limits and bounds, certainly does as much as that Being that sets a body in motion, that before was at rest. Now this Being, acting altogether of itself, producing effects, that are perfectly arbitrary, and that are no way necessary of themselves, must be Intelligent and Voluntary. There is no reason, in the nature of the thing itself, why a body, when set in motion, should stop at such limits, more than at any other. It must therefore be some arbitrary, active, and voluntary Being that determines it."Again Edwards ascribes the form of nature to the fiat of God, this time emphasizing His control of physics. Reason acknowledges not only that "a thing that begins to be cannot make itself," but also that nothing that continues to be can itself sustain existence. The complicated economy of the universe depends primarily on the continuous exertion of God's will, secondarily on natural law.[38]

Edwards's theory of continuous creation functions in *Original Sin* to substantiate his defense of the doctrine of imputation, which is, of course, the center of the controversy. Theological opponents, in particular the Scottish theologian John Taylor, argue that the imputation of Adam's sin to all subsequent generations of men is both unreasonable and unfair, and therefore inconsistent with divine justice. Among the many specific objections to the doctrine with which Edwards has to deal is the compelling one that children cannot in fairness have a moral responsibility for the sins of their fathers, and that the Bible on this point must convey a "dark, paradoxical, and hidden meaning" quite different from the obvious one. Edwards refutes this objection by arguing that Adam does not himself have the power to transmit his sin to posterity, but that his sinful disposition is maintained by God's continuous ordination of man's character; mankind is considered one with Adam not because mankind's "qualities and relations are derived down from past existence," as in a genealogy, but because of a "oneness that can be supposed to be founded on divine constitution." God, not Adam, is properly to be considered the author of man's nature, and to rail against the doctrine of imputation is not, as Taylor contends, to declare one's independence of a wicked earthly parent, but to renounce the heavenly Father.[39]

To establish the reasonableness of this defense, Edwards argues the necessity of God's creating man and the world out of nothing in every moment of their history: "God's upholding created substance, or causing its existence in each successive moment, is altogether equivalent to an immediate production out of nothing, at each moment, because its existence at this moment is not merely in part from God, but wholly from him; and not in any part, or degree, from its antecedent existence. For the supposing that its antecedent *concurs* with God in *efficiency,* to produce some part of the effect, is attended with the same absurdities, which have been shown to attend the supposition of its producing it wholly. Therefore the antecedent existence is nothing as to any proper influence or assistance in the affair: and consequently God produces the effect from *nothing,* as if there had been nothing *before.* So that this effect differs not at all from the first creation, but only *circumstantially;* as in the first creation there had been no such act and effect of God's power before; whereas his giving existence afterwards, *follows* preceding acts and effects of the same kind, in an established order."[40]

Edwards deduces logically that antecedent causes would have to be infinite in order for anything in nature to be self-generated, and this impresses the rational mind with the necessity of a supernatural first cause. In his discussion of continuous creation, he applies the same reasoning to the antecedent existence of a creature, arguing that just as all creatures originate ultimately from without nature, so must all successive moments of the creature's existence be caused by a supernatural agent. Reason concludes that antecedent existence is no more significant to continued existence than antecedent cause is to Creation, that just as "in creation something is brought out of nothing in an instant," so in existence is every moment vouchsafed by God's arbitrary decree. Natural antecedent can neither originate being in the genealogy of a species nor maintain being in the life of an individual. By showing how God's responsibility for the persistence of Creation follows logically from His responsibility for its origin, Edwards is able in *Original Sin* to answer "Arminian" objections to the doctrine of imputation, as in *Freedom of the Will* he attacks the notion of self-determination, without resorting to irrational faith in God's decrees.[41]

Thus, far from identifying nature with God, the theory of continuous creation places nature utterly at the mercy of divine sustenance, not unlike the spider of Edwards's Enfield sermon, liable at any moment to plunge into nonentity. All the great natural symmetries, beauties, and life-giving processes of the universe are held by God on the edge of nonbeing, for, as Edwards warns in the conclusion of the discussion in *Original Sin,* "it don't all *necessarily* follow that because there was sound, or light, or color, or resistance, or gravity, or thought or consciousness, or any other thing the last moment, that therefore there shall be the like at the next." God is certainly "related to all things that have finite existence," as Delattre contends, but not in a way that comforts man with a knowledge that God is close by. The relationship encourages feelings of suspense, not security. Like Atlas in Greek mythology, the continuously creative God holds up a world that would otherwise "drop into nothing upon the ceasing of the present moment."[42]

The impression that Edwards's theory of continuous creation in *Original Sin* is philosophically precocious can again be shown to derive much less

from Edwards's discourse itself than from the self-interest of modern interpretations of it, not only because Edwards's theory is not original—it belongs to a very long tradition of "occasionalist theory" that appears, even
before patristic writings, in the Old Testament, "If he should take back his
spirit to himself, and gather to himself his breath, all flesh would perish
together, and man would return to dust" (*Job* 34:14, 15), and runs through
not only the seventeenth- and eighteenth-century Puritan writings of Willard and Edwards but through the "enlightened" ones of Jefferson, who
concludes that that there must be "a wonder somewhere" to explain certain inexplicable facts of existence, and of Hamilton, who appeals to what
he clearly considers the entirely conventional wisdom that ungoverned
matter tends, like an ungoverned society, naturally toward chaos and that
form is self-evidently achieved only by the continuous exertion of external
force—but also because "occasionalist theory" is subjected by early romantic writers to the same kind of modern misprision to which they subject the
theist discourse of analogy. Perhaps the earliest example occurs in Kant's
General History of Nature and Theory of the Heavens, in which the con-
tinuousness of creation is connected through dialectical logic to the necessary inherence of the principle or primary motive force of creation.
Coleridge, in *Aids to Reflection,* probably the most widely read document of
romantic religious theory in the United States in the early nineteenth century, fundamentally redefines imputation, and adds to the controversy
between Edwards and Taylor a position that neither of them can possibly
state, by asking, rhetorically, "must not of necessity the FIRST MAN be a
SYMBOL of mankind, in the fullest force of the word, Symbol, rightly
defined—that is, a sign included in the idea, which it represents;—an
actual *part* chosen to represent the *whole,* as a lip with a chin prominent is a
symbol of man, or a *lower* form of species used as the representative of a
higher in the same *kind:* thus Magnetism is the Symbol of Vegetation, and
of the vegetative and reproductive power in animals; the Instinct of the
ant-tribe, or the bee, is a symbol of the human understanding. And this
definition of the word [symbol] is of great practical importance, inasmuch
as the symbolical is hereby distinguished *toto genera* from the allegoric and
metaphorical." Thus does Coleridge outline with comprehensiveness, if a
somewhat verbose and disorganized comprehensiveness, the universal
discursive context in which the discourses of the self-creation of material
and of human nature exist, dialectical causality being shown to have pene-
trated romantic exegesis, epistemology, ontology, and aesthetics, and to
differ "*toto genera*" from the linear causality that penetrates not only such
theist figures as allegory and metaphor but another universal discursive
context of theist discourse. In the United States, Coleridge's transformative
efforts are consolidated by Emerson when in a journal entry he distinguishes between a created and a creative universe, "I am of the Maker, not
of the Made," and also by Thoreau when in the celebrated passage from

Walden he witnesses continuous creativity at the seemingly unlikely spot of a cut taken out of a side of a hill to make room for the railroad, and again by Thoreau when in *Cape Cod* he asserts seeing matter dissolve and recohere daily in the margin on the beach between high and low tides, and, despite the lapse of years, by Lynen when in *The Design of the Present* he interprets Edwards's essay on the Trinity as anticipating both the Hegelian dialectic of becoming and the ultimate implication of this dialectical creativity, which is the sublation of God within Man.[43]

Although Edwards may feel "a direct and sensual pleasure in the beauties of nature," as a recent study contends, his interpretation of the religious significance of nature depends always on the distinction between Creation and Creator. His drawing of analogies does not anticipate romantic naturalism because it consistently deters identifications between nature and God that to Edwards would be both unreasonable and irreligious. Analogy as Edwards describes it allows enough of Divinity to be sensible to warrant study and enjoyment of nature without ever intimating the pantheism, or the "pan*en*theism," with which Edwards is lately credited. He never writes a phenomenology because, unlike Hegel and other romantic writers, he does not consider phenomena sufficiently expressive of truth to repay sanguine theological attention to them. Edwards's discourse on phenomena can be paraphrased in a sentence: The existence of the material universe argues the necessity of an immaterial first cause, and the order of the universe indicates the restraint of an extrinsic Governor.[44]

5. God's Chief End

How can Edwards determine God's chief end within these epistemological limits? Reason, properly employed, testifies to the existence of a Creator prior to His works. It teaches Edwards further that the chief end of such a Creator cannot possibly consist in making the world; because God's disposition to create, Edwards notes in the *Dissertation*, "is prior to the existence of any other being, and is to be considered as the inciting cause of giving existence to other beings, God cannot properly be said to make the creature his end . . . for the creature is not yet considered as existing." The creation of the world cannot reasonably be considered God's chief end, and may be only distantly related.[45]

Edwards believes, however, that proof of God's chief end is available to both the Christian heart and the rational mind. Revelation, properly heeded, and reason as well, so long as it continues rationally to acknowledge the superiority of cause to effect, teach that God is "infinitely, eternally, unchangeably, and independently glorious and happy: that he cannot be profited by, or receive anything from the creature." The will of such a perfect and independent agent can be chiefly disposed only to self-adoration, and all of His acts, including Creation, must therefore be subordinate to this chief end. As Edwards promises in the opening of the *Dissertation*, he bases this conclusion primarily on Scripture: "It is manifest, that the scriptures speak, on all occasions, as though God made *himself* his chief end in all his works; and as though the same being, who is the *first cause* of all things, were the supreme and last end of all things." Precisely the same conclusion is reached if reason alone is accepted as authority, which consistency within theist discourse is indicated by Plato and Aristotle's having come to the identical conclusion of the necessary self-sufficiency of a single Creator. The Bible and classical logic agree that, no matter how impressive nature seems to man, Creation represents an inferior end of God that cannot alone be expected to manifest His essence.[46]

What Creation can reveal, to reason and to observation and to Christian bibliophilia, is an ultimate end of God, inferior to His chief end of self-adoration but nonetheless valued "for its own sake," which Edwards calls God's natural sovereignty. In further application of dualistic epistemology Edwards analyzes God's greatness into moral, or internal, and natural, or visible, perfections. God's moral perfections are the unseen attributes of His character "whereby the heart and will of God are good, right and infinitely becoming and lovely; such as his righteousness, truth, faithfulness, and goodness; or, in a word, his holiness." God's natural perfections are analogous to His moral ones, but according to theist analogy are, as the expressions of God's will, inferior: "God's natural attributes or perfections . . . consist not in the holiness or moral goodness of God, but in his greatness; such as his power, his knowledge, whereby he knows all things, and his being eternal, from everlasting to everlasting, his omnipresence and his awful and terrible majesty." The difference between will and action is as crucial to Edwards's analysis of Divinity as to his analysis of man; the will is invisible, whereas actions can impress man's mind—in the case of God's activity by His rule over the "astonishing fabric of the universe" and by various providential miracles subsequent to Creation.[47]

The ultimate end served by Creation must therefore be the communication of God's will to minds that, as Locke shows, gain knowledge primarily through sensations of a material world, and that, Edwards elaborates, "can view nothing immediately," that is, can know the truth only through the mediation of lower analogues in nature. God translates His moral perfections into a medium that an audience of limited capacities can apprehend: "If we had strength and comprehension of mind sufficient, [we would] have a clear idea of the general and universal being, or, which is the same thing, of the infinite, eternal, most perfect divine Nature and Essence. But then we should not properly come to the knowledge of the being of God by arguing; but our evidence would be intuitive. . . . But we have not the strength and extent of mind, to know this certainty in this intuitive independent manner: but the way that mankind comes to the knowledge of the being of God, is that which the Apostle speaks of (*Rom.* 1:20), 'The Invisible things of Him, from the creation of the world, are clearly seen; being understood by the things that are made; even his eternal power and Godhead.' " Edwards believes his analysis of Creation to follow revelations like this famous one from the New Testament. He adds only an emphasis that, no matter how clearly God articulates Himself in Creation, He never makes Himself a creature; that to make sensible what is originally insensible is to create another thing, analogous but not identical to the source. Creation is not God but a diminution of Him suited rhetorically to a sentient audience, "a kind of voice or language of God to instruct intelligent beings in things pertaining to Himself."[48]

God's ultimate end manifested in Creation, the communication of certain aspects of His character, must agree with His chief end, which Edwards, like Plato and Aristotle, takes to be self-adoration. The relationship between the ultimate and chief ends of an agent can be obscure, Edwards insists, even in the infinitely simpler example of human behavior; it is infinitely harder to discern in divine activity. Edwards admits that the link between God's adoring Himself and communicating Himself can only be tentatively stated. After trying to reconcile God's creativity with His perfect self-sufficiency and self-love, Edwards confesses in the *Dissertation* that "there is a degree of indistinctness and obscurity in the close consideration of such subjects, and a great imperfection in the expressions we use concerning them; arising unavoidably from the infinite sublimity of the subject, and the incomprehensibleness of those things that are divine." The greatest difficulty lies in attempting to imagine an act subordinated not to an antecedent cause, as in human behavior, but to God's uncaused propensity to adore Himself. The creation of the universe, or any other specific act, seems inconsistent for a Being supposed to be perfect, and thus, according to linear causality, not disposed to act at all. Logically considered, such a Being would not benefit by creating a world, whose very existence might be cited as proof of His imperfection; as a particular act accomplished at a particular moment, Creation seems logically to have required some change in the Creator, and thereby seems logically to contradict His divinity.[49]

This argument is perennially a basis for agnosticism and inspires many ingenious refutations by pious Christian theologicans. Responding to its citation by the Epicurean and Manichean heretics, Augustine claims that since time originates simultaneously with Creation, the act of Creation occurs in eternity and therefore does not make God subject to time. In his notebooks Edwards attempts a defense by distinguishing between "decrees," which are eternally arranged in the mind of God, and "acts," which realize decrees in a temporal order that corresponds to the logic of the arrangement. Thus Edwards supposes that the whole structure of the exercise of God's will is present in His mind at once in a hierarchical diagram whose individual parts, like the creation of the universe, are subordinately related to the whole. Man experiences historically divine acts that are in the mind of God separated, however, only by rank.[50]

Edwards attempts another, quasi-rational solution of this mystery. He supposes that the very presence of perfect attributes within God may be a latent cause of their being exercised. Acting not because of an antecedent cause or at a particular moment in time, God is depicted as creating the universe out of a spontaneous delight in Himself: "If God both esteem and delight in his own perfections and virtues, he cannot but value and delight in the expression and genuine effects of them. So that in delighting in the *expressions* of his perfections, he manifests a delight in himself; and in making these expressions of his own perfections his [inferior] end, *he makes himself his* [chief] *end.*" Here Edwards tries to indicate that self-love and self-expression may be nonsubordinately related in God, the former not precisely caused by the latter but naturally accompanying it. That such an explanation represents a tautology, and is therefore illogical according to Edwards's definition of reason, confirms the necessity for faith in divine revelation for the determination of God's chief end. Edwards is too expert and consistent a logician to assume that tautologies—"There are many of the Divine attributes that, if God had not created the world, would never had any exercise"—are truly explanatory. Rather, he sees them as evidence that "language seems to be defective and to want a proper general word to express the supreme end of creation and all God's works," and thus as additional argument for religious belief.[51]

Figurative description gives him another means of dealing with the mystery, and this is the most intriguing approach for modern retrospect. Edwards conflates biblical metaphors comparing God to an overflowing fountain with the ontological surmises of such Neoplatonist ancient Greek philosophers as Plotinus to suggest the agreement between divine perfection and divine activity: "As there is an infinite fulness of all possible good in God—a fulness of every perfection, of all excellency and beauty, and of infinite happiness—and as this fulness is capable of communication, or emanation *ad extra;* so it seems a thing amiable and valuable *in itself* that this infinite fountain of good should send forth abundant streams." Although the literal meaning of this passage is virtually the same as in Edwards's quasi-rational attempts to reconcile the act of creation with Divinity—he implicitly begs the question in the second subordinate clause, "as this fulness is capable of communication," thereby turning what looks like an if-then construction into a tautology—yet logical inconsistency is camouflaged by a subtle stylistic maneuver. Multiplying the attributes contained in God's "fulness," a "fulness of every perfection, of all excellency and beauty, and of infinite happiness," in a long phrase in apposition, he both creates the impression of fullness swelling naturally toward an overflow and postpones the independent clause so as partly to conceal the grammatical logic of the sentence. The fountain image further blurs the logical distinction between the cause and effect of God's creativity by depicting both as the same substance; the "fountain of good" naturally sends forth "abundant streams." The style tries to mask the implausibility of the idea that God can possess a continual inclination to exercise that "fulness" whose expression is "amiable and valuable *in itself.*" Traditional Christian images of God as the sun, "emanating" or "diffusing" His light, as an overflowering "fountain of good," or as the "root and stock of a tree" naturally disposed to "communicate of its life and sap" are all used by Edwards to portray the mystery of Creation as a spontaneous, uncaused act of God.[52]

These passages are rhetorically examples of catechresis; taken literally they verge on theological heterodoxy. A dualistic epistemology cautions against identifying appearance and reality. The theist discursive pattern of which this epistemology is a part deems God incommensurately greater than His creatures. This compound prohibition makes impossible any genuine signification of Divinity. Edwards has no way to talk about God directly; language according to theist discourse is a "creature" adequate only when referring to creatures, and able to address God only through infinitely indirect connotation. As long as theist discourse is concerned just with creatures, these deficiencies are unimportant. But to reach beyond the creature is to exceed the expressiveness of language, and by so doing inevitably to confuse creature with Creator. There is no way for any theist writer to avoid this. Not only can no man look upon God and live, according to Christian piety, but can no man say *God* without instantly demeaning Him with a name that by definition is inarticulate of Divinity according to theist linguistics.

It is not surprising that the imagery to which Edwards resorts in attempting to state the inexplicable will of God prior to expression in creatures seems to imply an identity between God and His works that neither Edwards's epistemology nor his theology allows. Figuratively equated to sunshine, water, or sap, Creation may be mistaken as remaining somehow naturally a part of divine being. Although Edwards's analogical definitions of Creation can be shown to avoid pantheism, his metaphors for the unexercised "fulness" of God's will seem close to pantheism once more.

The chance that in pronouncing *God* Edwards talks himself into more intimate terms with Him appeals to modern interpretations. If Edwards had condemned man forever to an imprecise knowledge of spiritual things through ideas of their lower, material analogues, these supposedly pantheistic implications would be irrelevant. So long as the mind can be excited exclusively through the sensations of material things, as Locke's psychology contends, it cannot apprehend God directly no matter how close to nature God might be. But a central proposition of Edwards's theology is, of course, the notion that grace is introduced to the mind as a "new simple idea," and this makes the location of God a crucial issue. Because Edwards believes that God stimulates the minds of earthly saints immediately, communicating directly to the soul, and because he believes that the experience of grace reorients perception, his ontology is significant. Although the natural faculties of reason and observation, which the unregenerate never transcend and upon which even saints and theologians must depend for the most part, can never determine the disposition of God's will from Creation, the extraordinary light of grace might be able to discover God in His works if He is to be found there. Perhaps the mind assisted by grace can intuit what reason cannot accept, that immaterial cause and material effect can be ontologically the same. Perhaps, as Miller claims, the natural and supernatural are interwoven in Edwards's ontology.[53]

The resemblance between natural metaphors, such as are used not only by Edwards but by the Bible from which he borrows all of them, and the organicism of romantic ontology appears only in the context of modern retrospect; there it can be understood as a seed of future growth. In the context of theism, however, these passages have no such meaning; whatever monistic implications they convey appear in theist discourse as empty confusion. The potential errors of Edwards's thought need not today be evaluated as the near truths of modern culture. Because they either fall slightly outside or on the edge of theism, they can be used to plot exactly the outline of the theist discursive pattern. Modern retrospect has a special gift for this because what is peripheral to theism is central to humanism. Modern retrospect can devote this talent not to capturing the relatively undefended fringes of another discursive pattern, but to preserving the other's boundaries. Edwards's metaphors can fairly easily be torn from his corpus; a more difficult and interesting task is to attach them more firmly.

In order to see whether Edwards's natural metaphors can be made consistent with his theology, his descriptions of the way in which God creates the universe must be examined. If God creates in the manner that the image of the overflowing fountain suggests to modern restrospect, He seems to communicate Himself substantially to His creatures, thus possibly blurring any ontological distinction between His being and His works. Whether or not Edwards himself personally senses a confluence of the fountains of heaven and the streams of New England while under the influence of grace will be discussed in chapter 4 on Grace. Now the question is whether he depicts the way in which God "emanated *ad extra*" so as to make possible such a mystical experience.

Although the metaphors of the fountain, sun, and tree all imply likeness between the being of God and the being of His creatures, they need not contradict a fundamental distinction between the divine source and its emanations. Edwards emphasizes this distinction at the same time that he stresses the similarities between the internal and external glories of God. In the conclusion of the *Dissertation*, after an exhaustive etymological review of the Bible's use of *glory* both to connote the disposition and to denote the expression of God's will, Edwards again resorts to a figurative description of divine creativity, but this time explicitly qualifying the resemblance between God and His works: "The emanation or communication of the divine fulness . . . has relation indeed both to *God* and the *creature:* but it has relation to God as its *fountain,* as the thing communicated is something of his internal fulness. The water in the stream is something of the fountain; and the beams of the sun are something of the sun. . . . they have relation to God as their *object.*"[54]

The streams of the fountain, beams of the sun, or sap of the tree are not identical to their sources, but are rather attenuations of them, and Creation is therefore, by the metaphor, given not the same being as the Creator but "something" of it. Compared to natural progenitors in this way, God does not propagate Himself into beings that embody His essence, but rather differentiates Himself into lesser things that have subordinate "relation to God as their object," or origin. They must contain something of God in order for His creation of them to be consistent with His chief end; a perfect Being disposed chiefly to self-adoration would create and love only beings that possess something of Himself.

These subordinate beings must also actively participate in God's self-love, worshiping Him in answer to His creation and care of them: "In the creature's knowing, rejoicing in, and praising God, the glory of God is both . . . *received* and *returned.* Here is both an *emanation* and a *remanation.* The refulgence shines upon and into the creature, and is reflected back to the luminary. The beams of glory come from God, are something of God, and are refunded back again to their original." But this reciprocity is not one between equals. God's regard for the creature is proportionate to the degree of His being that the creature contains, and the creature in turn can "refund" only that degree of God's love which goes into his creation. "So much the greater the distance" between the being of God and of a creature, Edwards notes in *Religious Affections,* "so much the less the creature's respect is worthy of God's notice . . . for he can offer no more than himself, in offering his best respect; and therefore he is little, and little worth, so is his respect little worth." Man, possessing the least divine being of all intelligent creatures, can join only marginally in God's self-love. An earthly saint may feel inflamed with the love of God, but in the context of all of Creation his devotion burns no brighter than a "little sun, partaking of the nature of the fountain of its light," or a "jewel that receives [the sun's] light, and shines only by a participation of its brightness." This ontology is clearly consistently dualistic, and is exactly consistent with Edwards's epistemology. Just as Creation appears a diminished form of God's glory, so is Creation "of the same nature" as divine being yet "*infinitely* less in degree."[55]

Edward's natural metaphors are equivalent to what Coleridge scorns as merely allegorical or metaphysical conceits, but are examples of the only type of figuration possible in the theist discourse of Divinity, which is approximation. Puritan metaphysics are particularly insistent in announcing their imperfections. Willard states repeatedly that, in comparisons of the beings of Creator and of Creation, His "is the prototype, theirs but the copy; his the substance, theirs but the image or shadow; his the fountain, theirs but some few drops or small springs that issue from it." They are in fact so insistent that to make a case for their anticipating symbolism requires a partiality so extreme as virtually to constitute censorship, especially when compared to cases that can be made for the stylistic modernity of other kinds of theist figuration that are less scrupulous about announcing their limitations. Shea can argue that Edwards composes "the first organic metaphor, perhaps, in our literature" only by deleting the theist context in which the metaphor appears and replacing it with a humanist one whose organicism transforms the document into a part of a wholly other text. When Edwards writes in his notebooks the metaphor that so intrigues Shea—that "we had as good think that branches grow out of the ground without seeds, or that branches grow out of the trunk without buds; for seeds are but another sort of buds, that drop to the ground"—he is demonstrating in the context of his opera and of theist discourse nothing other than the principle of efficient causation, branches presupposing the prior existence of buds and trees presupposing the prior existence of seeds. Edwards adds at the conclusion of the entry, in a passage that Shea does not quote, that "the trees, or seeds, or whatever they were that God first created, were only the beginning of this process—enough to get it going," thus explicitly recalling that nature originates supernaturally.[56]

In the context of the humanist discursive pattern, the (truncated) passage signifies another meaning, that no cause is truly extrinsic or prior to nature, but that nature everywhere contains, in seeds growing into trees and buds growing into branches, the potential for self-generation. But although the (truncated) passage in this humanist context may communicate the spontaneous fecundity of nature, it is not bred spontaneously by some youthful insight into a reality that lies outside theist discourse by a young Edwards in closer touch with the natural world than the older Edwards would be, which is what Shea implies. Phenomenologically, no text is produced by such mystic communion with extratextual "realities," but is the product of specific significations, generated in this case by such signifiers as "bud" and "seed" and "branch" and "tree," all of which signify manifestations of organic, dialectical causality within, and only within, humanist discourse, which very unspontaneous systemic semiosis Shea himself unconsciously performs.

Theist metaphysics are consistent only with an ontology that classifies Creation as partial being. The being of God is diffused throughout Creation in regular stages, or, as Edwards terms them, "frames" of existence. These frames ascend hierarchically according to the amount of divine being they contain. The universe is "one vast general frame consisting of an innumerable multitude of lesser regular frames," of which man has knowledge of the "regular frames that constitute the body of an animal" or a plant, the "more general frame" of the entire "animate world," the "larger frame" of "this terraqueous globe, with its atmosphere," the still larger frame of the "planetary system," and, finally, the largest frame that mankind can perceive, of "innumerable enlightened systems, each from one fountain of light like the sun." Beyond this are still higher frames, the angelic host, the Trinity, and possibly other intermediate ones that God has not seen fit to reveal to man. This declension reveals Edwards's ontology to be a version of the great chain. It is in his thought perhaps more accurately called the great attenuation of being, wherein "an archangel must be supposed to have more existence, and to be every way further removed from nonentity," and closer to God, "than a worm." "The frame," according to Edwards's terminology, "is the Degree of Being." Pope articulates this ontology with diction that is the same as Edwards's, and adds a proviso in the form of the famous rhetorical questions from the opening of the first "Epistle" of An Essay On Man that differentiate this ontology precisely from the romantic one in which a part of existence can, paradoxically and synecdochically, contain all of existence: "But of this frame the bearings, and the ties, / The strong connections, nice dependencies, / Gradations just, has [man's] pervading soul / Look'd thro'? Or can a part contain the whole?" What is an absurdity to Pope and Edwards becomes visionary insight in romantic discourse, according to which partial being is precisely that which is unreal.[57]

In order to reconcile the act of Creation with the revealed chief end of God, Edwards frequently stresses the likeness between divine and created being. The latter must be "of God, and in God, and to God" if it is to help fulfill His self-love. This emphasis leads many modern critics to conclude, as Miller paraphrases Channing, that "by making God the only active power in the universe, Edwards annihilated the creature, [and] became in effect a 'pantheist.'" Miller acknowledges the efforts Edwards makes to avoid identifying God with nature yet goes on to imply that insofar as Edwards conceives all being to be divine in origin, he must believe, in his heart of hearts, that crude matter itself has no meaningful existence.[58]

But although nothing can substantively be other than God in Edwards's ontology, although all "positive existence is but a communication from Him," a real opponent to God's creativity is explicitly acknowledge by Edwards to be nonentity. The partial being of lower frames of Creation is not contaminated with something that is not God, nor does the attenuation of divine being necessitate a proportionate increase in some other substance. Rather, nonbeing, or chaos, gains as divine being diminishes. The order of the universe, as Edwards explains this order in his discussion of *concordia discors,* as well as the persistence of the universe, as he argues in proposing a continuous creation, depends wholly on the constant vigilance and exertion of God against a real force of chaos. The crude, sensible reality of all subordinate frames, like man's natural world, can therefore be taken to signify the relative absence of a higher, divine substance, and must be understood not as the "pasteboard mask" behind which the Absolute resides, a hope that Miller would have Edwards share with Ahab, but as unstable, barely existent stuff, liable to disintegrate at any moment's pause in the exercise of the divine will.[59]

Recognition of how fundamental hierarchy is to Edwards's ontology can lead to a different understanding of those few of his writings which concern themselves mainly with the observation of nature. The "Spider" essay has been noted as an instance of Edwards's precocious empiricism; this supposed gift and Edwards's supposed early inspiration by Locke have combined to aid modernist interpretations by implying that Edwards tends naturally to ground his thought in personal experience (a supposition based on the assumption that seventeenth- and eighteenth-century empiricism, such as Newtonian physics and Lockean psychology, is either modern or proto-modern, itself no longer a certainty). Both precocities have lately been contested on factual grounds, the "Spider" essay apparently having been written when Edwards was in or near his twenties according to the research of its latest editor, Wallace Anderson, and Edwards's reading of Locke apparently similarly having occurred after Edwards's childhood, according to the research of Anderson and also Fiering, who argues in addition that those ideas of Edwards ascribed to the influence of Locke by Miller and others could have been learned from a number of writers whom Edwards seems definitely to have read before he read Locke.[60]

These factual corrections, however, have not altered, but only qualified, what remains a basically modernist appreciation of Edwards's "scientific" or "psychological" texts. Anderson, for example, in his introduction to Edwards's *Scientific and Philosophical Writings,* although stating repeatedly that Edwards has neither any particular talent for nor any commitment to induction scientifically, states as repeatedly that Edwards tends toward "phenomenalist" idealism philosophically, implying that while the context of the mind is not prominent enough in his science to make him a precursor of modern experimenters, this context is sufficiently prominent in his philosophy to make him a precursor of modern phenomenologists. Moreover, Anderson's presentation of the "Spider" essay, although again admitting the incongruousness of the essay in an opera that almost nowhere else relies so heavily on observation, nevertheless evaluates the significance of the essay as lying exclusively in entomological descriptions of the spider.[61]

This assumption leads Anderson to dismiss as merely odd, and implicitly a bit embarrassing, a judgement Edwards makes, evidently in passing, toward the end of the notebook entry, a judgment that can, instead, be interpreted as revealing the entire, and entirely other than modern, character of Edwards's interest in the insect, and the consistency of this character with his theist ontology in general. Echoing Faust, who long ago derides this judgment as disclosing Edwards's unscientific ignorance, Anderson comments: "But probably the oddest of all the remarks Edwards offers concerning the phenomena of nature is that near the end of 'Of Insects,' that flying insects are 'little collections' of 'the corrupting nauseousness of our air.' " A bit later in the entry Edwards repeats this judgment, that it is "nauseous vapors which insects are made up of," and both expressions of the judgment reappear in what is presumably the finished version of the entry, the letter to a Fellow of the Royal Society in London, Judge Paul Dudley.[62]

The mention of this piece of evidently conventional eighteenth-century wisdom concerning insects need not be taken as a quaint or unfortunate lapse into superstition. Rather, it can be seen to indicate the presence in Edwards's writings, no matter how "scientific" or informal or how far removed from theology, of a hierarchical model of existence that does not privilege, that does not contain at all as a separate category, that cynosure of humanist discourse, "life." The links in the chain of existence, the "frames" in Edwards's and Pope's lexicon, are continuous from nonentity up to God. The spider, or insects generally, constitute a link that might possibly be intermediate between inert matter, whose highest form is "vapor," and living being, whose lowest forms are plants and insects. Spiders are interesting to Edwards not as forms of "life," but as manifestations of the continuity of this chain. They belong not to a category "life" nor to a class "arachnids"; they are but a small part of the entirety of being.

The continuity of the great chain of being allows for intimacy between what modern discourse celebrates as life and what it distinguishes fundamentally from life as inert matter. Such continuity does not allow, however—Lovejoy's dialectical analysis to the contrary notwithstanding—for the evolutionary metamorphosis of one into the other, nor the evolutionary transformation of lower links of one or the other into higher ones. The discursive potential for evolution does predate Darwin's and the other evolutionists' theoretical statements, in such romantic morphologies as Hegel's, and also that expressed in Emerson's 1849 motto for *Nature*, which concludes by claiming that a worm, "striving to be a man," can mount "through all the spires of form," an ascension whose discursive significance will be more fully discussed in the final chapter of this reading. Evolution is not possible, however, within theist ontology, at least not according to the regular order of things or in mimetic descriptions of this order, to which miracles, and the rhetorical exploitation of the miraculous in fables like those of Ovid and Aesop, relate only as deviations that indirectly show the power of order's rule. Thus when discussing "Productions,

Mineral, Vegetable, and Animal" in *Notes on the State of Virginia* Jefferson accepts the hierarchy of being as given and changeless, the rationale of which is "unsearchable to beings with our capacities," the alteration of which, even so small a one as the elimination of a single creature through extinction, Jefferson deems logically improbable. What is possible in theist discourse are connections between contiguous links in the chain of being, like one between vapor and insects, but no other, more far-reaching, connections, like one between apes and man. The etiology of theist natural philosophy is much more intelligibly to be classified the way Foucault does, as resembling only accidentally and superficially modern evolution, than the way Lovejoy *et al.* do, as inchoate versions of a modern dialectics whose roots can be traced all the way back to Platonic idealism.[63]

What Edwards supposes about the relationship between vapor and insects is of course a type of the speculations that abound in theist natural philosophy, not only up to but after the experiments of Joseph Priestley, which have come to be stigmatized as delusions of spontaneous generation. But such generation is not at all spontaneous; rather, generation is rigorously conditioned by the discourse of the great chain, only the very highest form of inert matter being perhaps capable of generating only the very lowest form of animate being, and no other. That the phrase has become a byword for ludicrous supersitions of an unscientific era says more about the insecurities of humanism than about the imprecisions of any such era. What is so repugnant to modern retrospect is not the flouting of empiricism but the implicit irreverence for "life." Edwards and other theists can casually accept the possibility that "life" is formed in so undignified a way because to them "life" has no priority, certainly none like that of the *ens entium* that is created by romanticism and that is refined and elaborated ever afterward. And theist opponents of spontaneous generation, such as Priestley, have nothing like the mission of their modern admirers who want to turn spontaneous generation into a laughing-stock of nonexperimental prejudice; theist opponents attack a proposition that is neither absurd nor inconceivable but that happens, according to what is genuinely a purely empirical objection, not to be confirmed. Whereas the stakes of the argument among theists are relatively low, they are enormous in the crusade fantasied by modern retrospect between itself and medieval ignorance. "Life" as described in humanist discourse cannot be allowed to have so ignoble an origin. "Life" may have been spontaneously generated—indeed, according to most visionary discourses of evolution "life" does arise spontaneously, and with a greater spontaneity than ever proposed by a theist proponent of spontaneous generation—but in the remote time, billions of years ago, and in the strange place, some "protean soup," and in the uncommon manner, that perfect, as yet unreproducible combination of chemical and thermal and electrical conditions, befitting an "object" to be worshiped. The nonchalance with which Edwards communicates to a personage whom he no doubt considers the highest scientific authority accessible to him personally that living being springs continually from corruption is today virtually inexpressible.

The closest Edwards ever comes to confusing nature with God is in attempts to reconcile God's creation of the universe with His perfect self-sufficiency. All theist theologians offend either piety or reason in this attempt, since the connection between the activity and perfection of God defies the logic of, and thus explication by, theist discourse. Edwards contributes to the record both a consistent recognition that the issue must remain paradoxical, and a remarkably consistent endeavor to preserve its ambiguities. He does not talk himself into the conclusion that God and Creation are one because to him such an identification is merely rhetorical, a symptom of the inexpressiveness of language and the inappropriateness of the natural experience of cause and effect on which language is based. And he strives to prevent his readers from being misled by the pantheistic implications of metaphors depicting God's relationship to His works. God may be to Creation as a fountain is to streams, but only insofar as the divine fountain can be imagined to remain paradoxically undiminished by overflow, like a river "that empties vast quantities of water every day and yet there is never the less to come"; when Edwards collects in his notebook examples of biblical water imagery like this one, he adds to the list an explicit reminder that even such figures as have scriptural authority represent "all temporal supplies," implying that even in their biblical contexts such figures do no more than suggest the dispensation of spiritual sustenance. The "omneity" of divine being may also be approximated spatially, as in the characterization of a circle whose circumference is everywhere and whose center is nowhere, a geometrical paradox often quoted in theist discourse and that Edwards ascribes in his notebooks to Skelton, or in Edwards's own simple equation of God with space in his *Notes on the Mind*. The paradox does not locate God, but in defying geometry removes Him from space, and Edwards's equation signifies not the secret worship of an immanent deity, as has been claimed, but that to him divine being must be tentatively stated to be something other than the natural or concrete; God is that theoretical and abstract Being which exists beyond Creation, "all the Space there is not proper to body, all the space there is without the Bounds of the Creature, all the space there was before the Creation." This is the prosaic meaning of the geometrical paradox throughout theist discourse, in Cardinal Nicolaus Cusanus's citation in the Middle Ages, and in Giordano Bruno's and Skelton's and Edwards's, and even in Poe's approving allusion to Pascal's citation which in "Eureka" serves the theist purpose of making the universe seem so vast as to chasten the mind's contemplation of the universe. Only in romantic discourse does the rhetorical status of the geometrical paradox change, radically, as Coleridge proclaims, again in *Aids to Reflection*, that the paradox confounds only the "Understanding," while remaining accessible to that higher, intuitive constituent of the mind that Coleridge, and Emerson, in another seminal contra-diction of theist discourse, call "Reason."[64]

When Edwards says that anything "being from [God] has some resemblance of him," the qualification must be taken seriously. In order to suggest the agreement between God's ultimate end in Creation and His chief end of self-adoration, Edwards has to insist that God is both ubiquitous and ontologically distinct from the natural world, and he carries this paradox throughout his writings. Although impatient with crude spatial representations of God as existing "up there," he does not correct them by situating Him down here. Rather, Edwards uses such metaphors to approximate the real disparity between God and His creatures. Because it is infinite, divine being remains separate and undiminished no matter how many lesser beings have been derived from it, and Edwards locates God, if not as a specific personality in a specific place, nevertheless as the center of undifferentiated supreme being from which all "frames" of Creation descend. Only by the entire collapse of this hierarchy could a vision of total being be achieved by Edwards or by any other saint occupying the subordinate frame of the natural world.[65]

6. The Trinity

The primary indication of the position of a frame of existence in the hierarchy of being is the degree to which God's creativity is immediately manifest in it. The natural world sees few occasions of this. Although Edwards believes the laws of nature to be upheld by the arbitrary decree of God, he can perceive divine influence only indirectly by recognizing that the behavior of animate and inanimate parts of Creation conforms to rational design. Insofar as natural cause and effect, "second causes," nearly always mediate divine influence in the universe, they betray its low status in the hierarchy of being. Further indication of its ontological subordination is noted by Edwards in the fact that all immediate acts of God that man experiences in the miracles of Providence happen through the humiliation of human or material nature.[66]

The Trinity, the highest frame, must accordingly be the one in which God's creativity is totally immediate, uncontaminated with second causes. Here, and here only, does Edwards hypothesize that the Creator and Creature must be one, the Son and Holy Spirit possessing the same being as the Father. God's initial, uncaused delight in Himself, Edwards imagines in his notebooks, requires Him to form an idea of Himself, which, because God's self-consciousness is immediate, itself acquires substantial being: "We cannot suppose that God reflects on Himself after the manner we reflect on things; for we can view nothing immediately. The immediate object of the mind's intuition is the idea always, and the soul perceives nothing but ideas. But God's intuition on Himself, without doubt, is immediate. But t'is certain it can't be, except His idea be His essence. For His idea is the immediate object of His intuition. An absolutely perfect idea of a thing is the very thing; for it wants nothing that is in the thing, substance nor nothing else." Edwards supposes that unlike man, who according to Locke's sensational psychology can have simple ideas only of tangible phenomena that are the "shadows of spiritual being," God knows spirit directly, without the mediation of a tangible analogue. Thus God's idea of His own spiritual essence can be considered to be the essence itself, wanting "nothing that is in the thing, substance nor nothing else," and He in effect duplicates Himself by contemplating Himself. The Being thereby created, named in Scripture "the image of God," "the form of God," and the "word of God," is God's Son.

The second member of the Trinity is thus created by the transmutation of thought into independent being. The third is made in a similar way, through the transmutation not of reflection, but of the affection that necessarily arises between the two members of God's duplicity: "If the Father and the Son do infinitely delight in each other, there must be an infinitely pure and perfect act between them, an infinitely sweet energy which we call delight. This [delight] is certainly distinct from the other two. The delight and energy that is begotten in us by any idea is thus distinct from the idea. So it cannot be confounded in God, whether with God begetting, or His ideal and image—or Son. It is distinct from each of the other two, and yet it is God. . . . The delight of God is properly a substance." Just as God's perfect idea of Himself acquires independent being, so the delight which Father and Son share, as an idea "distinct from" their ideas of one another, becomes independent being, the third in the Trinity, called the Holy Spirit.[67]

This is for Edwards pure speculation; it derives according to his theology from no experience he has, from no experience that ever any creature can have. Its meaning is contained in its departure from the experience of creatures, expressing not God but the inexpressibility of God, a description not of what God is but of what He, because infinitely superior to the Creation that defines the capacities of language, is not. God does not think of Himself as men do through the mediation of ideas, but in some immediate fashion that defies human thought. Neither does He love as men do but in some other way that is to men inimitable. To preserve God's superiority to and separation from Creation while attempting to imagine the increation of the Trinity, Edwards either implies such negations as these or overstates the reservations that must plague attempts to imagine the unimaginable. In a nonlyric, prolix, and more representative passage from Edwards's notebook entries on the Trinity that is not included in Harvey Townsend's still standard collection, *The Philosophy of Jonathan Ed-*

wards from His Private Notebooks, and that is never quoted in modern studies, Edwards goes on at great length to counteract any possible impression that he adequately describes the paradoxically nonlinear relationship between Father and Son: "It is very manifest, that the persons of the Trinity are not inferior to one another in glory and excellency of nature. The son, for instance, is not inferior to the Father in glory. . . . And though there be a priority of subsistence, and a kind of dependence in the Son, in His subsistence, on the Father; because with respect to his Subsistence, He is wholly from the Father and is begotten by him; yet this is more properly called priority than superiority, as we ordinarily use such terms. There is a dependence without inferiority of deity." Distinction between inferiority and dependence or between priority and superiority cannot be made in theist discourse, and so Edwards's analysis tortures both logic and language. The deterioration of style and punctuation in this passage is but a more obvious sign of the deficiencies of expression present throughout Edwards's essay on the Trinity.[68]

Edwards prefaces discussion of the Trinity in his notebooks with a denunciation of more timid theologians who dare not make such speculations, and with the promise to bring the mystery "within the reach of naked reason." He never publishes it and never integrates it in revised form, as he does so many other entries from his notebooks, in a published work. His uncommonly defiant introduction followed by the failure ever to publish may reveal that he lacks confidence; both the clarity and the piety of the description are at least suspect. This suggests that it, like attempts to reconcile the perfection and activity of God, lies at an extremity of the theist discursive pattern, and is perhaps even farther removed than these attempted reconciliations from the center of theism. Although its value and prominence to Edwards are apparently either slight or ambiguous, it cannot be ignored today; from the modern perspective affinities between it and humanist discourse are conspicuous. Seeming to prepare for a rational explanation of the mystery, Edwards portrays God's most perfect act of creation as a miraculous incarnation of the ideal that hardly conforms to reason as he elsewhere defines reason. The Father somehow thinks the Son into existence, and Father and Son somehow love the Holy Spirit into being. The triune God is thus identified by Edwards as an eternal reciprocity in which creative and created being participate equally, and are thereby ontologically identical. He tries to suggest that at the highest level of existence, unity and multiplicity combine so as to make God's chief end manifest; because the Trinity is an immediate consequence of God's self-consciousness, and since the members of the Trinity are accordingly divine, Creation in the highest frame is the very expression of God's chief end of self-adoration. The reconciliation of God's perfection and His creativity, or His chief and ultimate ends, can be seen, Edwards imagines, in the necessarily self-generative being of Divinity.

That this description resembles romantic portrayals of spirit realizing itself is obvious. Edwards is saying, hesitantly and inarticulately, that pure creative energy can be resolved into substance, and that substantial forms can, in turn, participate in pure creativity, which certainly sounds like an intimation of the dialectic and which certainly becomes one when described in this way and placed in the context of humanist discourse. Portraying the self-generation of divine being in another entry in his *Miscellanies*, Edwards says about God virtually what Hegel implies is the activity of a fully evolved *Geist;* "By God's thinking of Himself, the deity must certainly be generated" according to Edwards, in what seems a prestatement of Hegel's ideal, which has been called "thought thinking itself." Oliver Wendell Holmes supposes that Edwards's literary executors become dimly aware of this kind of precocity, which to their unenlightenment seems mere heterodoxy and which leads them according to Holmes to suppress the discussion of the Trinity. Nearly a century later Carse shares the similar opinion that, in imagining God thinking the Son into existence and God and the Son loving the Holy Spirit into existence, Edwards "is drawing the doctrine of the trinity out into an analogy with his conception of human agency" such as "to make it impossible for us to talk about God as though he were a being somehow apart and independent from the world of our experience" and thus to make the deity "all act," in which case Edwards's descendants do well to suspect heresy. Hegel himself establishes the precedent for the discovery in preromantic ruminations of thought, if not quite thinking itself at least guessing at itself, and in the preromantic ruminations of a much more distantly removed, if more illustrious predecessor than Edwards; in a not so grand gesture of philosophical deference in the preface to the *Phenomenology* Hegel admits only to be improving, albeit rather markedly, on Aristotle's description of Divinity as "love disporting with itself."[69]

These apparent similarities need not, however, reveal a genuine discursive continuity, any more than do Edwards's natural metaphors. In ascribing self-generation to God rather than to *Geist*, Edwards differs from Hegel not merely in diction. Direct incarnation of divine spirit may occur for Edwards only in the highest frame of existence, not throughout Creation, "for the perfect energy of God, with respect to Himself, is the most perfect exertion of Himself, of which the creation of the world is but a shadow." Romantic writers like Hegel claim to trace the generation of spirit, spirit's "becoming," in the forms of nature and the events of history. That Hegel should virtually repeat Edwards's description of divine being is evidence less of Edwards's precocity than of Hegel's misprisions of both Christian and pagan theology. Hegel, along with many other romantic philosophers, frequently derives his portrayals of the ideal as deflections from the theist discourse of Divinity. This allusiveness is not undeliberate, although neither is it fully self-conscious, and it certainly does not signify reversion to theism. Rather, it reflects a primary goal of romanticism, which is to repossess perfections that are, according to the romantic (mis)reading of theist discourse, mistakenly awarded to God only. Ludwig Feuerbach states the importance of this (mis)reading to the nineteenth-century humanist program in the 1840s, charging that the Christian religion benightedly surrenders man's own excellencies to a fictional being called "God," and then worships at the expense of human development. The theist description of Divinity is not so much corrected as appropriated by romanticism; the most significant change is in the relocation of divinity. Hegel's *Geist* may appear as awesome and mysterious as Edwards's God, but *Geist* is immanent in nature, available to human experience, present deeply within the Soul of Man. Despite ascribing similarly miraculous attributes to the original, uncreated source of being, Edwards and Hegel place the source differently, and therein lies a massive and fundamental distinction between Hegel's philosophy and Edwards's theology.[70]

Edwards's attempt to express God's immanence in the three members of the Trinity may be interpreted as a sublimation of his own ecstatic sense of union with God during intense religious experiences. But this judgment, which appeals to modern American cultural historiography, must ignore the subordinate relationship between God and Creation about which Edwards writes at great length and in unambiguous language. God is to Edwards emphatically not immanent in the frame of the natural world. That Edwards can entertain the possibility that God is immanent in Himself proves only the consistency with which Edwards denies any foundation for the immediate experience of God in nature, since, in granting a perfect communion with God only to the members of the Trinity, Edwards implicitly denies it to the elect even in afterlife, or to archangels for that matter, much less promising it to earthly saints. The joys of pantheism are not unimaginable to Edwards. They are not "hidden or potential" implications of his thought that he has "to hold in check . . . because he himself was so apt to become a mystic and pantheist," as Miller claims, but are rather excluded by him from the experience of any creature. Edwards may once try to imagine a "place" where God exists wholly, but to him this "place" is inaccessible, not a promised land. To depict him as trespassing there betrays an excessive, unexamined liking for the humanist discourse of the potential divinity of man.[71]

The revival of Puritanism is undeniably Edwards's own chief end, and he undeniable fails to achieve it; fundamental Protestantism is not long to be an ecclesiological or political reality at the time Edwards is preaching, as Parrington notes. The reconciliation of Calvinist doctrines with the science and philosophy of the eighteenth century is Edwards's ultimate end, and this end is largely realized. Although destined not to promote the higher end that Edwards so much desires, his ultimate success represents no small accomplishment. His exploration of the origin of the universe succeeds in uniting a conservative theology with a seemingly inconsistent epistemology. He shows convincingly how reason need not undermine but can sustain the primacy of revelation in the Christian knowledge of Divinity. He cultivates empiricism in a way that does not distract from God but establishes His supremacy over natural analogues. And Edwards lyrically celebrates the mysterious agreement between God's perfection and His creativity without confusing the being of God with that of His works.

The theist discourse of Creation cannot deny the limitations of nature that all theist writers describe as basic to the constitution of nature. Edwards usually explicates these limitations and always implies them; in returning to the origin of the universe he finds not immanent deity but a frame of being that is since the beginning only partial. The actions of God subsequent to Creation, the various salutary and punitive miracles of Providence, are portrayed by Edwards in a way that further emphasizes an ontological distinction between God and nature. Whereas Creation exhibits the separation of God from nature, Providence often shows Him acting dramatically against nature. This reading of Edwards's discourse of Creation, which differs from those performed by most modern scholars, has the virtue of making it fit well with his discourses of Providence and of Grace.[72]

3

PROVIDENCE

For the moral world is the end of the natural world; and the course of things in the latter, is undoubtedly subordinate to God's designs with respect to the former. Therefore he has seen cause from regard to the state of things in the moral world, *extraordinarily* to interpose, to interrupt and lay an arrest on the course of things in the natural world; and even in the greater wheels of its motion; even so as to stop the sun in its course.

—Edwards, *Freedom of the Will*

1. Introduction

Creation is not simply Edwards's word for nature. Creation is to him so far removed from truth as to be a thing entirely different from what is now taken to be self-generative. There is no genuine modern equivalent for Creation, which exists only within an ontology that distinguishes between the universe as an effect and God as first cause, and this distinction falls outside the humanist discursive pattern. Nor is there a genuine modern equivalent for analogy, since analogy represents a way of knowing that distinguishes fundamentally between reality and the appearance of reality in the sensible world, and this distinction is similarly apart from humanist epistemology. The resemblance between Creation and nature, analogy and science, is indulged in the last chapter only to expose its superficiality, and thereby to define precisely one difference between theist and humanist discursive patterns.

No more is Providence Edwards's word for history. He considers Providence much more expressive of Divinity than Creation, so he devotes much greater effort to its study—not only his several apocalyptic works and the series of sermons that he was about to combine into a history of the work of redemption before his death at Princeton, but all of his major treatises. It, too, differs fundamentally from what is now understood as

102

history. Providence is something wholly separate from and superior to time; its most revealing displays occur through interventions in historical process and violations of historical law. Although it is experienced by man in time and place, its often violent distortion of both teaches him to look beyond the world to know God, and thus articulates the same theist dualism as Creation. Like Creation it has no real modern equivalent because its meaning lies beyond sensible events and its study is concerned less with the events of history than the revelations of the Bible. Edwards is no more a historian than he is a scientist. To evaluate him as a historian shows another partiality to humanism.

But Edwards seems to be writing history, or almost to be writing history, not just to Bancroft in the nineteenth century but to Miller and a great many other modern scholars in the twentieth. This impression will be acknowledged in the same way and for the same purpose as the sense of Edwards's naturalism is indulged in the last chapter. It is not enough to say that Edwards writes history in ways that differ from modern historiography. He does not write history at all, because to him history does not exist as a subject of serious, theological inquiry. This distinction refers implicitly to the modern assumption of what history is in order by contrast to expose the other subject about which Edwards is so profilic, and thus condenses the meaning as well as illustrating the technique of this chapter. Difference from the humanist discursive pattern will again be noted continually to delineate the theist one to which Edwards's discourse of Providence belongs.

A text on Providence includes all of Edwards's published works. Each of the treatises attempts to reconcile with Providence some human knowledge, of feelings, the world, Scripture, that might appear detached from it. Edwards's greatest ambition is the Miltonic one of justifying all the works of God to man, as he indicates in a letter to the trustees of Princeton College explaining the scope of his projected history of the work of redemption and his reluctance to accept a post that might delay composition of such a theodicy: "This history will be carried on with regard to all three worlds, heaven, earth, and hell; considering the connected, successive events and alterations in each, so far as the scriptures give any light; introducing all parts of divinity in that order which is most scriptural and most natural; a method which appears to me most beautiful and entertaining, wherein every divine doctrine will appear to greatest advantage, in the highest light, in the most striking manner, shewing the admirable contexture and harmony of the whole." The study of Providence is to Edwards synonymous with theology. Its text is not to him one of three into which his writings can be divided, but the single one containing all of them worthy of publication. The modern text of Edwards omits most of these writings because humanism finds little in them that does not defer to Scripture and repeat, or at best refine, conventional Puritan exegesis. Some of Edwards's speculations on Creation may seem to shift to the subject of nature and stray into the method of science. Some of his speculations about Grace may seem to shift to the subject of personality and stray into the method of psychology. When writing of Providence Edwards relies little on humanity, neither his own personal experience nor the historical experience of the race, but writes almost always about revelation and almost exclusively as a theologian. The sovereign God is too much referred to in Edwards's discourse of Providence, so most of this discourse, an enormous archive quantitatively, is excluded from the modern text.[1]

The text of Providence that this chapter will compile comprehends most of Edwards's writings. It is today of no more than equal importance with texts of Creation and Grace despite being larger quantitatively. What it intends is the theoretical restoration of the majority of Edwards's works, not by proclaiming the fascination of pieties that will always bore modern retrospect, but by revealing their consistency with the rarer enterprises of Edwards's other discourses that so interest humanism. A regularity of considerable extent can be shown to join Edwards's discourse of Providence with those of Creation and of Grace, one that might impress modern retrospect with the exotic coherences of a theist discursive pattern.

2. Miracle

That the distinction between the miracles of Providence as better expressions of God's will and the miracle of Creation as a less clear expression of Divinity is an axiom of the Puritan theology of Edwards's time is indicated by Willard's stressing the distinction in his *Complete Body of Divinity*, the first comprehensive theological work written in New England and the one accepted by eighteenth-century Puritans in New England as a compendium of their religious principles. Edwards takes for granted that "God's works of providence are greater than those of creation," and cites the distinction frequently, especially in his sermons. This judgment is based less on differences between Creative and Providential acts than on the difference between the forces that must be overcome to accomplish them. Willard explains that chaos, or nonentity, is simply a "*Negative* contrary," and thus represents a less formidable opponent to God's creativity than evil, a "*Positive* contrary" willed by Satan, does to God's justice. Edwards agrees in the *Dissertation* that although the intrinsic formlessness of nature resists God's creation of the universe, an opposite will fights harder against His administration of the universe; "in this actual redemption of sinners, *the term from which, is more distant from the term to which,* than in the work of creation. The term from which in the work of creation, is nothing, and the term to which, is *being.* But the term from which, in the work of redemption, is a state *infinitely worse than nothing;* and the term to which, *a holy and happy being,* a state infinitely better than mere being. The terms in the production of the last, are much more remote from one another, than in the first." The divine will in both Creation and Providence defeats an opposing force; in the latter God's work requires greater effort.[2]

The militance of Providence redounds to God's glory. Edwards agrees with the interpretation of Luke 11:14 that likens the "strong man, fully armed" to Satan at his most formidable, and the stronger man who conquers him to God emphatically displaying His sovereignty. Dramatic confrontations between good and evil are common throughout Providence because God's "power never appears more illustrious than in conquering." The image of God as a "Boanerges playing the artillery of heaven against the hardy Sons of Vice," as Benjamin Colman characterizes Him, is a favorite one of Edwards and of many other eighteenth-century American Puritan theologians. Their preference is wholly scriptural, representing no peculiarly American tendency toward violent righteousness or evangelicalism. The Bible does not sanction various exegeses of miracle, but unmistakably supports a belligerent one; the very first extraterrestrial miracle recorded in the Old Testament, and arguably the most impressive one enacted by God since the Creation, stops the sun and moon to manifest God's sovereignty, not only by halting the natural cycles of the heavens but by cutting short, wholesale, the natural lives of men, the miraculous lengthening of the day permitting Joshua and his host to complete a slaughter of their and God's enemies that would otherwise have been interrupted by nightfall (Joshua 10: 12,13).[3]

Providence is not always so sanguine. God seems more benign when opposing less recalcitrant creatures, divine artillery being reserved for those who will be subdued by no more gentle means. A variety in the expressions of God's will is to Edwards a consequence of the structure of Creation; because the different frames of existence that creatures occupy and the different dispositions of creatures within the same frame together determine what kind of inspiration each can receive, God will continue to speak variously throughout the work of redemption; so may Grace be communicated as the terror of damnation to common laborers and simultaneously as a refined theological insight to "more knowing and thinking men." But every act of Providence, no matter how gentle, both teaches and occurs through the humiliation of the creature. Although the three stages into which Edwards divides the history of the work of redemption are defined by differences in the prevalent way God expresses His will, shifting from the "legal humiliations" of the Old Testament to the gracious inspirations of the Christian era, they do not reflect an improvement in the nature of man that would be necessary to alter the mortifying character of Providence. Because the hierarchy of being is coeval with Creation, mankind's ability to know and willingness to love God can never improve fundamentally, but only develop to their ordained limit. The old man who receives God's law in the Old Testament is not inferior to the young boy who feels His presence in New England, nor is Mount Sinai a less holy place than East Windsor. The thunder and lightning that humiliate Moses differ only rhetorically from the inspiration that humbles Edwards; in the former instance, God bends the necks of the Jews whereas in the latter He reveals the joy of bowing. Providence is designed always to urge men to renounce this world, and so always in some way subdues nature. To understand the order Edwards discerns in the providential plan, and to see why he endorses the chiliastic prophecy of Revelation 20, it is necessary to understand how he shows that just as Creation separates God from the creature, so does Providence proclaim the distinction between them.[4]

Edwards defines miracles as subjugations of nature, "by which the world was shaken, the whole frame of visible creation, earth, seas, and rivers, the atmosphere, the clouds, sun, moon and stars were affected." Nature betrays the direct influence of God upon it by behaving in a way that miraculously disobeys physics—the waters parting, the sun stopping, the bush burning without being consumed. Such unnatural happenings are for Edwards evidence of nature's being possessed by the spirit of God. Beyond disrupting the course of nature, miracles often serve Providence by actually destroying it. The best example of this in the Old Testament is the flood, which Edwards describes as a means of "lopping off" the corrupt branches of mankind. The virtuous root, Noah and his family, is saved and thereby winnowed from the rest of the world. Another type of miracle indirectly, and less violently, separates grain from chaff. Throughout the Old Testament God is reported periodically to sequester a chosen people in order to preserve them. Edwards notes a pattern in these miraculous sequestrations, beginning with the wanderings of Abraham: "God calls Abraham out of this idolatrous country, to a great distance from it. And when he came there, he gave him no inheritance in it, no not so much as to set his foot on; but he remained a stranger and a sojourner, that he and his family might be kept separate from all the world." Later, the entire Jewish people are not only separated from the world, but miraculously sustained in the wilderness by bread "daily rained down to them from heaven" and water sprung from a rock in a "continual miracle." Before the coming of Christ, the prophets are also "taken out of the schools" to maintain the purity of their vision, and in later times the true faith is similarly kept alive through the isolation of the Waldensians, who are "by natural walls, as well as by God's, separated from the rest of the world," the exile of the New England Puritans, and, Edwards modestly proposes, the even greater provinciality of Northampton, "being so far within the land, at a distance from seaports, and in a corner of the country."[5]

Each of these sequestrations reflects the ascetic character of miracles. They sustain a chosen people not through, but against nature, whose influence is counteracted by God's miraculously holding a few small, politically insignificant communities out of the mainstream. Prevented from discovering and destroying them, the world is defeated by these miracles much as it is destroyed by the flood. Accomplished miraculously, Providence operates entirely against the natural course of events: "It may here be observed, that from the fall of man, to our day, the work of redemption in its effects has mainly been carried out by remarkable communications of the Spirit of God. Though there be a more constant influence of God's Spirit always in some degree attending his ordinances; yet the way in which the greatest things have been done towards carrying out this work, always have been by remarkable effusions at special seasons of mercy."[6]

Edwards's distinction can be seen to differentiate between his discourse of Providence and modern historiography. He insists that advances toward God's end are miraculous, sudden and "remarkable" rather than gradual, happening at "special seasons of mercy" rather than at regular intervals. Providence is not embodied in a historical process and progressively unfolded, as it will seem to romantic historians and also, to a greater and lesser extent, to all their modern successors, but is imposed supernaturally. Its irregularity is the most essential feature of Providence because irregularity is proof of Divinity. The success of such a plan can be insured only by an omniscient and omnipotent Being: "The contrivance of our salvation is of such a nature that no one can rationally conclude that man had any hand in it. The nature of the contrivance is such, so out of the way of all human thoughts, so different from all human inventions." Divine rather than natural in origin, Providence flouts both nature and the human knowledge that is derived from nature.[7]

In advancing God's purpose circumstantially in the world, Providence serves a complementary doctrinal function for the faithful. Miracles not only rescue, they instruct; they not only defeat the world but discredit it. Miracles glorify God through discouraging worldliness. But as divine publicity "done in the open view of the world," they may not appear always to dignify their Author. In a variation of the old conundrum, unsolvable in theist discourse, that wonders why a perfect Being would be inclined to act, several Enlightened agnostics and atheists in the eighteenth century wonder whether a truly omnipotent Being need express Himself ostentatiously. Thomas Paine, for example, charges that miracles "degraded the Almighty into the character of a showman playing tricks to amuse and make the people stare and wonder." Edwards accepts the histrionic quality of miracles, but he ascribes their sensationalism to the insensitivity of the audience rather than the vulgarity of the Actor. Mankind's attention must be got with a blunt instrument. God stoops to sensational effects because of the obtuseness of the human sensibility and the recalcitrance of the human will, which explanation of the evangelical purpose of miracles fits Edwards's justification of the divine action, or inaction, that, at least to most modern perspectives, represents the greatest challenge to any Christian theodicy. Because miracles, as Edwards defines them, require opposition, their glory is proportionate to the power of their adversary. God must permit the forces of evil apparently to flourish in order the more dramatically to show His omnipotence in subduing them. A sudden victory against seemingly impossible odds is the most impressive one.[8]

The loosing of Satan in the world does not, therefore, represent an actual challenge to the work of redemption, but only an illusion of such a challenge, the background in contrast to which God's goodness shines more brightly: "Man's fall was God's opportunity to show how his contrivance and wisdom was beyond that of all creatures." God allows man to fall into a predicament so dire that only divine intervention can rescue him. When miraculous interventions occur, they impress man with the mercy of their Author. Edwards cites as illustration God's strengthening the enemies of the Jews to the degree that "it could be owing to nothing but a series of the greatest miracles" that the Jews are preserved. The pattern of hair's-breadth salvations in the Old Testament is designed to convince man that he is totally dependent on God, "so commonly things are in a state of great confusion before God works some great and glorious work in the church and in the world." Thus does God "harden Pharaoh's heart" against the Jews so that "I will get me honor upon Pharaoh" in the miraculous mass drowning of Pharaoh and his army in the Red Sea, and thus does God refuse to grant the Jews a victory when the Jews seem themselves capable of winning one, since "the people that are with thee are too many for me to give the Midianites into their hands, lest Israel vaunt themselves against me, saying, Mine own hand hath saved me" (Exodus 14:4, 17; Judges 7:2). And thus nearly two millennia later and a few generations before Edwards is born will the seventeenth-century New England Puritan Mary Rowlandson rationalize her captivity with what is to humanist retrospect the cruelly meager comfort that "when the Lord has brought His people to this that they saw no help in anything but Himself, then He takes the quarrel into His own Hand, and though [the Indians] had made a pit in their own imaginations as deep as hell for the Christians that summer, yet the Lord hurled themselves into it." This is offered as compensation for witnessing the slaughter of friends and family and having her baby girl die in her arms. The great problem of evil, which is more precisely to be called the problem of human suffering, over which humanist theology agonizes, simply does not exist as a commensurate obstacle to the theist discourse of Providence.[9]

The conflict between good and evil can take more subtle forms. Besides engineering last-minute rescues of His chosen people, God also reveals His beauty by contrasting it aesthetically with vice. Augustine argues that God permits evil in order to "embellish" Providence, to make "an exquisite poem set off with antitheses" whose effect is "achieved by the opposition of contraries, arranged, as it were, by an eloquence not of words, but of things." This kind of providential rhetoric is based on an aesthetic contrast between good and evil rather than an actual contest between them, and explains to Augustine why, in the prophecies of the New Testament, "things which have no signification of their own are interwoven for the sake of the things that are significant"; the structure of these narratives includes the dross of history as a "framework" in which the gold stands out in greater relief. This permits the inclusion of descriptions of the corrupt City of Rome in Augustine's own theological writings so as to give greater "luster" to the City of God.[10]

Edwards also notes the aesthetic value of "contraries" that "heighten the sense of one another," but he emphasizes more than Augustine how this antithesis affects man's moral sensibility, to which the "sense of good is comparatively dull and flat, without the knowledge of evil." And, because Edwards never loses sight of the primary doctrinal goal of Providence to show not only that good is preferable to evil but that good is entirely a gift of God, he stresses how the knowledge of evil brings man to "a more universal and immediate *sensible dependence* on God, than otherwise he would have [had]. . . . If man had not fallen, he would have had all his happiness in God, but not so sensibly . . . but now he is first sinful and universally corrupt, and afterwards is made holy. If man had held his integrity, misery would have been a stranger to him; and therefore happiness would not have been so sensibly a derivation from God." From man's point of view, the Fall is a calamity, but from God's it is an opportunity to intensify the piety of His creatures. A man "who never knew what evil was, but was happy from the first moment of being" would be less grateful to God for his salvation than one "who was brought to this happiness out of a miserable and doleful state."[11]

The dispassion with which Edwards treats human suffering may seem brutal. This impression is one reason for the exclusion of most of his discourse of Providence from the modern text of his works. But the impression can also be instructive of the disparity between the theism that controls his writing and the humanism that controls modern discourse. Suffering is meaningful to Edwards in the context of Creation; the ultimate significance of suffering, like that of all creatures, can be known only in the infinitely greater context of Divinity. As a theologian responsible mainly for the study of God, Edwards must evaluate the welfare of his own kind as contributing in only small and indirect ways to the glory of the Creator. One of the many strange consistencies of Edwards's theism is that it requires him to measure evil primarily in units not of human pain but of divine benefit.

Evil plays the role of straw man in the work of redemption, appearing threatening in order only to make God appear greater in victory. Though never genuinely competitive with God, evil, however, remains always opposed to Him. Edwards never implies that evil is transformed into good, as

romantic philosophy and some modern religious thought contend. Although Edwards says that Providence miraculously brings good out of evil,
this means in the context of the theist discursive pattern not that good is
caused to grow naturally from evil, but that good supersedes and replaces
evil. Miracles distinguish unmistakably between the opponents in the
providential battle and prove to man which one of them is holy.

The occurrence of miracles, according to Edwards, is the cause of the
earliest kinds of piety among men. God's first miraculous appearance after
the Fall causes Adam and Eve to cover themselves, which Edwards interprets as a primitive form of piety since modesty implies the effacing of
nature; clothing accordingly represents a war against the flesh because the
animal skins are acquired "at the expense of life." Sacrifice, to Edwards the
crudest form of worship, ceremonially destroys nature, and, he concludes,
must be inspired by the unnatural display of supernatural power:
"Sacrificing is not part of natural worship [since] the light of nature doth
not teach men to offer up beasts in sacrifice to God." Only the miraculous
revelation of a power superior to nature causes pagans to conduct these
symbolic humiliations of the flesh: "How came all the Heathen nations to
agree in the custom of sacrificing? The light of nature did not teach it to
them; without doubt they had it from tradition; and therefore, it need not
seem strange, that what of natural religion they had amongst them, came
the same way. I am persuaded, that mankind would have been like a herd
of beasts, with respect to their knowledge in all important truths, if there
had never been any such thing as revelation in the world."[12]

The pieties of the Jewish church are only more sophisticated, following
the same example set by God's miracles. According to the Bible, the commandments do not evolve from Jewish custom, but are delivered to Moses
in the wilderness, actually and figuratively cut off from the natural influence of his tribe, and, as Edwards points out, are imposed upon the
Jews afterward "in an awful manner, with a terrible voice, exceedingly loud
and awful, so that all the people in the camp trembled." The prohibitions
contained in the Law are enforced by a miraculous display of God's power
over nature, and the legalistic forms of worship that Moses institutes to
preserve the Law—consecration of a Levite priesthood that contributes
nothing to the natural welfare of the people, construction of a tabernacle
that diverts considerable human and material resources from the service of
the people to the service of God, establishment of an elaborate ceremonial
calendar that interrupts the economic schedule of the people—all reflect a
forced sacrifice of natural interests. "The church, under the Old Testament,
was a child under tutors and governors."[13]

But all of these miracles, all of these "many schemes and methods [that]
were tried of old, both before and after the flood," fail to redeem mankind.
The renunciation of the flesh ordered by the covenant of works is impressed upon man by the most spectacular of miracles, yet man persists in

worshiping the false gods of nature. Although in actual struggles with the forces of nature or evil God emerges miraculously triumphant, these struggles do not convince most men to live pious lives.[14]

This failure cannot to Edwards reveal a flaw in Providence. He interprets the backsliding of mankind as further indication that miracle is designed by God to distinguish His own excellency in contrast to the corruption of nature. The covenant of works is never intended to achieve a genuine, lasting change in the moral world; such an aim would imply that God is concerned chiefly with the welfare of His creatures, which Edwards shows in the *Dissertation* is a motive inconsistent with Divinity, and such an aim would also suggest that man can learn to be virtuous and thereby decrease his sense of reliance on God for salvation. Both of these implications show that had the covenant of works succeeded, it would have subordinated God to His creatures and actually discouraged piety.

Edwards justifies the only conclusion consistent with divine perfection, which is that the covenant of works is designed to fail, by comparing God's work of redemption from the Fall to the birth of Christ to a thousand years' labor devoted to clearing a weed-infested garden: "If there were a piece of ground, which abounded with briars and thorns, or some poisonous plant, and all mankind had used their endeavors, for a thousand years together, to suppress that evil growth, and to bring that ground by manure and cultivation, planting and sowing, to produce better fruit, but all in vain, it would still be overrun with the same noxious growth; [it would] be proof, that such a produce was agreeable to the nature of that soil, [and it could] be compared to that which is given in divine providence, that wickedness is a produce agreeable to the nature of the field of the world of mankind." The sense of the garden's badness is heightened by the amount of effort spent vainly cultivating, just as the conviction that the world is naturally wicked is strengthened by miracles that fail to reform the world. In this sense, miracle fulfills the doctrinal function indirectly by exposing man as reprobate. The radical distinction between the baseness of man and his world and the perfection of God is indicated first in the character of miracle and confirmed later when man persists in his disobedience even after witnessing God's most awesome enforcement of the law.[15]

Miracle shows, therefore, that even with the assistance of a divine champion and under the most propitious of circumstances, mankind persists in sinfulness. After their sequestration the Jews have no excuse for losing the faith—their worship is not disturbed by foreign aggression nor corrupted by the influence of pagan religion—and yet they fall. A more immediate and affecting example of miracle's indirectly exposing mankind's natural wickedness is observed by Edwards in the backsliding of the later generations of Puritans in New England: "When England grew very corrupt, God brought over a number of pious persons, and planted 'em in New England, and this land was planted with a noble vine. But how the gold became dim! How greatly have we forsaken the pious examples of our fathers." That New England Puritans grow impious even after being placed in a new world is to Edwards another of God's demonstrations of man's helpless inability to save himself.[16]

The particular circumstance of being a late eighteenth-century New England pastor, or the general condition of being an eighteenth-century Puritan theologian, is not the "cause" of Edwards's discourse of miracle, however, which is not at all peculiar—not to him, nor to Puritanism, nor even to eighteenth-century Christianity. It is but an instance of the discourse of Creation as partial being, or of the dualistic ontology of being as a whole, that pervades theism. The pervasiveness of this discourse and of the underlying theist pattern can be suggested by showing their consistency with a much celebrated passage from eighteenth-century secular American letters that has seemed so far afield from Edwards's writings as never before to have been discussed in the same context with them.

Modern interest in the "Natural Bridge" passage from Jefferson's *Notes on the State of Virginia* derives from the unusual specificity, present nowhere else in the *Notes,* of Jefferson's account of his emotions. The discursive foundation for this interest is the apparent naturalism and emotionalism, which is to say, since both apparent emphases are made possible by a single pattern of discourse, the humanism of the description. Here more than anywhere elso Jefferson seems to be mastered by the place, expressing an intimate, naturalizing relation between the American land and a self that is becoming American. Thus the passage is stressed in modern interpretations of the *Notes* and of Jefferson and is culled from the *Notes* by modern anthologies of American literature as inevitably as is Edwards's personal narrative.

That the natural bridge and Jefferson's description of it have special status is a judgment not only of modern retrospect. Jefferson himself singles out both as anomalous at the beginning of the passage, indicating that the bridge fits no known classification, much less the one, "Cascades," of the Query in which, having no more appropriate heading, he places it. The bridge interrupts Virginia's topography and Jefferson's discourse; it is remarked because it is remarkably out of the course of nature. This special status within the context of the *Notes* does more than just differ from the special status awarded by modern retrospect. Far from being unusual because of conforming to a pattern in which man is acclimatized to his environment, the natural bridge is curious to Jefferson because it deviates spectacularly from the order of things, and accordingly will promote a response from him that is entirely other than an attachment to his surroundings.

The sequence of Jefferson's description is familiar. He begins by declaring that the bridge is the "most sublime" of nature's works and continues with measurements that fail to convey, or postpone the conveyance of its sublimity. Seeming inconsistencies like this one recur throughout the *Notes*—in Jefferson's descriptions of the Ohio and Wabash rivers, for example, declarations of a river's beauty, "the most beautiful river on earth," are immediately followed by statistics, "a very beautiful river, four hundred yards wide"—and they can be interpreted as signifying a genuine structure rather than occasional inconsistencies. The aesthetics of the bridge, or of the rivers, or of any feature of nature, belongs to an emotional reality that is only indirectly related to material reality. Beauty is perceived by the immaterial faculty of the perceiver's soul, or will, or feelings. The bodily eye and the material bodies seen by the eye are the vehicle and analogues of this immaterial faculty while remaining ontologically separate and inferior. Thus a systemic dualism can be seen positively to dictate what might appear as simple error. The beauty of Virginia is peripheral to the subject of the *Notes*, which are those realities of the region which interest an eighteenth-century scientist or entrepreneur, and so is properly only mentioned in passing amid descriptions of things that remain, both the things and the discourses about them, related obliquely to accounts of the delight or disgust of a traveler's sensibilities.[17]

But the description of the natural bridge is unique because it returns, after measuring the dimensions of the bridge, to relating the awe of the perceiver, even his "rapture": "It is impossible for the emotions arising from the sublime to be felt beyond what they are here; so beautiful an arch, so elevated, so light, and springing as it were up to heaven! the rapture of the spectator is really indescribable." Just prior to this eulogy Jefferson describes the sickness he feels while looking from the arch of the bridge into the "abyss" it spans. His sickness and his rapture are versions of a single response, which is not the ecstatic kinship with nature that characterizes romantic visionary experience of places but, rather (and this distinction may apply to all examples in the eighteenth century and, in American culture at least, in the early nineteenth century as well, of the *sublime* as the term is originally understood), an ecstatic subordination to the supernatural power not immanent in but responsible as Creator for such prodigies as a natural bridge. Subjectively, Jefferson is prostrated by the bridge, both physically in his sickness and stylistically in his inarticulately repetitive genuflections to its grandeur (a particular mimesis for wonder that will be shown also to be practiced, almost identically, in the theophanies of Edwards's personal narrative). Objectively, the bridge as Jefferson describes it commands this response not only by its size but by its shape, which humbles the very nature of which it is anomalously a part by providing an example of how the imperfections of topography may be overcome through artifice, how the irregularities of rivers and valleys may be mended by the construction of bridges. The natural bridge is, of course, an oxymoron, a case of nature miraculously acting against nature, and Jefferson's awe concerns him less with the material reality of the bridge than with the immaterial reality to which the bridge, with a kind of natural piety of its own, defers.

The passage concludes with what might appear just a transition back to the dispassionate empiricism that dominates the *Notes*—the bridge is located in Rockbridge county; the stream that flows under it is named Cedar-Creek; the creek flows regularly enough to "turn a grist-mill." But the way in which Jefferson regains his balance prior to this dry list of geographical and economic attributes recalls an earlier passage, one from the same Query describing the bursting of the Potomac river through the Blue Ridge, and illustrates further how Jefferson's discourse can be understood as a reflection of the theist discourse of miracle. In both descriptions the foreground—the abyss under the bridge and the "riot and tumult" of the Potomac canyon—produces vertigo; the background, however, toward which Jefferson's gaze is drawn to relieve his immediate sensation of peril and perception of chaos, is serene, the distant horizon in each description seeming, especially in contrast to what lies nearby, a welcome alternative prospect. Thus the whole structure of miracle that is explicit in Edwards's writings is contained implicitly in Jefferson's. Not only does Jefferson's description of the bridge correspond in emphasizing unnatural qualities, and not only does Jefferson's description of his reaction correspond in emphasizing humiliation, but even Jefferson's concluding shift of attention from the prodigies themselves to the horizon above them corresponds to the doctrinal hermeneutic of miracle according to theism, that miracle is designed to encourage an ascetic withdrawal from this life and from this world.[18]

The theist discourse of miracle can thus be seen to join apparently disparate writings, including nontheological ones, like the "Natural Bridge" episode from Jefferson's *Notes on the State of Virginia*, or one from the writings of James Madison that ascribes the unlikely agreement of delegates to the Constitutional Convention to the miraculous restraining force of a "finger of that Almighty Hand," as well as apparently kindred ones, such as one from the opening of the *Magnalia* in which Mather ascribes the coincidence of the invention of movable type, the Protestant Reformation, and the discovery of the North American continent to the antihistorical intervention of God's Providence. Edwards's and these other theist discourses of miracle are best appreciated not as momentary lapses from or delays in intellectual progress but as positive embodiments of the theist discursive pattern whose capacity to explain the world is equivalant in its way to that of modern historicism.[19]

During the pre-Christian era the church is prevented from falling wholly into the hands of its enemies or wholly into idolatry by God's miraculous restraint of the natural course of events and the natural tendencies of men. The preservation of the church is not of primary importance, however. It contributes to the work of redemption by providing a background against which divine intervention appears more illustrious and necessary. God miraculously "intercedes for fallen man" and "governs the church and the world as a king" throughout the Old Testament to show that the ingratitude and unworthiness of man is such that only the most unexpected and unnatural miracle of all can save him.[20]

3. Christ

To members of the original Jewish church, the convenant of works seems final. God gives them many signs that they are His chosen people and that His blessing may be earned through obedience to the Law. They can conclude only that the fate of God's kingdom depends on their fidelity. To Christians trying to explain the Old Testament in light of the new covenant, this assumption is of course shortsighted. They see the Jewish church as an unwitting harbinger of Christ. Such typological interpretations of the Old Testament imply that the history of the church prior to Christ's birth has little intrinsic significance and is worthy of attention for the sake only of the great future event that it anticipates. Christian typology therefore subordinates all the persons and events of the Old Testament to the Incarnation that supersedes them. This anticipatory aspect of typology is the one that Edwards stresses.

Like many Puritan exegetes, including John Bunyan, Edwards distinguishes three kinds of type in the Old Testament; "The types of Christ were of three sorts: instituted, providential, and personal. The ordinance of *sacrificing* was the greatest of the *instituted* types; the redemption out of *Egypt* was the greatest of the *providential*; and David the greatest of the *personal* ones." All three kinds of type are similar in that each signifies an asceticism that to Edwards will represent the proper doctrinal interpretation of Christ: "instituted" types sacrifice things of carnal value; "providential" ones negate the influence of worldly powers; and personal types of Christ such as Moses and David preach humiliation of the flesh as the path to holiness. The types differ in the degree to which the piety they represent is self-consciously and willfully practiced.[21]

Sacrificing is prompted by miraculous displays of divine sovereignty and is instituted in pagan and Jewish religions through custom. It arises in recognition of God's power over nature, acquires form through crude attempts to imitate this example, and is preserved for generations through repetition. Because it is enforced by God's "legal humiliations," and subsequently by religious sanctions rather than by the free consent of man, and because its figurative appeal to renounce the flesh is largely ignored by both pagans and Jews, sacrifice reflects to Edwards the least self-conscious kind of piety and hence the lowest kind of type.

The providential redemptions of the Jews constitute a higher kind because they reveal more clearly that sacrifice of worldly things is essential to the pursuit of holiness. Unlike sacrifice, which shows only idolatrous respect for supernatural power, redemptions indicate that abandonment of the world, represented in the Jews' escape from Egypt and all the miraculous salvations in the Old Testament, is a moral duty, not merely a legal one. But although the doctrinal relationship between otherworldliness and virtue is more evident in redemption than in sacrifice, the sequestrations of the Jews are accomplished by the miraculous interventions of God rather than by the intrinsic piety of the people, whose wickedness reemerges even while they are isolated from the heathen nations. The providential type is ranked by Edwards as an intermediate kind because it still does not represent a voluntary preference for God over the world.

The personal types are closest to Christ because these Old and New Testament figures are freely and self-consciously pious. The perseverance of Ruth, to which Edwards devotes a sermon, "Ruth's Resolution," qualifies her as a personal type since it lies in her sacrificing the natural ties she feels to her own people for the holy ties she feels to the God of the Jews. Her piety exiles her from the world, as the Jews are sequestered, but she achieves this redemption without the aid of miracles, at least of the outward sort. In freely choosing the virtuous life, she shows evidence of possessing a truly virtuous disposition and therefore foreshadows not only Christ but the Christian church as defined by the covenant of Grace. The other personal types are distinguished similarly by their voluntary love of God. David is the greatest of the personal types because his piety is the most joyful, as expressed in the Psalms, and the least dictated by the prohibitions of the Law.[22]

The qualitative distinctions Edwards draws among these three kinds of type define a structure for the first period of the work of redemption that is neither progressive nor organic. The nature of persons who anticipate Christ is not gradually improved; they do not comprise the stem from which Christ flowers. Rather, the nature of personal types declines as the moment of the Incarnation becomes imminent, so as to reveal dramatically that Christ is born not of natural generation but of divine intervention.

The increasing otherworldliness of the personal types is indicated by a more and more self-effacing tone in their prophecies. They foreshadow Christ not only through their voluntary asceticism, as is the case with Ruth, but also through the prophetic subordination of themselves to His coming. Edwards notes that the prophecies of the Old Testament speak not of present but of future times, not of the wisdom that can presently be acquired but of the visionary truth that will later be revealed: "And therefore we find that the great and main thing that the most of the prophets in their written prophecies insist upon, is Christ and his redemption, and the glorious times of the Gospel. And though many other things were spoken of in their prophecies, yet they seem to be only as introductory to their prophecy of these great things. Whatever they predict, here their prophecies commonly terminate." These personal types prostrate themselves before the greatest of all prophets, and urge their listeners to ignore the current circumstances of the church and the world and devote all of their attention to an impending miracle that will totally overshadow all past and current history. Their most inspired utterances are those which deny themselves in rapturous anticipation of Christ: "And in what an exalted strain do they all speak of these things! Many other things they speak of in men's usual language. But when they enter upon this subject, what a heavenly sublimity is there in their language."[23]

The more passionately forward-looking these personal types become, the less important become their personal identities; as truth waxes in their prophecies, so does nature wane. Their personalities become less and less prominent until, just before the Incarnation they have so long predicted actually occurs, they disappear altogether: "Thus the Old Testament light[s], the stars of the long night, began apace to hide their heads, the time of the Son of righteousness now drawing nigh. . . . The time of the Great Prophet of God was now so nigh, it was time for the typical prophets to be silent." During the iniquitous times that characterize most of the history of the church under the covenant of works, the personal types of Christ, such as David and the other great Jewish kings, shine individually and distinctly as stars in a night sky. These personal types are great in worldly as well as internal attributes. The progression of personal types is defined by Edwards as an extinction of their individuality, the "stars of the long night" beginning "apace to hide their heads," before the miraculous dawning of a spiritual light of which theirs is but a pale fire. John the Baptist, last of the personal types, is quoted by Edwards from John 3:30 to summarize the direction of this movement: "He must increase, but I must decrease."[24]

Immediately before the coming of Christ, the prophets, whose prophecies have contained for some time a crescendo of anticipation, fall abruptly silent. The world meanwhile has become particularly vicious. This sudden moral darkness is ordained the better to contrast with and thereby glorify the perfect virtue that Christ will represent: "So the world, as it were, travailed in pain, and was in continual convulsions, for several hundred years together, to bring forth the first-born child, and the only begotten Son of God." Vice reigns as a background against which Christ stands out in sharp relief; the prophets are silent before Christ begins His public ministry in order to allow His prophecy singly to oppose the world's apostasy. Edwards stresses the decline of morality prior to the Incarnation to show that this, the greatest of all works of redemption, distinguishes even more sharply than previous miracles between God and nature. Christ comes suddenly, unexpectedly, at the eleventh hour, in order that the salvation that He offers will be understood to derive entirely from God, and not at all from even the most virtuous and enlightened prophets who precede Him.[25]

Believing Providence to serve God's chief end of self-glorification, Edwards must demonstrate how the Incarnation, the central work of redemption, is particularly illustrative of this end. God's assumption of human nature is seen by Edwards primarily to benefit Divinity, only secondarily to benefit man. That Christ is born when the forces of evil prevail reveals that the Incarnation is designed to glorify God, and all subsequent appearances of the Son on earth, Edwards assumes, will occur at times of iniquity so as similarly to presage a glorious victory over evil: "Each of these comings of Christ is accompanied with a terrible *destruction* of the wicked, and the enemies of the church." The way in which the Incarnation achieves this victory is especially miraculous, however, because of the lowly state that God assumes to do battle. After permitting evil to flourish, God accepts the additional handicap of confronting evil in the weak person of a single human being: "Creature-wisdom would have thought that Christ, in order to perform this great work, should deck himself with all his strength; but divine wisdom determined, that he should be made weak, and put on the infirmities of human nature." The Incarnation is the best example of Providence taking an unexpected course, and is therefore the clearest illustration of God's glorifying Himself in contrast to nature. Disdaining to exercise His power directly, God reveals the sovereignty of His will by showing He must triumph even when working through the limited strength of man. The Son, as Christ, discards the armament of Divinity so as to be at a disadvantage in His struggle, and thus appears unmistakably superior in His ultimate victory.[26]

The Incarnation improves upon previous miracles by heightening the impression of God's vulnerability to the forces of evil, which are allowed to assault Divinity stripped of omnipotence. Although the success of Christ's struggle is inevitable, it glorifies God, like all other miracles, by granting evil a seeming opportunity to prevail. In order to serve God's chief end, the Incarnation must not repair the fundamental imperfections of the human nature that God assumes. Christ cannot be merely disguised as man, nor can He transcend man's weakness; the gloriousness of His victory over sin depends upon the reality of the handicap under which He fights.[27]

Because Edwards equates the miraculousness of works of redemption with the resistance they encounter, he accounts the Incarnation the greatest of these works insofar as it shows God succeeding in spite of the greatest difficulties. He interprets the Incarnation not as a deification of human nature, but as a miraculous combination of two different natures, human and divine, that remain distinct and, implicitly, conflicting in the person of Christ. The human nature of Christ is inhibiting since human being prevents the direct expression of Divinity; ontologically a man, Christ is exposed to the weaknesses of the flesh; culturally a Jew, He is bound by the moral and ceremonial laws of His tribe. Christ never frees Himself from these restrictions; He remains subject to pain and desire and obedient to the covenant of works that governs Judaism. Rather, in revealing new principles of religion that voluntarily sacrifice the flesh and so replace those of the old covenant, He achieves the most glorious manifestation of Divinity by successfully instituting these new principles despite being personally in thrall to the old principles they renounce. His human nature must remain a formidable obstacle to His prophecy in order, according to Edwards's discourse of miracle, for the realization of that prophecy to be glorious. Christ's Divinity appears in contrast to His human nature and the forces of evil, both of which He must conquer to fulfill what Edwards calls the "mediatorial" office of communicating the new covenant: "Christ's righteousness, by which he merited heaven for himself, and all who believe in him, consists principally in his obedience to this mediatorial law: for in fulfilling this law consisted his chief works and business in the world. . . . This part of his obedience was attended with the greatest difficulty; and therefore his obedience to it was most meritorious. What Christ had to do in the world by virtue of his being Mediator, was infinitely more difficult than what he had to do merely as a man or as a Jew."[28]

Christ fulfills the mediatorial law by establishing the new covenant, which is the most impressive of His actions and capable of being accomplished only by God Himself; more difficult than all other tasks, such as obeying moral or religious law, the establishment of the new covenant must overcome not only the weakness of one human will, but the influence of all previous history and religious custom. To be virtuous, a Jew has only to restrain his pride. To be Mediator, Christ has to overcome the pride of the world. The glory of this divine work depends for Edwards on having been done despite the great disadvantage of Christ's being incarnated as an "inconceivable" mixture of "natures so infinitely different, as the divine and human nature, in one person." The duality of Christ's being is no overfine metaphysical quibble spawned by Edwards's overfinely metaphysical mind, but is the basis for Christ's heroism, and is thus a basic assumption of all theist Christology; Willard, for example, agrees that Christ is compounded of "two natures infinitely disproportionate" and can therefore be classified teratologically as "God-man."[29]

Edwards demonstrates how the Incarnation conforms to God's chief end of self-glorification by consistently stressing the duality of Christ's nature. This emphasis is apparent also in his analysis of Christ's subordinate role as the savior of man. Salvation is one means by which God's chief end is realized, and it requires the merciful concessions to human nature implied in the new covenant. Although Christ's placing love of God above fidelity to the law may seem to broaden religion to allow for the participation of the whole human being, the new obligation represents to Edwards a reduction of man's religious duties to fit man's limited capacity for obedience. The old covenant counsels a more difficult course than man unaided is able to pursue, and serves indirectly to reveal man's inability even in part to earn his own salvation: "The great thing wherein the first covenant was deficient, was, that the fulfillment of the righteousness of the covenant, and man's perseverance, was entrusted to man himself, with nothing better to secure it than his own strength." In promoting the new covenant that replaces self-reliance with total dependence on God, Christ exemplifies the pious subordination of His human nature to His divine one, and thereby distinguishes between them in all of His evangelical works.[30]

Thus the most important example Christ sets is the sacrificing of human nature to divine principle, which consummates all typical subordinations of nature to God that precede Christ: "The greatest thing that Christ did in execution of his priestly office, and the greatest thing he ever did, and the greatest thing that ever was done, was the offering up himself a sacrifice to God. Herein he was the antetype of all that had been done by the priests, in all their sacrifices and offerings, from the beginning of the world." Edwards begins the "history" leaving no doubt about his view of the primary significance of Christ's career. Christ's virtue lies in His willingness to endure the humiliation of His human nature in order to accomplish His providential mission, so all Christians ought similarly to renounce the flesh for love of God.[31]

The way that Christ communicates to man distinguishes between His two natures no less than the meaning of His sacrifice. The pious gratitude inspired in many by God's deigning to incarnate Himself depends for Edwards on constant recognition of the infinite difference between God's divine nature and the unworthy form that God briefly inhabits. In Edwards's consolatory letter to Lady Pepperell, he explains that Christ's humanity is correctly to be understood as a concession to the limitations of human perception: "Infinite wisdom has also contrived, that we should behold the glory of the Deity, in the face of Jesus Christ, to the greatest advantage, in such a manner as should be best adapted to the capacity of poor feeble man. . . . For Christ [has] by his incarnation come down from his Infinite exaltation above us, and become one of our kinsmen and brothers. And his glory shining upon us through his human nature, the manifestation is wonderfully adapted to the strength of human vision." Christ appeals to man's affections by condescending to human weakness, and man responds by keeping always in mind the disparity between the awesome magnificence with which pure Divinity would appear and the meekness that Divinity assumes in the human nature of Christ. The sense of this disparity contributes specifically to man's acceptance of Christ's sacrificial example. The suffering of God is more affecting than that of a man because God's state is felt to be ordinarily so far removed from that of victim, and God's willingness Himself to endure humiliation and death convinces man more persuasively than the agony of any human martyr of the justice of sacrifice: "So the majesty of God appears much more in the sufferings of Christ than it would have done in the eternal sufferings of all mankind. The majesty of a prince appears greater in the just punishment of great personages under the guilt of treason, than of inferior persons. The sufferings of Christ have this advantage over the eternal sufferings of the wicked, for impressing upon the minds of the spectators a sense of the dread majesty of God." The righteousness of God is glorified more in the punishment of a Being who takes upon himself the sins of the world than in that of "inferior persons" who are guilty only of personal transgressions, and the virtuousness of sacrifice is better evidenced in the suffering of a Being who is omnipotent in His normal state than in the suffering of men who are naturally slaves to pain. Both of these impressions depend on the recognition that the human being that dies on Calvary is part of the cross accepted by Divinity to further the work of redemption.[32]

This presentation of Edwards's discourse of Providence, of the role of the Incarnation in Providence, and of the fitness of the Incarnation to God's chief end of self-adoration, is prompted by the inevitable tendency of modern retrospect to overlook or to (mis)read differently each of these expressions of theism in Edwards' writings. The assumption that Providence leads incrementally up to the climax of Christ's ministry and continues to develop in the subsequent history of the Christian religion belongs to a humanist discursive pattern. So do those assumptions that Christ represents the apotheosis of human being and that the chief end of God is the salvation of man. None of these propositions has positive value in theist discourse. To keep prominent such differences between theism and humanism is the chief end of this reading.

Edwards perceives Christ not as divine man, which view is consistent with the romantic conclusion that Christ reveals the potential divinity of the race, but as God burdened by human nature. To neglect this distinction results to Edwards in no philosophical breakthrough, but in confusion and sin, in what he would condemn as idolatry. Even in a passage in which Edwards seems careless about the distinction, a note, just recently published, on Psalms 8:4 from his "Blank Bible," in which he describes the Incarnation as "an actual uniting of the human nature with the divine, whereby the human nature was exalted not only to an honor and dominion that was an image of God's, but actually to God's honor and dominion." What seems an unmistakable identification of Divinity with humanity is so only when transferred from theist to humanist discourse. The feature of this passage that appears most inconsistent with Edwards's Christology is the insistence that Incarnation creates not just an "image" of God's "honor and dominion," which in theist diction means a lower analogue, but an "actuality," which must in this comparison mean rather a much closer connection, perhaps even an identity. That this implication seems inconsistent with everything Edwards publishes on the subject of Christ, and almost everything else he writes on the subject that survives in manuscript, not to mention all of Edwards's other writings on all other subjects insofar as they constitute a theist discourse as theism is being defined here, might justify dismissing this one passage as somehow an exception that somehow proves the rule, a mere lapse that does not propel Edwards toward a more advanced discourse on Christ but that detracts from the high standard of consistency set by the rest of his Christology. But a way more persuasively of reconciling the passage with theism is available with reference to a discursive context no wider than that of the note. The Psalm upon which Edwards is commenting is exclusively concerned with the "honor and dominion" of God over nature and, particularly, over man, about whom the well-known fourth verse asks, rhetorically, "What is man, that thou art mindful of him? and the son of man, that thou visitest him?", the answer being, of course, nothing, or at least nothing sufficient to require any solicitude of an omnipotent and sovereign God. What the Psalm takes to be the absolute standard of condescension, the very hyperbole of condescension, is from Edwards's Christian retrospect only a type and thus still an insufficiently exaggerated form of the antetypically utter condescension represented by the Incarnation. Edwards's exegesis does not substitute any new meaning for the original piety of the verse from the Old Testament but just amplifies this piety to an even greater pitch, an intensification that depends upon God's appearing even more benificent, and thus superior, and man's appearing even more a beneficiary, and thus inferior, in the Incarnation than in any dispensations granted to the Jews.[33]

One more, stylistic discrimination can be added further to suggest how this note does not contradict theism, not even through some inattention that might be expected in a manuscript as voluminous as Edwards's notebooks. In Edwards's note man is raised, according to a distinction that is implicit whenever Edwards is discussing the actions or attributes of either God or man but that must be made explicit to a humanist readership accustomed to interchanging the internal existence and the external manifestation even of supreme being, not to the essence but to the "honor and dominion" of God, which are even more clearly than most of God's attributes to be distinguished from His essence since they are entirely negative; God "will get me honor upon Pharaoh" by annihilating Pharaoh and his host in the verse from Exodus that defines miracle according to Old Testament theist usage, and God rules the world just as, in a delegation that is the lower analogue of divine sovereignty, God "madest [man] to have dominion over the works of thy hands" according to the very Psalm Edwards is commenting on in this apparently precocious note (Psalms 8:6). So, for man to enjoy precisely the "honor and dominion" of God does not necessarily imply even a casual, vagrant, involuntary merging of human and divine beings, not, that is, in the context of theist discourse.

As a man, Christ, like anything else that is visible according to Edwards's dualistic epistemology, is understood properly as the lower analogue of Christ's will. Worship of the historical Jesus mistakes flesh for spirit, man for God, the impiety of which is implicitly warned against by Christ Himself. Abandoning His human form after the Ascension, Christ discourages the natural desire of His followers to cling to His person: "It would not have been proper for Christ constantly to dwell among men after his resurrection. Men would be exceedingly apt to fall into idolatry, and, because they *saw* the man Jesus Christ, would be apt to direct their worship to the *human* nature." Despite Edwards's appreciation of Christ's personal beauty, he never overlooks the distinction between apparent and essential Divinity. Even the most excellent product of nature can be no more than the shadow of spiritual perfection: "Christ's spiritual glory is that wherein his divinity consists; and the outward glory of his transfiguration showed him to be divine, only as it was a remarkable image or representation of that spiritual glory." In the context of a discourse that generates qualifications like this, the claim of a recent critic that according to Edwards the meaning of Christ is to be apprehended primarily through visual images is, perhaps complexly, but nonetheless certainly mistaken.[34]

In His role as the Savior of mankind, Christ reveals more of Divinity than is ever before or afterward seen on earth, at least until the Day of Judgment, but He does not perfectly manifest God to Edwards, for whom even this most "remarkable image or representation" suffers from the fundamental inexpressiveness of visible things. Neither are Christ's evangelical efforts on earth universally effective. Although He provides an example from which man might "learn and be animated, to seek the like glory and honor, and to obtain the like glorious reward," the example has no more effect on the reprobate than all the "many schemes and methods" of Providence that precede it. The limited success of Christ's ministry no more damages the perfection of the whole work of redemption than does the failure of the covenant of works, however, since the conversion of man is subordinate to God's chief end of self-glorification. In simplifying man's religious responsibilities and promoting virtue through the most gentle and affecting appeals, Christ fits salvation precisely to man's limited capabilities to show that man's disobedience betrays wicked inclination rather than natural weakness. The new covenant proves that nothing can excuse man's failure to obey, that God is righteous in the damnation of sinners, that God's virtue shines in contrast to vice.[35]

The work of redemption is thus to Edwards less a crusade in which God, through the Incarnation and other miracles, solicits men's souls than a pageant in which salvation contributes to the display of God's glory. Edwards equates the success of evangelical works not with the number of men they convert, but with the degree to which they radiate Divinity. That from the modern perspective he seems inhumane cannot be denied, but this impression can be exploited to sharpen a perception of the theist pattern that organizes all of Edwards's writings. With God's chief end always in mind Edwards can explain both why evil exists on earth before the Incarnation and why evil is permitted to persist in the Christian era. The pious admission that God, not man, is the end of all things enables Edwards also to follow Christ's example in fighting sin while recognizing that sin is predestined to survive as a necessary part of God's Providence. An understanding of this can help answer a question that puzzles the modern scholarship of both Edwards and Puritanism in general: How can a predestinarian theology be consistent with an activist church government?

4. Church Government

An apparent contradiction between the sovereignty of God and the evangelism of preachers is noted by virtually every modern student of Puritanism. Puritan justifications of energetic preaching and strong administration of the church seem to most modern scholars at best dialectically contradictory, if not specious or dishonest. Strong government is politically imperative in colonial New England, even though it may be hard to defend theologically, so it seems often to be instituted by bending religious principle.

This conclusion is generated by humanist discourse. Assuming man to be the origin of all human culture, his interests concealed behind those of some "god" and superstitiously mistaken for them, modern retrospect projects into Puritan theism a reality alien to it and then either patronizes or castigates it for failing to acknowledge what to its theism is unreal. But as long as the work of redemption is taken to glorify God, in spite and often because of the damnation of men, theist ecclesiastical activism can be patterned after the acts of Providence. The governing of the church can be genuinely reconciled with predestination so long as the end of governance, like that of the providential government of the world, is understood to be the glorification of God rather than the salvation of man.

Edwards admits that legal humiliations, such as the miracles that precede the coming of Christ, fail to convert mankind. He accounts for this by noting that they serve God's chief end by exposing the wicked and confirming God's justice in punishing them. But although no threat of punishment nor the most terrible execution of punishment can redeem wicked creatures—even the pains of hell Edwards considers incapable of causing the damned to "hate sin on its own account"—legal sanctions can successfully restrain them. As governor of the world, the Son acts not to eradicate evil but to prevent evil from overwhelming the church: "Those lusts of pride and covetousness" that motivated Pharaoh "were never really mortified in him" by God's assisting the captive Jews, but they were "violently restrained" so as to permit the Jews' escape.[36]

All truly wicked souls are, like Pharaoh's, obdurately inclined to evil. God's chastisement is not, therefore, intended to rehabilitate, but to restrain. In the same way that His eternal vigilance is required to prevent the material universe from falling into nonentity, so is it necessary to prevent the moral world from turning into hell. Edwards defines evil not only as irremediable, but as constant and relentless. In an imprecatory sermon like "Sinners in the Hands of an Angry God" he can terrify his listeners with the idea that many of them, like Milton's Satan, carry a hell within them, that "there is laid in the very natures of carnal men a foundation for the torments of hell," that is suppressed only by the "restraining hand of God." As this warning implies, the severity of divine restraint does not in any way diminish the essential wickedness of an evil soul. What it does affect is the capacity of an evil soul for self-expression. Devils in hell are no more depraved than the reprobate on earth, but their depravity is there totally unleashed: "But when wicked men come to be in hell, there will be no new corruption put into their heart; but only old ones which then break forth without restraint. . . . A natural man has a heart, like the heart of a devil; only corruption is more under restraint in man than in devils."[37]

Because Edwards considers sin to be ordained as a fact of existence, and man's propensity for sin to be as automatic as the "tendency of the nature of an heavy body, if obstacles are removed . . . not only to fall with a constant motion, but with a constantly increasing motion," he has to concede that the struggle against evil in the world can be but marginally successful. The forces ranged against goodness are portrayed by this clever, one might say even playful, allusion to the "new" science from *Original Sin* as being no less irrevocable than Newton's laws. Natural law reminds Edwards continually of man's moral depravity, and the experience of nature provides him with countless examples that he recalls in the most affecting images of his sermons: the tendency of all men toward moral corruption, despite differences in their worldly states, can be seen in the fact that "one rotting, putrefying corpse is as ignoble as another; the worms are as bold with one carcass as another." Gravity figures largely in "Sinners in the Hands of an Angry God" in metaphors emphasizing the ineluctable attraction for sinners of hell; in the sermon sinfulness is likened, much as in the "new" scientific metaphor from *Original Sin*, to a weight as "heavy as lead" that tends naturally to "sink and swiftly descend and plunge into the bottomless gulf." As much a statute of moral law as gravity or biological decay are of physical law, sin is thus no less an ordination of God that men are powerless to repeal.[38]

Regardless of the ingeniousness of their conception or the rigor of their execution, all of Edwards's efforts to combat evil and promote virtue in

New England have limited objectives. To aspire toward a more perfect felicity in this world constitutes a vain and proud opposition to the divine order, and results in the administrative error, and worse, that Edwards and other radical Protestants believe they can expose in both more and less radically Protestant ecclesiologies. Because Edwards believes on the one hand that neither church nor civil policy can purify the world, and yet on the other that both can be inspired by God indirectly to assist in the advent of His kingdom on earth, Edwards assumes as the leader of a church the difficult task of finding "the right path in the middle" between the extreme quietism of the Quakers and the extreme activism of the church of Rome.[39]

Edwards's insistence that visible things should never be mistaken for their spiritual analogues would be expected to make him careful about the administration of traditional sacraments in Puritan congregations, and especially careful about the institution of new ones. If even the most genuine and beautiful manifestation of Divinity, the person of Christ, were liable to encourage idolatry, how much more dangerous are man's representations of God or ceremonial devotions. Why, then, does Edwards support the rather ostentatious innovation in Puritan church policy, proposed by Puritan ministers in Scotland in 1744, that would initiate concerted prayer for the coming of the Millennium in all Puritan congregations throughout the world? Such a universal uplifting of the voices of the faithful seems to imply that the climax of God's Providential drama can be hastened by a sufficiently loud summons from earth, which presumption would challenge the sovereignty of God's will and invoke retributions like the ones exacted upon the evidently pious and well-meaning Samuel, who improves upon God's commandment to slaughter the Amalekites and their cattle by reserving their king and few choice animals for sacrifice and for his trouble is rebuked by God as a rebel (1 Samuel 15:22–23), and upon Uzzah, who tries to steady the Ark on the mules and is struck dead for his zeal (2 Samuel 6:7).

Edwards is aware of this danger, and in advocating the proposal in "An Humble Attempt to Promote Explicit and Visible Union of God's People in Extraordinary Prayer" (1748), he insists that it should be instituted not with the great expectation of the Millennium but with a more modest ambition to counteract the "sloth, carnality, or fulness of our own worldly and private concerns" that are natural in even the most pious of church members. Extraordinary prayer will take the form of a petition not in the vain hope that God will be prompted to ordain the Millennium in response to human wishes, but with the sad knowledge that man needs the contrivance of a specific reward to long for to assist his fragile piety. Because there is no causal relationship between a particular form of worship and an act of God, the institution of a church policy ought not to be guided by a concern for what is most persuasive to God; to believe that "the precise order of worship . . . what shall precede, and what shall follow; whether praying or singing shall be first, and what shall be next, and what shall conclude" has any bearing on divine behavior "would be superstitious." But although "it would not be reasonable to suppose, that merely such a circumstance as many people praying at the same time, will directly have any providence with God; yet such a circumstance may reasonably be supposed to have influence on the minds of *men*." Edwards distinguishes between the formal object of extraordinary prayer, which is the coming of the Millennium, and its ecclesiastical purpose, which is the encouragement of a general mood of prayerfulness among church members, and thus can support it. There is nothing equivocal about "An Humble Attempt . . . ," nor about Edwards's ecclesiology in general, which becomes inconsistently both "optimistic" and "pessimistic," or an example of Edwards wanting to "have his cake and eat it" or becoming "the master of a quick-working and voluble tongue," as a recent critic has charged, only when subjected to an unself-consciously humanist reading that assumes all discourse to be centered on man.[40]

How disappointed, when the Millennium fails to come to pass, is Edwards, or Cotton Mather before him, or any of those apparently sanguine millennial prognosticators of the seventeenth and eighteenth centuries who have the temerity to specify, either in public or in private, their predictions of the imminence of latter days? Or, to broaden the skepticism of this rhetorical question, how "optimistic" and "pessimistic" are, respectively, the post- and premillennialists of these centuries? And how premeditated on the intricate and ambiguous dynamics of human expectations are the imprecations of the jeremiads that are cited for their psychological profundity by Miller and Bercovitch and others? To concentrate on the impact on human beings of the apocalyptic speculations of theism is once again to introduce humanism to a discourse that is better read as not containing it. The reactions of mankind to any act of Providence, including of course the ultimate or penultimate acts, are far from insignificant to theists. But they are not paramount. The chief importance of these reactions is measured not in units of human happiness or misery but in the degree to which these reactions glorify God. Concerted prayer for the coming of the Millennium is ordained by God to glorify Himself, and only may be ordained in advance of His subsequent ordination of the Millennium, so to feel moved toward concerted prayer is to join successfully in God's self-glorification whether or not the Millennium eventuate; the value of the exercise, like that of all genuine prayer, like that of all genuine religious duty, is intrinsic, and is totally independent of prophetic accuracy. To have failed to forecast the actual schedule of Providence would be reason for despair only to a false prophet or an idolator whose chief end is not witnessing Judgment but witnessing the fulfillment of his prophecy, a distinction that under theism amounts to the absolute moral one between virtue and sin. Theism supplies no other, positive content for this disappointment. Modern scholars who have sympathized with the risks and anxieties of seventeenth- and eighteenth-century millennialism invest theism with a humanity to which theism is unentitled, but they also divest theism of a stoic resolution that modern humanism lacks. They ought rather to feel sorry for the Emerson of "Fate," whose faith in nature's capacity and inevitable propensity for self-perfection makes him liable to the truly disillusioning recognition in the nineteenth century that as yet no man has realized nature's goal, and that therefore perhaps no man ever will. This is the *angst* invented by humanism, and which need not be exported to a discursive pattern that allows for more than enough suffering of other kinds.[41]

As long as sacraments and forms of worship in general are recognized as assisting the piety of the human heart rather than getting God's attention or approval, they can properly be reviewed and changed by church leaders. With no more hope of benefiting God than of giving benefit to a "fountain by drinking at it, or to a light by seeing," as Augustine characterizes the independence of God's excellency from human praise, the church can nevertheless experiment, for example, with the "vocal tone" in which prayers are recited, that Edwards believes might be orchestrated so as to "help religious thoughts." But although innovations in forms of worship might be piously defended as having no direct influence on God's will, might they not permit the impression that the religious affections encouraged by them are sure evidence of election? Will not congregations be led to mistake the piety inspired by the exhortations of their churches for that inspired by God, especially while joining in such remarkable devotions as extraordinary prayer?[42]

Edwards tries to guard against this confusion by recalling the distinction between truth and its visible analogue: "If one [is] present in a worshipping assembly, and sees their external behavior; their *union* with him in worship, he does not see; and what he sees, encourages him in worship, only as an evidence of that union and concurrence which is out of sight." Physical propinquity and vocal unison are but the analogues of genuine union, and should be viewed not as confirmation but as suggestion. Edwards's description denies both a causal relationship between human petitions and divine dispensation and a necessary correspondence between visible and invisible churches. True Christians praise God in forms suitable "to affect our own hearts, with the things we express, and so to prepare us to receive the blessings we ask."[43]

But the distinction between being "encouraged" to join the ranks of the faithful in communal prayer and being enlisted in them is a fine one, and that between "preparing" men through prayer to receive God's grace and winning it is finer still. "More knowing and thinking men," to whom Edwards claims are granted such refined theological insights, might not forget the inefficacy of visible devotions, but less gifted eighteenth-century New England Puritans are liable to. Edwards is too often reminded of the depravity of the human will and the weakness of the human intellect not to suspect that some, perhaps many members of Puritan congregations are under the delusion that great shows of piety on earth earn great rewards in heaven.

Edwards can countenance this possibility by sacrificing the nonelect to ecclesiastical necessity, and he can do so on no less conservative authority than the ecclesiastical theory of Increase Mather. The nonelect, according to Mather, can contribute to the community's temporal welfare, which, although having no direct influence on its spiritual health, must nonetheless increase if the faithful are to have the security and the leisure to live the life of the spirit. Mather's policy would presumably allow the nonelect to share in the temporal rewards of the community, as this would be necessary to secure their participation in the economy. Mather balks at extending what he would probably consider further spiritual bribes, such as full church membership; Stoddard, under whom Edwards serves his apprenticeship in the administration of a major Puritan congregation, is perhaps not so principled. Stoddard justifies his further liberalization of the half-way convenant by arguing that since no visible profession of faith is certain proof of faith, no standard can be devised to exclude the nonelect, and that churches ought accordingly to extend the sacraments to all who desire them, at least in the Connecticut River Valley, and piously leave the task of distinguishing true from false believers to God in the hereafter. Stoddard's policy, however, can be seen also as a logical extension of Mather's. Full church membership has cash value, providing temporal benefits if not necessarily eternal ones, and membership has disciplinary value as well, adding the control of spiritual leaders to that of civil magistrates. Liberal standards for church membership admit the nonelect not for their own good, but for that of their virtuous neighbors, and therefore exploits them in the way that Mather recommends. Stoddard has been characterized as an eighteenth-century Puritan Grand Inquisitor, using the false promise of a peace that passeth understanding in order to keep the peace on earth, but his policies can be made to appear, in the theist context of Puritan ecclesiology, as neither glamorous nor sinister, and their departure from those of the Mathers can accordingly be made to seem much more a small tempest than the titanic struggle that many of their modern critics perceive. Beyond turning Increase Mather's words against him, Stoddard might have cited the even more revered authority of John Cotton, who characterizes the reprobate among church members as goats, as opposed to pigs, in order to say not only that hypocrites are impossible to distinguish from true saints, in contrast to easily exposed porcine sinners, but also that hypocrites are useful to the church and are safely left unmolested. The stakes in the controversy between more and less liberal theories of church membership are in theist discourse technical, and perhaps sometimes personal, and thus often productive of acrimony, but they are not nearly so enormous as they seem to modern retrospect, whose humanism is infinitely more fastidious about the precise discrimination of sheep from goats, or goats from pigs, in the classification of men.[44]

There is no evidence that Edwards fashions church policy deliberately to fool the children of Satan into believing themselves children of God. The liberal standards for church membership instituted by his predecessor Stoddard eventually trouble him enough to make him risk the anger of his congregation by tightening them, which action focuses the opposition to him in Northampton and helps unify the faction that eventually deposes him. But although he follows the Cambridge Platform in distinguishing the role of magistrates from that of ministers, he does recognize a relationship between civil and church government: "The civil authorities have nothing to do with matters ecclesiastical, with those things which relate to conscience and eternal salvation or with any matters religious, [yet they are] reconcilable still with their having to do with some matters that, in some sense, concern religion." The sense in which civil government assists religion is for Edwards similar to the way in which the miracles of Providence assist the work of redemption. Just as God chastises the wicked in the times of the Old Testament in order to permit a remnant of the faithful to survive, so must Puritan commonwealths control the nonelect to prevent them from hindering the worship of the faithful. Because the necessity of "heads, princes, or governours, to whom honour, subjection, and obedience should be paid" is justified by Providence itself, the governance of the outward man is properly a concern of theologians.[45]

Edwards's political theory takes for granted not only that the "inferior principles" of mankind cannot be fundamentally improved, but that selfishness is vital to the health of society. "Self-love and natural appetite," he says in *Original Sin*, are necessary for the survival of all creatures, and carnal love, he repeats in *The Nature of True Virtue*, is "implanted in men for the preservation and well-being of the world of mankind." The love of self and of a mate is extended to affection for "party or particular friends," with the beneficial effect of preventing "acts of injustice towards these persons." Although to Edwards even the most general benevolence is a species of self-love only, and not to be mistaken for a sign of grace, it is valuable to him insofar as it can help unite the community. The duty of civil magistrates is therefore not to discourage this affection, but to harness it: "These inferior principles are like a fire in a house; which we say, is a good servant, but a bad master; very useful while kept in its place, but if left to take possession of the whole house, soon brings all to destruction." This mention of the ineradicability of selfishness and the subsequent concession that selfishness can only be moderated and redirected through what eighteenth-century moral philosophy calls "*storgé*," a borrowing from ancient Greek philosophy that signifies the expansion of self-love into love of kind, join Edwards's relatively few comments on civil government with the large archive of theist political theory, including Madison's stipulation in the *Federalist Papers* that faction, as a corporate form of selfishness, can be eradicated only by annihilation of the race or revocation of the character of the race, which undesirability and impossibility show that the art of governance is one of management rather than of reformation.[46]

One of the most gifted managers of the inferior principles of mankind in eighteenth-century Northampton is Edwards's uncle, Colonel John Stoddard, whose death in 1748 removes Edwards's most powerful political ally in the congregation and inspires Edwards's sermon, "God's Awful Judgment in the Breaking and Withering of the Strong Rods of a Community." In eulogizing his uncle, Edwards identifies the qualities he believes most important in temporal leaders: they must have "great natural abilities," "insight into the mysteries of government," and an ability to "discern those things wherein the public welfare or calamity consists and the proper means to avoid the one and promote the other"; they must "have obtained great actual knowledge. . .great skill in public affairs and things requisite to be known in order to their wise, prudent, and effectual management . . . and great understanding of men and things, a great knowledge of human nature and of the ways of accommodating themselves to it, so as most effectually to influence it to wise purposes." Edwards qualifies each of these attributes—"natural abilities," "actual knowledge," "understanding of men and things"—in a way that avoids claiming them as evidence of his uncle's sainthood. Whatever Edwards thinks of the state of his uncle's soul, and he certainly owes a lot to his uncle's political skill, he does not once in the sermon praise Stoddard for a gracious disposition. The ideal magistrate as Edwards portrays him does not seem to need the enlightenment of grace, which, insofar as grace might tend to estrange one from the world, might actually impair a magistrate's performance. Edwards may be less willing than his Grandfather Stoddard to involve the church in the *Realpolitik* of Puritan New England, but he seems in this sermon to endorse a virtually Godless administration of temporal affairs. This administration has no spiritual goals whatsoever, and serves the church only by standing between it and the "inferior principles" which, unrestrained, would consume it. "Government is necessary to defend communities from miseries from within themselves; from the prevalence of intestine discord, mutual injustice and violence; the members of the society continually making a prey one of another." This identification of government as a system of wholly negative restraints perhaps seems merely subjective in the discourse of an other than civil leader, especially one whose political skills and even whose pastoral ones are obviously less than Machiavellian, as has recently been pointed out by Tracy and Carse and other modern scholars interested in the efficacy of Edwards's pastorate in Northampton. But the significance of Edwards's political theory is not personal, and not restricted to Edwards and other similarly unworldly and unsuccessful eighteenth-century managers, but is discursive, present in the writings of Puritan magistrates noted for their political acumen, such as even John Winthrop, who probably epitomizes Puritan magistracy, who likens government to "the brake of a windmill:w'ch hathe no power, to move the running work: but it is of speciall use, to stoppe any violent motion, w'ch in some extraordinary tempest might endanger the wholl fabricke," and in the writings of political leaders known for their advocacy of strong government, such as even John Adams, who concedes in *Discourses on Davila* that "laws and government, which regulate *sublunary* things . . . appear baubles at the hour of death," and in the writings even of such "free-thinking" secular activists as Thomas Paine, who concedes similarly, in what might seem a surprisingly biblical monition from "Common Sense," that "government, like dress, is the badge of lost innocence." Meiotic depictions of government pervade theist discourse, including the writings of individuals who have the greatest personal and professional cause to exalt government.[47]

Although delegating responsibility for civil discipline to magistrates, Edwards may use the pulpit in ways that implicitly confuse the distinction between obedience imposed by "strong rods" and piety inspired by God. If the powerful appeal of "extraordinary prayer" might cause unsophisticated congregations to mistake roused affections for true grace, the heavy cudgel of Edwards's imprecatory imagery is even more likely to impress them with a false humility. Edwards warns against this error frequently; his notebooks are full of entries insisting that "the best and most able men in the world, with their greatest diligence and labouriousness, most eloquent speaking, clearest illustrations, and convincing arguments, can do nothing towards causing the knowledge of the Gospel." Nor does he keep this warning to himself. His sermons also contain reminders that the word of God, no more than the words of preachers, communicates "these and those doctrines" to the intellect only; "it is the cause of the notion of them in our minds, but not of the sense of the divine excellency in our hearts. Indeed a person can't have spiritual light without the word. But that don't argue that the word properly causes that light." But the cold logic of this conclusion might escape a parishioner in the heat of the Enfield sermon. Assuming that a great deal of conscious artistry goes into the composition of a sermon like "Sinners in the Hands of an Angry God," and that the sermon is designed to exhort congregations to spiritual self-examination, how can Edwards justify to himself such "conjoining of theological objectivism with a call to human effort," as one modern critic has named the apparent contradiction?[48]

A true theological objectivist like Edwards cannot claim that evangelism causes revivals. There is for him only one possible explanation for the fact that revivals sometimes follow evangelical efforts. Just as he argues in his analysis of the laws of nature that effect follows cause in nature not because of the actual priority of natural cause, but because God sees fit continuously to ordain both in tandem, so does he argue that the evangelism of preachers and the revival of congregations are each inspired independently of one another by God. Thus extraordinary prayer for the Millennium does not summon the Millennium, but the fact that "God gives an extraordinary spirit of prayer for the promised advancement of his kingdom on earth" suggests that He might be ready to ordain the Millennium, giving some reason to hope that "the fulfillment of the event is nigh." The relationship between the petitions of the faithful and the dispensation of God is often harmonious but never subordinative: "When God decrees to give the blessing of rain, he decrees the prayers of his people; and when he decrees the prayers of his people for rain, he very commonly decrees rain; and thereby there is an harmony between these two decrees." Thus imprecatory eloquence in preachers can be inspired by God simultaneously with awakenings in congregations. Although "the power of enmity of natural men against God, is so great, that it is *insuperable* by any finite power," awakenings will be inspired by God. Edwards cites Scripture (Rev. 14:6–8) in testifying to the role of such powerful, though finite, preachers of the Gospel as himself: "The great work of God shall be brought to pass by the preaching of the gospel. . . . before Babylon falls, the gospel shall be powerfully preached and propagated in the world." Babylon will not be felled by evangelists, but may fall after a revival, both events constituting independently ordained acts of Providence.[49]

The Millennium does not follow hard upon the awakenings in New England in the late 1730s, nor does it accompany the proposal to institute extraordinary prayer for it in 1744. Edwards has to admit that neither his preaching nor his church policy presages a general awakening, and that many individual testimonies are undoubtedly inspired merely by his efforts, and are therefore false. Yet despite these failures he continues to promise salvation and threaten damnation. He continues to cudgel and exhort, knowing that the spiritual welfare of sinners and saints alike is beyond the influence of his preaching.

When Edwards goes to Enfield in 1741 he is entering a lions' den of resistance to the Awakening. The conversion of sinners in a particularly sinful town is not his primary goal, nor is the extension of the political influence of Northampton's evangelicalism. His chief end is the glorification of God, and this is accomplished as much through the selfish terror of the damned as through the selfless awe of the saved. The groans of the wicked testify to God's glory no less than the groans of the virtuous. Edwards's seemingly truckling appeals to civic pride and primitive fears and personal jealousy do not, as a modern critic has claimed, implicitly contradict predestination; rather, they function like the "many schemes and methods" of Providence to make salvation so compelling that only fatally intractable creatures can resist, and thereby glorifies God by revealing the justice of his damnation of the wicked. Nowhere in the sermon does Edwards offer the false hope of man's being able to earn his eternal reward; everywhere in it he torments the wicked with their helpless inability to love despite every selfish reason for doing so. Far from concealing the doctrine of predestination, Edwards brandishes predestination about the heads of saint and sinner alike, and creates a spectacle in which both are prostrated before God in a foreshadowing of the Day of Judgment.[50]

Nor is this example of Edwards's most sensationalist figuration anticipatory of modernism stylistically, a differentiation that can be made clear by comparing Edwards's imprecatory imagery with the scarifying imagery of humanist discourse. The vertiginousness of Edwards's metaphors in "Sinners in the Hands of an Angry God", like that of the settings of Poe and Brockden Brown and other theist Gothic writers, is designed to impress man with his moral helplessness precisely through analogy to his physical helplessness; the sensation and the doctrine both depend on the objectivity of the world, both physical and moral. The chasms of romantic discourse, however, reflect the abysmal depth not of an external world, but of the self, as is the case with the "dark labyrinth" that Hester's mind becomes during her unrestricted meditations in Hawthorne's *The Scarlet Letter* or the legendary chasm into which Curtius throws himself in the Forum at Rome and that is elaborated by Hawthorne's later fiction into a symbol of self-consciousness as Kenyon and Miriam confront Miriam's deep past at that very spot in *The Marble Faun;* because these depths are in romantic discourse specular, they can ideally be sounded, as in Wordsworth's crossing of the Simplon Pass in *The Prelude* or Natty's negotiating Glenn's Falls' slippery footing, described in virtual (mis)quotations of Edwards's "Sinners," in Cooper's *The Last of the Mohicans,* or in Thoreau's converting the precariousness of life from a denial to the proof of man's self-sufficiency— "What risks we run! famine and fire and pestilence, and the thousand forms of a cruel fate,—and yet every man lives till he—dies." To interpret all or part of Edwards's "Sinners" as "a projection of Edwards' own state of mind," or to interpret Edwards's sensationalist rhetoric in general as immediately an end in itself, such that "we can still hear the stirring 'Now!' that electrified his congregations," as two modern critics suppose, is to superimpose romantic *mis en abîme* over what in theist discourse is real abyss, created by, and the embodiment of, otherness.[51]

Controversy over church government is the predominant genre of seventeenth- and eighteenth-century Protestant theology, not just among sectarian rivals but among theologians who consider themselves members of the same church. It spreads because of disagreement over the best and most proper way to serve God, not over whether man or God, or some monstrous combination of both, is the proper object of worship. Modern histories of Protestantism, especially of the eighteenth-century Protestantism that chronologically precedes the humanist theology and ecclesiology of the next century, tend to imply that, at least potentially, the ends of disagreeing theologians differ radically, and that the heat of debate is generated by the debate's potentially revolutionary outcome. But arguments over means can seem the most divisive, because they speak the same language to a relatively homogenous audience, because theirs is a kind of civil warfare. Increase Mather and Solomon Stoddard are bitter personal rivals. Edwards is seen in Boston as Stoddard's *protégé*, but his actions after Stoddard's death show that he has, or comes to develop, his own opinions on the administration of a church. Each of the three differs about how best to glorify God in this world, not in spite of their agreement that as theologians and church leaders their first duty is to glorify Him, but because of that agreement. A great latitude in hermeneutics, even of so crucial a subject as religion, can be seen as evidence not of the self-destructive permissiveness, but of the fundamental integrity of theist discourse.

5. The End of the World

The meeting of a Puritan congregation, Edwards states in his "Farewell Sermon," is analogous to the final gathering of all mankind. The difference between the two is that on earth men remain uncertain about the true state of their own and their neighbors' souls, whereas on the last day they will be sure: "now, ministers have no infallible discerning of the state of the souls of their own people . . . . nor are the people able certainly to know the state of their minister, or one another's state. . . . but at the day of judgment they shall meet in God's most immediate presence" and expose their true inclinations before him.[52]

One reason why Edwards preaches on this subject is to strike fear, or at least doubt, in the hearts of those parishioners who support his dismissal. Without charging that their motives are less virtuous than his, he invites them to anticipate divine judgment with as clear a conscience as he implicitly possesses. But his comparison is designed also to show how both the presiding over a congregation and the adjudication of the Day of Judgment similarly, though unequally, glorify God. The Day of Judgment is not a trial at which men can plead their case. The sentencing is foreordained and beyond the power of human effort to affect; it is executed only to make the equity of God's judgment apparent to all intelligent creatures: "And therefore though God needs no medium whereby to make the truth evident to himself, yet evidences will be made use of in his future judgment of men. And doubtless the *evidences* that will be made use of in their trial, will be such as will be best fitted to serve the ends of judgment; viz., the *manifestation* of the righteous judgment of God, not only to the world, but to men's own consciences." God does not cross-examine mankind, nor does He listen to mankind's testimonies of faith. He simply displays Himself, with the result that the elect immediately reveal their affinity and the damned immediately reveal their enmity. "The design of the day of judgment is not to find out what is just, as it is with human judgments, but it is to *manifest* what is just."[53]

In continuing energetically to preach the Gospel regardless of the consequences in this world, Edwards follows the examples of the covenant of works, of Christ, and of the Day of Judgment. He strives to display God in as glorious a light as imagination can invent and language can convey, just as God displays Himself in the works of redemption, trusting not that it will unify a congregation in salvation, but that it will separate, to the degree that "finite power" can accomplish the winnowing, the elect from the damned. The failure to elicit genuine professions of faith from a majority of any congregation would simply presage the great division of mankind to occur at the end of the world, when "shall an everlasting separation be made between [the elect] and wicked men. Before, they were mixed together, and it was impossible in many instances to determine their characters; but now all shall become visible." Edwards's evangelical efforts, both as preacher and as church leader, are designed piously to expose the moral division between saints and the nonelect. He makes no compromises with the wicked, but rather goads them to emerge in order that they might be openly and gloriously humiliated. His willingness ultimately to sacrifice civic calm for ecclesiastical upheaval is evident in his role in the unsettling of Northampton and other Puritan communities during the 1740s and 50s.[54]

As long as the welfare of human beings is accepted as secondary to the glorification of God, the historical antecedents and consequences of a display of His glory, whether the great one of the Day of Judgment or the small one of a sermon at Enfield, are relatively unimportant. A man's life, whether apparently virtuous or apparently vicious, is irrelevant to a discovery of the state of his soul on the occasion of Edwards's sermon. The aftermath of the sermon, whether provoking mass conversion or mass hysteria, is equally unimportant from the eternal perspective. Similarly, the history of mankind in no way determines the outcome of the Day of Judgment, on which guilt and innocence are not ascertained from past events, but proclaimed; and the division that follows may be of great concern to individuals, but matters little to God, who is glorified equally by the regret of the damned and the gratitude of the saved. The end of the world is achieved outside the context of history, on the Last Day and on any sabbath, each of which is called by the seventeenth-century Puritan Thomas Shepard "the abridgement of eternity," including an eighteenth-century one at Enfield, when God is glorified in ways that anticipate the Last Day.[55]

The work of redemption does not in any reading of theist discourse other than a partisanly or unself-consciously humanist one lead progressively toward the Day of Judgment, but foreshadows it in various "openings" whose structure differs fundamentally from historical process. Periods of God's greatest glory on earth do not emerge from prior events, but are prophesied by events that, in looking forward, efface themselves. This is clear in Edwards's typological interpretation of the Old Testament. The episodic structure of the Book, which is "large in the account of the re- demption out of Egypt, and the first settling of the affairs of the Jewish church and nation in the time of Moses and Joshua; but much shorter in the time of the Judges," abbreviates time by narrating only those events which typify the coming of Christ; Cotton Mather similarly cites, as prece- dent for the superabundance of religious in comparison to secular matter in theodicy, the structure of Genesis, in which "that for the Description of the *Whole World . . .* that *First-Born of all Historians,* the great *Moses,* employes but *one* or *two* Chapters, whereas he employes, it may be *seven times* as many Chapters, in describing that one little Pavilion, The Tabernacle," disproportion being a good indication of discursive identity in any dis- course, such as, conversely, in Bancroft's devoting about as disproportion- ate space to the American Revolution in his *History.* Edwards's and Mather's accounts describe a Christian era punctuated by occasional foreshadowings of the next great manifestation of God on earth, which will be the Millennium, the church continuing to wax and wane, suffering through many periods of iniquity and enjoying a few golden ages, such as those of Constantine's reign and of the Reformation, each flourishing of the true faith being a "prelibation" of the Millennium, but none progress- ing directly to the Millennium. Only "after numerous vexations, disasters, and disappointments" will "the church of God, in the time of Luther and other reformers, revive on a sudden, in a wonderful manner, when such an event was least suspected, to the surprize and amazement of their anti- christian enemies," and such revivals will be extinguished as suddenly until the Millennium is ordained."[56]

Any more direct relationship between Providence and time would sub- ordinate God's ways to the ways of the world. Edwards interprets the irregularity of Providence as it is experienced by men as another example of the disruption that accompanies any divine use of nature. The work of redemption, as a product of the divine will, is perfect, existing whole in the mind of God from eternity. The registration of it on an imperfect world inevitably disrupts the world, and the apprehension of it by the imperfect intelligence of man inevitably astonishes. The ahistorical structure of the work of redemption should impress man, like the unnatural character of all miracles, with the infinite disparity between God and nature; its intermit- tence is apparent only, a result of translating a perfect plan into an imper- fect medium, and fortunate as well, since "if all that glory which appears in these events had been manifested at once, it would have been too much for us."[57]

Recognition that time is the instrument rather than the ally of Providence implies recognition that man is helpless either singly or collectively to save himself, and thus promotes piety, keeping the faithful continually in suspense and thus intensifying their feeling of dependence: "It is the manner of God, to keep his church on earth in hope of a still more glorious state; and so their prayers are enlivened, when they pray that the interest of religion may be promoted, and God's kingdom may come." Any more predictable pattern risks complacency, and reduces the pious worship that contributes to God's chief end of self-adoration. Again, because piety fulfills God's chief end, rewards for piety are promised and, in due time, granted only as secondary inducements. Divine dispensations like the Millennium are unpredictable because they represent concessions to creatures whose faith will endure only while encouraged by God and His ministers "to think that such times are coming, wherein Christianity shall prevail over all enemies."[58]

Edwards cites the biblical metaphor of Ezekiel's chariot to show how the revolutions of the world are connected to the progress of the work of redemption in a way that no man can discern: "The whole universe is a machine, or chariot, which God hath made for his own use, as it is represented in Ezekiel's vision, Ez. I,22, 26–28. The inferior parts of creation, the visible universe, are the wheels of the chariot. God's providence, in the constant revolutions, alterations, and successive events, is represented by the motion of the wheels of the chariot, by the spirit of him who sits on his throne in the heavens, or above the firmament." The revolutions of the wheels of time are propelling the chariot of God's Providence toward the end of the world, but that the movement is toward this goal is evident only to God on his throne "above the firmament." Mankind, on the rim of the wheel, sees only the revolutions in which periods of virtue and periods of vice alternate without apparent order: "We live in a world of change, where nothing is certain or stable; and when a little time, a few revolutions of the sun bring to pass strange things, surprizing alterations, in particular persons, in families, in towns and churches, in countries and nations."[59]

The theism of Edwards's exegesis can be made to stand out in greater relief by differentiation from humanist interpretation, which again can be provided by Coleridge's *Aids to Reflection*. Much as Coleridge interprets as proof of the continuity of man what in Edwards's theist discourse proves the timelessness of God in his discussion of imputation, so does Coleridge interpret as a symbol of the inherence of eternity in time what in Edwards's theist discourse is a metaphor of the disparity between them in his discussion of Ezekiel's vision. Coleridge fastens on a verse to which Edwards does not allude, "Whithersoever the Spirit was to go, the wheels went, and thither was their Spirit to go: for the Spirit of the living creature was in the wheels also" (Ezekiel, 1:20), since this verse in the context of humanist discourse means that the unaccomplished plan of the world and the accomplished part of the plan, that Providence and history, or will and expression, or any of the host of pairings that theist discourse is designed to keep apart, are fused. The wheels that to Edwards signify the ineluctable imperfection of time are by Coleridge made to mean precisely that time is ultimately perfectible. Of these two readings Coleridge's is of course the modern one, but Edwards's seems more consistent with the discursive pattern of the Bible. The complexity of the chariot is marked—pulled by four beasts, each with four faces and four wings, mounted on wheels with a throne above, and a jewel above the throne, and a voice emanating seemingly from above even the jewel. The expressiveness of even so intricate an image is explicity qualified as being thrice removed from the tenor being conveyed—"This *was* the appearance of the likeness of the glory of the LORD" (Ezekiel 1:28)—and Ezekiel's reaction, "And when I saw it, I fell upon my face," is not one that suggests an intimate conferring between Divinity and humanity, all of which combine to make more plausible the theist exegesis that reads biblical imagery to characterize Providence as inscrutable and overwhelming. Bancroft's interpretation of Edwards as latently a progressive historian is as modern as Coleridge's reading of Ezekiel, and equally inconsistent with the pattern of Edwards's discourse of Providence. And Hegel's famous historiographical aphorism, that time is cunning, is meaningless in the context of Edwards's discourse.[60]

Edwards is himself a casualty of revolution when he reminds his rebellious congregation of the uncertainties of life in the "Farewell Sermon." How the disgrace of his dismissal from Northampton or the suffering of his family's impending exile contributes to the advent of the Millennium that he so often anticipates from that pulpit must seem a particularly agonizing mystery. That he goes into the wilderness with continuing dedication, which eventually issues from his Stockbridge cabin-study in a series of major theological treatises, suggests that his belief in the ultimate justification for the uncertainty of life holds him in good stead: "God's providence may not unfitly be compared to a large and long river, having innumerable branches, beginning in different regions, and at a great distance from one another. . . . The different streams of this river are apt to appear like mere confusion to us, because of our limited sight, whereby we cannot see the whole at once. . . . but if we trace them, they all unite at last, all come to the same issue, disgorging themselves into the same great ocean." Having been banished to a rather obscure branch himself, he has faith that this removal from the apparent mainstream of Puritan life in New England follows, in another of Pope's well-known phrases, a direction unperceived.[61]

The first important identification of Edwards as latently a modern historian is probably Bancroft's brief mention of him in the *History* as a proponent of what Bancroft takes to be a characteristically American progressive historicism: "the inference that there is progress in human affairs, is also warranted. The trust of our race has ever been in the coming of better times. Universal history does but seek to relate 'the sum of all God's works of providence.' In America, the first conception of its office, in the mind of Jonathan Edwards, though still cramped and perverted by theological forms not derived from observation, was nobler than the theory of Vico. . . . The meek New England divine, in his quiet association with the innocence and simplicity of rural life, knew that, in every succession of revolutions, the cause of civilization and moral reform is advanced. 'The new creation'—such are his words—is more excellent than the old." This is a good summary of Bancroft's nineteenth-century romantic historiography. It describes a discourse that differs fundamentally from Edwards's theism, according to which every revolution in the wheels of Providence advances not civilization and moral reform, but God's self-love, and in a way that is incomprehensible to man. Edwards derives none of his insights into Providence from observation of events, in innocent and simple New England or anywhere else, but from just those "perverting and cramping theological forms" that Bancroft regrets. Edwards does long for the "coming of better times," and does believe the "new creation" superior to the old, but his longing is proportionate to his inability to perceive how or when better times emerge from worse ones, which to him must persist until God unpredictably ordains a revolution in the wheels of His providential chariot.[62]

But Bancroft's evaluation remains still the predominant one, and since him both Miller and Heimert discern a protomodern historiography in Edwards's typology. Analyzing Edwards's use of natural imagery in the introduction to *Images or Shadows of Divine Things,* Miller argues that, "by an unavoidable compulsion," the typological interpretations of Edwards and other Puritan theologians force them "to seek for a unity greater than that of the Bible, a unity of history, nature, and theology." Such "compulsive" improvements on the Bible lead inevitably, according to Miller, to a view of history progressing in a comprehensible way toward the end of the world. Heimert agrees with Miller and follows his lead to the conclusion that Edwards "had a vision of history as the progressive enlargement of the realm of the spirit" according to which "in the last analysis cataclysm was inconsistent." After Miller and Heimert there is a chorus of agreement, including C. C. Goen's that Edwards's postmillenialism "allowed no discontinuities in history" and that "the victory was to be won gradually," Ursula Brumm's that "it is the early theological version of the nineteenth-century American view of history which looked rather to the future than to the past," William Scheick's that it describes "the continuity of divine providence as disclosed by history," Lowance's that its "progressive and evolutionary view of prophetic fulfillment was fully developed . . . making [Edwards] the most prominent exponent of millennial utopianism in America before the revolution," Stein's that its "interpretation was based on a belief that God works through the historical process to achieve his will, not in spite of or apart from that process" so as to "underscore the gradualness of historical process," Davidson's that it reflects a "gradualism much like the one incorporated by the secular idea of progress," and Bercovitch's both that it "envisioned a continual increase of moral, spiritual, and material goodness in this world—an age of sacred wonders within history" and that it "welded the whole progression [of history] into an organic human-divine (and natural-divine) whole." Assuming such dissents as Gay's that Edwards's "history" is merely Augustinian or medieval to be occasional and insubstantial and prompted by disagreement with proposals that it is a great deal more than Augustinian or medieval, there is presently no position on Edwards's "postmillennialism" in modern scholarship other than that it complexly is (or simply is not) modern.[63]

The misprision according to which Edwards's discourse of Providence is read as one in which God's plan is realized progressively through time— that is, realized historically—represents no simple error. The source of the reading lies in the romantic interpretation of *postmillennialism* as a very privileged form of Protestant exegesis that anticipates romantic historiography, which is the assumption behind Bancroft's and all subsequent praise for Edwards as a historian, and which can be made to exemplify the complex ways in which not only oeuvres or texts or passages but even single words are phenomena whose meanings depend radically on the discursive system that they occupy. One word in particular, which is used seldom by Edwards to describe the structure of Providence and often by modern interpretations to describe his descriptions, has positively different meanings in the theist context of Edwards's writings and in the humanist one of modern interpretations of them. When Edwards, infrequently, calls Providence "gradual," he uses the word according to the Latin root that has become vestigial in modern usage. When modern interpretations call Edwards's eschatology "gradual" they use the word according to another definition, whose difference from Edwards's appears slight semantically—the two meanings seem to coexist in seventeenth- and eighteenth-century writings, although some efforts are being made by seventeenth- and eighteenth-century writers to distinguish between the meanings, especially in theology—but that can be understood to be very significant discursively.

That Edwards uses *gradual* in a way that is other than standard according to modern usage is obvious in a commentary on Revelation from his notebooks. Referring to verse 8 of chapter 18, "Therefore shall her plagues come in one day," Edwards writes that "though Antichrist's fall be very gradual, yet the great and finishing stroke shall be very sudden, as indeed shall every one of the seven strokes that shall be given him, as have the two past." What Edwards takes to be a qualification constitutes, according to modern usage, in which *gradual* and *sudden* are antonyms, a contradiction. Either Edwards in indulging the luxury of writing poorly in the privacy of his notebooks or he understands *gradual* to permit degrees of intermittence and not just the absence of it. A review of the etymology of the word suggests the latter. Coming from the Latin for "step," *gradual* does originally mean not the uninterrupted ascent or progress of the modern definition but ascent or progress in degrees. Present in modern usage only in a rare verb, to *graduate* an instrument of measurement, and in an archaic noun, the *Gradual* of the Mass, whose figurative derivation from the stairs of the alter is moreover of course largely forgotten, this original meaning is current enough, however, in seventeenth- and eighteenth-century English to make Edwards's distinction proper; Providence occurs in stages or steps whose individual advances toward the Day of Judgment are more precipitous than regular.[64]

An enlargement of the definition of *gradual,* and, more important, a perception that this enlargement permits confusions that must be avoided, at least in theological writings, occurs also in the seventeenth and eighteenth centuries, when the modern definition exists alongside the Latin one. It is clear, for example, that when Locke advises in *Some Thoughts Concerning Education* (1692) that "by a gradual progress from the plainest and easiest Historians, a student may at last come to read the most difficult and sublime of Latin authors," or when Defoe advises in *The Family Instructor* (1715) that "you must understand it gradually, my dear, a little at a time," both are using the word to mean an ascent in regular increments, connoting less a stairway than an incline. But whereas within theist discourse advances in learning might safely be considered to be so small as to be imperceptible as separate units, the gradations of being cannot be safely mistaken as so "gradual" in this sense. Pleonastic supplements to *gradual* when it is being used in the original sense begin to appear in some theological writings in the seventeenth and eighteenth centuries to specify that those distinctions whose maintenance is essential to the preservation of the hierarchy of being, and thus of the sovereignty of God, must not be allowed to fade. For example, the word *specifical,* to emphasize that the step or stage is, like a species, distinct from all others in a chain, is sometimes added to *gradual* so as to prevent confusion on those theological subjects where confusion might constitute impiety.[65]

Thus the "same" word can have a great deal more than just variant meanings, and the contemporaneity of usages is no good measure of their likeness. When Milton writes two generations before and an ocean removed from the time and place of Edwards's birth that "flowers and their fruit/Man's nourishment, by gradual scale sublim'd/To vital spirits aspire," his pleonasm, viewed in the context of *Paradise Lost* and in the whole context of his oeuvre, indicates that he is using the word to support the same hierarchical ontology that Edwards upholds. When, a bit later, Increase Mather writes that "*Gradually* become the *Kingdoms of Christ,* until the whole World is become Christendom," his meaning is the same. But when Joel Barlowe writes about a generation after Edwards's death that "Now twenty years these children of the skies Beheld their gradual empire rise," his alliteration in the context of *The Columbiad* and of his oeuvre suggests that he defines it according to the discursively different, historical sense that is accepted in modern usage. And when at about the same time that Barlowe is writing *The Columbiad* the American Quaker John Woolman writes in his *Journal* that "in the history of the reformation from Popery it is observable that the progress was gradual from age to age," the historicism of Providence is become theologically expressive.[66]

Although the typological interpretation of the Bible makes sense to Edwards, it does not make historical sense. The structure that typology reveals can be apprehended only in retrospect. Even the most enlightened persons of the Old Testament cannot perceive it from events themselves; only those prophets who are granted the miraculous equivalent of retrospect through divinely inspired visions can see the future, and even they cannot predict how or when their prophecies will be fulfilled. Typology instructs a theist like Edwards that time makes sense in a way that cannot be appreciated through temporal experience, and thus exposes the futility of attempting to discover a pattern in time.

A cataclysmic end of the world is inconsistent with modern historiography (though not necessarily with modern physics or modern international relations), since such an end implies antagonism rather than harmony between meaning and time. That Edwards always foresees the total destruction of the world accompanying the Day of Judgment is further proof that to him Providence operates through sudden catastrophe rather than gradual (in the modern sense) improvement. Not only will the world end, but it will end in a way that Edwards and other theist chiliasts imagine as totally unnatural and startling. It will not wither away according to the laws of natural decay, nor will it be dispatched through natural calamities, which Edwards sees as "but little, faint shadows" of the final destruction. In order that there will be no doubt that God Himself is executing this judgment, God will use no secondary, natural means, but will directly revoke the existence of the universe: "God will destroy the world by an arrest of the laws of nature everywhere . . . by an entire new disposition and mighty change in all things at once. . . . the arbitrary interposition [is] entirely beside and above [the laws of nature] and in some respects contrary to them and interrupting their influence. . . . very many of the laws of nature will be utterly abolished." Disdaining nature altogether, God will "immediately interpose to put the world to an end, and destroy it suddenly," emphatically, with a bang.[67]

Edwards's insistence on this kind of climax is predictable, given his determination of the chief end and subsequent structure of Providence. Every individual work of redemption is preceded by a period of iniquity that God remarkably terminates so as to glorify Himself in distinct contrast to evil. Before the Golden Age of Constantine He allows heathenism to reign in the Roman Empire the more gloriously to humble it. Before the coming of the Millennium, "infidelity, heresy, and vice" is permitted to dominate for the same purpose. And the Millennium will be followed by a brief, but violent, revival of viciousness so as to make "the state of things . . . most remarkable to call for Christ's immediate appearance to judgment." This last reversion is predicted by Edwards not because he blindly accepts a chiliastic interpretation of Rev. 20:9,10 but because his definition of the way God glorifies Himself requires always the conquering of an opposing force. Should the Millennium proceed directly to the Day of Judgment, salvation can be claimed by mankind as reward for its thousand-year obedience. To be thoroughly convinced that God alone is responsible for salvation, mankind must be reduced to helpless iniquity one last time. If the Devil were not allowed one final reign, as Augustine explains, "his malicious power would be less patent, and less proof would be given of the steadfast fortitude of the holy city: it would, in short, be less manifest what good use the Almightly makes of his great evil. . . . [God] will in the end loose him, that the city of God may see how mighty an adversary it has conquered." But even if chiliasm did not exist in Christian tradition, implied in Revelation, explicated in Augustine, and supported by such Puritan theologians as Moses Lowman, whose eschatology Edwards is known to have read, Edwards would still have deduced an equivalent, so consistent with his entire discourse of Providence is the unnatural chiliastic prophecy.[68]

An epic struggle between *pre-* and *postmillennialism* is as much the creation of modern interpretation as is the one between spontaneous and infraspecial generation. Pre- and postmillennialism are both versions of theist eschatology, and the latter articulates, in a form that varies from that of the former in ways that are discursively inconsequential, the same miraculous, ahistorical structure of Providence. The premillennial ordering of the final stages of Providence—Christian era, Day of Judgment, Millennium, End of the World—and the postmillennial variant—Christian era, Millennium, Day of Judgment, End of the World—appear significantly to differ only when the transition between history, the Christian era, and utopia, the Millennium, is emphasized, and this emphasis is totally the product of humanist discourse. Only a discursive pattern that privileges history, as it privileges life, to be intrinsically a source of value would distinguish so invidiously between a theory that separates earthly misery from earthly happiness with divine intervention, as premillennialism does, from one that brings happiness out of misery without so interrupting the historical process, as postmillennialism, according to modern retrospect, seems to do. But if postmillennialism were, in the context of theist discourse, to link the Millennium as closely to the Christian era as modern interpretations wish, postmillennialism falls into precisely the heresy that

Origen condemns, that of constituting a "carnal Jewish dream," an idolatrous, unChristian reversion to the covenant of works, which claims not just that a man can earn his way to heaven through good works but that mankind can earn the way to heaven on earth through collective virtue. Edwards and other theist postmillennialists are very anxious about this charge, striving to distinguish finely between the piety, in service to God's chief end of self-adoration, of promoting the fervent anticipation of the Millennium inspired by the postmillennial schedule, and the apostasy, in service to man's selfishness, of allowing fervent anticipation of the Millennium to degenerate into the greed that might also be prompted by the postmillennial schedule. This fastidiousness is apparent throughout Edwards's "An Humble Attempt . . . ," and is apparent also in the trouble Edwards puts himself to in attempting to reconcile his discourse of Providence—which requires that some calamity precede every dispensation, even and especially as climactic a one as the Millennium, no matter whether the Millennium precede the Day of Judgment—with his evangelizing on the basis of hope for the imminence of the Millennium, which must be preceded by just such a dreaded reversal, such as the prophesied "slaughter of the witnesses," the precise date and form of which is much discussed but is undecidable in theist discourse. The best Edwards can manage to still his own or his congregations' fears that prayer for the Millennium may be prayer for their own destruction is to equivocate, in the safety of his notebooks, over the meaning or the timing of calamity. Perhaps what from the perspective of eternity are periods as separate as day from night appear, from the perspective of human experience, to be separated by the intermediacy of morning, implying both that catastrophe may seem gradual (due to the elongating distortions of time) and that the calamity Edwards never doubts must somehow precede the Millennium may already have occurred. Such a weak and unsatisfying defense reveals that the explanation that instantly occurs to humanism—latter days emerge organically from present ones—is unspeakable to Edwards in any utterance other than heresy, and that theist reconciliations of the ways of God to man must arrive finally at a confession that humanist discourse never makes, not at least as the culmination of mere theology, which is dilemma. What bothers modern retrospect most about Edwards's eschatology is that Edwards's chiliasm has God interposing inexplicably, with discouraging otherworldliness, to proclaim the Day of Judgment after Edwards's postmillennialism supposedly describes reality as merging, with apparently promising historicity, into the ideal. His postmillennialism, however, becomes inconsistent only when transformed into humanist discourse; read as an expression of theism, postmillennialism is structurally consistent with chiliasm.[69]

The structure of the work of redemption is for Edwards an expression of God's sovereignty and any suggestion that Providence is realized "gradually" rather than abruptly is inconsistent with Divinity as Edwards describes Divinity. This agrees with his discourse of Creation, which reckons nature wholly subordinate to a supernatural cause, and also with his discourse of Grace. The structure of a life is evaluated by Edwards according to the tension between divine and human wills. Just as Creation works against nature and Providence against time, so does Grace work against personality. Just as the places of science and history are taken in the theist discursive pattern by the theology of subjects that have no true modern equivalents, so will psychology be displaced in the ensuing reading of Edwards's writings on Grace.

4

GRACE

God ordered it so that nothing paradisiacal should be any
more here. And though sometimes there be great appearances of it and men are ready to flatter themselves that they
shall obtain it, yet it is found that paradise is not here, and
there is nothing but the shadow of it. Those things that look
most paradisiacal will have some sting to spoil them.
—Edwards, *Notebooks*

1. Introduction

A brief account of his conversion, written years after the (supposed) fact in
a personal letter to satisfy the curiosity of an admirer, represents Edwards's
only attempt to relate directly his own experience of Grace. In *Religious
Affections, The Nature of True Virtue,* and "The Distinguishing Marks of the
Works of the Spirit of God," writings that deal with Grace theologically
rather than personally, Edwards approaches Grace "by, First, observing
negatively, in some instances what are *not signs* of conversion." Edwards
does not restrict himself to giving a few instances of false signs; each of
these works disqualifies virtually all sensible evidence as proof of conversion and each identifies the experience of Grace only speculatively as a joy
that transcends both understanding and articulation. In writings that report his acquaintance with persons he believes to be saints—the *Faithful
Narrative* of the conversions in Northampton, the editorial commentary on
David Brainerd's diaries, and the short complimentary paragraph ad-
dressed to his future wife, Sarah Pierrepont—Edwards does not presume
to convey the religious ecstasy felt by his subjects but only reports, with
clinical dispassion, its external manifestations. The account of personal
awakenings constitutes a tiny fraction not only of Edwards's complete
writings, but of his writings about Grace.[1]

The only major work of Edwards concerned mainly with the personal
experience of Grace is the *Faithful Narrative;* its relative brevity, and the

relative lack of commentary in it, suggest that he does not consider it a major theological effort. The account of his own conversion is informal and is never meant for publication; similarly unfinished and intended only for private reading are the notebook entries in which Edwards attempts to describe the emotional content of his enjoyment of God or His works. But all of these fragments, along with the *Faithful Narrative,* occupy a central position in modern interpretations of his writings; prominent even is the love note scribbled by a teen-aged Edwards on a schoolbook to his then thirteen-year-old future wife. Although all interpretations add to the document of a writer's work, that modern ones of Edwards adds disproportionately is suggested by comparing the number and length of modern interpretations to the number and length of Edwards's writings to which modern interpretations pay close attention.

The following reading of Edwards's discourse of Grace will attempt no more than the previous ones of Edwards's discourse of Creation and of Providence to restore some original meaning. Like them it will try to create a new phenomenon by emphasizing the difference between Edwards's discourse of human being and the significance of human being in existence, which he calls virtue, and the modern discourse of the personality, including the humanist science of psychology. Like them it will propose that what seem now indispensable categories in the analysis of the self, and what seem now the primary literary forms of this analysis, are either marginal or absent in the theist discursive pattern that governs Edwards's writings.

Modern scholars have difficulty praising Edwards's writings for their romantic, or their pre- or protoromantic qualities. Edwards never writes a whole spiritual autobiography—even the account of his conversion contains much that is neither spiritual nor autobiographical, or, what is more important, omits precisely the events and feelings that are essential to spiritual autobiography. Rather, he writes an occasional paragraph that, when collected with other similar fragments, is said to constitute one. That the modern text of Edwards's personal writings on Grace is something entirely unlike any text that can be found intact in Edwards's corpus does not necessarily discredit it. But it can be made to seem tendentious in having to fetch from so far the statements that together comprise a meaning in Edwards's work that he barely, if ever, articulates. It has made him seem the novice of a profession he can never master, forever the apprentice of modern philosophy, or modern autobiography, or modern poetry. The purpose of this chapter is not empirically to correct modern interpretations but to show that a different reading can more economically attach Edwards's personal writings to theism, and also to the majority of his writings, without sacrificing the curiosity of modern retrospect. As before, there will be no pretension of eliminating modern perspective, only the attempt to exploit modern perspective indirectly in order to reveal the

strangeness of Edwards's writings rather than directly to show their familiarity. No pure reproduction of the document of Edwards's writings is
possible, not even in verbatim quotation. This is the third part of a
phenomenology that competes with modern interpretations and hopes to
replace them.

2. A New Simple Idea

Locke argues that ideas originate from sensations of tangible
phenomena. Although he proposes that simple ideas can be generated by
reflection as well as by sensation, his analysis of the mind implies that
reflection is subordinate to sensation. The mind cannot be impressed with
an idea of itself before acquiring the force of an object, and probably cannot
gain objectivity before being furnished with simple ideas through sensory
experience. A blank slate, that is Locke's well-known metaphor for the
original character of the mind, probably cannot generate ideas; when the
mind is inscribed with simple ideas of sensation, it becomes an object of
experience that can inspire ideas of reflection. Complex ideas, which Locke
defined as combinations of simple ones, can similarly be traced back to
sensations. Some modern commentaries on Locke have fastened on a
seeming inconsistency of this discourse on the mind, which is that the
capacity to apprehend sense data and to formulate complex ideas must be
prior to the actual experience of the former and the actual performance of
the latter; this occurs to modern retrospect because such "innate" potential
of the mind suggests that the mind is latently, and more importantly,
defined by Locke as self-generating, which intimation makes Locke into a
protophenomenologist.

Locke is relatively silent about the original character of the mind not,
however, because he senses an embarrassing contradiction of his sensationalist discourse of experience, but because the origin of the mind is by
him, as by any theist, taken for granted to refer to the priority of a Creator
whose creative processes are not only unsearchable but not particularly
interesting to man. What is "innate" to the mind or any other creature is
what the Creator arbitrarily makes of them, and thus betrays self-evidently,
in ways so obvious that they need not be elucidated and that are unproductive of much discourse in theism, the dependence of the mind on an other.
What interests Locke and is productive of *An Essay Concerning Human
Understanding* are the consequences of this dependency, which are all of the
operations of the mind. That a totally inexperienced mind still can think,
that there is such a thing as pure thought, is of course theoretically possible
according to Locke's discourse, not as a potential but as a hyperbole of
human thought, that, like much theist hyperbole, approximates Divinity.[2]

According to Locke's discourse of experience, a simple idea can be new only in the context of an individual mind. Someone can acquire as many new simple ideas of sensation as there are tangible things in the world that he has yet to experience, and he can acquire as many new simple ideas of reflection as there are unperformed mental operations, inspired by new sensory experiences or new intellectualizations about old ones. But because sensation ultimately determines both experience and reflection, and because the abundant sensible things of the natural world are nonetheless finite, a truly new idea can be inspired only by the appearance of something radically original. Locke associates the phrase *new simple idea* in the *Essay* with what he considers to be the illusion of a thought not derived from reality: "It is not in the power of the most exalted wit or understanding, by any quickness or variety of thought, to *invent or frame one new simple idea* in the mind. . . . [Man's power] reaches no further than to combine and divide the materials that are made to his hand." To Locke, both the "great world of visible things" and the "little world of man's understanding" that is based upon it determine a fund of ideas to which the mind is limited.[3]

Edwards's definition of the process by which new simple ideas are impressed upon the mind seems precisely to follow Locke's. He agrees that the mind is fundamentally passive and incapable alone of generating original ideas. This assumption requires him to grant both priority and objectivity to nature. The suggestion, which modern histories of philosophy often associate with Berkeley, that the world might lack objectivity is illogical to Edwards, whether or not he actually reads Berkeley's supposedly Kantian conjecture, because it presumes self-creation and thereby violates linear causality. If the world has no being separate from the mind, "then the sensations themselves, or the organs of sense by which sensible ideas are let into the mind, have no existence but only in the mind. And those organs of sense have no existence but what is conveyed to the mind by themselves, for they are part of the sensible world. And then it would follow that the organs of sense owe their existence to the organs of sense, and so are prior to them, being the cause or occasion of their own existence—which is a seeming inconsistence with reason." Edwards recalls again the *in infinitum* regression that refutes any assumption of self-creation. When he says that "the world is an ideal one," or that "the Material universe exists only in the mind," he means not that nature is phenomenologically a projection of the mind, but that nature can be experienced by men only through the mind's ideal impression of nature's objective being. That man's idea of nature differs from the essence of nature is likely, due to the limitations of the mind, but man's idea represents an imperfect record of a given object, not the fabrication of a new one.[4]

Edwards is especially concerned with emphasizing that the particular new simple idea of Grace is passively received by the mind, not just because this agrees with Locke but because this agrees also with the sovereignty of God. A confusion of subject and object in the understanding of the formation of this idea threatens divine sovereignty; to suppose an innate idea of Grace is to suppose the soul author of its own salvation. But, although Edwards can derive the process by which Grace is communicated to men from Locke's analysis, he identifies the source of this simple idea as something other than material reality. Whereas Locke traces all ideas back to sensations of material things, Edwards proposes that an equally fundamental idea can be impressed upon the mind by an immediate immaterial communication from God.

According to Edwards, Grace, like all simple ideas, is sensible. It is not apprehended, however, through the experience of tangible things. In *Religious Affections* Edwards always qualifies the contention that Grace is sensed with the reminder that its sensation differs from those of natural objects. The text that he chooses as the motto for the treatise is 1 Peter 1:8, "Whom having not seen, ye love," and his improvement on the verse notes that even in the earliest Christian times "there was nothing that was seen, nothing that the world saw, or that Christians themselves ever saw with their *bodily* eyes, that thus influenced and supported them, yet they had a *supernatural* principle of love to something unseen." He stresses consistently, no less in *The Nature of True Virtue* and the sermons that discuss the experience of Grace than in *Religious Affections*, that "there is no necessary connection in the nature of things, between any thing that a natural man may experience while in a state of nature, and the saving grace of God's Spirit." Edwards equates the purity of an awakening with its dissociation from conventional ideas. An affection is more apt to be truly religious if not connected with any experience of nature. The inspirations of Grace "are things entirely different in their natures from strong ideas of shapes and colours and outward brightness and glory, or sounds or voices," and his own awakening is made implicitly to seem more genuine, as reported in his account of his own conversion, by the fact that it is occasioned by a particularly unsensational passage from Scripture: "Now unto the King eternal, immortal, invisible, the only wise God, be honor and glory forever and ever, Amen" (1 Tim. 1:17). The "inward sweet delight" that Edwards claims to feel upon reading this passage appears independent of any experience of nature because the passage is totally abstract and makes no appeal stylistically to natural affections.[5]

Because Grace to Edwards is an idea initiated by the impression of an immaterial thing, the recollection of it should be uncontaminated with conventional ideas. Edwards knows that religious affections seem frequently to stimulate the imagination, and that testimonies are often embellished with images from nature. The imaginativeness of a testimony is to him irrelevant, however, and may even damage the credibility of the testimony. One of the most reliable criteria Edwards devises in *Religious Affections* to distinguish between enthusiasm and Grace is that the former usually consists "in the exciting [of] external ideas in the mind, either in ideas of *outward* shapes and colours, or *words* spoken, or letters written, or ideas of things external and sensible." Conversely, the validity of a conversion like Brainerd's stems for Edwards in large part from the unimaginative quality of Brainerd's conviction, which "did not arise from any frightful *impression* of his *imagination*, or any external images or ideas of fire and brimstone." Although Grace is inscribed upon the mind like any idea of sensation, its immaterial source makes of it a wholly different sort of idea that can be neither experienced nor described in images. The new simple idea of Grace is to Edwards so different from other ideas, which are continually reinforced and refreshed by the experience of nature, that a saint may not be able to recall it even to himself: "Those spiritual ideas are of such a nature that [even if] a person has once had them in mind, having obtained them by actual sense, yet it may be impossible for him to bring the idea into his mind again distinctly, or indeed at all. We can't renew them when we please, as we can an idea of colour and figure."[6]

That imaginings often accompany the experience of Grace reveals only that the mind, even after awakening, cannot fully transcend the limitations of natural experience: "[Religious] affections do not arise from the imagination, the imagination is only the accidental effect or consequent of the affection, through the infirmity of human nature." Unable adequately to express or remember the feeling of Grace, the saint resorts to his fund of conventional ideas to approximate his joy. Edwards's discounting of the imagination as a contributor to awakening signifies his consistent refusal to identify truth with natural analogues of truth. Defining the imagination simply, classically, as the picture-making ability of the mind, he dismisses it as a religious faculty because to him visible things, no matter how vividly reproduced or refined by the mind, cannot embody Divinity. The imagination can become religiously and philosophically significant, "may be defined as the use which the Reason makes of the material world," according to Emerson's genuinely Kantian definition in *Nature*, only after nature, and hence images of nature, are redefined as capable of directly manifesting spiritual truths; it does so in later romantic writings because of this fundamental redefinition. Imagination is to Edwards what it is to Willard before him, properly no more than "the porter, which takes in the species of things, as they are offered to it," or what it is to Hamilton after him, improperly a juggernaut that "may range at pleasure till it gets bewildered amid the labyrinths of any enchanted castle, and know not on which side to turn to escape from the apparitions which itself has raised," to give two more disparate versions of a definition that runs throughout theist discourse and that Edwards does not once qualify by "nevertheless [bespeaking] an important place for the faculty," as an imaginative modern scholar contends.[7]

Edwards reads Locke's discourse of the mind as subordinating the mind to external forces and describing knowledge as a series of recognitions impressed upon the mind by these forces. The mind is therefore determined by its ideas, and bears the imprint of the forces that generate ideas. To suppose, as Edwards does, that ideas can be inspired by God without the medium of material reality is to suppose the existence of minds formed, at least in part, independently of the experience of nature. Genuine testimonies avoid reference to conventional ideas not just to obey some formal rule of piety, but because they express a disposition for holy rather than natural things. As a new simple idea, Grace creates an essentially new mind.

The institution of the covenant of Grace is accompanied by a greater intimacy in the way God communicates to man, and Edwards interprets Grace as implying more evidently than "legal humiliations" that "t'is but an immediate step from the soul to God." But this change does not alter the meaning or intent of Providence, which forever distinguishes radically between God and His creatures. The difference between the two covenants lies for Edwards in the different contexts in which they operate: "With the Jews, election, their redemption out of Egypt, their creation, was a national thing; it began with them as a nation, and descended as it were from the nation to particular persons. . . . But it is evidently contrariwise in Christians. With regard to them, the election, redemption, creation, etc. are personal things. They begin with particular persons, and ascend to public societies." The Jewish church is protected and instructed by God through a series of miraculous subjugations of nature; the election of the Jews as a chosen people, their redemption from their enemies, and their maintenance as an independent theocracy all occur through divine restraint of natural antagonists, both within and outside the Jewish church. The Christian church is sustained through the gracious inspiration of the elect rather than through miracles, but the new simple idea of Grace is described by Edwards as being communicated miraculously by God and as having consequences similar to those of the miracles of the Old Testament.[8]

Edwards frequently cites the traditional Christian metaphor likening Grace to a second birth. His fondness for it may have been unselfconscious; it occurs often in Scripture, especially in the New Testament, and is dutifully repeated by seventeenth- and eighteenth-century ministers in their descriptions of Grace. But the ways in which Edwards expands upon it suggests that it has special appeal for him. A second birth connotes the denial of the first one, in which the principles of the flesh originate, and thus sharpens the distinction between man's holy and natural identities. The experience of Grace does not perfect what is old and natural in a man; rather, Grace makes him into a new creature whose new virtuousness is unrelated to his former self. The remarkable and unnatural character of this is emphasized by Edwards through his claim that Grace not only revokes the natural identity of an individual, but in an instant counteracts the long historical development of man's natural principles, which are ascendant since the Fall: "When God made man at first, he implanted in him two kinds of principles. There was an *inferior* kind, which may be called natural. . .and there were *superior* principles, that were spiritual, holy, and divine . . .which are called in Scripture the *divine nature.*" The superior principles are moribund except when assisted by Providential miracles, but they are revived, Edwards supposes, by the gracious inspiration of God; in conversions, "those principles are restored that were utterly lost by the fall." This revival occurs against all human culture, and therefore shows God acting against nature as dramatically as in the miracles designed to enforce the old covenant. The unnatural implication of the metaphor of the second birth is what makes it a proper one for describing the experience of Grace. Edwards argues that it implies not only the suppression of natural origin, but a direct incarnation so miraculously out of the course of nature as to be similar to the birth of Christ: "The ingenerating of a principle of grace in the soul, seems in scripture to be compared to the conceiving of Christ in the womb" (Gal. 4:19)[9]

Another similarity between Grace and the miracles of the old covenant is that they both have a similar effect on man. Much as miracles confound natural law in order to display God's excellency, so does Grace overwhelm all that is natural in a man remarkably to display God's generosity: "Gracious influences. . .not only differ from what is natural, and from everything that natural men experience, in degree and circumstance, but also in kind; and are of a nature vastly more excellent." Because the distinction between the old natural principles of the mind and the new divine ones is radical, the old principles stand in contrast to the experience of Grace, as nature and events stand in contrast to miracles, to help enhance the glory of God. The experience of Grace "must be wholly and entirely a work of the Spirit of God, not merely as co-working with natural principles, but infusing something above nature," if the sovereignty of God is to be evident. Lest the elect become complacent about their supposed intimacy with God, they must testify always to the fact that the state of Grace is initiated through God's miraculous defeat of what is intrinsic to their natural identity, and is preserved through His continual restraint of the sin that "remains in the heart resisting."[10]

Although Edwards seems fully to concur with Locke's determination of the character of the mind, and although he seems to agree with Locke's epistemological assumption that the mind is instructed by a coercive external reality, he expands the world of sensations to include sensations of immaterial things, and thereby allows for the formation of a new mind. Whereas Locke restricts his study to the analysis of minds habituated to nature, Edwards proposes the existence of minds as fatally habituated to God. Edwards refers to Locke in his descriptions of the way these new minds originate because he recognizes in Locke's writings a persuasive explanation of how knowledge is gained. The value of sensationalist epistemology for Edwards is that it can be applied to show how men become convinced not only by natural fact, but by immaterial truth. It serves him as an empirical justification for religious certainty.

The equation of Grace with a new simple idea enables Edwards to base the conviction of the elect on the common sense not just of Puritan theology but of "enlightened" science: "The prophet has so divine a sense, such a divine disposition, such a divine pleasure; and sees so divine an excellency, and divine a power, in what is revealed, that he sees as immediately that God is there, as we perceive another's presence, when we are talking face to face. And our features, our voice and our shapes, are not so clear manifestations of us, as those spiritual resemblances of God, that are in the Inspiration, are manifestations of him." Edwards is less interested in portraying what the prophet perceives or how the prophet is granted the vision than in claiming that the experience is as influential and undeniable as the most basic sense impression. Sight functions in this description to convey the reality of the prophet's vision and the certainty of his recognition. He does not see anything visible, nor does his apprehension resemble natural sight in any way other than its simplicity. He is miraculously granted an idea of the immaterial attributes of God, God's excellency and power, and the sensation is stronger than that gained through the natural sense of material things. Edwards uses sight in his descriptions of the experience of Grace to suggest how a fundamental impression of the supernatural can be received through a sixth sense, "the opening to view, with such a clearness, such a world of wonderful and glorious truth in the gospel, that before was unknown, being quite above the view of the natural eye." The addition of a sixth sense to permit Grace entrance to the mind seems superflous to modern epistemology that wants access to the ideal to require no more than refinement of man's natural endowment. The superaddition of senses occurs throughout theist discourse of visionary experience, however, even as late of the writings of Poe, who requires not just a sixth sense but the replacement of all five by "five myriad other alien to mortality."[11]

The opening to the saint of a new world through new simple ideas acclimatizes him to this new world as irresistibly as his simple ideas of material things acclimatize him to nature. And because what is sensed by the saint is holy, his gracious disposition competes with his natural one. Although the saint senses reality and is formed by it in the manner that Locke describes, his reality differs from that of natural men, by which he is determined before his conversion and to which he may periodically revert due to natural imperfection. At his best, most religiously inspired moments, he becomes a stranger both to natural men and to his own natural self. Having simple ideas of things that remain insensible to most of his fellows, he acquires perspectives and inclinations that are not real to them. Although using more subtle, personal means, God sequesters him as evi-

dently as ever God sequesters a prophet or a people under the old covenant, and manifests divine glory through the contrast between the
Christian saint's asceticism and the carnality of natural men much as God
glorifies Himself in the times of the Old Testament by contrasting the
cultural isolation of the Jews with the worldliness of the heathen.

Far from implying or even permitting an inference of an association
between religious inspirations and impressions of nature, such that the
new simple idea of Grace might properly be defined as "composed of
nothing but what nature supplies" as Miller claims, Edwards's portrayal of
the experience of Grace as the receipt of a new simple idea reinforces the
otherworldliness of its origin. The operations of a mind that has been
inscribed with the new simple idea of Grace, the gracious formation of
ideas of reflection and of complex ideas, differ consequently from those of
natural minds. Edwards expands Locke's definition of understanding,
which identifies understanding as the agreement of ideas in the mind, to
allow for a "union" in the gracious mind between ideas that are not logically related: "It is not impossible to believe, or know, the Truth of Mysteries, or propositions that we cannot comprehend. . . . we may perceive
that [ideas] are *united,* and know that they *belong* to one another; though we
do not know the manner *how they are tied together.*" Here, in an entry from
his notebooks, Edwards lays the foundation for the saint's special feeling
of cordial consent and his special recognition of beauty. The apparent
agreement or disagreement between ideas constitutes the basis both of
natural understanding and of aesthetic standards. The invisible union or
disunion between them apprehended by the saint bestows a different,
superior judgment that cannot be taught to natural men. The understanding of a saint is incommunicable and incomprehensible; understanding
does not, however, represent merely a blind acceptance of the ineffable.
The certainty of the saint is equal to the certainty of his new simple idea of
Grace, and derives from his experience as surely as does that of natural
men. Again, Edwards accepts sensationalist epistemology, but harnessed
to his claim that Grace is supernatural and thus enlarges the potential of
experience to include supernatural impressions.[12]

Those modern scholars who contest Miller's linking Edwards's writings
on Grace to an early, and procociously comprehending reading of Locke's
Treatise—most recently Fiering and before him Erdt and, implicitly, Gay—
are correct in pointing out that Locke's epistemology is not so original as to
make an awareness of it on Edwards's part either a necessary or a sufficient
reason for Edwards's sensationalist definition of Grace, to indulge for a
moment the positivist illusion that the mere fact of a discourse being read is
any kind of legitimate explanation of another discourse being written,
especially by a strong reader, as Edwards must be assumed to be; Erdt
notes that Calvin and Augustine write of Grace sensationalistically, and

Fiering notes that sensationalist characterizations are so pervasive in medieval Christian and later Protestant writings on Grace that they cannot possibly be attributed to any single source, certainly not to Locke. But the issue here is not when or how Edwards comes by writing of Grace as an idea, but how to classify sensationalist epistemology. Miller's intention is not to portray Edwards as a follower of even so eminent a figure as Locke, is not to portray Edwards as a follower at all, but to portray him as having as clear a foreknowledge as Locke, whose "enlightenment" Miller identifies conventionally as very bright, of the modern naturalism that Miller takes sensationalist epistemology in its entirety to anticipate, a syncretism not only shared by Fiering *et al.* but even more obviously practiced by them in connecting not just Edwards and Locke but many more and much earlier sensationalists to the great post-Enlightenment luminaries of modern science and philosophy. What is not supposed by any of their interpretations is the possibility that sensationalist epistemology,—even when applied by such "enlightened" writers as Locke or Edwards, much less Calvin and Augustine and medieval Catholic pietists—is better classified as other than modern, a possibility that is supported by contrasting it with the epistemology of the romantics, the earliest among whom are critical of precisely the sensationalism that modern scholarship so often cites as a precursor of romanticism. Kant goes to great lengths to redefine *idea* so as to enlarge Locke's definition, amplifying that *ideas* are not only formed by the passive receipt of sense impressions and by secondary operations performed on remembered sense impressions, but are generated also, and, Kant says, essentially, as purely mental phenomena, which redefinition is, of course, consistent with modern usage. Consequently, Kant identifies as the basis for thought not experience but "intuition," constituted by "ideas" according to the second, modern definition; after Kant, Hegel even more forcefully dismisses "sense-certainty" as the foundation of knowledge in any but the least self-knowledgeable of modern epistemologies. When Emerson calls the highest form of knowing one "that fastens attention upon immortal, necessary, uncreated natures, that is, upon Ideas," he is best read as neither refining nor building upon Locke's sensationalism, but as expressing a wholly different epistemology in wholly different terms, including *Idea*, which only appear, but semiotically are not the same words when used in the discourse of Locke or Edwards. A conventional romantic wisdom, expressed by James Marsh in his "Preliminary Essay" to the first American edition of Coleridge's *Aids to Reflection*, is that Locke's epistemology supports the old theology of the "Scottish Metaphysicians" in implicitly denying the freedom of the will, and that Locke denies, vainly, the new religiosity of such romantic writers as Coleridge, to whom an unfree will seems as patently a contradiction in terms and an offense to Reason as, conversely, a free will seems to Edwards. Stripped of invidiousness, this distinction differentiates systemic-ally between theist and humanist epistemologies, as well as between the different ontologies underlying them.[13]

Once the perspective of a saint is altered by the experience of Grace and "Divine things now appear excellent, beautiful, glorious, which did not when the soul was of another spirit," he begins to be drawn automatically toward them. Edwards compares this attraction with "the desires of appe-tite, the thirstings of a new nature, as a new-born babe desires the mother's breast; and as a hungry man longs for some pleasant food he thinks of; or as the thirsty heart pants after the cool and clear stream." The inclination is involuntary and irresistible because aroused by an idea as basic as that of nourishment acquired through the sense of taste, and it becomes "as natu-ral to a holy nature as breathing is to a living body." But although originat-ing sensationally, in the same way as natural desires, the objects of gracious inclination are holy and therefore replace the objects of natural appetite.[14]

Edwards compares gracious longing also with an aesthetic response to beauty. Despite seeming to imply a more refined and deliberate inclination than appetite, the enjoyment of beauty is used by Edwards as an illustra-tion of religious affection in order to suggest that the cordial consent of a saint to God is passive and automatic. And aesthetic sensibility implies better than appetite a mysterious affection for invisible things, which is why Edwards cites this affection so often when attempting to distinguish true virtue from mere morality. Just as he portrays the acquisition of Grace as the apprehension of a new simple idea in order to stress its supernatural origin, so will he depict the state of Grace as a kind of "relish" to emphasize its ascetic character.

3. The Aesthetic Metaphor

Edwards's comparing Grace to aesthetic pleasure is as striking as his identifying it as a new simple idea. He speculates often in his notebooks that a gracious disposition is best described as a taste for Divinity, and he begins in *Religious Affections* to use the aesthetic vocabulary that he de-velops more fully in *The Nature of True Virtue*. Miller is the first to suggest that this vocabulary signifies the beginning of advancement from Puritan theology, and Delattre follows the suggestion by devoting an entire book to beauty and sensibility in Edwards's thought. Delattre argues that in em-phasizing the beauty of God, Edwards makes God more accessible both emotionally and intellectually than God is to Calvin: "Divine majesty was for [Edwards] a lovely rather than an awful or awesome majesty," in the sense of being more enjoyable, and divine beauty is according to Delattre defined by Edwards "to be primarily objective, structural, and relational," so as to be comprehensible even to natural men "who cannot themselves lay claim to a savory acquaintance with the divine beauty." There is a small dispute among modern scholars over the originality of Edwards's likening religious affections to aesthetic ones. Lee agrees with Miller and Delattre that this is among the best evidence of Edwards's distinctive precocity, implying the active participation of sensibility in the production of beauty and so proving that Edwards has "of course . . . gone far beyond Locke's view that the mind is 'merely passive' in the perceptual process," whereas Fiering wants, typically, to correct the provinciality of such estimates by showing that a broader perspective on intellectual history discovers the development of aesthetic imagery in theology to be ancient and seamless, supposing that "the notion that virtue was beautiful has, of course, ancient Platonic roots and was a concept current among seventeenth-century philosophers." Fiering's point is again not that Edwards's aestheticism is to be dissociated from modernism in being associated with that of these earlier writers, but that his aestheticism along with that of these earlier writers merges more gradually into modernism than narrow studies of just Edwards's imagery realize, and thus supplements arguments for Edwards's modernity.[15]

Edwards begins *The Nature of True Virtue* by denying, at great length, any identity between the beauty of virtue and the beauty of visible things. He goes farther to distinguish it also from those invisible natural attributes of the mind, such as understanding and speculation, which may be considered beautiful. Both of these distinctions seem to indicate that if Edwards were about to define virtue as an "articulated reality," as Delattre contends, he is not planning to do so. When, after listing all the beautiful things with which true virtue must not be confused, he arrives finally at a positive definition, he calls it "the beauty of the qualities and exercises of the heart, or those actions which proceed from them." Had Edwards never inserted this demand that true virtue be beautiful, his definition would have identified it simply as the sensibly virtuous acts of the will. By interpolating the aesthetic criterion, he distinguishes virtue from morality, and thereby makes it harder to discern. Announcing at the beginning of the treatise that not just obedience to the Law but a sensibility for holiness will be required of the truly virtuous soul, Edwards promises neither an easily identifiable nor an easily fulfilled standard for true virtue.[16]

This complication persists throughout *The Nature of True Virtue* because Edwards perceives only an approximate and uncertain relationship between virtue and natural beauty. Although there is analogy between the visible and invisible just as there is analogy between nature and truth, and although an appreciation of natural beauty may "*assist* those whose hearts are under the influence of a truly virtuous temper to dispose them to the exercise of divine love, and enliven in them a sense of spiritual beauty," the beauty of true virtue remains infinitely superior to natural beauty and causally independent of nature. The enjoyment of spiritual beauty is always granted to the saint prior to his exploiting aesthetic pleasure of natural beauties to cultivate spiritual beauty in his mind. Because the saint must have received the new simple idea of Grace before he can begin to delight in it, his feeling is no more closely related to the aesthetic response to natural beauty than God, according to Edwards's ontology, is related to Creation: "As bodies, the objects of our external senses, are but the shadows of beings; that harmony, wherein consists sensible excellency and beauty, is but the shadow of excellency. That is, it is pleasant to the mind, because it is a shadow of love." The same radical distrust of visible things that controls Edwards's epistemology and ontology guides his analysis of divine beauty as well, preventing him in *The Nature of True Virtue* from proposing a formal aesthetic to define it. Much as the hierarchical complexity of motivations functions to deny any certain relationship between action and inclination in Edwards's analysis of the will, so does the introduction of an aesthetic standard complicate the relationship between true and apparent goodness in his analysis of virtue. While he insists that true virtue is beautiful, he emphasizes that it is invisible. Thus he discourages the identification of apparent morality, which "approves the *very same things* which a spiritual and divine sense approves," with Grace, which approves them also, "*though not* on the same grounds."[17]

Because Edwards believes that spiritual beauty is "far purer than anything here upon the earth" and "that everything else, was like mire, filth and defilement in comparison of it," his aesthetic vocabulary must be understood as self-consciously inadequate, capable merely of suggesting a divine beauty that surpasses nature and man's experience. This style is the least adequate way of writing for Edwards, because it is used to describe what language is least able to express. Words, Locke says, are like every aspect of human culture derived from simple ideas of nature, and can describe truth, Edwards adds, only analogously: "Words were first formed to express external things; and those that are applied to express things internal and spiritual, are almost all borrowed, and used in a sort of figurative sense. When they are most of 'em attended with a great deal of ambiguity and unfixedness in their signification." When describing the operations of the mind, such as reasoning or understanding or imagining, Edwards can refer to simple ideas of reflection experienced by all men, and his style, though abstract, derives from these ideas and is therefore relatively straightforward. When describing natural depravity, he can recall a host of simple ideas of the unpleasant sensations to which the flesh is heir, and his imprecatory style is vivid and concrete, to which virtually any image from "Sinners in the Hands of an Angry God" attests. Descriptions of Divinity represent to Edwards a use of words to convey meanings about which words are fundamentally inarticulate, and his rhetoric in those passages accordingly, and explicitly, strains language.[18]

This strain inheres in the figures Edwards uses most often to portray divine beauty, all of which are forms of hyperbole. The grandeur of nature can be exaggerated to suggest how God's grandeur "unspeakably exceeds them," and the deformities of nature can similarly be magnified to simulate the moral ugliness of sin. Words that derive from the experience of nature can denote only the attributes of nature; by hyperbolically inflating the natural qualities that words denote, Edwards implies that divine beauty cannot be experienced in the conventional way and that it cannot be described precisely by language originating in natural sensations. His frequent use of paradox and oxymoron acknowledges this limitation of language in a similar way. The religious vision that Edwards has in his father's pasture is conveyed in his account of his conversion through a series of paradoxes that imply divine beauty to exceed the natural beauties unavoidably denoted by his aesthetic vocabulary. The "sweet conjunction" of opposites that Edwards fashions—"majesty and meekness join'd together," "a sweet and gentle, and holy majesty," "an awful sweetness," "a high, and great, and holy gentleness"—celebrates the beauty of God by compounding it of qualities that ordinarily cancel one another and that cannot be embodied in even the most fetching natural object. The repetition of these paradoxes functions not to specify the sense of Divinity that Edwards experiences in the pasture, but to abstract it so from natural sensations as to make it ineffable.[19]

Another, related, technique that exalts God by implicitly admitting the incapacities of language is the simple multiplication of terms. Throughout *The Nature of True Virtue* Edwards pairs "beauty and excellency" to connote the attractiveness of God to a gracious sensibility. This pairing represents a near paradox, since "excellency," which Edwards uses in the biblical sense, suggests an omnipotence that "beauty" alone does not; "excellent" is a hierarchical adjective in the Bible—"O Lord, our Lord, how excellent is thy name in all the earth! who hast set thy Glory above the heavens!" (Ps. 8:17)—whereas "beauty" might be understood as a comeliness that is accessible and familiar. Edwards combines the terms because neither alone communicates the quality of divine beauty. Neither do they together add up to an articulation of Divinity; rather, they create the impression that no word nor any combination of words, no matter how comprehensive or various, can express the miraculous character of Divinity. Edwards uses a "variety of expressions" in his analysis of divine beauty and fails to arrive at "any short definition" of it so as to promote stylistically the pious belief that God is incomparably beautiful. The right word or phrase will never be discovered because, as the rhetorical question of Isaiah instructs, God can be likened to nothing, and Edwards's multiplication of terms sustains the pious expectancy that an appropriate one will remain forever "at the tongue's end."[20]

Edwards is continually at war with "those dreadful enemies of mankind called words," and never more than in his descriptions of the beauty of God. His figuration is expressly ineloquent, and his "tropes"—less than those of some other Puritan writers, such as Thomas Hooker and Cotton Mather, both of whom seem more to indulge rhetorical extravagance— nearly always contain a reminder, either explicit or implicit, that the concrete image is but a shadow of the truth to which it is compared. Edwards's metaphors are designed so as to encourage a shift of attention from the vehicle, the visible, lower analogue, to the tenor, which is invisible and infinitely superior. Thus the self-effacing, hesitant quality of Edwards's aesthetic metaphors represents not a flaw in style, but the adoption of a technique that inherently reflects the dualism of theist discourse. All of his aesthetic vocabulary has the status of a vehicle—unimportant intrinsically, significant only as a suggestion of the inexpressibly excellent attributes of God and the inexpressibly delightful sensation of Grace.[21]

Although the aesthetic metaphor for Grace is not perfectly articulate, it evidently seems to Edwards particularly valuable. Virtually obsessed with the problem of having "no word that clearly and adequately expresses the whole act of acceptance, or closing of the soul or heart with Christ," Edwards's choice of the aesthetic metaphor is a careful one, and reflects his discerning a special resemblance between the enjoyment of beauty and the feeling of Grace. The resemblance is, however, not formal. The beauty of an object to aesthetic sensibility does not help to substantiate God to religious sensibility because all objective beauty is defined by Edwards as mysterious and inexplicable. The religious value of the aesthetic metaphor lies for him not in providing a structural definition of the beautiful, but in dramatizing the revelation of a taste for the beautiful: "That form or quality is called beautiful, which appears in itself agreeable or comely, or the view of which is immediately pleasant to the mind." Edwards is more than simply negligent about establishing formal aesthetic principles; he emphasizes the sort of aesthetic response that is immediate and unprincipled, that is not educated by the "argumentation or connection and consequences" of aesthetic theory, and that reveals not the objective beauty of an idea but the "frame of our minds, whereby they are so made that such an idea, as soon as we have it, is grateful, or appears beautiful." An aesthetic response manifests not the object that sensibility approves, but the character of an approving sensibility.[22]

Edwards compares true virtue to aesthetic sensibility less to envision Divinity than to expose the soul. To "relish" God is to love Him spontaneously and undeliberately, which feeling certifies, as far as words can describe, a truly gracious disposition: "It is impossible that any one should truly relish this [divine] beauty, consisting in general benevolence, who has not that temper himself. I have observed, that if any being is possessed of such a temper, he will unavoidably be pleased with the same temper in another." Religious sensibility is aroused by the instantaneous recognition of kinship with the holy object, whether the latter be the infinite holiness of God or the kindred holiness of another saint. Aesthetic pleasure resembles religious affection because it is instinctive and nonrational, surprising the beholder with a joy that immediately reveals his predisposition to delight aesthetically in the object before him: "There is such an idea of religion in [the saint's] mind when he knows he sees and feels that power, that holiness, that purity, that majesty, that love, that excellency, that beauty and loveliness, that amounts to his idea of God. Now no man can say such a thing cannot be. A man may see a beauty, a charmingness, and feel a power that he can no way in the world describe. T'is so in corporeal beauties, in beautiful charming airs, etc." About the objective beauty of God Edwards is characteristically inarticulate, celebrating Divinity through a list of abstract excellencies that is the stylistic equivalent of speechlessness. About the saint's response to this divine beauty he is explicit and illustrative, preaching the doctrine of free Grace by likening Grace to aesthetic rapture. Edwards fastens upon the aesthetic metaphor because he finds it a persuasive means to explain the immediacy and irresistibility of cordial consent.[23]

The aesthetic response implies the absence of man's generic motive, and this is what makes it useful to Edwards for clarifying his complicated definition of religious love as "cordial consent to being in general" in *The Nature of True Virtue.* The most sophisticated aesthetic sensibility may consult rules of proportion before acknowledging beauty, but would never consider mere selfish interest; the primitive sensibility that Edwards's aesthetic vocabulary presumes is apt in the moment of aesthetic pleasure to forget in an even more spontaneous way all selfish concerns. To love the beauty of an object is to love qualities that have no material value, and aesthetic sensibility represents therefore the most disinterested and unselfish of natural affections. Edwards cites this affection in order to show how love can be intense without being self-seeking, and then magnifies it according to his metaphorical technique to suggest how "cordial consent to being in general" is so radically unselfish as to be unnatural. Less associated with self-preservation than metaphors of thirst or hunger, Edwards prefers the aesthetic metaphor when attempting to relate the miraculous joy saints receive in abandoning themselves to the experience of Grace. Edwards's use of the aesthetic metaphor is unusual in reflecting a thorough recognition of the metaphysical implications of the figure, in being consistent throughout his writings on Grace, and in being practiced freely and confidently in descriptions of what to Edwards is not only difficult but risky to describe, an affection for God that neither contradicts man's natural experience of love nor diminishes God to the status of a natural object of love. But it is not at all unique in theist discourse, which often rates love of beauty as the most widespread and generous kind, not only in other religious and philosophical writings, such as those cited by

Fiering, but also in secular, and even ribald ones, such as, for example, Brackenridge's *Modern Chivalry*, in which the crude satire directed against early Irish emigrants to the United States is qualified by the patronizing compliment that "simple and ignorant nature will fasten on beauty, as well as the most instructed in the principles of taste."[24]

Although the excited aesthetic sensibility may be unruly according to Edwards's figuration, the feeling need not be promiscuous. Edwards's distinction between tutored and spontaneous aesthetic pleasures does not require that the latter arise haphazardly, but that the latter obey an emotional command that supersedes the dictates of reason. Aesthetic sensibility may approve precisely the same things emotionally that aesthetic theory approves intellectually, and when this simultaneous approval occurs, delight in beauty most closely resembles the cordial consent of grace. Religious affection for being-in-general does not ignore the structure of Creation, which can be apprehended through a rational understanding of Scripture or even the rational study of nature; rather, Grace approves without deliberation the same hierarchical ontology that Christian theology deduces after pondering revelation and natural history for centuries. Consent to being-in-general does not, therefore, imply an impartial love of everything equally. Edwards never, not even implicitly, contradicts the discourse of the Great Chain; he describes a gracious love for things that is spontaneously graduated according to their ranks in the hierarchy of being. A love of God rather than of the self prompts the saint ecstatically to abandon his worldly concerns, or at least to reduce them in proportion to their insignificance relative to being-in-general. Love of God resembles love of beauty to Edwards only insofar as both overlook natural interest. It is not Edwards's aestheticism that signals departure from theist discourse; rather, it is Kant's aestheticism, which constitutes a great deal more than a pattern of imagery with which to approximate the ideal, but is the very manifestation of the ideal according to Kant's romantic philosophy and is appropriately the very first topic discussed in the *Critique*. What represents to Edwards a fairly good gauge of either the viciousness or the virtuousness of created wills, all of which to Edwards can in their essences be fitted into no more than these two categories, represents to Kant the phenomena of Reason, which in Kant's humanist discourse contains plentiful, perhaps infinite, diversity. Modern interpretations of the protomodernism of Edwards's aesthetic metaphors are Kantian readings that would be better, and more fully employed reading Kant.[25]

What is most remarkable about Edwards's applications of Locke's idealism and of aesthetic metaphors to the analysis of Grace is that in neither does he deviate at all from a discourse centered on a sovereign God. That he departs from this discourse when discussing personal religious experience seems likely to modern retrospect because the personal experience of God is a primary concern of modern religion, which narrows or eliminates

the gap between divinity and humanity. The intention of the present reading is to show that when writing on this subject Edwards successfully
traverses the edge of the theist discursive pattern and does not fall away
toward the center of the humanist one. The same intent will guide the
following reading of those documents which have been seen by modern
scholarship as most clearly anticipating humanist discourse. Edwards's
descriptions of what God feels like to him, and his attempts to describe
what God feels like to others, appear most to resemble the visionary experiences described in modern religious writings, and they have accordingly
been seized upon by modern studies. The final argument for Edwards's
theism must expose the familiarity of these documents, apparently the
most accessible of his writings, to be superficial.

4. Conversion

The structure of the work of redemption is comprised of "very unequal
divisions" of time in Edwards's discourse of Providence. This form reflects
the distinction that temporal importance, determined by the prominence of
events or by the lengths of historical periods themselves, is no measure of
true importance. Edwards's account of the process by which the individual
Christian is redeemed implies a similar disparity between biography and
conversion. A likeness exists between the ahistorical redemption of the
world and arbitrary salvation of a soul: "The increase of gospel light, and
the progress of the work of redemption, as it respects the church in general, from its erection to the end of the world, is similar to the progress of
the same work, and the same light, in a particular soul, from the time of its
conversion, till it is perfected and crowned with glory. Sometimes the light
shines brighter, and at other times more obscurely; sometimes grace prevails, at other times it seems to languish for a great while altogether; now
corruption prevails, and then grace revives again." The irregularity of conversion denies any relationship between it and personality. It originates
independently of the natural origin of a person, and it develops independently of his subsequent natural experience. The lives of the saints,
whether reported in the Bible or testified to by New Englanders during the
awakenings of the eighteenth century, are characterized by the conflict
between their natural selves and the divine inspirations that intermittently
and unpredictably supersede them.[26]

Edwards hesitates to confirm conversions that are said to have occurred
in a progressive series of steps for the same reason that he suspects testimonies of particular religious experiences that are recollected in sensational imagery. Both kinds of testimony confuse divine with natural
agencies; the former implicitly challenges God's sovereignty by subordinating the dispensation of Grace to a rational schedule, just as the latter

implicitly does through an idolatrous emphasis on the beauty and power of natural things. Testimonies need not contain "an account of the particular steps and method, by which the Holy Spirit . . . wrought and brought about those great essential things of Christianity" because conversions are more apt to occur through "those manifest evidences of a supernatural power, wonderfully and *suddenly* causing a great change." This defense of abrupt conversions in *Religious Affections* amounts to a defense of the entire Great Awakening against those critics to whom any excessive display of religious emotion automatically betrays enthusiasm. It does not contradict Edwards's own warnings, both in *Religious Affections* and elsewhere, against the enthusiastic indulgence of ecstasy for ecstasy's sake; rather, it states another dualism of theist discourse, according to which divine actions interrupt rather than complement the course of nature. Much as Edwards cannot express Providence as working gradually toward the Day of Judgment, so can he not say that Grace grows incrementally in the heart of a saint: "The conversion of the heart is not a work thus gradually wrought, but at once appears by Christ's converting the soul."[27]

Both Providence and Grace are brought to pass unnaturally because both are destined to accomplish the perfect segregation of Divinity from nature. Edwards can estimate the validity of particular evidences of Grace, despite his admission that election cannot be determined with certainty in this world, by asking how clearly they seem to anticipate this goal. All "prelibations" of the joys of a holy afterlife ought to foreshadow the abrupt removal of the soul from earth to heaven, and all should therefore noticeably loosen natural ties. A person is more evidently a saint as he is recognized to be more farsighted, and less attentive to his immediate interests, since "as grace increases, the field opens more and more to a distant view, until the soul is swallowed up with the vastness of the object." The exchange of a near for the distant prospect is not recommended by Edwards to encourage actual migration from home to a more religiously and philosophically inspiring wilderness; the resemblance between Edwards's description and the solitary contemplation of nature recommended by later romantic naturalists is another phenomenon of modern retrospect. The "distant view" is for Edwards figurative, representing the absence of all visible things that to him merely distract from religious devotion. Although the saint's conversion draws toward a Divinity that is periodically as sensible to him as any natural object, its manifestation to others, even those who may themselves be among the elect, is seen mainly in his being drawn away from even the most essential and gratifying pleasures of natural life.[28]

Because Edwards assumes that the virtue of a person is not just unrelated to his natural life but frequently opposed to it, he is especially skeptical about the importance of those circumstances which seem most influential in the formation of natural identity. Thus birth and childhood, which are celebrated as sources of inspiration by the romantics, possess no intrinsic religious value for Edwards. At best, the child may serve as a representative of the relative absence of corruption, juvenile meekness signifying not so much a positive humility as a lack of the vanities that are acquired in later life. More often Edwards mentions children as examples of a vitality and a closeness to nature that inhibits piety. "Young people are especially apt to be taken with the pleasing things of this world" he admonishes in one of his sermons, and the sudden and unforced willingness of the young people of Northampton to leave off "frolicking" seems so miraculous to him that he cites the reformation as one of the most dramatic signs of the advent of the awakenings in the town.[29]

The same concern that leads Edwards to discount the religious significance of youth prompts him to pay greater attention to the experiences and testimonies of old age. Deathbed utterances acquire virtually oracular authority for theists because spoken from the perspective of persons who are "between two worlds." Edwards considers one nearly dead to be "the most capable to look on things as they are and judge aright of 'em" because he believes in a radical and qualitative distinction between this world and the next; someone on the verge of passing over from the lower to the higher realm is least distracted by the flesh and most likely to glimpse, and perhaps communicate the truth. Another instance of dualistic ontology, this fascination with the moment of death, or with near- or semi-dead states such as zombiism and somnambulism and catalepsy, remains prominent in later theism, present in the works of Gothic writers who, although evidently yearning for a greater certainty than theist epistemology allows, nevertheless cannot forget the theist distinction between nature and truth. The morbidities of Brockden Brown, Washington Irving, and Poe suggest that theism persists chronologically alongside humanism well into the nineteenth century in the United States. Humanist discourse eventually predominates, of course, and with this comes the disappearance of discourses of the metaphysics, and the physics, of the moment of death. To theists like Edwards, however, wisdom is especially likely to be available in the words of the dying, or of ascetics, or of the aged, who are closer than most to that vast metaphysical gap between earth and heaven.[30]

Dualist assumptions underlie Edwards's evaluations of all the individual conversions he considers to be genuine, and they also determine the style and structure of his reports of conversions, leading to consistent emphases of certain aspects of the lives of saints and to consistent, often surprising, omissions of others. David Brainerd provides Edwards with perhaps the most persuasive, and certainly the most extensive testimony of a gracious awakening and a gracious disposition. Edwards claims, in his commentary on Brainerd's *Journal*, to be personally convinced of Brainerd's election, and to be desirous of communicating this conviction in his editing and publication of the *Journal*. The result does not seem very compelling according to modern biographical or autobiographical standards. Edwards makes little attempt to select among the repetitious entries, including so many as to give the impression of a moment-by-moment record of the waxing and waning of divine inspiration in Brainerd's heart, nor does he try more clearly to organize the journal by giving the biographical details that Brainerd invariably leaves out. A typical entry that Edwards reproduces without comment merely reports the gist of a religious thought and gives the time and place of occurrence: "Dec. 16: Rode to Derby; and had some sweet thoughts on the road; especially on the essence of our salvation by Christ, from these words, *Thou shalt call him home, Jesus,* etc." Modern interest in the appearance of the New England countryside through which Brainerd travels and of the New England Indians with whom he becomes acquainted during his missionary ordeals is satisfied neither by Brainerd's account nor by Edwards's editing.[31]

What may seem careless or unsophisticated inattention to certain kinds of detail represents a pious obeisance, on both Brainerd's and Edwards's part, to the supremacy of divine inspiration over natural cause in the conversion of the soul. The fact that one of Brainerd's religious affections is felt on December 16 on the road to Derby is not elaborated upon because the fact has no influence on the kindling of the religious affection. The meagerness of this description is not without purpose; it fulfills the aim of having the event appear miraculously out of the ordinary. Like all traditional anecdotes of marvelous happenings, revived in the twentieth century by Robert Ripley, Brainerd's entry gives a few circumstantial details not so as to explain the happening through them, but to imply the independence of the happening from such common determinants as dates, names, and locations. This kind of description shows an event to be historically a fact and at the same time historically inexplicable, a kind of description whose prototype in the theist discourse of Judeo-Christian antiquity can be taken to be the Book of Ezekiel, which introduces the most bizarre vision of the Old Testament with the mundane specification that "it came to pass in the thirtieth year, in the fourth month, in the fifth day of the month, as I was among the captives by the river of Chebar" (Ezek. 1:1).

Each of the episodes of Brainerd's *Journal* individually demonstrates the discontinuity between his natural and gracious life. The listing of them, which amounts to the structure of the *Journal,* upholds the same distinction. That his life "is a constant mixture of consolations and conflicts" is declared by Brainerd not as an admission of having failed to discover any form in his life but as the implicit claim that Grace comes to him unsummoned, granted by God rather than simulated by his own enthusiasm. Edwards approves this desultory structure, and comments in his afterword to the *Journal* that he considers it one of the primary evidences of the validity of Brainerd's testimony: "I am far from thinking, and so was [Brainerd], that clearness of the *order* of experience is, in any measure, of equal importance with the clearness of their *nature.*" Brainerd's individual religious experiences are manifestly disconnected from any particulars of his natural life, so their collection in his *Journal* properly denies any gradual, orderly progression toward salvation. God shows His work so evidently in Brainerd's conversion that God not only comes to Brainerd unexpectedly, but in inverse proportion as God is sought. God reveals Himself to Brainerd and through Brainerd to Edwards only after Brainerd has left off striving for Grace: "While he opposed [sin], he was the subject of no such mercy; though he so earnestly sought it, and prayed for it with so much care, and strictures in religion: but when once his opposition is fully subdued, and he is brought to submit to the truths . . . then the mercy he sought for is granted." Broken-hearted and nearly despairing in his fruitless search for Grace, the Christian who suddenly and effortlessly receives salvation becomes convinced of his own helplessness and God's omnipotence in the redemption of sinners. So affectively increasing piety and thus promoting the glorification of God, this kind of conversion is especially plausible to Edwards, leading him to endorse Abigail Hutchinson's almost identical experience in his *Faithful Narrative* and to trust the validity of his own, similarly unexpected awakening as described in the account of his own awakening.[32]

Only after the disappointment of Brainerd's expectations is recognized as indirect proof of God's intervention in his life can Edwards's description of Brainerd's death be understood. Ecstatically anticipating the final leave-taking, Brainerd is seized by several false paroxysms. Hoping to end his life, symmetrically, on the sabbath, having been awakened on one, he is made to die on a Friday, the dating of the advent and termination of natural life being irrelevant from the eternal perspective, a distinction reflected by what seems today the overly fastidious piety of those seventeenth-century English Separatists who record dates only of conversion and never of birth. Most pathetically, Brainerd's wish to die peacefully is brutally denied: "He said to those about him, that it was another thing to die, than people imagined; explaining himself to mean that they were not aware what *bodily* pain and anguish is undergone before death." That Brainerd's final hours are actually characterized by these events and utterances does not oblige Edwards to report them, who elsewhere shows no such fidelity. Edwards chooses to include this information because to him this information illustrates the religious truth that the request of even so faithful a servant as Brainerd need not be granted by a sovereign God. Edwards can relate that Brainerd's mouth is full of pieties at one moment—" 'Oh that dear book! that lovely book! I shall soon see it opened!' "—and that it is full of pus at the next—"what he brought up by expectoration, seemed as it were mouthfuls of almost clear pus"—not because he is naively unaware of the apparent incongruity of the two images, but because he believes Brainerd's salvation is complemented and confirmed by the physical torment he suffers. In ignoring Brainerd's particular, and somewhat vain hope that his death conform to pattern, God fulfills Brainerd's general, and truly pious desire to surrender himself wholly to the divine will.[33]

The conversions that Edwards selects to represent the awakening in the Connecticut River Valley in his "Faithful Narrative" are similar in many ways to Brainerd's. As is the case in his editing of the *Journal,* he omits all circumstantial details of saints' lives that are not directly associated with their religious experiences. After saying virtually nothing about Abigail Hutchinson's background in a brief introductory paragraph (her name is mentioned only once in the eight pages Edwards devotes to her case) he proceeds with a surprising and seemingly fastidious regard for detail to report that her first religious experience occurs on a Monday. The sudden mention of a date, especially following such a cursory review of the entire span of her former life, functions as does the scarce particulars of Brainerd's *Journal* not to subordinate the moment of awakening to calendar time but implicitly to distinguish the awakening as a miraculous intervention. In addition to being unrelated to the circumstances of her natural life, Abigail's conversion comes, as Brainerd's does, independently of her seeking; the Holy Spirit foreshortens her energetic striving for Grace, arriving before she feels she earns salvation by religious duties. The result of her awakening is an increasing asceticism, and a growing desire for solitude that resembles Brainerd's assumption of missionary duties: "She told her sister that had lived near the heart of town, that she once thought it pleasant to live in the middle of the town, but now, says she, 'I think it much more pleasant to sit and see the wind blowing the trees, and to behold what God has made.'" Both Brainerd's travels and Abigail's less extensive wanderings are portrayed more as escapes from the distractions of life than as journeys to an unspoiled region that positively assists religious contemplation, which is another reason why Brainerd's descriptions of the wilderness are so scant, and which explains why Abigail identifies the value of the countryside as the absence of men as much as the presence of God. And, in keeping with the ascetic character of her awakening and subsequent religious duties, Abigail's death dramatizes, perhaps even more climactically than Brainerd's, the warring of virtue against the flesh that election requires. Edwards relates the symptoms of her diphtheria with the same clinical detachment with which he relates those of Brainerd's tuberculosis because in both cases he interprets the humiliation of the body as proof of the exaltation of the soul. Abigail's agonies are particularly illustrative; the swelling of her throat first prevents her from eating, anticipating the liberation of her spirit from fleshly appetite, and eventually prevents her from speaking as well, anticipating her passage into a higher realm from which there is no direct communication with those left behind.[34]

The account of Phoebe Bartlett's awakening follows in a similar manner. Stricken by the Holy Spirit, she retreats immediately to the solitude of a closet for "secret prayer." This sequestering is remarkable because of Phoebe's youth; Edwards considers children to be by nature unwilling to isolate themselves from the pleasures of play and company. Again, the first evidence of awakening is withdrawal, the spontaneity of which is strikingly exemplified in the action of a child whose natural affection for the world is presumably more intense than that of either the melancholy Brainerd or the sickly Abigail, and whose understanding of the virtue of self-denial is doubtless not so sophisticated nor so strongly held as that of the two elder saints. But even a child may absorb a sufficient idea of the form of piety to closet himself in an ostentatious show of religious duty, a childish vanity that Edwards confesses is behind his own retreat to the "booth" in his report of his early awakening, so Phoebe's solitary prayer is followed not by the reward of religious ecstasy, but by continuous fits of hysteria. (Edwards interpolates an irrelevant detail in this description as well, noting that she had "four times of crying" during a particular day.) Rather than answer the summons even of Phoebe's primitive self-abasement, the Holy Spirit brings satisfaction, as it does to Abigail, when least expected: "she continued thus earnestly crying [despite her mother's entreaties], and taking on for some time, till at length she suddenly ceased crying, and began to smile, and presently said with a smiling countenance, 'Mother, the kingdom of heaven is come to me!' "[35]

The "faithful narrative" is designed as a public defense of the awakenings in and around Northampton to an informed Puritan audience. Edwards can anticipate charges that he is condoning enthusiasm in publishing the testimonies, and his choice and description of them are undoubtedly calculated to be least offensive to pious skeptics. A private, and much less deliberated account of the demeanor of one whom Edwards believes to be a saint is his complimentary portrait of his future wife, Sarah Pierrepont, jotted down in a youthful, and probably not just religious surge of admiration. If Edwards were ever tempted to confuse natural and holy attributes, he is in this "lyric panegyric," as one modern critic calls the paragraph, which is identified by another modern critic as a protoromantic poem inspired by a vision of the interpenetration of carnal and heavenly beauties as yet uninhibited by the Puritan theology that Edwards later allows to prohibit such joys. But despite having no need to demonstrate his orthodoxy—moreover, a compliment meant for Sarah's eyes seems better to promote Edwards's suit by praising her than by praising God—he says no more about her person or her accomplishments than he does about either Brainerd's, Abigail's, or Phoebe's. The particular person, Sarah Pierrepont, disappears, in the second clause of the first sentence of Edwards's description, as another Presence becomes more apparent: "They say there is a young lady in ———, who is beloved of that Great Being, who made and rules the world, and that there are certain seasons in which this Great Being, in some way or other invisible, comes to her and fills her mind with exceeding sweet delight, and that she hardly cares for anything, except to meditate on him—that she expects after a while to be received up where he is, to be raised up out of the world and caught up to heaven." Edwards's attention shifts immediately from the historical facts of Sarah's age and home, which seem as irrelevant as the circumstantial details of Brainerd's or Abigail's awakenings, to the religious truths signified by Sarah's piety. In humbly effacing herself before God and in removing herself from the world the better to worship Him, Sarah herself encourages disregard of her nature. The most ardent praise Edwards can bestow is to acknowledge her piety and to imply that she assists his own. He recognizes that since she is destined for heaven, her soul is most clearly revealed in actions that antici-pate her taking leave of earth: "She will sometimes go about from place to place, singing sweetly; and seems to be always full of joy and pleasure; and no one knows for what. She loves to be alone, walking in fields and groves, and seems to have some one invisible always conversing with her." Her pleasure derives entirely from an appreciation of invisible things, the places she wanders through having no effect on her serenity, and her most characteristic utterances are in a mysterious tongue to an invisible compan-ion. Even assuming Sarah an exceptionally pious thirteen-year-old, and thus liable to be taken by Edwards's discovery in her of an asceticism beyond her years, it is remarkable that he woos her in this love note without even a passing reference to the lesser beauties of her intellect and person.[36]

When he is least defensive, and presumably far from wholly mature, in a piece of juvenile marginalia intended to be read only by its recipient, Ed-wards's boyish flattery in every stylistic and structural particular still pre-serves the dualism of his latest and most circumspect theological treatises. A discursive pattern like theism is deeper and more pervasive than even the most fervently held opinion. Edwards is not just mindful that God is sovereign. God's sovereignty is to him the condition of thinking and writ-ing. To Edwards, beyond God's sovereignty is nothing, nonthought and silence, against God's sovereignty only sin, rebellion, and blasphemy. Ed-wards does not avoid the pantheism or the lyricism or the symbolism that modern critics find in passages like this one. He positively thinks and expresses otherwise. What ought most to strike modern scholarship is that writing of all sorts, from theological treatises to imprecatory sermons to *billet doux*, can be accomplished according to a pattern other than its own humanist one.

The love note to Sarah is no more simply "found" and then simply reproduced than are any of the many other unpublished writings of Ed-wards that are translated from Beinecke Library manuscripts into such collections as Miller's *Images or Shadows of Divine Things* or, most recently, Stein's *Apocalyptic Writings* and Anderson's *Scientific and Philosophical Writ-ings*. This industry helps foster the illusion that Edwards's writings, more than those of other, more fully published writers are "objective" because some significant quantity of them remains as yet unavailable and thus seem liable, by deviating from or conforming to the already published corpus, to alter or to confirm at some future moment the current understanding of Edwards. Phenomenologically, all "discovery," including even that of the physical sciences, reveals only the conditions that make "discovery" possible, and so, phenomenologically, the documents of Edwards's writing, including especially the ones he seems never to have intended publishing, are the products of consciousness, not just that of Edwards, who enjoys the mere chronological priority of having written them, but of others who read them and deem them sufficiently worthy of being read by others to preserve them, and of still others who continually select among them, according to the same criterion, those to be published. No additional entry from Edward's notebooks simply happens to become known, nor does an entry, through some immanent, "objective" meaning, either detract from or contribute to any interpretation of Edwards; rather, interpretations always already possess the writings, and genuinely differing interpretations will make of the same documents genuinely different phenomena.

The love note to Sarah is selected by Aldridge as entries are selected by Miller, Stein, and Anderson, so as to supplement, or, in the case of Stein's and Anderson's collections, to qualify and complicate, the modern text of Edwards's writings. Similar principles of selection guide the editing of all of Edwards's manuscripts. Before publishing the fifth volume of the Yale edition for Edwards's works, Stein chooses a separate entry from Edwards's notebooks for publication in *New England Quarterly*. His critical commentary appears modest to the point of invisibility, in keeping with the unobtrusive, apparently just heuristic style preferred by modern editors. But the choice of the entry, which discusses a prodigy of nature, the rainbow; the title of the article, which links Edwards's exegesis to the romantic faculty of "poetic imagination"; and the concluding comments, which suggest how Edwards does at times set aside traditional Protestant strictures against the medieval four-fold hermeneutic of Scripture so as to show "a delightfully different," and interpretively more adventurous side of his mind when thinking figuratively about Grace—all show that Stein presents the entry as yet another phenomenon of Edwards's precocity.[37]

The present reading of Edwards's discourse of Grace seizes the entry differently, and in so doing turns it into a different phenomenon. Edwards's analysis of the rainbow does allude to physics in the optical diffraction of the sun's rays, to the meteorological association of the rainbow with storm, and to the physiological constitution of the rainbow as droplets of water. But Edwards's analysis consistently subordinates nature as providing only passive and imperfect media for, in the order of his presentation, the beauty, action, and being of God. Thus it consistently represents experience according to the theist pattern; in such an informal comment again the pattern can be made to seem inescapable and adherence to the pattern made to seem reflex, as in the note to Sarah.

Edwards begins by comparing the declension, sun—rainbow—mankind, to the declension God—Christ—man: "the Light of the Sun is more beautifull & pleasant to our weak Eyes appearing thus in a Cloud where the Dazzling brightness of it is Removd and its pleasantness Retained & illustrated then when we behold it in the Sun Directly. So the Divine Perfections as appearing in [Christ] God man are brought down to our Manner of Conception & are represented to the Greatest advantage to such weak Creatures as we are appear[ing] not Glaring and terrifying but Easy Sweet and Inviting." Neither the rainbow nor Christ contains, ontologically, nor can man's experience of them perceive, aesthetically, the beauty of their sources. Rather, both diminish the essence of their origins in refracting them; the rainbow becomes the lower analogue of the sun, just as all of nature is the lower analogue of the Creator, which implies also that the rainbow, no matter how remarkable, indeed, because of its special beauty, is no more to be appreciated for its own sake than is any creature idolatrously to be worshiped. Edwards continues by noting the association between the bow and the rain that accompanies or precedes it, but he does so in a way that similarly deemphasizes the physics of the rainbow in the process of stressing its metaphysics. He ignores the meteorological connection between the bow and its natural cause and cites instead only the contrast between the two and the sucession in which they occur. That Edwards is interested in and knowledgeable about the physics of the rainbow is indicated in another, and even longer notebook entry that analyzes it exclusively from a scientific perspective. That he would omit any such analysis in this one indicates once again his distinguishing radically between secondary, natural etiologies and the primary, supernatural one in the religious apprehension of nature. Just as Creation and Miracle happen in spite of nature according to Edward's theism, so does the rainbow according to its theological hermeneutic, established in the Bible in the story of the flood, represent a sudden, arbitrary, and surprising intervention by God in the naturally stormy way of the world. Edwards concludes his commentary by likening the unusual, almost monstrous combination of light and water in the composition of the rainbow to the miraculous grafting of spiritual goodness onto natural corruption that Grace achieves: "The Drops of Rain Reflecting the Light of the Sun in the Rain bow fitly Represent the Saints for in them fire and water are mixed together which fitly Represents the Contrary principles that are in the Saints flesh & Spirit." Again, Edwards's careless, unguarded commentary is perfectly consistent with his best-armed theology. The saint is created by an addition to his nature that is no more intrinsic, or even compatible to his nature than fire is to water. The relatively incongruous makeup of the rainbow suggests the absolute duality of the makeup of a saint.[38]

Modern interpretations of the humanism of Edwards's discourse of Grace take many forms, including the apparently least tendentious one of collections of unpublished entries from Edwards's notebooks. In addition there is Miller's contention that the ways in which preparation for Grace is described by Edwards and other seventeenth- and eighteenth-century Protestants insinuate that "the leap to a saving understanding proceeds out of the natural," and that in promoting awakening in the New World Edwards has to abandon a theory of Grace "that would not work in the American wilderness" in favor of a more naturalistic one, and there are the similar, later conclusions of Delattre that the love of man is to Edwards the avenue to the love of God, and of Tracy that the conversions in Northampton are not at all "surprising," despite the title of Edwards's narrative of them, because they are so well prepared by Edwards's working "strenuously to revitalize the faith of his flock." And there are also the contentions that Edwards's writings on Grace imply the integration of the personality, which is also perhaps first and probably most influentially stated by Miller and repeated in slightly altered form by Carse and Fiering, to both of whom a gracious disposition becomes habitual, consolidating action and intention in ways that anticipate modern existential philosophy or behavioral psychology. These interpretations must either ignore or transform into some subtle kind of indirection many passages in which Edwards explicitly contradicts these interpretations. Sometimes he does this in words that are the same as or similar to ones they use, such as that "to speak of a habit of grace as a natural disposition . . . seems in some respects to carry a wrong idea with it . . . [for] if God should take away His Spirit out of the soul, all habits and acts of grace would of themselves cease as immediately as light ceases in a room when a candle is carried out," or "that which is commonly called the *covenant of grace,* is only *Christ's open and free offer of life,* whereby He holds it out in His hand to sinners, and offers it without conditions. Faith cannot be called the *condition* of receiving, for it is the *receiving* itself; Christ holds out, and believers receive." Statements like these are consistent with one another and with everything Edwards says about Grace with the confidence of being definitive, and they can be made to appear consistent with everything else he says or implies on other subjects. They are certainly most easily read as exemplifying his discourse of Grace, and as doing so expressly.[39]

5. Personal Narrative

Finally, there is Edwards's account of his own conversion, several of whose paragraphs seem best to support arguments for his supposed modernity. The final task of this reading of Edwards' discourse of Grace is to attach to the theist discursive pattern the document that is central to humanist interpretations.

What Edwards considers to have been his true conversion is related without any mention of time, place, or persons. Companions and locales are associated with preceding false awakenings. The founding of the cult of the booth in the swamp represents an ostentatious, and therefore false asceticism; Edwards concludes this because the virtuousness that accompanies the retreat is short-lived and represents but an adventurous competition among Puritan boys for whom heroism is no doubt associated with pietism. A second false awakening is reported to occur during his student years at Yale, where the pressure to experience Grace is no doubt intense, at least among pious classmates. These two incidents, which take up just the first three paragraphs of the account, are all that Edwards says about his childhood and adolescence. Because he intends to describe conversion rather than maturation, because he believes conversion to occur outside the course of personal history, he skips immediately to the time when his "concern [was] now wrought more by inward struggles and conflicts, and self-reflections," upon which external events have no apparent effect.[40]

The circumstances of the genuine conversion are not given. It is described as a miraculous acceptance of the doctrine least acceptable to human nature: "From my childhood up, my mind had been wont to be full of objections against the doctrine of God's sovereignty, in choosing whom he would to eternal life, and rejecting whom he pleased. . . . It used to appear like a horrible doctrine to me. But I remember the time very well, when I seemed to be convinced, and fully satisfied, as to this sovereignty of God, and his justice in thus eternally disposing of men, according to his sovereign pleasure." The abandoning of self-interest is perceptual as well as religious. Edwards describes none of the particulars of this central event because to him they are irrelevant. He goes on to claim that the abstract style of the description reflects his unspecific recollection of the conversion: "But never could [I] give an account, how, or by what means, I was thus convinced; not in the least imagining, in the the time of it, nor a long time after, that there was an extraordinary influence of God's spirit in it." Nature does not contain the means by which to convince the mind of the equity of predestination, because nature is governed by the preservation of the self, so the most pious account Edwards can give of "that wonderful alteration in my mind" that has endured "from that day to this" is no specific account at all. This account is neither careless nor off-hand. Edwards omits those aspects of biography which are inappropriate according to his lights.[41]

The subsequent descriptions of visionary experiences are designed to illustrate the new perception that Grace bestows. Some details of time and place are included, but they function, as the style of the account of the conversion anticipates, to distinguish by contrast the more excellent, holy things to which Edwards has become sensitized.

After noting his mysteriously ecstatic enjoyment of the passage from 1

Timothy that pays homage abstractly to God's sovereignty, Edwards recalls a special fondness for another, more sensational passage from The Song of Solomon, 2:1: "I am the Rose of Sharon, the lily of the valleys." Edwards's affection for this Scripture may tend toward a confusion between the beauty of flowers and the beauty of Christ; but Edwards's explanation of the mood with which this passage is associated shows that it helps detach him from nature: "[I] found, from time to time, an inward sweetness, that used, as it were, to carry me away in my contemplations; in what I know not how to express otherwise, than by a calm, sweet abstraction of soul from all the concerns of this world; and a kind of vision, or fix'd ideas and imaginations, of being alone in the mountains, or some solitary wilderness, far from all mankind, sweetly conversing with Christ, and wrapt and swallowed up in God." The sensational imagery from Solomon does not encourage Edwards to smell flowers; rather than wedding him to nature, it refers him to an "inward sweetness" whose sensation is derived from nothing tangible, a taste cited often in theist discourses of Grace to connote less a sensation than an instantaneous, nondiscursive, and hence ineffable communication from God, as in Thomas Shepard's use almost a century before Edwards, in which sweetness is figuratively "a most clear evidence of truth, as tasting of honey is to the tongue, Wherein without the discourse the soul knows certainly honey is sweet." Edwards likens spiritual enjoyment to the solitude of a desert, which he describes, as he does the sites of all truly pious sequestrations, as being void of things that might distract the awakened mind with natural ideas and pleasures. And, because he is concerned about distinguishing an invisible state from the natural locale to which language must refer it, he calls attention to the imprecision of his metaphor, knowing "not how to express" the spiritual preoccupation of the saint other than by comparison to "a kind of vision, or fix'd ideas and imaginations" of waste places, all of which, because they refer to natural sensation in approximating the absence of natural sensation, cannot precisely depict a mind emptied of conventional ideas while being "wrapt and swallowed" by the new simple idea of Grace. Edwards' figurative setting implies distinctions that are made repeatedly explicit in the famous biblical description of the miracle wrought to confirm the piety of Elijah in contrast to the idolatrous sacrifices of the pagan priests of Baal: "and a great strong wind rent the mountains, and brake in pieces the rocks before the Lord; but the Lord was not in the wind: and after the wind an earthquake; but the Lord was not in the earthquake: / And after the earthquake a fire; but the Lord was not in the fire: and after the fire a still small voice." (1 Kings 19:11). God speaks in a voice so as to dissociate His message from the noises of wind, earthquake, and fire, and in a "still, small" voice so as further to dissociate Himself from the natural clamor He has so effortlessly and contemptuously caused. Edwards's setting is discursively identical to this ancient theist one, and implies, no less clearly than the Scripture declares, the placelessness of God, as well as the insensateness of the graciously inspired saint.[42]

"The appearance of everything was altered" to Edwards after his awakening in a way that diminishes the vividness of his perception of the natural settings where his visionary experiences occur. An intimate, moving discussion may have taken place between Edwards and his father immediately before his vision of God's majesty in the pasture; only a brief mention of the conversation is included, however, because Edwards believes his subsequent religious affection to be independent of his filial one. The pasture itself may have powerfully affected Edwards's natural sensibilities, but the "clouds and sky" above it are barely glanced at because Edwards believes that he apprehends the spiritual beauty of God independently of the natural beauties of the place. The vision itself is portrayed in a list of paradoxes—a necessary indulgence of " 'mixed modes' (as Mr. Locke calls them) that appertain to moral and spiritual matters" and that must hence contradict man's simple ideas of nature.[43]

After the vision in the pasture Edwards's "sense of divine things gradually increased" at the expense of his sensitivity to nature. He no longer needs the emptiness of waste places to assist religious concentration; his perception has itself begun to overlook the material reality of natural things and to regard them only as shadows of Divinity: "there seem'd to be, as it were, a calm, sweet cast, or appearance of divine glory, in almost every thing. God's excellency, his wisdom, his purity and love, seemed to appear in every thing; in the sun, moon and stars; in the clouds, and blue sky; in the grass, flowers, trees; in the water, and all nature; which used greatly to fix my mind. I often used to sit and view the moon, for a long time; and so in the day time, spent much time in viewing the clouds and sky, to behold the sweet glory of God in these things: in the mean time, singing forth with a low voice, my contemplations of the Creator and Redeemer." Nature in this description is inert and unprepossessing. Only a single adjective is attached to a part of nature, and no part of nature takes a verb. Prominence is reserved for God alone, by the listing of His invisibile attributes—"excellency," "wisdom," "purity," and "love"—and implicitly by the listing of the many diverse natural things that all are recognized as subordinate to His glory. To Edwards's awakened mind the features of the landscape have a hyponotic effect. Like a swaying pendant, they inspire not a lucid examination of themselves, but a trancelike communion with invisible things. Edwards does not delight in nature naturalistically, but rather stares at nature with a fixity that decreases his attentiveness to his immediate surroundings. This kind of contemplation leads to a mode of expression that not only omits mention of the natural beauties of the earth, but aspires, through the stylization of incantation and song, somewhat to transcend the natural roots of language. Incantation attempts to conjure a meaning that transcends the explicit meaning of words; Edwards notes Abigail

Hutchinson's continuous repetition of "wisdom, justice, goodness, and truth" as a sign of her conversion in the *Faithful Narrative*. To sing words also implies an attempt to say more than words themselves can convey; Edwards interprets the spontaneous breaking into three-part harmony by a congregation not tutored in the art as a miracle that signals the beginning of awakenings in Northampton. The solitary singing that is the fruit of Edwards's own new sense of things represents his search for a medium more adequate than language to express his supernatural joy. Inarticulateness is the predominant style of all theist discourse of the ideal, whether the Pagan one of classical antiquity, the Hebraic one of the Old Testament, or the Christian one of the New Testament, or of such later Christian writings as Edwards's, or even the quasi-secular one of such decadent theists as Poe. Poe's heterodox but still theist idealism declares the existence of "supernal," transcendent realities no more accessible to his mind or words than God is to Edwards's, glimpsed only in "a class of fancies, of exquisite delicacy, which are *not* thoughts, and to which *as yet* I have found it absolutely impossible to adapt language." Poe's own discourse of Divinity, though marginal to his oeuvre, contains stylistic humilities that would not appear anomalous if inserted verbatim into Edwards's theology, such as that words, Poe complains, like " 'God,' 'spirit,' and some other expressions of which the equivalents exist in all languages [are] by no means the expression of an idea—but an effort at one. It stands for the possible attempt at an impossible conception."[44]

The overcoming of a fear of thunderstorms that Edwards cites to illustrate his converted perception is one incident in which nature seems to take an active role. But in the context of the discussion of his coming to love the doctrine of predestination, the thunder represents not the power of nature, but, as in the famous verse from 1 Kings, the power of God acting against nature: "And scarce any thing, among all the works of nature, was so sweet to me as thunder and lightning. Formerly, nothing had been so terrible to me. I used to be a person uncommonly terrified with thunder; and it used to strike me with terror, when I saw a thunder-storm rising. But now, on the contrary, it rejoiced me. I felt God at the first appearance of a thunder-storm. And used to take the opportunity at such times to fix myself to view the clouds, and see the lightnings play, and hear the majestic and awful voice of God's thunder: which often times was exceeding entertaining, leading me to sweet contemplations of my great and glorious God." The thunder is the natural emblem of God's sovereignty, and Edwards's sudden coming to rejoice in it is equivalent to the reversal of his attitude toward God's sovereignty. In both cases the change is instantaneous and inexplicable by any natural cause; there is no selfish reason for a man to love the Being that arbitrarily disposes his eternal welfare, nor is there any selfish reason for him to love a natural force that can accidentally kill him. The thunderstorm is not tamed by Edwards's description of it, nor does his sense of his own strength grow to make him feel equal to it, both of which transformations would promote a greater attachment to nature. He is neither Whitman in *Song of Myself* nor Ahab in the typhoon—"At that moment in one of the intervals of profound darkness, following the flashes, a voice was heard . . . and almost at the same instant a volley of thunder peals overhead. 'Who's there?' 'Old Thunder!' said Ahab." In Edwards's account both the lethal potential of the storm and Edwards's vulnerability remain, making his affection reveal no defiance but an abandonment of self-interest and a willingness to leave this earth behind. As is the case in the presence of less imposing natural settings, Edwards comes finally to ignore the thunder and, in a "still small voice," to "sing or chant forth [his] meditations; to speak his thoughts in soliloquies, and speak with a singing voice."[45]

Considering the principles Edwards states for defining the new simple idea of Grace and the way he judges the testimonies of others, his account of his own conversion is not exceptional, either in parts or as a whole. It is virtually silent about the circumstances of his life, even when they must have been striking, as during his removal to the unfamiliar territory of New York during his first ministry, because the activity of his personal life is inversely related to that of his soul. It is most expansive about those times when Edwards is cut off from temporal affairs—in sickbed, in solitary meditation—because then he is farthest from the wickedness that predominates when he is most "in himself." The paragraphs of Edwards's account seem disconnected because most of them report the behavior of a God who obeys no creature, not Edwards, not plausibility, not time. Discontinuity signifies no merely superficial appearance of Edwards's account, as one modern critic claims; discontinuity is the very structure of theophany according to the theist discursive pattern, and theophany is the proper theist name for what has come to be called in modern scholarship Edwards's "personal narrative."[46]

The visionary experience whose description is most detailed in Edwards's account of his awakening occurs in the woods during one of many solitary horseback rides. Although the situation and the landscape promise to be vivid, they vanish immediately as Edwards receives the new simple idea that derives from neither: "Once, as I rid out into the woods for my health, *Anno* 1737; and having lit from my horse in a retired place, as my manner commonly has been, to walk for divine contemplation and prayer; I had a view, that for me was extraordinary, of the glory of the Son of God; as mediator between God and man; and his wonderful, great, full, pure and sweet grace and love, and meek and gentle condescension. This grace, that appear'd to me so calm and sweet, appear'd great above the heavens. The person of Christ appear'd ineffably excellent, with an excellency great enough to swallow up all thought and conception, which continued, as near as I can judge, about an hour; which kept me, the bigger part of the time, in a flood of tears, and weeping aloud. I felt withal, an ardency of soul to be, what I know not how to express, other than to be emptied and annihilated; to lie in the dust, and to be full of Christ alone."[47]

The facts that the vision occurred in 1737 and lasted for "about an hour" are irrelevant; that it happens on a particular date implies only that it can happen on any date, and that it has a duration measurable by the clock similarly implies its timelessness. Edwards's regular combining of religious duty with physical exercise cannot appoint a meeting with Christ; his religious meditations in the woods are habitual, whereas they are so rewarded by Christ only once. The vision itself is all the more conspicuously abstract after having been set in so specific a time and place. Christ is portrayed fulfilling the invisible function of "mediator" and embodying a string of abstract perfections: "glory," "wonderful, great, full, pure and sweet grace," "meek and gentle condescension." Edwards multiplies the attributes to make Christ appear not comprehensibly, but "ineffably excellent." And, in case this expression of divine beauty is not sufficiently supernatural, Edwards continues to mix the modes of his description, insisting paradoxically that those lovely features of Christ are at the same time awesome and distant, His Grace appearing "calm and sweet" and at the same time appearing to tower "great above the heavens" and to be "great enough to swallow all thought and conception." The emotional power of this vision stems from Edwards's experiencing the annihilation of both human and material nature that results from any intervention by God in the world. The "emptying" of the self is what leaves Edwards "weeping aloud" at the conclusion of the vision.

Edwards's account of his conversion is said not to have "vitalized" all of his recollections "through personal expression." It is said to reveal that "the lyric expression that Edwards wanted and needed to declare the work of God was captured for the future, for us, by those who knew it to be the art of man," which judgment stigmatizes Edwards as "a religious philosopher of abstractions, majestic and disembodied, and without poetry." These evaluations imply that Edwards might specify the emotional or circumstantial content of his religious experience, and that not to do so amounts only negatively to a failure to live up to "lyric," "poetic" standards inherent in all personal accounts of religious experience, which is to evaluate Edwards's account of his conversion according not to some neutral measure, the chimerical disinterest that exists only within the most successfully partial and widespread system of values, but to the romantic, and subsequently the modern principles of narrative and poetic art. Experience, of God or of any other phenomena, becomes "vital," or "lyric," by which is meant accessible both to the writer and, by him, to his readers, only when the objectivity of the world is taken to be potentially conquerable, and is achieved by romantic writers in ways that can seem to make Edwards's account of his conversion particularly disappointing; precisely the "mediatorial" function of Christ that Edwards cites to deter any possible impression of the visibility of Christ is asserted by Emerson in "The Lord's Supper" to be Christ's most human attribute, the one most deifying to man, whose example "teaches us to be like God," and precisely the paradoxes Edwards uses to abstract the ideal from nature are asserted by Thoreau in *Walden* to be sensible in everyday experience of ordinary nature, as in the many descriptions of the pond as manifesting simultaneously different and even opposite attributes, various colors, light and darkness, sky and earth, near and far, summer and winter, activity and passivity, whose example places ubiquity, quantifies infinity, dates the eternal. But the theist discursive pattern does not permit the kind of "personal expression" that modern criticism is taught by romanticism to demand of writers; "personal expression" is no more to be found in Edwards's few personal writings than in his voluminous other ones. The goal of his account of his conversion is reached in the sporadic final entries, in which both speaker and situation disappear: "On one Saturday night in particular, had a particular discovery of the excellency of the gospel of Christ, above all other doctrines." Not only is the irrelevance of the date and circumstances of this vision implied by the mention of the single detail that the vision occurs on a Saturday; the insignificance of the particular visionary is implied by the omission of the personal pronoun.[48]

Edwards's account appears faulty or underdeveloped only when forced to aspire toward the "personal expression" of the romantics. In the context of theism it is adequate, even artful, and belongs to a company of theist personal writings that can be made to intrigue modern retrospect because of their surprising, at first glance seemingly impossible lacunae, characterized by a recent phenomenological critic as an emphasis according to which "experience, personal experience, was largely beside the point." This classification is not *outré;* it comprehends a great number of writings, including those whose literary excellence is less controversial, according to modern criticism, than is that of Edwards's account, such as for example Poe's "Ligeia," in which the narrator's attempt to know his wife, and even to know himself, can be made to appear governed by the same epistemological and stylistic restraints that govern Edwards's descriptions of God—restraints that seem even more striking to modern retrospect in Poe's story, since they are applied to the knowledge and description of the more proximate ideals of the self and the self's closest kin, a beloved—and this classification includes writings that seem ideologically and generically unrelated to Edwards's account, such as for example Bartram's *Travels,* in which the self is described as ecstatically extinguished by illness in terms virtually identical to those Edwards uses to describe his prostrations, and also Franklin's so-called *Autobiography,* in which an exclusive concentration on behavior gives no more certain proof of inclination than that allowed by Edwards's analysis of the will.[49]

The account of Edwards's conversion proves the steadfastness of Edwards's theism. Whatever tendency there might be to make God accessible in recalling his own awakening is absent. Whatever interest he might have in analyzing the natural influences on the formation of his personality is not there. The account is unique only insofar as it bases its exploration of Divinity, more than any of Edwards's other writings, on his own awakening. That he relies on his own awakening only once, only after having been implored by an acolyte, and in so brief an account never meant for publication indicates the consistency with which Edwards doubts man's ability to gain or to communicate knowledge of God through even the most careful and inspired recounting of personal experience. According to this reading, the account of his conversion shows better than any other single one of Edwards's writings the difference between theism and humanism. The familiar discourse of personality that defines humanist autobiography and biography serves in this reading to distinguish by contrast the very different, lesser thing a person is according to the theist pattern of Edwards's reminiscence.

5

THEISM AND HUMANISM

One of the most essential features of the new history is probably this displacement of the discontinuous: its transference from the obstacle to the work itself; its integration into the discourse of the historian, where it no longer plays the role of an external factor that must be reduced, but that of a working concept.

—Foucault, *The Archaeology of Knowledge*

1. Introduction

This last chapter will expand the contention introduced in the first that theism be considered a separate discursive pattern in American literature. This position generates the intervening chapters on Edwards's discourses of Creation, of Providence, and of Grace, in that each of these chapters distinguishes between the theist discursive pattern of Edwards's writings and the humanist one that his writings are seen by modern retrospect to anticipate. Modern criticism will be opposed once again directly in the following, as it is in the first chapter, initially in readings that find a discursive affinity between the writings of Edwards and Franklin and a discursive difference between the writings of Edwards and Emerson, both of which findings will contest in various ways the unitary model of American culture, and finally in a deconstruction of the unitary model that will attempt to elaborate the reasons for its persistence in modern American cultural historiography, which analysis will reveal its limitations and preview another, differential model for the culture.

The reorganization of American culture will command reinterpretation of all documents so as to place them in the different contexts prescribed by a new model. Once this is complete, assuming this is begun, the model will no longer be new and will be as full extended and probably as ready for demolition as the unitary model may be now. To begin just with Edwards, or just with Franklin or Emerson, is not only a first step toward this goal;

thus to begin represents a departure from the dominant way of writing about American culture whose importance cannot be measured by the distance actually traveled, by the number of writers or writings actually covered. The phenomenology of American culture that this reading attempts is catastrophic methodologically to modern American cultural historiography, serving, as does John Carlos Rowe's proposing a "strategic intertextuality" among only six "anomalous" nineteenth-century American texts, "to defamiliarize the critical conventions that continue to govern even the most avowedly revisionary interpretations of American literature." It can transform instantly, even before every particular analysis is complete, not only a way of looking at American culture but the phenomenon of American culture. It creates a culture different from that created by modern American scholarship, one that includes this scholarship not as criticism of the culture, but, in ways of which the scholarship cannot be cognizant, as product of the culture. If this reading is successful, it is so not just about Edwards, or about Franklin or Emerson, but by implication about literature written in the English colonies of North America and the United States. It constitutes not only a revision of Edwards or of Puritanism or even of theism, but the beginning of the end of the modern historicist phenomenon, America.[1]

Anticipating the stakes to be so high, the following chapter will attempt to discover theism where theism seems least apparent, to disprove the presence of humanism where humanism seems unquestionably there. Franklin is chosen to compare with Edwards because their contemporaneity seems to modern retrospect problematic, their writings seeming so unlike. Emerson is chosen to contrast with Edwards because their lack of contemporaneity seems to modern retrospect not problematic enough, the chronological gap between them seeming shortened or even eliminated by their supposed intellectual kinship. The definitions of both relationships epitomize modern American cultural historiography. The following effort to contest them aspires to a significance equivalent to theirs.

2. Franklin and Edwards

Franklin and Edwards are frequently mentioned in the same context. Comparisons between them rely mainly on the chronological and circumstantial accidents of their being born in the same decade in New England and their both winning international repute, although of different kinds, simultaneously; as long ago as the 1880s Oliver Wendell Holmes cites worldwide fame as a shared attribute superficially linking the two, and John Opie recalls it as recently as 1969. The contemporaneity of Edwards and Franklin inspires several relatively weak arguments for their more substantial affinity, such as those of Aldridge, Heimert, John Smith, and

Minter, all of which contend essentially that although Edwards promotes good behavior less expressly and less centrally, he does so in ways that are nonetheless similar in effect to those recommended by Franklin's pragmatic moralizing. More common and stronger are arguments that contrast Edwards and Franklin as representing contrary tendencies of colonial American culture. Van Doren contrasts them in his early twentieth-century anthology of short works and excerpts from longer works by each, which is organized to demonstrate the opposition between the "defeated Edwards" and "Franklin, chief among the victors," the former holding a "mystic's" vision of man's lowliness while the latter leads the "generation that was unlearning that vision in its discovery of human dignity and self-sufficiency," a view generally seconded not long ago by Fiering, both in an article, in which he rejects the notion that "Franklin would have any interest whatsoever in the kind of painstaking discrimination of degrees and qualities of religious affections that Jonathan Edwards agonized over for four hundred pages in his book on the subject," and, later, conversely, in his book on Edwards's moral thought, in which he says that "although some interpretations might argue that Edwards believed that true virtue consists ultimately in doing good in the world, I am inclined to think that Edwards identified Turnbull and his ilk as the archenemy." The disagreement between arguments linking Franklin and Edwards and arguments separating them is not fundamental, since the latter contrast them as representative of dialectical oppositions; Van Doren implies that Edwards's "mysticism" survives him, and Puritanism, to become an unencumbered ideal of American romantics; Fiering implies that Franklin is properly to be identified as embodying an ancient and international moralism that conflicts dialectically and continuously with the more austere variety embodied by Edwards; and a third, recent critic, John Lynen, says that the difference between Franklin and Edwards is the very one that is ongoing in American culture and so constitutes the culture, both Franklin and Edwards envisioning a single "world in which thought must choose between the same set of alternative viewpoints." Thus even in opposing one another Franklin and Edwards unify "America," personifying the struggle between practicality and idealism, or between experience and hope, or between tough-mindedness and tender-mindedness, which are names for the same epic duel, fancied by neoromantic historiography, from whose throes neoromantic historiography fancies "America" to be born. The latest and most theoretically self-conscious expression of this dialectical continuity is Bercovitch's, which acknowledges the manifest differences between Edwards's personal narrative and Franklin's memoirs, and also Thoreau's *Walden*, to which Bercovitch, significantly, believes the two earlier works are comparable, but accounts the differences as "options offered by and for the culture," as "symbiotic oppositions, mirror inversions of what is basically the same set of social needs and social beliefs," such that, determined by the secret conservatism and chauvinism that Bercovitch sees underlying virtually all American discourse, "the three autobiographies represent changing forms of authority in an organically-developing free enterprise culture."[2]

The goal in establishing a new phenomenon of Edwards's writings in the preceding three chapters is to substitute new regularities for the ones that attach him to modern discourse. The theist discursive pattern is defined in these chapters as more than a belief in God, or in God's sovereignty, or in the dogmas of Puritanism or of any other religion; theism is defined as a discourse that pervades all early American literature in ways that make this literature alien, and potentially interesting to modern retrospect. The ability of theism to compete with other patterns devised by modern American cultural historiography depends ultimately on its comprehending not just more documents of Edwards's writings than other patterns comprehend, but in comprehending so many documents of early American writers along with those of Edwards that together they add up to a discourse comparable in size and complexity to that of humanism. The contention that theism is a sufficiently broad and meaningful context to reconcile the supposedly modern Edwards with the supposedly medieval Edwards speaks to modern students of Edwards, and perhaps to students of American Puritanism. To show that it is so broad and meaningful as to reconcile Edwards with Franklin in a more than superficial and other than dialectical way addresses the modern scholarship of early American culture. This section, and the next one contrasting Edwards with Emerson, are not appendixes. They attempt to develop more fully the several observations made previously in passing, that Edwards can profitably be associated with a number of apparently disparate theist writers—Hamilton, Jefferson, Paine, Poe—and dissociated from a number of apparently similar humanist ones—Thoreau, Hawthorne, Melville—and so to suggest that the theist discursive pattern revealed in Edwards's writings represents a single phenomenon differentiated from humanism in American literature.

Edwards's account of his conversion is said by a modern critic to be "as revealing in its way as Franklin's *Autobiography*." This compliments Edwards by associating his account with what is generally considered to be among the finest autobiographies, certainly the best in colonial American literature. But although worthy in its "way," the method of Edwards's account, glorification of God in the annihilation of the self, appears unrelated to Franklin's, which can here be summarized as giving service to man, both Franklin and his fellows, through the management of the self. Franklin seems to reveal himself in the ways that Edwards does not, in a vivid, detailed, consecutive discourse that seems much better than Edwards's account to fulfill modern requirements for the exposition of the personality.[3]

The value of Franklin's writings to modern retrospect is more than literary. Their appeal is based on the impression that they constitute a humanist discourse. Beneath the reserve that prudence requires Franklin to maintain in the company of less enlightened contemporaries, he appears to be a philosophical revolutionary eager to substitute for piety a reverence for man. Franklin's career and writings receive little obvious tailoring from modern criticism to make them fit the unitary model. In his wordly ambition, his public service as both scientist and statesman, his moral philosophy and seemingly off-hand theology, Franklin appears not just humanist but even anti-theist, sly and subversive and always discrete but nonetheless so apparently a champion of man as to seem to Kant a romantic ally, "a new Prometheus who has stolen fire from heaven."[4]

The resemblance between Franklin's memoirs and modern descriptions of personality depends on the assumption that Franklin's intent in them is to express himself. This is not the purpose he states in the opening. He says there that he will explain "the means which I employed" toward the acquisition of wealth and fame. This restriction may seem part of a conventional apology, a pretense of humility to disarm those who would criticize his vanity and a defense of the claim that a description of his life is useful to others. But Franklin's introduction may be more than a formality. In it he alludes to the criteria that will be applied consistently throughout the memoirs to determine which aspects of his self to include. More important, it implies exclusions that are easily overlooked and that, once revealed to modern retrospect, should make strange this discourse that has been made to appear so familiar. The structure of the memoirs is that of the conduct book, containing cautionary tales and ways to wealth. Although the memoirs have elements in common with modern biography and autobiography, they represent another form governed by another discursive pattern. They are, in their presentation of the self and of the way in which the self is manifested, surprisingly like Edwards's account of his conversion.[5]

The chief end behind the composition of the memoirs is admitted by Franklin to be ineffable. He can give only their ultimate ends, the education of his son and of all young men who would make a way in this world, ends sincerely pursued, perhaps, but uncertainly related to Franklin's chief end. The complexity of motives that Edwards deduces in the beginning of the *Dissertation* on God's chief end in Creation is implied in Franklin's cheerful admission in the first paragraph of the memoirs that selfishness may well be their primary motivation. This remark can be seen ironically to disparage the lengthy protestations of selflessness that are, in fact, the most conventional apologies for moral treatises in Franklin and Edwards's time. It amounts to disbelief in the possibility of demonstrating convincingly, in words or actions, a fundamental inclination, and thus agrees with the skepticism of the dualistic epistemology that is so marked in Edwards's writings.

Franklin is concerned with means rather than ends, with actions rather than inclinations. These dualisms are as essential to his writing as they are to Edwards's; he takes for granted that a concentration on the visible is exclusive, that it is defined by its omission of the invisible. He announces an emphasis in the memoirs that will be strictly partial, excusing him from the responsibility of examining the whole self. He leaves out what Edwards finds so difficult to express in the account of his conversion and so difficult to discover in *Religious Affections* and other theological works about Grace. The absence in Franklin's memoirs of any attempt to state the intrinsic state of the will is the reason why they seem more articulate than Edwards's writings about conversion.

An awareness of this exclusion leads to the notice of alien qualities in Franklin's descriptions of his origin. He says he has a "bookish inclination" as a child that may possibly be inherited; he notes that an uncle Thomas, though bred a blacksmith, teaches himself to read and write and so becomes a scrivener, and that an uncle Benjamin writes poetry and devises a shorthand. It is tempting to see in these comments the beginnings of a theory of hereditary identity. The family is of course central to humanist discourse, and is as obviously peripheral to theism, and so Franklin's apparently hereditary explanation of himself would represent an important sign of discursive allegiance. But the resemblance between Franklin's reference to his ancestors and modern theories of hereditary identity can be shown rather easily to be insignificant. Franklin's comments are not only brief; they are casual, almost flippant. The amateur poet who is Franklin's namesake dies "four years to the day" before Franklin is born, occasioning the idle speculation of Franklin's son that if the ancestor had died four years later, " 'one might have supposed a transmigration.' " The source of inclinations, such as a "bookish" one or the public spiritedness that seems also to be common among Franklins, is so uncertain that Franklin's discourse of family inclination is joking or superstitious. The collective and continuous disposition that a family according to modern definition represents is marginal to the subject of Franklin's memoirs; his mentions of this type of inclination are always aside. The relationship between Franklin's character and the characters of his ancestors is coincident, not causal, no more subject to reason than is a hypothetical coincidence of his birth with his uncle Benjamin's death. Such continuities or regularities are to Franklin prodigious, fitting no knowable pattern, anomalies to thought, parenthetical.[6]

What Franklin is most articulate about, what is exclusively the subject of the memoirs, is action, an emphasis that can be recognized even in his short, introductory guesses about hereditary origins. The inclination of Thomas and Benjamin is no more describable intrinsically than is the possibility of their having transmitted it. The sensible remains of both men, the record of Uncle Thomas's career and a specimen of Uncle Benjamin's poetry, is the subject of Franklin's description. Franklin never attempts to state what they feel or think or what talents they possess; he identifies them strictly through ideas, in the Lockean sense, of whatever evidence of their behavior survives them. This dualistic analysis of character is applied immediately afterward in the memoirs in Franklin's depiction of his family's Protestantism during the persecutions in England. He illustrates the family's resistance through the anecdote of the false-bottomed stool, where according to family legend a Bible is hidden from Catholic authorities. The contrivance may seem to testify to the piety of the makers of the contrivance. Franklin, however, never makes the claim. He says nothing about the family's dedication to God or Reformation, following the anecdote with a two-sentence review of the churches to which family members profess allegiance after the Revolution. The episode contains a precise description of the historical circumstances of the persecution and the aftermath and of the mechanics of the stool. Missing from the episode is a conclusion, even a conjecture, about the significance of the act of preserving the Book to the intent of the family. This is the first of several passages in the memoirs in which Franklin consistently narrows his discussion of religious zeal to concrete manifestations.[7]

Edwards would no doubt condemn such singlemindedness as worldly and complacent. He would have no difficulty understanding it, however, since it is governed by the same logical distinction that guides his own analysis of the will. Like Edwards, Franklin distinguishes always between inclination and activity. Unlike Edwards, Franklin ignores inclination because he is content to devote himself entirely to the affairs of this world, to which an unexercised inclination is irrelevant. Franklin's scope is incomplete, even perversely and cynically short-sighted. The wit and eloquence of the memoirs result not from a revolutionary broadening of man's horizon. They are made possible rather by tacit resignation to the one prescribed for him by theist discourse. The memoirs appeal to modern retrospect because they seem to glorify nature in nature's modern guise as the repository of all being and thus of all truth. But they are admittedly profane. They can be seen also to accept with an equanimity that is foreign to humanism the mysteriousness of a world conceived as the creation of a superior Being, whatever His ends or methods, and can be seen in their analysis of behavior to be the obverse of Edwards's personal writings, not the different phenomenon represented by modern self-expression. The hypothetical controversy between Edwards and Franklin, controversy in general, does not preclude nor even qualify the discursive affinity of the opponents, but rather confirms their writing within the same discursive pattern, a "network," in Foucault's words, whose "positivity renders an interplay of simultaneous and apparently contradictory opinions possible."[8]

Franklin's native inclinations can only be inferred from the resemblance between a liking for books and leadership he asserts to have in childhood and the literary and political accomplishments of his uncles and, to a lesser extent, his father. About his youth, the stage during which these inclinations are most apparent, he is not only unforthcoming or unconcerned but monitory. The way in which he portrays his early literary and political tendencies shows that he considers neither intrinsically to be a gift. The wharf-building adventure reveals that his eagerness to be of public service as a child, or, perhaps, his eagerness to be high in the esteem of his playmates, leads him to steal. The writing of poetry that is the first result of his bookishness tempts him to pursue the unprofitable vocation of poet. Both examples imply the danger of inclination. If the unexercised will is irrelevant to success in this world, the unrestrained will is a threat to success. Franklin's description of his early childhood is expressed in a dualistic discourse of the self and is designed to encourage the suppression of its natural constituent. Although his description of this stage is more detailed, because he is concerned with his natural talents and accordingly with their evidences, his description of childhood is not unlike Edwards's. To neither is the child an example of positive innocence or purity. To neither occurs the revolutionary proposition that the child is father to the man.

The rational constituent of the self is not only preferred by Franklin, it is what makes possible the writing of the memoirs. His youthful inclination becomes expressive only after being tutored by reason, at first his father's and later his own, into following the regular pattern of a career. The alternatives to this, running away to sea or pursuing the noncareers of thief or poet, are insubstantial, pure rebellions against the normal conduct of life. Restraint of the will is not only prudent or moral; it provides the structure of the memoirs. Without it there is no life capable of articulation. Inclination, whether unexercised or unrestrained, defies description in the memoirs, whose form necessarily excludes inclination.

Only when Franklin begins to channel his inclinations into productive activities, those which produce sensible effects, does he begin to succeed both as a printer and as a memoirist. The "bookish inclination" is a single phrase; it appears once and is never elaborated upon. The literary dexterity that represents Franklin's rationally harnessing his inclination inspires an episode, developed over several pages, in which his acquisition of literary skill is fully exposed. The learning of diction, a "stock of words" accumulated through the composition of heroic couplets, and of rhetoric, through the laborious transposition of issues of the *Spectator* into poetry and back to prose, along with the canny assumption of the Socratic pose, are actions with tangible consequences. They give Franklin something to write about, something to denote. Missing from this description is any expression of emotion; nowhere does Franklin mention dedication to the task of becoming a writer, or inspiration, or love of literature, or any literary feeling at all. This lack ought to be startling to modern retrospect. So strong is the modern assumption that descriptions of early literary ambition must contain assertions of commitment that they are often assumed to be implicit in Franklin's dispassionate portrayal, and sometimes unconsciously supplied. The difference between what Franklin says about himself and what the modern conception of the self requires must be said can constitute an interpretation of the memoirs. Such differentiation can discover a curious absence of any protestation of sincere modesty or righteousness in, for example, Franklin's exploitation of the Socratic method to win arguments, or a similar lack of statements of sincere bibliophilia in his evaluation of his library as large enough quantitatively to win a young tradesman the notice of William Burnet, Royal Governor of New York and New Jersey. This same kind of exclusion applies, even more strangely, to Franklin's descriptions of personal and family ties throughout the memoirs.[9]

It can also be shown once again to reveal an obverse relationship between Franklin's memoirs and Edwards's personal writings. The discontinuous structure of Edwards's accounts results both from his emphasis on Grace, which he identifies in part to manifest the arbitrariness of God's operations, and also from his concentration on the inner life, which, even in cases of unholy wills, resists discovery and articulation. A dualistic definition of the self authorizes neither a rhetoric nor a narrative of feeling; to attempt either is to introduce a form that is foreign to theism. Edwards's account of his own awakening is thus not a "personal narrative"—the name of the account, which he leaves untitled as well as unpublished, is added after his death—insofar as he defines person theistically, according to the original Greek derivation. He is seeking to convey not the mask or apparition of his self, but the essence of his self. The latter is to Edwards insufficiently manifest to support a narrative structure and so can only be suggested through a collection of entries recording the desultory incidence of feeling in tentative language. Franklin's memoirs are truly a personal narrative in this theist sense of the phrase, but they differ from Edwards's account only in which of the two aspects of a self dualistically defined they choose to express. Both documents, Franklin's no less than Edwards's, can be understood as omitting realities that must be present according to the modern definition of person, a word that like so many others loses the originally exclusionary meaning in the context of humanist discourse and comes to connote, even to denote, every possible aspect of a manifold but nonetheless integrated self. Such an entity does not exist in theist discourse and so has no literary form; in the context of theist discourse such an entity would be monstrous, whose literary form would be no genre but some kind of teratological grafting, such as perhaps the one that would result from attaching Edwards's account to Franklin's memoirs. Even more than biography, autobiography, that at least implies the most complete self-expression, is a humanist invention. Hence the retitling of various theist discourses of the self represents no mere innocent updating by modern editors. Simply to call Franklin's memoirs, or Edwards's account of his conversion, or Thomas Shepard's records autobiographies is already to commit humanist misprision.

About his parents Franklin says in his memoirs that both provide examples of good health and that his father provides examples of asceticism in preferring conversation to eating and of prudence in his handling of Franklin's childish inclination to run off to sea; concerning their deaths, Franklin reproduces the inscription composed by him for their tombstone. About his brother James he regrets the *"erratum"* of leaving before the term of his apprenticeship expires, but notes later the compensation of apprenticing his nephew to his own printing business in Philadelphia. About his friends he lists their contributions to and detractions from his worldly estate. His amatory relations consist of a series of escapades cursorily alluded to and regretted later for their exposing him to disease, an engagement to Miss Godfrey which Franklin ends after her parents make the mistake of believing him "too far engaged in affection" to bother haggling over a dowry, and, finally, marriage to Miss Read, which Franklin evaluates as a correction of the *"erratum"* of abandoning her earlier and as the acquisition of a "good and faithful helpmate" who "assisted me by attending the shop." About an illness that nearly kills him he regrets going through all the "disagreeable work" of dying only to have to do the work all over again. On the occasion of a son's death by smallpox he regrets failing to have the child inoculated. At the site of the massacre at Gnadenhut he devotes a sentence to describing the half-interred bodies and the rest of the passage to itemizing the building of a new fort, including a determination of how many seconds it took on the average to fell a tree.[10]

This list is not intended to make Franklin appear heartless but to stress that dispassion is a structural principle of the memoirs, that dispassion governs with a consistency that can be shocking. A similar impression can be gained from reading Marcus Aurelius's *Meditations*, where, in a passage very like Franklin's description of his parents, Aurelius claims to be honoring his father by impersonally listing a group of entirely impersonal attributes that he says he admires most, which is not to suggest that Franklin is "influenced" by the *Meditations* nor that Aurelius is to be considered personally an "influence" on Franklin or on eighteenth-century American letters, but that the theist pattern will produce similar discourses on similar subjects no matter how widely separated theist writers happen to be. Whether creating the impression of a comic deadpan or a chilling detachment, Franklin's memoirs always restrict themselves to the sensible behavior of persons, even when describing events that are assumed to provoke reactions—respect, sorrow, joy, horror—whose sincerity seems unquestionable. The most salient feature of the memoirs from the modern perspective ought to be their speaking always other than emotionally.[11]

The essential self is beyond the reach of human culture to Franklin, either that of the language of the memoirs or that of the many schemes he describes in them to improve behavior. It is impossible to conclude from the memoirs that Franklin is generous or industrious or humble; it is equally impossible to prove that he is greedy or lazy or proud. What is known is that he insists on paying the oarsmen who ferry him to Philadelphia despite helping them row, and that he later gives away two of the three rolls he buys there to a mother and child despite being penniless himself. Also certain is that he burns his candle late in his shop window and carries paper at all hours in a wheelbarrow, and that he never speaks in ways that might give him the "air of positiveness." The ostentation of these acts, of most of the anecdotes Franklin tells about himself in the memoirs, seems to encourage the suspicion they are hypocritically designed to benefit Franklin. But this is no more sure than is the humility of the acts. Franklin is concerned with manifestations and consequences, which concern excuses him from speculating on motivation. That there is motive lurking invisibly behind all of these actions is indicated by Franklin's insinuation that the motive may be other than selfless. The impression is identical to the one Franklin creates in his apology at the beginning of the memoirs that inclination is mysterious, that the most vehement declarations of inclination are the most likely to be false, but that there are forms, such as the conduct book or cautionary tale or way to wealth, whose exclusive secularity makes irrelevant the chief end of the author. Although Franklin may appeal to modern retrospect as a harbinger of humanism, his isolation of behavior is no more existential philosophically than is Edwards's analysis of the will. If anything, Franklin's discourse of the self implies an even more radical division, according to which the truth of persons is so remote from the experience of persons as to permit the cultivation of forms, both literary and political, that are defined by willingness to settle for much less than perfect felicity. A decadence of theism, perhaps, Franklin's dualism is, however, no revolutionary advance toward the unities of humanist discourse. The affectionate image of Franklin as a merry shape-changer, which probably originates in Carl Becker's profile for the 1943 *Dictionary of American Biography* and is preserved by such later and more intensive studies as that of Robert Sayre, transforms the complex indeterminacy of a simply dipartite self in the memoirs into the simple role-playing of a complexly manifold self, and so modernizes Franklin by turning a strange epistemological difficulty into a familiar psychological one.[12]

Supposing that Franklin's portrayals of himself and others can be made to agree with Edwards's analysis of man, Franklin's theology, though a very small fraction of his writings, seems irreconcilable with Edwards's. The final test of the utility of a theist discursive pattern in the comprehension of the writings of Franklin and Edwards will be to determine whether it has the capacity to join "free"-thinking about God with piety. A discursive affinity between Edwards's and Franklin's theology seems most unlikely. To demonstrate the existence of one would be an argument for granting theism the status of a major pattern in American literature.

The memoirs contain no theology according to strict theist definition. Franklin in them is as consistently disinterested in the invisible character of God as he is in the invisible motivations of men. He explicitly warns against metaphysical speculations in his recollection of the consequences of one venture into theological controversy, the "Dissertation on Liberty and Necessity, Pleasure and Pain," which he publishes in 1725 in response to the anti-Deist lectures sponsored by Robert Boyle in 1692. The abstract truthfulness of his essay or the Deism that it espouses is never denied, although Franklin admits that an error might have "insinuated itself unperceived into my argument so as to infect all that followed, as is common in metaphysical reasonings." But its practicality is to Franklin's hindsight clearly dubious, having produced injurious behavior in himself and others "infected" by the doctrine. God and religion enter the memoirs the way everything else does, through sensible manifestations.[13]

The consistency with which Franklin holds to this emphasis can be comical or deliberately impious. The Quaker meeting house that he visits after arriving in Philadelphia is a good place to nap. Behavior prohibited by the commandments is bad not because the Bible forbids it but because it is "bad for us," and behavior encouraged by the Bible is good because "beneficial to us." "The most acceptable service of God was the doing good to man." The "apparently extempore" sermons of a visiting preacher are good because, despite being exposed as not only memorized but plagiarized, they promote good works; after the preacher is discredited, Franklin organizes a collection on his behalf. Whitefield's evangelical efforts in Philadelphia are successful because of the effectiveness of his thespian manner—Franklin paces off the distance over which Whitefield's voice can be heard and calculates the number of people he can reach in one sermon—and because of the good works that follow, the speedy construction of a meeting house in Philadelphia and the establishment of an orphanage in Georgia.[14]

The meaning of each of these judgments, as well as their rhetorical power, depends on the clever inversion of a wisdom that Franklin can assume to be conventional. Each is designed to contradict a common theist understanding of religion as something to be evaluated for its eternal, invisible consequences with the comic one of attending exclusively to its temporal results. Because his irony and polemics indirectly recall the immaterial rewards of Grace and unknowable workings of Providence, Franklin's judgments implicitly confirm the existence of these intangible, and for his purposes irrelevant, and to his taste uninteresting, but nonetheless real things. The fundamental literary technique of the memoirs is substitution, not transformation. Franklin does not transform good works into Providence, citizenship into Grace, earth into heaven. Rather, he maintains the tension between them by always neglecting one through the affirmation of the other, and thus preserves the dualism basic to theist discourse. God is not an after-thought to the memoirs. He is that which must be forgotten in order to think and communicate the meaning of the memoirs. God is as much the condition indirectly of Franklin's morality as God is directly that of Edwards's theology.

When Poor Richard says that "in the affairs of this world, men are saved, not by faith, but by the want of it," the introductory phrase represents not only an important qualification but the basis for understanding what follows and for appreciating Franklin's wit. The apothegm requires an immediate, even an instinctive recognition that this world is not the next, that the relationship between them is often one of opposition. An implication of Franklin's advice is that there is no way to bridge the gap between worlds and consequently that success here may occur at the expense of eternal salvation. This is the implication also of the admitted partiality toward "the affairs of this world" of all of Franklin's writings. It is one with which Edwards would agree, that would enable him perfectly to comprehend Franklin's work and exactly to formulate his inevitable condemnation. The disagreement between Franklin and Edwards can be surmised because such controversy is a long- and well-established genre of theism. The crux would be what obligation man, defined as the creature of God, owes his Creator. Edwards believes that all behavior can ideally be turned into adoration of God and strives to reduce to a level commensurate to man's lowly position in Creation his service to his own kind. Franklin believes that no fidelity on the part of so lowly a creature as man can much benefit an omnipotent and eternal God and so recommends that man modestly limit his efforts to his capabilities, which extend to but do not exceed the improvement of human welfare. Franklin's position relies no less than Edwards's on an assumption of divine sovereignty, and in a sense an even more radical one. Although Edwards would probably call Franklin's moralism impiety in disguise and call his religion a camouflaged rebellion against God, and although modern retrospect might agree with the substance of Edwards's accusation that Franklin's piety is sophistical and skin-deep, Franklin can respond in no other way than by defending his theology as being better, or at least as being as well suited to a universal order in which God reigns. The disagreement between Franklin and Edwards occurs over how best to be consistent with theist ontology. The controversy, although permitting a variety of opinions and an attendant virulence, is bounded by theism. The supposition that man may occupy the position held by God, that the disparity between Creator and creature is an illusion, is no more serious a possibility to Franklin than to Edwards.[15]

The theism of Franklin's memoirs is mainly implicit. It is stated explicitly, however, as the foundation of what little theology he attempts, not only in the scattering of theological comments included in his works but in the Deistical tract he renounces for immorality in the memoirs and that he tries to exclude from his literary remains. The "Dissertation" begins with a sentence that could easily be transposed to the opening of one of Edwards's theological treatises, stating that "God is the First Mover . . . Maker of the Universe," and continues to deduce, according to the same logic Edwards uses, that "to suppose any Thing to exist or to be done, *contrary* to the will of the Almighty, is to suppose him not almighty; or that something is more mighty than the Almighty," which is both absurd and unscriptural. That Franklin applies this assumption and the rational extension of the assumption to reach a conclusion, that genuine evil does not exist, with which Edwards would disagree does not indicate any discursive difference between them. Franklin's beginning from the assumption of divine sovereignty represents more than a convention or a devious attempt to entrap the pious with their own piety. He begins with what theistically is the original, irrefutable truth, apparent to the common sense of all sane men regardless of their religious principles, regardless even of their morality, from which all corollaries must descend, against which all must be tested for their validity. This is the only way rhetorically and structurally for a theist to begin, whether he is a so-called free thinker contesting the existence of evil or a Puritan invoking the doctrine of human depravity. Both sides in the controversy arise from the same discursive foundation. Again, the controversy is bounded, is made possible, by theism.[16]

Franklin's deduction that a God who is both omnipotent and good cannot be supposed to cause, or to suffer evil without implying flaws in either His power or His virtue or both is a rational one according to Edwards's definition of reason. It is consistent also with the justifications of evil proposed by Edwards in his writings about Providence, and with those accepted by even the most bibliophilic eighteenth-century Protestants as orthodox. Insofar as evil is defined as a genuine threat to God's sovereignty or goodness, evil is no more real to Edwards than to Franklin; Edwards strives to distinguish between apparent challenges to Providence, which serve indirectly to glorify God in their inevitable defeat, and actual challenges to Providence, which are impossible. Franklin's distinction between pain, on the one hand, which can be said to contribute to the plan of the universe, and evil, which would seem only to disrupt the plan, is in essence the same as Edwards's, designed in more secular and utilitarian language to reconcile the appearance of opposition to God with the omnipotence of the Creator. Although the wording of Franklin's essay suggests that he can derive further conclusions about the moral responsibilities of man, or their lack, which Edwards would dispute and which would lead Edwards to suspect Franklin's premises or motives, a suspicion that Franklin himself confesses in his report of the "Dissertation" in the memoirs, Franklin's theology is expressed, no matter in how untrained or ill-considered a way, theistically.

In one other, briefer work of theology, written a few years after the "Dissertation," Franklin attempts to summarize all of his religious principles. The "Articles of Belief and Acts of Religion" (1728), which is included in Franklin's collected works, hypothesizes the existence of a seemingly polytheistic confederation of gods, one of whom creates and rules over the world, headed by a single, omnipotent, eternal God whose distance from the affairs of man is made to appear immeasurable by the interposition of the subordinate god between. What is most extraordinary about this speculation, which seems in its quasi-pagan reversion from Christian monotheism to be even more dangerous and worthy of retraction than the "Dissertation," is not that Franklin feels free to question the very basis of Judeo-Christianity, but that he goes to such a length to contrive a theology that is consistent both with theism and with the dedication to good works that to him is man's primary responsibility. Franklin's scheme does not constitute a true polytheism. The created gods of Franklin's pantheon are not omnipotent or eternal or ubiquitous, are not truly divine, but are the instruments of the sovereign God who creates them. In supposing their existence Franklin personifies intermediate agencies that are represented in Edwards's theology by natural laws, operating according to a regularity and controlling according to a power that appears to be their own but that is delegated to them by the continuous ordination of God. The difference between Franklin's created god and Edwards's mechanisms is that the former, being a sentient creature rather than a collection of the properties of matter, can more easily command affection and allegiance, and thus reinforce the self-love that naturally attaches man to his world with a principle, which Franklin believes to be equally natural, "which inclines [man] to Devotion, or the worship of some unseen power." The similarity between Franklin's theological contrivance and Edwards's radical monotheism is that Franklin's contrivance supports the existence and absolute independence of Creation of a single creative God whose being is required by experience and reason and revelation, by every discourse of the theist pattern. When Franklin states in the memoirs that the best way to serve god is by serving man he refers not to the sovereign God who according to Franklin's delegated Divinity is beyond the reach of human reverence, but to the created god who is imperfect and thus can delight in the care of his human creatures for one another. To Franklin this is the god in whose image man is made, a god who shares in some superior form the compassion, curiosity, vanity, and all the natural strengths and weaknesses of man. That Franklin would have to suppose that only such a vassal can be the object of a religion governed by human values shows the impossibility of his conceiving or expressing a unity between Divinity and man. All he does is to interpose another "frame," to use Edwards's term, of existence that widens further the ontological gap between created and creative being. This widening may open the way toward impiety, or the immorality that Franklin concedes as a fault of his Deism, but it does not authorize, is not even the first step toward the authorization of any repossessing of the attributes of Divinity for man. Edwards again would no doubt condemn Franklin's scheme, but again, both positions appeal to the same irrefutable truth. The condition of all discourse in the British Colonies of North America before the assimilation here of romanticism is that somewhere, somehow a Power exists prior to all creatures. In Franklin's writing no less than in Edwards's, "there is no other way." Theist discourse is expansive enough to accommodate both the Enlightenment and the revealed religion, which to Peter Gay's modernist perspective seem "wholly incompatible." The young Franklin who speculates on the existence of a lower house of gods is no less a theist than the ancient Franklin who admonishes the Constitutional Convention not to forget "that God governs in the affairs of men. And if a sparrow cannot fall to the ground without his notice, is it probably that an Empire can rise without his aid?"[17]

3. Emerson and Edwards

A link between Emerson and Edwards represents more than a hypothesis advanced in a single article by a noted scholar of early American culture. Perry Miller's combining in a short essay of two major American writers separated by nearly a century is based on his overall theory of American cultural history, a theory that assumes the presence of unity and that is shared by most modern American cultural historians. What exists "From Edwards to Emerson" is a theoretical unit belonging to a pattern of continuities that not only makes possible but requires the assigning of such topics. This section will challenge Miller's essay not as an isolated proposition but as an important expression of modern American cultural historiography. It seeks to contest not the particular combination but the theoretical unit. Its grounds are not factual but phenomenological.

The connection between Miller's comparison of Edwards and Emerson and the rest of his work—on Edwards, Puritanism, and Transcendentalism—is evident within *Errand Into the Wilderness*. Although including articles published over a span of more than twenty years, the collection exhibits a theoretical integrity of which "From Edwards to Emerson" can be seen as an epitome. The argument of the collection is whole, following the transition of Protestant theology from an abstract wish imported from Europe, an intent stated in advance of and isolation from its realization, an errand in prospect only, to an actuality that the environment, the wilderness, makes over into the new thing that is American culture. Miller's description of this transformation is distilled in his comparison of Edwards and Emerson. Edwards is to him the child both of the abstract theology and the American frontier, of which in the eighteenth century the Connecticut River Valley where Edwards grows up and serves as minister in Northampton is a part. Emerson is more completely the child, or man, of nature. Together they stand in Miller's unitary model of American culture for the beginning and end of American cultural development. Between them is a difference only of degree. Miller begins the essay by stating the basic desire, the "effort to confront, face to face, the image of a blinding divinity in the physical universe," and he concludes the essay by stating the common "energy" that unifies not just Edwards with Emerson, but Puritans with a host of mid-nineteenth-century artists and thinkers in New England. Whatever change occurs is circumscribed by the unitary model of American culture, of which Miller is one of the founders.[18]

Another conclusion results from contrasting Emerson with Edwards according to the three subjects used in the three preceding chapters of this reading to expose the discursive pattern of Edwards's writings. In place of Creation Emerson writes of nature, which as the embodiment of both cause and effect is another phenomenon. In place of Providence Emerson writes of history, whose possession of inherent meaning makes of it another phenomenon as well. Instead of Grace Emerson writes of the heart, which as the source of divinity is another phenomenon, too. Emerson's writing is governed by a discursive pattern in which God is replaced by man, theism by humanism. Whereas theism is merely apart from the humanism that to theism is of course nonexistent and inexpressible, Emerson's writing and the humanist discursive pattern his writing helps to establish in the United States departs semi-knowledgeably from a discursive predecessor. Whereas Edwards's writing can be understood as merely other than humanist, Emerson's must be understood as attempting to deny, and thus to contain, the theism that precedes. Modern discourse has both the imperative and the opportunity to assimilate theism in an agreeable form. A corresponding privilege is not enjoyed by theism, and this imbalance must be compensated for to realize the difference between the two discursive patterns.

It is difficult today to appreciate the revolutionary character of Emerson's *Nature*, especially in the United States of 1836, by which time romanticism has yet fully to dominate either religion or philosophy here. The modern discourse of the world, nature according to the modern definition, originates in American literature in works like Emerson's. Many of the flat declarations that today seem familiar and at least plausible—"All things are moral," "Each creature is only a modification of the other," "I am part or parcel of God"—represent confounding assertions in the context of the theist discourse still being written in the United States when Emerson's essay is first published. It is doubtful whether many of Emerson's American contemporaries who are unfamiliar with German romantic philosophy or English romantic poetry and criticism can read these assertions well enough even to express clear objections, since Emerson not only challenges the theist discourse of the world as a creature of God but in doing so also violates theist diction and usage. The most important redefinition is that of nature, and this is applied immediately and tacitly in the beginning of the essay.The epigraph Emerson chooses for the original publication of *Nature* quotes Plotinus without comment, as if the motto, " 'Nature is but an image or imitation of wisdom, the last thing of the soul; nature being a thing which doth only do, but not know,' " summarizes his own meaning. But Plotinus's statement in the context of the rest of Plotinus's writings reflects the dualistic definition of the world that *Nature* is dedicated to replace. Plotinus distinguishes "wisdom," the "last thing of the soul," hierarchically from nature, which as an "image or imitation" is an analogue, inarticulate of truth, that possesses physical laws but is the slave of a higher unseen power dictating the laws, a nature "which doth only do, but not know." The motto must be subjected to misprision before becoming consistent with the essay that follows. The pejorative connotation of *image* and *imitation* must be ignored, and the referent of the appositive phrase that ends the first clause must be considered ambiguous, either or both *nature* and *wisdom* rather than wisdom distinct from nature. The final clause must be inferred to celebrate man, the highest product of nature, who knows the truth in nature by contemplating nature, rather than to remind that nature, material and human, as a creature lacks the intrinsic resources necessary for self-knowledge. Emerson's romanticism is negligent of tradition even when appearing most respectful, perhaps most negligent then because the respect is patronizing, like that of other romantic writers for their heritage—Blake's for the Bible, Wordsworth's for Milton in the preface to *Lyrical Ballads*, Coleridge's for Shakespeare in the criticism.

The difference between what Emerson means by nature and the theist definition of nature is never explicated in the essay. Although consistent with a new definition, and although containing proclamations that seem gnostic, or merely odd, the passages about the stars and the "transparent eyeball," the beginning of the essay does not define nature but rather begins without introduction to apply the new definition. Over ten years after the original publication Emerson finally provides an appropriate motto in the three couplets used as the epigraph for the 1849 edition; or perhaps it would be better to say that Emerson replaces quotation from Plotinus with quotation from Schiller, the worm of Emerson's poem being clearly brother to the worm of Schiller's "Ode to Joy," whose "lust" is indistinguishable from the adoration of the "cherub [who] stands before God." The contrast between the nature of Emerson, and Schiller, and that of Plotinus's motto is marked. Whereas Plotinus supports a chain of being, Emerson suggests a radically different ontology, "A subtle chain of countless rings / The next unto the farthest brings," which substitutes for the hierarchy of existence a sort of protean, collapsible cord. Emerson may be considered to be conversing with the theist discourse of the great chain in his reference to a "subtle" one, almost to be parodying the great chain by emphasizing flexible properties rather than segmentation. His use of the image subverts the earlier meaning, which holds the frames of existence to be forever separate and distinct, with the mysterious connotation that nature is of such a structure as to permit a worm, "striving to be man," to mount "through all the spires of form," as the final couplet attests. The differences between this proposal and Edwards's comment in *The Nature of True Virtue* contrasting worms with archangels could not be more drastic. In supposing an archangel "to be in every way further removed from nonentity" and closer to God "than a worm" Edwards states hyperbolically what all reasonable theists, like Plotinus, would conclude, that the Creator is superior to and separate from the creature, a distinction that is true in all cases and only very blatantly true in the comparison of archangels with worms. Emerson's poem polemically implies another ontology, according to which even so seemingly irrefutable a distinction as one between worms and men, or worms and cherubs if Emerson believes in such beings and if he could have fitted them metrically, is false. Emerson's hyperbole serves to make thinkable the apparently, superficially absurd. Edwards' serves to expose the apparently, superficially, sane as nonsense. Emerson's, and Schiller's, discourse of nature flies in the face of theism. His ontology, that is more properly called a phenomenology, is revolutionary.[19]

And so, accordingly, is Emerson's epistemology, which the poem suggests and which the opening passages of *Nature* continue to demonstrate. The middle couplet, "The eye reads omens where it goes,/And speaks all languages the rose," refers both to nature being the source of truth, not the "image" or "imitation" of truth as in the quotation from Plotinus, and to the consequent accessibility of this truth to observation, that to Emerson unlike Plotinus, is, rather than some abstract, contemplative, "wisdom," the highest philosophical endeavor. Even so common a phenomenon as a rose communicates all knowledge, "speaks all languages," to the mind that perceives the rose correctly, the "eye" that "reads omens where it goes." Only as applications of this epistemology based on this ontology, or, again, as a phenomenology, do the opening descriptions of *Nature* make sense. The stars that communicate to Emerson the "perpetual presence of the sublime," the "bare common" that makes him "glad to the brink of fear," and the woods that restore "perpetual youth" are each equivalent to the rose of the 1849 epigraph, seemingly ordinary phenomena that contain extraordinary meaning. The way in which Emerson regards them, looking at each as if for the first time, as "if the stars should appear one night in a thousand years," shows a perception capable of "reading omens where it goes." This continuous emphasis on the clarity of perception, throughout

Emerson's *Nature,* in all of his other works, and in the works of romanticism in general, relies on defining nature, what is perceived, as inherently truthful. Edwards's continuous skepticism about the validity of perception is based on defining Creation as an effect separate from the Creator. Both Emerson's epistemology and his underlying ontology differ from theism and attempt to improve upon the knowledge of the past and to restore to man a self-esteem that Emerson and other romantics believe to be lacking in the self-consciousness of their predecessors.[20]

The disparity between the discourse of Emerson's *Nature* and that not only of Edwards's writings but of theism generally can be further exemplified by noting another of Emerson's misprisions, one used to incorporate into the essay the most celebrated English author of the past. At the end of the fourth section on language Emerson cites proverbial wisdom as evidence of the "analogy" that exists between facts and truth. He goes on to support this relationship by implying that it is supported by Shakespeare, who, as quoted by Emerson, seems to declare the perceptual corollary of this "analogy," that man should attend with proper awe to the quotidian: " 'Can such things be, / And overcome us like a summer's cloud, / Without our special wonder?' "

The lines are from the fourth scene of the third act of *Macbeth* and they are spoken by Macbeth in reaction to seeing Banquo's ghost at the banquet. In the context of the scene, which is redundantly, almost tediously constructed so as ironically to disclose the disorderly and unnatural consequences of Macbeth's disorderly and unnatural murder of Banquo, the cloud of Macbeth's metaphor obviously represents an unwanted, and— according to the rhetoric of the figure, which is a sort of understatement— even an unnatural eclipsing of the radiance of the sun. What Emerson would take as a reference to the diurnal and seasonal is in the context of Shakespeare's play (and, arguably, although this is not the occasion for the argument, in the context of Shakespeare's oeuvre) a reference to something emphatically out of the ordinary. The cloud, and Banquo's murder, and the apparition of the ghost, and Macbeth's distraction, represent simultaneous breaches in the cosmological, moral, ontological, passional, and social orders. The cloud is a precise, albeit to modern retrospect an unlikely figure for the un- or supernatural. It is made into a symbol of the immanence of spirit only by quotation out of context, as is the case in Emerson's enlisting Plotinus to support his revolutionary redefinition of nature by originally attaching Plotinus's phrase to *Nature* as a motto. And, again, the "analogy" between spirit and nature that Emerson sees Shakespeare to support is redefined by Emerson's modern usage as a synonym for identity, thus making "analogy" conform to the monistic ontology, the phenomenology, of modernism. The relation between Emerson's "analogy" and the "analogy" that appears in Edwards's writings to signify the tenuous link between spirit and nature, and the consequent limitations of knowledge, is merely alphabetical. What may seem the simple repetition of a word in the discourses of Edwards and of Emerson can be seen in this light to signify a complex and potentially confusing transdiscursive pun.

These misprisions appear in Emerson' earliest important essay. That they constitute seminal differences from theist discourse, and not just mis-statements, is suggested by a third example from the late essay "Fate." The passage in which Emerson claims that heightened perception, a "sufficient perspective," can make the spectacle of universal predation, "the whole circle of animal life," palatable can be seen similarly to alter a superficially synonymous passage in *The City of God,* in which Augustine states that the cycles of nature appear cruel and ugly only from within their midst, whereas from the vantage of omniscience they must seem "harmonized with the most accurate fitness and beauty." Emerson's point is that "sufficient perspective" is epistemologically a potential of natural life. Augustine's is that no terrestrial witnessing of nature can transcend the "mortal frailty" of being "so involved in a part of it" and that the inequities of life, "some perish to make way for others that are born in their room, and the less succumb to the greater," are balanced not on earth but elsewhere, where faith in revelation knows, but no experience of nature can confirm, that supernatural reciprocities prevail. Other theist descriptions of the turmoil of nature in the writings of major early American writers include John Adams's genuinely Augustinian reminder that "animal life is a chemical process . . . carried on by unceasing motion" and that "the mutability and mutations of matter, and much more of the moral and intellectual world, are the consequence of laws of nature, not less without our power than beyond our comprehension," and Jefferson's portrayal of the optical illusion of looming as evidence of the "whimsical" vagaries of natural experience, a particularly valuable example of theist discourse that can be economically contrasted to romantic portrayals of the same illusion, ones by Cooper, Thoreau, and Melville, for example, that invariably interpret looming as a means symbolically of visualizing the infinite. Emerson's humanist description of nature's mutability in "Fate" is discursively to be associated with others by romantic writers, such as Hegel's lyric evocation of ceaselessly self-consuming and so ceaselessly creative *geist,* "the soul of the world, the universal life-blood, which courses everywhere, and whose flow is neither disturbed nor checked by any obstructing distinction, but is itself every distinction that arises, as well as that into which all distinctions are dissolved; pulsating within itself, but ever motionless, shaken to its depths, but still at rest." Emerson's description is also discursively akin to Thoreau's less grandly occasioned but equally olympian justification for the devouring of a pigeon: "the same regard for Nature which excited our sympathy for her creatures nerved our hands to carry through what we had begun. For we would be honorable to the party we deserted; we would fulfill fate, and so at length, perhaps, detect the secret innocence of those

incessant tragedies which Heaven allows." Consolation is deeply imbedded in life for Emerson, Hegel, and Thoreau, is distantly situated outside and after life for Augustine, Adams, and Jefferson. The latter view
appears an intimation of the former only within the former's discourse, as
a misprision. The relationship between the two can be understood less
partially as systemic, each possessing the equal status necessary to differentiate them, as signs or as parts of signs in sign systems or in individual
semioses, each completely dependent on the differentiation between it and
the other for its meaning. Emerson's misprision represents an important
mark of his humanism, but is no longer an unavoidable phenomenon of
retrospect. Once identified, this type of misprision can no longer be practiced innocently. The relationship between Emerson and Augustine, or
Emerson and Edwards, or ourselves and writers of theist discourse, can be
considered differential, conventional, synchronic, the consequence of
nothing external to or other than our attention to and interest in them.[21]

To understand Edwards and the theism he represents as the prelude to
Emerson's romanticism is to see Edwards through Emerson's eyes, to ro-
manticize, to help consolidate the past according to romantic discourse. It
is to read omens not only in the rose or stars or the outdoors in general, but
in cultural history, in the writings of Edwards, and thus not really to
criticize either Edwards or Emerson but to continue to write the modern
text that, with *Nature*, Emerson is beginning in the United States. Statements of continuity between Edwards and Emerson, or between pre- and
post-romantic writings in American culture, are less analyses of either
discourse than they are humanist manifestos.

The knowledge obtained from Emerson's visionary experiences in *Nature*
is absent from even the most inspiring and legitimate awakenings that
Edwards describes in the account of his conversion or anywhere else. The
stars impress Emerson with the transparency of the atmosphere separating
them from him, making them not distant but near, transforming them from
an emblem of the comparative insignificance of man to one of man's ability
to share in their vastness, to reach into heaven himself. The ecstasy
kindled incongruously by "crossing a bare common, in snow puddles, at
twilight, under a clouded sky," teaches conversely that even the meanest,
apparently earthbound sensations can propel man beyond his mortality to
the height of religious consolation, a supernal "gladness" that intimates
immortality. The final vision of the opening section of *Nature* reveals most
audaciously Emerson's revolutionary finding. In the woods, "these planta-
tions of God," he feels not the passionate abasement that is impressed on
Edwards and other theists in contemplation of a sublime landscape, whose
grandeur is as Edwards insists still that of a creature and thus "but a little,
trivial, and childish greatness in comparison of the noble, refined, exalted,
divine" greatness of the Creator; rather, Emerson feels a kindred stature
that makes him instantly a colossus, "standing on the bare ground—my

head bathed by the blithe air and uplifted into infinite space," himself figuratively spanning the supposed gap between upper and lower realms and thereby denying the reality of the gap, himself a part of the meaning he perceives. The ultimate insight of this highest form of perception to Emerson is the marrying of subject and object, creator and creation, God and man, into the new ubiquity, eternity, and omnipotence that is nature: "I become a transparent eyeball; I am nothing; I see all; the currents of the Universal Being circulate through me; I am part or parcel of God." Epistemology and ontology here converge, being and knowing become one. The eyeball, insistently corporeal image of perception, in seeing becomes ideal, transparent, sees itself as no thing apart from its object, obliterates the distinction between itself and what it sees. Epistemology and ontology are here replaced by phenomenology in the romantic, Hegelian sense, a new discourse predicated by the eradication of all the dualisms, Creator and Creation, cause and effect, subject and object, of theism, dissolving all of them into phenomena. This is the union that is unutterable to Edwards, that is not even a remote descendant of his discourse of Creation, neither stated nor implied in his theology or his philosophy or his personal writings. The significance of both Edwards's and Emerson's discourses can be said to lie precisely in this difference. What Edwards describes as Creation is not a subject of Emerson's discourse. What Emerson describes as nature supersedes Creation, demoting Creation into an icon of the past and the discourse of Creation into superstition, the "creationism" of our own contemporary educational Luddites.[22]

Emerson is iconoclastic also toward the belief in a Providence governed by extraordinary breaches of natural law. His criticism of miracles as they are described theistically is directed in "The Divinity School Address" not only at the nineteenth-century Unitarians at Harvard who would excommunicate anyone who doubts the literal truth of the Bible's account of the parting of the seas. It rejects a discourse of Providence that identifies Providence primarily through un- or anti-natural catastrophes, and so speaks apart from theist discourse. Emerson may have more immediate theological opponents in mind when he addresses the graduating class of the Divinity School in 1838, but he speaks against Edwards and all theists in charging that Christianity until his time misinterprets the significance of miracles: "Christ spoke of miracles; for he felt that man's life was a miracle and all that man doth, and he knew that his daily miracle shines, as the man is diviner. But the very word Miracle, as pronounced by Christian churches, gives a false impression; it is Monster. It is not one with the blowing clover and the falling rain." In the context only of the time and place this statement is made, Emerson is quarreling with the "cold, lifeless negations" of Unitarianism, one of which prohibits questioning of the literal truthfulness of the Bible. But by redefining miracle as a true perception of the commonplace rather than an ancient report of the monstrous, Emerson not only renounces the legalistic standard for membership in the nineteenth-century Unitarian church and replaces this standard with one that certifies as Christian all men who are religiously inspired by their personal experience. He also implicitly discards, as he does in *Nature*, the dualism between Creator and Creation. Whatever God can be distinguished in this passage resides within, not above, the nature of man and works through, not in spite of, the processes of material nature. In the passage neither man nor the world is a creature. Rather, each contains and displays to the enlightened observer the origin of being. The Christ Emerson describes teaches men not to worship an unseen Creator but to adore, with a sensitivity that can perceive "daily miracles," phenomena no more superficially remarkable than the "blowing clover and falling rain," or the " 'summer's cloud,' " once transposed by Emerson from the terrorized conscience of Shakespeare's Macbeth to the serene curiosity of the perceiver of *Nature*. Emerson's Christ teaches man to look at the stars as if they come out only once in a thousand years. He differs fundamentally from Edwards's Christ, whom Edwards would have removing Himself from the world on the third day after His resurrection to prevent the idolatrous worship of His fleshly manifestation. Emerson's phrase, "daily miracles," would strike Edwards also as evidencing either poor diction or mental distraction.[23]

Providence is no more a subject of Emerson's humanism than is Creation. In place of Providence stands history, in the modern sense, which defines Emerson's understanding not only of secular institutions but of religion; or, more accurately, its subject comprehends all human experience, acknowledging no distinction between worshiping and living. Therefore the Incarnation, which to Edwards's theism represents the single, dramatic culmination of all miraculous interventions by God in natural process, to Emerson represents the continuous realization of divinity in the natural event of birth, not just that of Jesus but of all men. Jesus is to Emerson not singular but representative, a member of "the true race of prophets," prophesying not implausibly against all human reason and conjecture an incredible way toward redemption but naturally in a way that appeals to human experience as a clearer sight and better articulation of the truth that always inheres in life and will continue always to remain there, "the greatness of man," that "God incarnates himself in man, and forever goes forth anew to take possession of his World." Emerson insists that the truth of the past, the divinity of history, is "incarnated" in the events of the past, man's "forever going forth anew." To Edwards Christ defeats the world and substitutes for worldly wisdom a teaching that is astonishingly negligent of the world; His victory commands the renunciation of this life and humble awe. To Emerson Christ champions what is best in nature and refines a vision that is intrinsic to human culture, encouraging man to look within and about him, to reattach himself more passionately to nature, and to have the confidence that he can attain the same insight, to "become like God."[24]

History is described by Emerson as nature, possessing intrinsic meaning, again in the romantic philosophical sense of a phenomenon. Emerson's study of history is another phenomenology, a regard for the past that combines the being of the past with an epistemology of the past. The image of time's "becoming" that is central to romantic phenomenology and that is eleborated radically by subsequent phenomenological analyses, such as Heidegger's finding temporality to be a way of knowing rather than a limitation on what can be known, is common in Emerson's writings. The image implies that a timeless pattern exists immanently at every moment of time's passing, that the present is the unfolding of the past, and that the future lies folded in the present. The meaning of time, understood according to this image, need not be communicated as a revelation apart from time, a separate utterance of time's Creator, but can be comprehended through the apprehension of time from within time; because time is making itself continuously, it reveals its own truth continuously, because nature and history are not creatures but are rather phenomena to Emerson and other romantics, they can be studied exclusively through what they present to experience.[25]

Emerson indicates his faith in the potential unification of the temporal and the eternal in many different versions of the image of becoming. One appropriates from classical rhetoric the technique of synecdoche, inverting its original purpose of stylistic economy into a new one of perceptional expansion. The classical figure, usually exemplified by Homer's famous sails, refines the profusion of reality into the selectivity of art. It belongs to the same discursive pattern as Aristotle's aesthetics, whose unities impose order on a world that is implicitly disorderly and inherently inartistic. It is discursively akin also to the distinction between nature and wisdom implied in the quotation from Plotinus that Emerson uses for the 1836 motto of *Nature*. The synecdoche of the romantics, that can be found not especially in Emerson's works but throughout romanticism, ascribes the refinement to nature and alters man's responsibility from that of the artificer, rhetorically or aesthetically to reproduce the world in more seemly fashion, to that of the perceiver, to recognize that the whole of existence can be seen in parts of nature, even the most ordinary parts such as the stars or a wet common or the woods outside of Concord. Emerson uses this kind of synecdoche implicitly in all his writings and applies this kind to interpretations of all experience to correct what is to him a foolish acceptance of the limitations of an individual's perspective. Romantic synecdoche serves always to overcome space or time, or both; in *Nature* Emerson justifies his generalizing from apparently meager particulars with the assumption that "each particle is a microcosm, and faithfully renders the whole," and in "The Poet" he defends the ability to generate fine and philosophically significant works out of an apparently limited experience with the assumption that "there is no fact in nature which does not carry the whole sense of nature." In the study of ancient culture romantic synecdoche makes accessible all periods, no matter how remote, to the historian whose perception is inspired to "watch the monad through all his masks as he performs the metempsychosis of nature," who sees that time is compressed in the simplest artifacts of material culture, that "the Chinese Pagoda is plainly a Tartan tent."[26]

Another romantic technique of expressing the unity of time is the organic symbol, which is really only a form of romantic synecdoche but is one of the most conspicuous features of romantic discourse and has become one of its hallmarks for modern retrospect. Organic symbols occur often in Emerson's writings, most frequently in early ones, but also in the later essays in which Emerson is said to have lost his optimism about visionary experience and the inspirational qualities of nature. In "Experience" he notes with interest the discovery that the embryo evolves "not from one central point, but coactive from three or more points," which observation suggests to him that being does not originate at a single moment and place, and develop in a linear way that would make time the measure of the increasing estrangement between past and present, but that it originates continuously, so as to prove that "life has no memory," no impression of a gap between past and present, that life is simultaneous. In one of his last essays, "Works and Days," he still has the sense, referring with approval to the French proverb, that "God works in moments." Nature teaches Emerson as a historian that just as the "creation of a thousand forests is in one acorn," so do "Egypt, Greece, Rome, Gaul, Britain, America, lie folded in the first man." They remain by implication deeply imbedded in the latest one and thus accessible to the historian who looks inward. By extension the future is there also, ready to be known by the prophet whose insight sees deeply enough into his own potential.[27]

Organic figures are so closely associated in modern criticism with the romantic use of them to imply the absence of distinction—not only between past and present, but, what is the ontological dualism underlying the temporal distinction, between cause and effect, Creator and Creation—that it is difficult now to understand metaphors whose vehicles are living things or natural objects as serving any other purpose. This is the problem in evaluating Edwards's likening God's creativity to an endlessly overflowing fountain or to a river with an inexhaustible source, or in evaluating Winthrop's comparing the snake he finds behind a pulpit as representing Satan in the Garden, that Feidelson hails as revealing the "symbolic perception that pervaded the life of the American Puritans." It is difficult also to describe in other than neoromantic, humanist terms the biblical metaphors from which Edwards's and Winthrop's are almost literally copied. Edwards so qualifies the attributes of the natural objects he cites, however, as to concede their inability to convey the whole meaning of their tenor, which is the final truth of the world, God's chief end in Creation; nature contains no endlessly flowing fountains or rivers. Rather than uniting the infinite with the finite, the eternal with the temporal, Edwards's metaphors violate nature in using nature as the vehicle of Divinity, and Winthrop's metaphor is prompted not by any symbolic readiness, such as that present in Emerson's ability instantly to extract meaning from the mundane experience of walking across a common, but rather by a chance coming upon a rare happenstance, the small theist miracle of a snake in a pulpit. Theist figuration agrees with the metaphysics of theism, even resembling God's Providence by suppressing nature in modest imitation of the suppression of nature by miracles, and so is to be defined as including the imagery of the Bible, and of Edwards and Winthrop, and as differing from that of Emerson and other humanists, including Feidelson.[28]

A third, and the most complex, expression of the romantic image of becoming is the dialectic, which despite the pretension of romantic discourse to discover dialectic in all writing from antiquity onward, differs profoundly from the conflicts permitted in theist discourse, from the antinomies of Greek philosophy and from the dualisms of Christian theology, including those of heresies like the Manichean one, and which is essential to phenomenology as a humanist discourse. Emerson portrays the dialectic in various forms throughout his writings, from *Nature* to "Experience" and "Fate." The opinion that his philosophical confidence declines in later years derives from notice of the greater emphasis he places on the violence of dialectical change in the last essays. This emphasis is consistent with his phenomenological approach to historical experience and represents no mere personal depression.

Mutability is to Edwards and to other theists the stigma of imperfection that the world wears even to the carnal eye; change is the destiny of the most fetching natural beauty and accompanies theist pleasure in it even while that beauty is in its prime. An important victory of romantic discourse is the idealization of the flight of time. The theme of *tempis fugit* is taken over by romantic writing to encourage a response opposite from the one that, theistically, *tempis fugit* is intended to recommend; romantically, the flight of time invites the wedding of the self to nature rather than asceticism. The most beautiful quality of the panorama of the sunrise Emerson describes in *Nature* is "rapid transformation," because this is to him the most kindred; he "partakes" of transformation and reciprocally "dilates and conspires." The changeableness of the landscape neither leaves him behind nor reminds him of his mortality, both of which reactions are invariably present in theist descriptions of the sublime, such as in Jefferson's description of the "Natural Bridge." But the possibility of such reactions, which are in romantic discourse mistaken ones, is implied by the corrective tone of Emerson's delight. His teaching assumes an audience of the uninitiated, of those still benighted by the unnecessary and false pieties of the past. The rhetorical strategy of this celebration of time passing, and of Emerson's essays in general, is to "unsettle" what he considers the merely hidebound theological and philosophical conventions against which any romantic must revolt. This is his purpose when he praises the movement of nature for very movement's sake, "shooting like rays, upward, downward, without center, without circumference," "the great principle of Undulation in nature" in "The American Scholar," or when he castigates the stasis of a "foolish consistency" in "Self-Reliance" and later in the same essay praises "Power," no matter how unruly, as the "essential measure of right." The strength of these statements lies in their opposition. All of Emerson's predicate nominatives suppress qualifications that are implicit and can be easily supplied; time and change are not *memento mori* that resign man to death and advise him to look away from the world for consolation, but are the symbols of a vitality that man shares and that shows life to be interminable, life being intrinsically the site of immortality. Romanticism intends finally to subdue the antagonism of all philosophical opponents. But there is little evidence that better indicates the difference between humanism and theism to phenomenological retrospect than the implied negations of romantic pronouncements.[29]

Dialectic is the best means of portraying history as self-created and self-revelatory. It takes the place of the analogy used by Edwards and other theists to understand the way of the world as an imperfect record of Providence. Dialectic looks beneath and within events in time rather than above and away from them. It intensifies perception of the concrete rather than shifting attention to the immaterial. Emerson's description of it in "Circles" combines the impression of an abstract diagram—a thought inspiring a "circular wave of circumstance" that expands to the limit of the energy of the thought to congeal into a perimeter of institutions that remains until a stronger thought inspires another wave to wash the old institutions away—with that of a natural event, the dropping of a stone into still water. His description of the dialectic in "Fate" combines impressions of the harshest facts of life, that "the diseases, the elements, fortune, gravity, lightning, respect no persons," with the knowledge that inherent in this turmoil is a meaning that man can recognize and to which he belongs, that in the "savage accidents" of fate there is nothing imperfect or threatening or "objective" to man, but that man himself constitutes a "stupendous antagonism" equal to the assault of circumstance; that man can "compare advantageously with a river, an oak, or a mountain"; that in struggle life is "mellowed and refined for higher use" and can be apprehended and can even "please at a sufficient perspective." Dialectic unifies the ideal with the real. It has been said, from the humanist vantage of intellectual historians like Lovejoy and Miller, only to develop and further analogy. It seems, rather, in the insistent polemical tone of its articulation by romantics like

Emerson, here in one of his latest and supposedly less rebellious essays, to replace analogy in service to the humanist cause of supplanting all theist ways of writing. The significance of these passages from Emerson's "Fate" lies primarily in their comprising a text that is nowhere to be found in any of the writings of Edwards or of other theists. When Edwards speculates in his notebooks that God may hold the entire plan of Providence in His mind simultaneously, or when before him Augustine speculates similarly, neither bases his hypothesis on any sensation that can ever be received by any man from the material universe; their words convey the latency of dialectic only after having been transported to the alien context of humanism. When Edwards approximates the attributes of God by magnifying infinitely the most impressive features of Creation, or when before him Milton portrays Paradise and Heaven and Hell as hyperbolic magnifications of gardens and charnel houses, both present the ideal as so far exceeding place and time as to annihilate them in the mind of man, and do not anticipate romantic idealism except in the romantic imaginations of Perry Miller and William Blake. The significance of Edwards's discourse of Providence and of Emerson's discourse of history resides precisely, semiotically, in the difference between them.[30]

To abstract a discourse of humanity from Emerson's writings, even as the conclusion of this reading of them, represents as violent a rearrangement of Emerson's writings as the abstraction from Edwards's of a discourse of Providence. As God is the center of the theist discursive pattern, all experience a testimony to God's sovereignty, and all writing thus ultimately about Providence, so is Man the center of humanism, experience proof of Man's dominance, all writing a discourse of Man. Emerson's discourse of humanity is artificially separated and placed at the end of this reading so as to make the analysis of his writings symmetrical with that of Edwards's, to distinguish his "deep Heart" or "Over-Soul" or "genius" in contrast to Edwards's Grace, and thereby to reveal Emerson's particular discursive identity in unusually sharp relief. The value of stressing the difference between theism and humanism lies not only in preserving the distinctness of the former but in revealing to modern retrospect the peculiar character of its origin.

The source of Emerson's delight in perceiving the various landscapes he describes in the opening of *Nature* derives from his not sharing the theist impression that because they are the creation of God they are beyond comprehension and thus a sign that man, too, is God's creature. Emerson's discourse of history does not contain the theist sense that time is the instrument of this same God and thus another indication of God's sovereignty. Rather, Emerson sees in both nature and history an extension of himself; the world is but the "externization of the Soul," all history "properly" speaking biography. There is no "object" in Emerson's ontology that is external to Man, no genuine objectivity at all, but only the semblance of objectivity in "things" whose humanity has yet to be discovered. There is according to the same radical humanism no true subject and therefore no real analysis of subjectivity. Man is both ubiquitous and indistinguishable in Emerson's writing; he has infinite significance but no particularity, at least not to the highest, most philosophical perception. Emerson distinguishes what he calls the "mean ego"—which reckons the self isolated and projects the insecurities of such an isolated self into the world, even into the self, as dangers to be guarded against, individually by self and collectively by social government—from what is usually capitalized but given no single name in his writings, the true Self that senses its belonging always and everywhere and whose occupation is the ever-widening, ecstatic recognition of its presence. The perspective of the former views human culture in the limited sense, studying individuals and nations for what can be learned about the preservation of individuals and nations. The latter regards mankind and his works as expressions of Universal Being, present also and equally in woods or village commons or worms or, according to Whitman's natural extension of Emerson's phenomenology, "dung and dirt." Human science is not a category of Emerson's thought. The lives of men constitute one, but not a special revelation of the Life of Man.[31]

"Infancy is the perpetual Messiah" to Emerson for precisely the same reason that childhood is theologically an image of worldliness to Edwards and morally suspect to Franklin. Proximity to nature connotes impiety to Edwards and recklessness to Franklin because neither describes nature as an immediate source of ideals. Emerson's celebration of youth, which is continual throughout his writings and a major theme of romanticism, again replaces theist metaphysics with a revolutionary appreciation of nature. Humanistically, the birth of man signifies the origin of man's whole being, not just the carnal or temperamental half. But Emerson is disinterested in the moment of birth and the chronological period of childhood. Youth is "perpetual," both in the fact that it is always replenished through successive generations and, more important, in the perception that forever sees with the freshness of an original impression. Youth is nature's symbol, shown as a fact bounded by the circumstances of time and place but signifying an unbounded truth. It is not just a period of life nor is it only the property of the young. For Emerson it is a paradisaic integration among all apparent diversities of life that is lost only to those who permit the mean ego to dominate over their perception and thereby estrange themselves from the union that can be retained by anyone who looks correctly within and without to see the same deep Self. Emerson may adopt this particular symbol from nature, and refine the symbol to the degree of illuminating meaning without distortion, because his experience of youth is primarily of childhood and children. But within humanist discourse this emphasis represents neither a projection of humanity onto the world, a pathetic fallacy, nor an exclusion of the nonhuman. Man is to Emerson no more one of a variety of subjects for philosophy than to Edwards God is one of several topics for theology. He is all there is to know and the author of knowing. He is at the center and defines the periphery of thought; there is nothing other than or beyond him. Childhood is much closer to the center of the humanist discursive pattern than it is to the theist one of Edwards or Franklin, and it receives more attention from Emerson and other humanists. This attention does not, however, constitute in Emerson's thought a separate discipline, a philosophical obstetrics or pediatrics, nor does it promote nostalgia, because childhood, like all phenomena, ultimately possesses no discrete objectivity. Rather, it is a manifestation of the vitality that is self-creative, belongs everywhere, and that is self-knowing, like all parts of nature, which from the highest perspective has no parts. Youth is always the condition of the universe and is always aware of its ubiquity.

The true maturity of man similarly transcends particulars. Man's development proceeds as a recognition of the universality of attributes that are mistakenly restricted to himself alone. The life of a man not only represents the life of the species, biography being to Emerson the essence of history, but stands as a romantic synecdoche, an organic symbol, for nature, embryogeny being to Emerson identical to evolution. Thus, for example, there are no truly separate vocations of scholar and poet in Emerson's essays but only complementary pursuits of a single truth; "The American Scholar" and "The Poet" are devoted to the redefinition of scholarship and poetry not as specialized skills but as superficially different versions of the same activity. But a more audacious extension of Emerson's humanism, and one that must be recognized to signify its status as not just a preference or an emphasis but a whole discursive pattern, is his comprehending, explicitly in these two essays and implicitly throughout his writings, human culture within a culture of "things." Scholar is to Emerson a name for "Man Thinking," which is his most characteristic activity, so scholar is a synonym for Man. Because Man identifies to Emerson not only all men but all "things," including the nonhuman and the apparently insensate, the synonymy of scholar is infinite. Scholarship is a name for the occupation of the universe, "Man Thinking" has a vision in nature of Man Thinking: "[Nature's] beauty is the beauty of his own mind. Nature then becomes to him the measure of his attainments. So much of nature as he is ignorant of, so much of his own mind does he not yet possess. And, in fine, the ancient precept, 'Know thyself,' and the modern precept, 'Study nature,' become at last one maxim." Scholarship is to Emerson thought thinking itself. Similarly, "the poet is representative," standing "among partial men for the complete man, and apprises us not of his wealth, but of the common wealth"; and the meaning of poet, like that of scholar, extends beyond the human race to material nature. Poetry exists both in verse and in things: "Nature offers all her creatures to him as picture-language. . . . Things admit of being used as symbols because nature is a symbol." Emerson professes to find authority for these assertions throughout the history of aesthetics, from the sayings of the Neoplatonist Jamblichus to the poetry of Spenser. But his citations are as partial as those of Plotinus and of Shakespeare in *Nature*. The aesthetics of Jamblichus, or Spenser, or Edwards can be made to agree with Emerson's only after their mention of nature, and the various equivalents of nature according to theistic usage, such as "body" and "flesh," are interpreted to connote something more than a Creation logically and ontologically distinct from and inferior to the Creator, which is what nature according to romantic usage has become. The poet of Emerson's essay is the creative principle that inheres in all things; poet is one of the countless names, inspired by the countless impressions of nature, for immanent deity.[32]

Perhaps the most obvious sign of Emerson's humanism, and one of the attributes of romanticism most frequently noted by modern scholarship, is an emphasis on feeling. This may seem the most narrowly anthropocentric of all his emphases, but, because of the infinite breadth of Man as Emerson conceives him, it is no more, or less, introspective than any other kind of emphasis, nor does it discover an exclusive domain for human science, for the humanities or social sciences as they are usually defined in curriculums today. Emotions confined just to men are for Emerson by definition venial, effects of the mean ego, and beneath visionary notice. "Sensibility" and "temperament" inhibit genuine feeling according to Emerson's terminology and are defined in "Experience" and "Fate" as among the "lords of life" that set the physical limits of existence and exploit the personal weaknesses of individuals. Genuine feeling is to be distinguished from them by its greater depth and intensity. It is not, however, as Emerson insists in the "Divinity School Address," again in clear opposition to Edwards and to whatever residue of theocentricity remains in Unitarianism in the 1830s, an additional, unprecedented feeling for something imperceptible in nature, but rather a "sweet and natural goodness, a goodness like thine and mine," which, raised to a high enough pitch, becomes "divine and deifying"; what is entirely the subject of Edwards's *Religious Affections*, how to distinguish between merely natural and truly holy feelings, is no subject at all in Emerson's "Divinity School Address." This address repeatedly dismisses such theist discrimination as false and demeaning to man (as discrimination defined pejoratively according to the modern political connotation) and repeatedly defines religious affection as indistinguishable from an intense love of man and nature, of "Epaminondas, or Washington," or of "a true orator," or of "a dear friend," no less than of "the true God in all ages."[33]

The omission of the recipient and quality of emotion from the truth of emotion is a result of Emerson's describing it not as exclusive to human beings but as the property—moreover as the essence—of all nature. The distinction between emotion and motion is to Emerson a linguistic trace of a dualism that his philosophy rejects. Both are to him incidents of the single creative energy that animates not men on the one hand and things on the other, but a whole universe. The "aboriginal Self" once aroused exerts a magnetism equal to the gravity of heavenly bodies, and a passionate belief is as "much a fact as the sun" in "Self-Reliance." The geological catastrophes during which "new continents are built out of the ruins of an old planet" and the social ones during which civilizations are destroyed and built are no more tempestuous than "invisible thought" in "Circles," and the eruptions of Etna, which "lighten the capes of Sicily," and of Vesuvius, which illuminate the towers and vineyards of Naples," are no hotter or brighter than the light of the "one soul which animates all men" in "The American Scholar." When the Poet allows "the ethereal tides to roll and circulate through him . . . his speech is thunder." The "pulses" of affection by which Man lives are not only equal to the accidents of the external world but are identical to them, enabling Man to "thrive" on never-ending contest in "Experience." The "opinion of the million" in "Fate" exemplifies the same explosive power as steam, and the will of even a single man "appears to share the life of things, and to be an expression of the same laws which control the tides and sun, numbers and quantities" in "Character." To feel deeply, as feeling is described in all of these essays, is to participate in the creativity of nature. Emerson does not recommend that emotion be volcanic. He refuses to distinguish between human and material eruptions. His emphasis does not represent an emotionalism, such as that of the "Age of Sensibility," since this implies an exclusive attention, first to man (in the restrictive sense) and next to one aspect of humanity, emotion instead of reason. Rather, the humanist discourse of emotion declares a universal truth, shared by the human and the other than human, including the inanimate, by Man as Emerson describes Man. Emerson, and romantics in general, do not select one category from theist discourse to stress above all others. They write in a new pattern that wholly takes the place of theism. Although often using the same words, romantics speak another language. Emotion has an entirely different meaning to Emerson and to Edwards, to humanists and to theists. The relation between them is ultimately not even one of contradiction, but of difference.[34]

The entire career of humanism, including the self-consciousness of humanism that modern phenomenology constitutes, is contained, or at least suggested, by Emerson's writings. The later essays, although not retracting the philosophy of the early ones, yet display the eventually fatiguing and demoralizing circularity of humanist discourse. This destiny is probably not peculiar to humanism, Franklin's cynical moralism signifying perhaps a similar end for theism, as may also be signified by the near-aphasia brought on by Edwards's encounters with Divinity. Nor is the destiny of humanism only or best expressed by Emerson; the querulousness of both Hawthorne and Melville suggests more evidently than any of Emerson's misgivings the end of humanism, including— among other implicitly deconstructive passages from their writings, a few of which will be examined in the next section—Hawthorne's meticulously itemizing the morbidities of Zenobia's dead body at the end of *The Blithdale Romance* so as with cruel irony to expose "how much Nature seems to love us! And how readily, nevertheless, without a sigh or a complaint, she converts us to a mean purpose." The complaint is directed not at nature but at a perception of nature that pretends to see in "the whole circle of animal life" anything pleasing or consolatory. And Hawthorne's resigned endorsement of Hilda's vocation as a copiest in *The Marble Faun* is less a positive evocation of character than a characterological retort to the romantic ideal of originality expressed in "The Poet" and other romantic aesthetics. Similarly deconstructive of humanism is Melville's subtle parodying of the apotheosizing potential of human courage when, in the beginning of *Pierre*, he describes the naming in perpetuity of "Saddle Meadows" in memory of Pierre's grandfather—a general shot dead while sitting wounded, unhorsed, on just a saddle, and still urging his troops onward— a spectacle that anticipates Babo's diabolically anti-romantic symbolism in refashioning the figurehead for the slave ship after the rebellion in "Benito Cereno" and that seems directed in particular at Melville's own preceding novel, whose climactic image is of a dead arm hammering in eternal defiance, as much as abstractly at the romantic ideal of heroism.[35]

But Emerson's romanticism is earlier than that of Hawthorne or Melville and at least initially less qualified, and so his queries, although never so bitter, appear within his corpus in relatively sharp relief. One is especially striking. Emerson says in "Experience" that the Fall of Man occurs not when Man exceeds the limit of his authority, as in the theist interpretation of the Judeo-Christian myth, but when Man realizes the full extent of his power. Emerson begins the essay by asking "where do we find ourselves?" and continues in the opening pages to suggest that mean selves inevitably look for and find themselves in meanness. The Deep Self is not conducting this search, however, and is presumably still capable of finding more; despite an unusually glum tone, the essay does not begin by conceding the impossibility of experience in the higher sense. But later Emerson implies a different, more serious, prophetic concession, not just that half-men are short-sighted or that mean spirit, or indigestion, colors perception. A single poignant statement from "Experience" suddenly, and almost pellucidly, exposes the whole structure of humanism in admitting that Man may tire of looking at himself: "It is very unhappy, but too late to be helped, the discovery we have made that we exist. That discovery is called the Fall of Man. Ever afterwards we suspect our instruments. We have learned that we do not see directly, but mediately, and that we have no means of correcting these colored and distorting lenses which we are, or of computing the amount of their errors. Perhaps these subject-lenses have a creative power; perhaps there are no objects. Once we lived in what we saw; now, the rapaciousness of this new power, which threatens to absorb all things, engages us. Nature, art, persons, letters, religions, objects, successively tumble in, and God is but one of its ideas. Nature and literature are subjective phenomena; every evil and every good thing is a shadow which we cast." The sadness of this passage is transitory. Emerson concludes "Experience" by encouraging himself to abandon the comforts of middle-aged prosperity and to continue venturing against the risks of solitude—"never mind the defeat; up again, old heart!" The passage foreshadows, however, the yearning for "objectivity" that in various forms and in varying degrees haunts postromantic humanist discourse, especially in American culture. Having proclaimed a Self that includes everything, romanticism bequeathes both the philosophical confidence that Man can know all and the philosophical claustrophobia of all mirroring Man, the fear that "there are no objects," that "every evil and every good thing is a shadow which we cast." Ironically, it is while suspecting the value of self-consciousness that Emerson becomes most self-conscious, most truly critical of his own writing. This brief doubt makes visible for a moment the humanism that as the discursive pattern of Emerson's writing is elsewhere so profoundly implicit.[36]

4. The End of Humanism

The phenomenology of humanist discourse begins when romanticism becomes problematic, when it no longer seems what humanism wants it to seem, which is in humanist discourse a period or movement, of unusual brevity and accomplishment, to be sure, but still comparable as a classification to those longer and less illustrious periods coming before and after. That romanticism is so odd in comparison to the various other periods in the modern genealogy of the intellect as to appear a phenomenon wholly anomalous to genealogical classification is manifest structurally. Romanticism is conventionally depicted as never quite new, but as containing more of what preceding periods possess less bountifully, and as never quite old, but as preserved in a variety of less purely romantic descendents. Thus it is made to be at once determinate and infinite, momentary and eternal, a period without precise beginning and ending, with no history of his own, but with vast, really universal breadth—a period among periods and at the same time the period that represents all periods. Romanticism can thus be identified as itself a romantic synecdoche, which is to say that it is more than a symbol, that it is the *Ur*-symbol, the symbol *par excellence*, since in enjoying this stature romanticism has a privilege—that cannot be shared by any other, genuine period, because this stature is by definition nonperiodic—which is that of creating itself. Thus in modern historiography romanticism produces itself with endless, inescapable circularity, and the questions, What is romanticism? or How does romanticism originate? are in modern historiography always begged. Romanticism is according to modern historiography always already there, history becoming the record of the varying of its presence. There is no history of romanticism, nor can one ever be written; within the confines of historicism, romanticism can only be practiced. What can be written, as these paradoxes become evident, are deconstructions of romanticism, and these do exist in significant number, although always controversial and often embattled, outside the scholarship of American culture.

The mildest and least consequential form of the deconstructive criticism of romanticism is that which recognizes the romantic character of modernism. This identification is fairly common in literary criticism, and alone seldom serves any revolutionary intent to disclose romanticism to be the contrivance devised by modern humanism to deny any specific origin and thus pretend to be the legatee of all that is best throughout human culture: Henri Peyre quotes Michel Butor on the romanticism of modern literature in the midst of a very conventional analysis of romanticism, designed primarily to compliment it according to its modernist leanings; Harold Bloom, despite otherwise abrasive tendencies, casually praises romanticism similarly in *The Anxiety of Influence;* and Todorov, with somewhat more the intent of making a revelation, confesses that "the romantic ideology . . . is not yet dead; we share in it. . . . I am perhaps a part of the picture I am drawing of the romantics; but that is because they are a part of me." More agressive analyses note that the romanticism of modern humanism is misunderstood, and sometimes note also that this misunderstanding may be essential to the persistence of the structures of modern culture: Bergson charges that modern historicism continues unself-consciously to commit the romantic (self-)deception of projecting romantic ideals into a preromantic past and thus "retroactively . . . created its own prefiguration in the past and an explanation of itself by what had come before"; Derrida says in agreement with Gerard Genette that "we have not yet been delivered from the Romantic heritage," whose grip is still so tight that even the attempt to attack romanticism "remains itself a part or effect of Romanticism"; a recent article in *PMLA* counts "more than six hundred books and articles published during the first half of this century attempting to define Romanticism," the very number of which is accounted evidence of at least the failure and perhaps the impossibility of the venture; and de Man mentions in a variety of contexts the elusiveness of the residue of romantic structures in modern discourse, such as the almost ghostlike trace of Hegel ("Few thinkers have so many disciples who never read a word of their master's writings") and the equally spectral curse that seems to linger over modern attempts to explain romanticism historically, romanticism stubbornly refusing to submit to precisely the discursive structure that it so effortlessly applies to any other subject, that of the narrative—"The ultimate test or 'proof' of the fact that Romanticism puts the genetic pattern of history in question would then be the impossibility of writing a history of Romanticism. The abundant bibliography that exists on the subject tends to confirm this, for a curious blindness seems to compel historians and interpreters of Romanticism to circumvent the central insights that put their own practice, as historians, into question."[37]

Perhaps the most conspicuous result of these suspicions about romanticism is the attempt to reject romantic historicism, to turn against organic or dialectical explanations not only of change in general but, especially, of what now can be suspected to be the most crucial change that brings romanticism itself into being. The catastrophist explanation of historical change is probably most successfully promoted in current American intellectual historiography by Kuhn. He is noted for emphasizing so vast a disparity between scientific paradigms that, in unsettled periods during which an early one is being succeeded by the next, "a law that cannot even be demonstrated to one group of scientists may occasionally seem intuitively obvious to another." Catastrophism is most successfully promoted in international historical theory by Foucault of course, who is even more conspicuously the champion of "ruptures" in the course of intellectual history caused by the "irruptions" of new discursive patterns. Although Foucault sees two major breaks in the history of Western thought, the first occurring roughly between medieval and classical thought, the second is by far the more controversial, since this break corresponds roughly with the advent of romanticism and inaugurates modern thought with a violence and arbitrariness that calls into question all of our certainties, including even those of the existence of "man" and "life," which Foucault forever brackets with quotation marks and whose mere exclusive relativity within humanist discourse Foucault (in)famously declares. Had Foucault interpreted change to be "sudden and thorough" between medieval and classical "epistemes" only, his catastrophism would be of only academic interest—Foucault himself acknowledges that such modeling of history has a long and diverse group of proponents, none of whom, significantly, ever attains the celebrity of Foucault. But his application of this theory to humanism—his modest proposal that "the second great discontinuity" of intellectual history "at the beginning of the nineteenth century marks the beginning of the modern age"; or, as the simply corollary, that "man—the study of whom is supposed by the naive to be the oldest investigation since Socrates—is probably no more than a rift in the order of things . . . only a recent invention, a figure not yet two centuries old, a new wrinkle in our knowledge"; or, more specifically, that "anthropology constitutes perhaps the fundamental arrangement that has governed and controlled the path of philosophical thought [only] from Kant until our day"—such a proposal offends modernism's neoromantic claim to an ancient and honorable descent and so makes likely the widespread esteem and condemnation that Foucault does in fact receive. Although his detractors are many and often illustrious, his demystifying of romanticism and its legacies in modern humanism is by now incontestibly a major position in intellectual historiography, to which even the considerable opposition to him testifies indirectly, but which is indicated obviously by an equal or greater number of supporters. The latter include Todorov, who states flatly and without any immediate effort at substantiation or clarification that, around 1800, "a viewpoint that had been dominant for centuries in the West gave way to another that, I believe, still reigns today," which recognition requires that the study of discourse produced before 1800 be a "heterology" rather than the "homology" recommended by romantic historiography. Other supporters are John O. Lyons, according to whose identical timing "the turn appears to come toward the end of the eighteenth century," and also James Engell, according to whose narrower study of the imagination the modern definition "developed in the Enlightenment and triumphant in Romanticism, marks the end of an epoch stretching back 2500 years and introduces a new stage of thought and letters, now two hundred years in progress," and also D. W. Robertson, who warns that the lesson of catastrophist theory is that "what we call the past is, in effect, a series of foreign countries inhabited by strangers. . . . Concealed self-study through the inadequate medium of the past only stultifies us within the narrow confines of our own naively envisioned perspectives. The specious and easy 'relevance' achieved by positing 'universal humanity' and thus imposing our own prejudices on the past is not merely detrimental to understanding. It will soon become absurd in the light of a growing awareness of the complexity of historical processes." Even *PMLA* concedes the inevitable, a former editor not long ago polling the footnotes of recent submissions and discovering that Foucault and "structuralist" critics of his ilk have become predominant, an indication that Kuhn guesses to be an early sign of paradigm change and that the former editor of *PMLA* does not quite succeed in being facetious toward, and recent *PMLA* articles dealing with romanticism generally at least demonstrate awareness of Foucault, and occasionally show reverance, as in an article that praises Foucault's catastrophism as hardly molesting the corpus of intellectual history at all, since Foucault metaphorically wields "a knife that never needs sharpening because it glides through the natural divisions without ever touching muscle or bone. Foucault's periodization is not new, but he justifies it subtly, precisely, and plausibly."[38]

Although the radical questioning of humanism and the theory of historical discontinuity on which such radical questioning is often based are relatively new to literary criticism, especially in the United States, both are prevalent in modern philosophy, at least as early as the beginning of the twentieth century, and perhaps, if modern phenomenological literary critics are correct, in even the earliest romantic discourse. The status of "things" is problematic in the epistemology of Kant, is provisional in the phenomenology of Hegel, and remains at least equivocal in even the least phenomenological modern discourse, thus making unstable all modern citations of "externality" or "objectivity," including the neoromantic claims of humanism to be descended genealogically and historically from some "other." Modern phenomenology claims to do no more than make this implication explicit and pointed, such as when Husserl tries to correct the "naturalistic misconceptions" of modern empiricism by noting that "we have an infinitude of knowledge previous to all deduction, knowledge whose mediated connections . . . have nothing to do with deduction." Or when, anticipating Kuhn, Husserl states the ontological paradox, in essence eliminating the possibility of a truly philosophical ontology, that " 'the real world,' as it is called, the correlative of our factual experience, then represents itself as *a special case of various possible worlds and non-worlds*," such that "we must not therefore let ourselves be deceived by any talk of the thing over against consciousness or about 'Being in itself.' " Or when, again anticipating Kuhn, Husserl states the consequent epistemological paradox, similarly eliminating the possibility of a truly philosophical epistemology, that "discoveries are *predesignated in accordance with their essential type*, and are, in brief, motivated."[39]

That ontology and epistemology have no real place in a humanist discourse that grants no genuine being to otherness is implied also by Heidegger when he rejects both "realism"—the attempt to prove the existence of an other by explaining the interactions among "things," the physics of motion, for example—and "idealism"—the distinguishing of an "indefinite" and "un-Thing-like" subjectivity or consciousness—in favor of a phemomenology that does away with the existence of either as any more than illusion. Beyond undermining the romantic and neoromantic discourse relating past to present, origin to outcome, progenitor to offspring, such phenomenological reductions undermine the even broader romantic and neoromantic discourse relating the environment, "life," to culture, allowing for cultural phenomenologies that can startle and outrage conventional, unself-consciously humanist interpretation. It becomes possible, for example, to understand the subjects of art as the consequence of nothing in "life," neither the life of the artist nor of anybody else, but of the prefigured patterns of signification organized in particular semioses, as in Jaques Lacan's insolent reversal of Goethe's famous dictum (which reverses the famous, preceding dictum from John 1:1: "In the beginning was the Word. . . .") " 'in the beginning was the action,' is itself reversed in its turn: it was certainly the *verbe* that was in the beginning," and in de Man's deconstructing an infralinguistic compulsion toward such ambivalent figures as chiasmus in the style of Rilke as the best explanation of the predominance of the theme of loss in Rilke's poetry, and de Man's similar deconstruction of the rhetorical gift for making excuses intrinsic to Rousseau's style as the best explanation of the predominance of the confession in Rousseau's writings, and Michael Fried's astonishing phemomenology of two paintings by Courbet that transforms the apparently superrealistic slices of life shown in "After Dinner at Ornans" and "The Stonebreakers" into covert *mises en abîme,* the former composed of nothing other than specular images of the artist himself, the latter covertly presenting the two proletarian laborers so as to signify the artist's left and right hands.[40]

Finally, there is Derrida's characteristically extreme and comprehensive summation that textuality is radically insular: "this interweaving, this textile, is the *text* produced only in the transformation of another text." Even more expansively, Derrida deconstructs the pretense that nature is the origin of romantic discourse like that of Rousseau: "there has never been anything but writing; there have never been anything but supplements, substitutive significations which could only come forth in a chain of differential references, the 'real' supervening, and being added only while taking on meaning from a trace and from an invocation of the supplement, etc. And thus to infinity, for we have read, *in the text,* that the absolute present, Nature, that which words like 'real mother' name, [has] always already escaped, [has] never existed; that what opens meaning and language is the disappearance of natural presence."[41]

Phenomenology encourages the polemic denunciation of all forms of positivism in interpretation, leading both Todorov and Jonathan Culler to criticize modern aesthetics for taking for granted, in their overwhelming concentration on the metaphor, that this figure preserves the "object" in various forms of verisimilitude and "thereby makes it easier to defend literature as a mode of vision whose language is functional." It also leads both Todorov and Derrida to criticize modern theology for an unexamined acceptance of deity as the "objective," "ultimate" or "transcendental signified," and Lacan to deride positivist psychoanalysis as tending toward Plato's ancient satire on realism, the embracing of trees, or, worse, "a reciprocal sniffing between analyst and subject." Phenomenology opens the Pandora's Box of humanism; the demon ridiculing the paternity of humanism is only one of the demons to escape, and is joined by others challenging every supposed absolute whose unshakable "objectivity" humanism believes necessary for support.[42]

What probably offends modern positivist interpretation most is phenomenology's claim to find Pandora's box in the very heart of humanism. Methodologically committed to the nonessential entity of "things," phenomenology cannot without fundamental inconsistency allow its own procedures to appear truly foreign to the subjects to which they are applied. Thus the catachresis of coining the term *deconstruction* is apt, signifying more than a mere negative, and thereby ultimately self-defeating inversion of or opposition to structure, a mere destruction. The coinage signifies rather a positive addition whose very superfluity reveals the arbitrary and intrinsic phenomenality of structure, the unwieldy and unfamiliar addition of a prefix to a sign that makes manifest how all signification takes place. Deconstruction, and Derrida's even more fastidious catachresis, *"différance,"* are perfectly significant of the whole enterprise of phenomenology, representing in semantic form a methodology that adds artificially onto meaning and then builds artifically onto form so as to show how (un)naturally meaning and form are generated. This is the principle behind Nietzsche's famous oxymoron, the *"strong* pessimism" arising from a "plethora of health, plenitude of being," whose fullness is required to counteract the "influence" of classicism and to support genuine analysis of the historicist notion of classical antiquity as an ancestor of modern culture, and behind Nicolai Hartman's perverse hypothetical discipline of "aporetics," a science of the barriers to science, a knowledge of what is impossible to know, and behind Heidegger's paradoxical justification of the violence of his method as necessary only to reveal common sense to common sense, which, without such apparent assaults on reason as Heidegger's, will forever "misunderstand understanding." This is the principle also behind the sublimations of modern phemomenological critics like René Girard, Eugenio Donato, and John Lyons of their scorn for the "pieties of commencement speeches" and the platitudes of book reviews into "a more searching and ruthless method of analysis"; or behind analysis that "can only seize violently an interpretation that is already there, and that it must overturn, overthrow, shatter with the blows of a hammer"; or behind "a medicinal argument" that "might be considered harsh by many." *Deconstruction* is inflammatory in large part because of its profession to reach the incendiary resolution that "the motif of homogeneity, the theological motif *par excellance,* is decidedly the one to be destroyed" directly through and not in spite of the modern discourse of immanence, the "quality and rigor" of deconstruction thus being "measured by the critical rigor" with which its own inescapable "relationship to the history of metaphysics and to inherited concepts is thought."[43]

The most carefully guarded of the "inherited concepts" is that of man, or self, and this is the one accordingly whose deconstruction seems, initially, most baffling and—eventually, once the purpose of the deconstruction is recognized beneath terminology that often is so very technical and specialized and reflexive that the revolutionary intent is obscure—most outrageous to humanism. This deconstruction goes beyond noting the phenomenality of mankind as the subject of discourse, as a category of philosophy, or a character in fiction, or a perspective in poetry; the problem of the self is simultaneous with the apparition of the self, as de Man notes in discussing Hegel's discourse on selfhood. And examples of what Geoffrey Hartman calls "surnomie" exist as themes self-consciously presented throughout romantic and especially neoromantic literature, arguably being even the dominant theme in Hawthorne's fiction, reappearing continually in such forms as an ancestor's portrait that cannot be removed from the wall, the transformation of *heimlichkeit* into claustrophobia, entrapment in a portrait gallery or by oversized effigies at a carnival, complaint against the English countryside as being too crowded with Tennyson's talking oaks. The theme is present also in such essays by Emerson as "Experience" and "Fate." Skepticism about man becomes acute in phenomenological analyses when not only the humanity of subjects of discourse, but also that of writers and readers of discourse is questioned; this is the implication of Husserl's complicating both diction and syntax so as to depersonalize knowledge, fussily preferring "eidetic worker" over thinker or subject, for example. This is the basis for what is probably the most difficult terminological abstraction in modern phenomenology, Heidegger's usurpation of *Dasein* (specified or determinate being) to name the phenomenon of knowing so as to include that which is known along with that which knows, and his conversely investing the common signifer *care* with multiple signifieds so as to construct a sign representing virtually all relation, not just relations including persons or those requiring affection. This is also the implication of current phenomenological theories of reading, that not only "orphan" texts, as Fish and Culler describe the impersonal designation of the status of textuality, but also dehumanize the reader, transforming reading into a systemic process the understanding of which does not require, and is even impeded by, the assumption that a person is doing the reading.[44]

The methodological purity of phenomenology is hardest to maintain in analyses of man, however, for the very reason that man is the center of humanist discourse and deconstruction of man is in the context of humanist discourse unavoidably contaminated by negation, the merely destructive force of misanthropy and cultural pessimism. The studied banality of some of Fish's sloganlike titles: "Is there a text in this class?" "Who's afraid of Wolfgang Iser?" "With the compliments of the author," lapses into mere irreverence, and so do the more impassioned and lengthy polemics against man delivered by Foucault: "[Anthropology] is essential, since it forms part of our history; but it is disintegrating before our eyes, since we are beginning to recognize and denounce it, in a critical mode, both a forgetfulness of the opening that made it possible and a stubborn obstacle standing obstinately in the way of an immanent new form of thought. To all those who still wish to talk of man, about his reign or his liberation, to all those who still ask themselves questions about what man is in his essence, to all those who wish to take him as their starting-point in their attempts to reach the truth, to all those, who, on the other hand, refer all knowledge back to the truths of man himself, to all those who refuse to mythologize without anthropologizing, who refuse to think without immediately thinking that it is man who is thinking, to all those warped and twisted forms of reflection we can answer only with a philosophical laugh—which means, to a certain extent, a silent one."[45]

Foucault's rhetoric, as extravagant as his rhetoric can become, seldom turns against him, so the unmistakable impression that this passage is shrill rather than bemused, and is certainly not silent or even terse in denouncing humanism, represents an uncharacteristic vulnerability of Foucault, himself, to a deconstruction that exposes him indirectly testifying to the power of precisely the humanism he condemns. This lapse allies him not with some "immanent new form of thought," but with the old neoromantic *triste* of writers whom he prefers to outstrip, such as Claude Lévi-Strauss, whose most famous book ends with a similar paean to inhumanity, the urge to "grasp the essence of what our species has been and still is beyond thought and beneath society: an essence that might be vouchsafed to us in a mineral more beautiful than any work of Man; in the scent, more subtly evolved than our books, that lingers in the heart of a lily; or in the wink of an eye, heavy with patience, serenity, and mutual forgiveness, that sometimes, through an involuntary understanding one can exchange with a cat." Such *mensch-schmertz* imprisons Foucault in the discourse he would escape, and can be found in texts earlier than those of Lévi-Strauss, and in texts that cannot possibly yet be directly concerned with the problems of modernism. It can be found, for example, in the very earliest, still romantic expressions of dissatisfaction with the romantic idealization of man, such as in Melville's *Pierre,* where a character's illegitimacy and orphanhood surprisingly inspire a yearning not for attachment to but rather for withdrawal from humanity: "my spirit seeks different food from happiness . . . . I pray for peace—for motionlessness—for the feeling of myself, as of some plant, absorbing life without seeking it, and existing without individual sensation." And it can be found in neoromantic American literature not much later, in the poetry of Emily Dickinson, for example, which in one poem invokes a "quartz-contentment" indistinguishable from the stoicism of Melville's Isabel and from the stone- and flower- and cat-worship of Lévi-Strauss.[46]

Another, related pitfall of phenomenological polemics is that in contesting neoromantic etiologies, deriving from the discourse of man as discourses of the evolution of man's presence, it sometimes unwittingly substitutes another, and even cruder form of neoromantic causality for the one it often so angrily wishes to displace. This, too, is exemplified in Foucault's writings, in his impatient and elliptical explanations of the connections among the three major sections of his periodization of Western discourse. Foucault tries to conceal the absence in his theory of a way to account for change by implying that change is so precipitous and massive as to humble all attempts at causal explanations, change being so "sudden and thorough" that "the traditional explanations—spirit of the time, technological and social changes, influences of various kinds—struck me for the most part as being more magical than effective. In this work, then, I left the problem of causes to one side." Lacan is equally negative, conceding that "it is the principle of analysis that nobody understands anything of what happens" and that, accordingly, "the idea of the unifying unity of the human condition has always had on me the effect of a scandalous lie." Kuhn is only a bit more forthcoming, saying that since the causes for paradigm shifts are multiple and desultory—including such nonscientific factors as the personal repute of individual scientists, the accidents of the dramatic confirmations of particular theories, the rhetorical impact of the ways in which certain theories are presented, and the aesthetic values of theories, how "neat" or "elegant" they are apart from their truthfulness—the explanations of paradigm shifts are subsequently no more than tentative and "impressionistic," which is to admit more openly than Foucault or Lacan that the "magical" character of causality is not just left to stand but is indirectly supported.[47]

Other phenomenologists throw up their hands even more obviously and submissively when confronted with the problem of cause. De Saussure confesses that linguistic change "comes about through sheer accident" and that "language is a mechanism that continues to function in spite of the deterioration to which it is subjected." Lyons states similarly that "it is impossible to say exactly why this change came about, why the very nature of men's consciousness and the concept of how things were known was altered toward the middle of the eighteenth century." These failures do not simply leave gaps in the arguments that are forced to acknowledge them; they reserve a place for the crudest kind of "otherness," "fate" or accident, to occupy, and they permit the deconstruction of themselves as unselfconsciously patterned after the crudest form of narrative based on the most implicit acceptance of the reality and power of "otherness," which is the melodrama. Foucault is merely defensive and not very threatening when he attacks historians who continue to believe in continuity as "those agoraphobics of history and time," because he is no more than their opposite, the thrill-seeker of history and time, the erstwhile melodramatic protagonist of his own historiography who affirms the "objectivity" of history and time even more hyperbolically than the historians whom he denounces for their timidity.[48]

The anti-romances of discontinuity written by Foucault and others can rather easily be deconstructed as disguising synchronic semioses as diachronic plots, as melodramatizing systemic difference as catastrophic "rupture." The problem of cause disappears not when cause is secretly idolized, as in Foucault's catastrophism, but when cause is overtly replaced with differentiation as the true phenomenology of history and when attention is shifted from "events" as the repository of the meaning of history to the consciousness that determining the meaning of "events" creates history, the *"Dasein"* in which being and knowing, and thus the truth of both history and consciousness, are the same. Radical synchronism is always the implication of humanism, whose emergence is only especially delayed in modern historiography because the "object" of study seems for so long and so obviously "objective" and diachronic; recognition that the phenomena of history are always already coded, either immediately in the form of texts or mediately in the form of other data that, prior to and as the condition of being converted to historical discourse, must be encoded, and that the study of history is consequently always some form of reading, some form of phenomenology, and that the most mimetic historiography is finally not narrative but semiotic, is slow. This recognition is relentless, however, becoming commonplace in ethnography and anthopology since Lévi-Strauss, whose analyses of families and tribes replace the "fact" of generation in genealogies with the phenomenon of intelligibility in the scientific study of them; and in historical linguistics at least since Jacobsen, who as early as 1927 discards the humanist assumption that the relationship between modern poetry and medieval poetry is "the same as between the machine-gun and the bow" in favor of the phenomenological one that all parts of the whole of literature are related according to a structuralism inherent to the consideration of literature as a whole, which is to say, the very constitution of literature as a phenomenon; and in narrative theory at least since Barthes, who deconstructs the temporal structure of stories as an elaboration of the *post hoc* fallacy and whose history of narrative accordingly makes fun of all source-hunting; and currently in the semiology of Culler, who points out in terms more accessible than those of Derrida that the condition of intelligibility is codification, that codification "can only originate or be originated if it is already encoded in a prior code" and that to search for an original "ultimate signified" prior to codification is to deny in the act of reading the condition that permits reading to occur. Other well-established literary applications of semiotics are Julia Kristeva's theory of intertextuality; Bloom's theory of "influence," which is more self-consciously a dramatic figure for the synchronic "roads" that connect texts than is Foucault's catastrophism; and Riffaterre's theory of "filiation," so radically synchronic that Riffatterre can defiantly reveal at the end of an analysis of a text that its "intertext," that which contains the "hypograms" of meaning from which the meaning of the subsequent text departs and on which the subsequent text's meaning depends, is written fifteen years after the text that, according to Riffaterre's semiosis, the "intertext" "influences."[49]

Derrida sums up the progress of the revolution: "For over a century this uneasiness has been evident in philosophy, in science, in literature. All the revolutions in these fields can be interpreted as shocks that are gradually destroying the linear model. Which is to say the *epic* model. What is thought today cannot be written according to the line and the book, except by imitating the operation implicit in teaching modern mathematics with an abacus. This inadequation is not *modern*, but it is exposed today better than ever before. The access to pluri-dimensionality and to delinearized temporality is not a simple regression toward the mythogram; on the contrary, it makes all the rationality subjected to the linear model appear as another form and another age of mythography. The meta-rationality and meta-scientificity which are thus announced within the meditation upon writing can therefore be no more shut up within a science of man than conform to the traditional idea of science. In one and the same gesture, they leave *man, science,* and *line* behind."[50]

This last is Foucault's goal as well, but the violence of his pursuit paradoxically makes the goal forever elusive, which paradox is recognized by Derrida and prompts him to disbelieve in "discursive ruptures, in an unequivocal 'epistemological break,' " and to insist, rather, that "breaks are always, and fatally, reinscribed in an old cloth that must continually, interminably, be undone," a "cloth" representing not continuity, not what Derrida stigmatizes as the "epic" or "linear" model nor what this reading stigmatizes in modern American cultural historiography as the unitary model, but synchronism. The melodramatizing of the semioses among the parts of any semiotic whole, among the characters of the alphabet, for example, produces more sudden and unexpected shifts between opposition and allegiance than even the bloodiest and most eventful melodramatic plot.[51]

That this rich and various phenomenological discourse, only barely adumbrated here, is just beginning to be read by modern American intellectural historians and remains virtually unread by critics of any other than the most contemporary American literature represents no mere deficiency in American scholarship, no cultural lag. The resistance of modernism to phenomenological analysis, to the reflexive terminologies and the claims to find the tools for deconstruction within modern discourse and the attacks on "man" and "life," is most intense in American culture because phenomenology threatens the identity of the culture and the profession of its students, threatens what that rare, phenomenological critic of American literature, John Rowe, calls the "protective defenses that govern the various schools of American studies." Phenomenology brackets, puts in quotation marks and thereby reveals as no more than a part of a sign, what is acutely hypostatized and acutely in need of punctuation that redundantly calls attention to its status as a signifier: "America," itself. Thus in the United States phenomenology seeks to do battle with humanism allied to nationalism. This coalition enjoys an extraordinarily successful neoteny, and although appearing ungainly and infantile in the broader field of contemporary literary theory, remains master of the limited one of American culture. Not only are foreign invaders excluded, but native variants are ultimately either driven out or forced to conform. After saying in the climactic part of the climactic essay in *Errand Into the Wilderness* that reports of the Hiroshima bombing, the "event" *par excellence,* may derive more from the conventions of eschatological literature than from the eyewitnessing of even so unprecedented and cataclysmic an "event" (which claim represents a revolt against the dictatorship of American environmentalism more daring than the one implied by claiming that even mercantilist colonial Virginia has a "mind," and as daring a one as that implied by the claim that Rilke writes about loss out of rhetorical compulsion and Rousseau writes about guilt out of stylistic compulsion) Miller submits elsewhere, meekly, that the "land" or the "wilderness" is, "in the final analysis," the progenitor of American culture and the sire of Jonathan Edwards. "America" is "nature's nation," to be sure, not only in spite of contrary "facts" that Miller knows can be made to show "America" acting viciously against nature and that, after Miller, Bercovitch knows can be made to show "America" as acting viciously against people, but in ways that ironically differ from and sadly dominate the interpretations of modern American cultural historiography.[52]

Examples of the application of unitary theory in modern American scholarship are cited in the first chapter of this reading and recalled here not with the hope of proving that a single model silently reigns; the field is as yet far from capable of such a proof. These examples are designed to provoke; the more objectionable they manage to be, the more real and powerful and determinate, and potentially deficient, becomes what this reading so grandiloquently and repeatedly calls modern American cultural historiography, and the more real, and necessary, become alternative theories of American culture. This reading occupies the sacrificial position of an *avant garde* that lures superior force into accepting the possibility that a real challenge is possible, the acceptance of which constitutes instant vulnerability. Or it occupies the devious position of the riddler of folklore who lures some figure of omnipotence into answering to a proper name, usually complex, polysyllabic, and thus unique, like "Rumplestiltskin" (or "modern American cultural historiography") the acceptance of which constitutes instant mortality, just as being tricked into answering to the title *humanist* would acknowledge the possible existence of a genuinely different predecessor, a theist, perhaps, as well as of a genuinely different successor, maybe a phenomenologist. This reading measures its effectiveness in units of rejection. Its positive justification will seem to modern American cultural historiography of a slight and rarefied value, that of showing how American culture is a conveniently limited and particularly concentrated instance of humanism, and so serves well the heuristic purpose of deconstructing the supranational, semiotic phenomenon of humanism. It will no doubt only further annoy by claiming the potential support of several modern commentaries on "America" by several much-celebrated modern American writers, including Faulkner, whose insistence that he writes about the South arbitrarily, simply because the South is what he happens to know best, amounts in this context to a great deal more than fencing with simple-minded or philistine critics. Similarly deconstructive implications can be found in the works of a number of other major modern American writers whose writings are customarily seen as contributing most to the independence and the reality of "America." By making explicit several of these deconstructive implications this reading will end.[53]

5. The End of "America"

"The land," or the "wilderness," or the "frontier," or "America," no matter how eclectically defined, are all names for the same chimera; they are to modern American cultural historiography what infinitist theology is to modern religion, or first cause to modern etiology, or "ultimate signified" to modern semiotics—expressions of theism that devolve in humanist discourse into incantations of self-forgetfulness. Phenomenology, from its earliest articulation in the epistemology of Kant, knows that there is no place for *pre-* or *a*-systemic "things as such" in truly philosophical modern thought, and all truly philosophical modern thinkers realize this, from Nietszche, who knows what happens to "God," to Foucault and Derrida, who know what is happening to "man." But the hypostatizing of otherness is a necessary delusion of humanism, as Hegel and Husserl and Kuhn all demonstrate, and the fecundity of modern American cultural historiography constitutes enormous proof of both the practical utility and the theoretical unself-consciousness of hypostization. "The land" is always already appropriated, or civilized, or defiled, or just plain lost, as the condition of the existence of the land in humanist discourse, and the yearning for some American environment that is anterior to signification only seems to represent modern American culture's nostalgia for a paradise lost while in actuality representing modern American culture's unself-conscious urge for nonentity. Death, as Freud finally comes to say, is not extrinsic to, is no less instinctual than life. Deconstruction is no French disease threatening to pollute our own homegrown method. Deconstruction is the implication of humanism from the outset of humanism, no less in American culture than elsewhere. To realize that belief in the presence of the land is the peculiarly American humanist fantasy does not require superimposition of Derridean "grammatology" on modern American cultural historiography; such a deconstruction can be performed using nothing other than the earliest of modern American materials, the writings of that group canonized over a generation ago by Matthiessen: Emerson, Thoreau, Hawthorne, Melville, and Whitman.

That the disappearance of the "object"—"the land" or whatever—may identify the very process of cognition, and not just some meanly egotistical, false, or partial kind of cognition, is implied by Emerson throughout his writings, not just in supposedly pessimistic essays like "Experience" and "Fate." What he regrets in these essays as mere "temperament" represents nothing substantially different from the clear perception idealized in earlier writings, no genuinely foreign opponent, but only a decadent form that, like all decadent forms, exposes the structure that lies hidden in more vital ones. Thus the subjectivity, the error, the sickness lamented in "Experience" and "Fate" can be seen in the context of subsequent developments in humanism to prefigure phenomenology, truth, health. Emerson's negations signify only the philosophical inchoateness of his humanism, which at this stage is mistaking itself for another.

Thoreau and Whitman seem less to suffer from misgivings, the relative paucity of which in their writings can be cited as evidence that their humanism is even less mature. But Emerson's doubts concerning subjectivism have their equivalent in the perceptual insecurities implied by Thoreau's and Whitman's repeated and exaggerated assertions of the fusion of nature and the self, a paradoxically dehumanizing tendency of early humanism that is condemned by, among many neoromantic critics of romanticism, George Santayana. Commenting in *Character and Opinion in the United States* on the romantic ontology of Josiah Royce, Santayana charges that in Royce's equations of man with nature or God, "the terrible Absolute had been simply translated to the self. You were your own master, and omnipotent; but you were no less dark, hostile, and inexorable to yourself than the gods of Calvin or Spinoza had been before." Santayana's point is the simply moralistic one, repeated by a host of anti-romantic writers— such as, in the United States, Mark Twain, William Dean Howells, Emily Dickinson, and Henry James—that romanticism can be cruel. Santayana goes on first to deduce that Royce's olympian perspective ought to make him negligent of the human cost of the sinking of the Lusitania, and then, after reporting Royce's actual outrage over the event, accounting his reaction "an honest lapse from his logic," and thus does no more than negate a type of humanism present in Royce's writings. Santayana's criticism discovers a phenomenological implication of the bravado of Royce and other early humanist writers, however, and suggests how, once the moralistic impulse has subsided, this bravado might be deconstructed. Royce grimly admits into the self the same phantom that Emerson resignedly excludes, and both operations occur in behalf of the same wish of humanism to forget itself by hypostitizing an other, whether indirectly by assimilating a "dark, hostile, and inexorable" reality, and so, as Santayana accuses Royce, paradoxically imply the inhumanity of the world, or directly by conceding like Emerson that a truth lies "objectively" beyond man's "temperamental" ability to know.[54]

Instances of the former are very numerous in the writings of Thoreau and Whitman, and many approach the self-consciousness, if not the moralism, of Santayana's criticism. Thoreau often celebrates the self by emphasizing its strangeness, even to itself, as, for example, in the conclusion of *Walden* where he likens himself not only to the world, and not only to the New World, but to the newest, unexplored part still "white on the chart." Whitman is even more expansive, although at times his breadth would seem to become mysterious and self-daunting; on several occasions he admits, usually after an especially exhaustive list of capacities or accomplishments, to not knowing who or what "Walt Whitman, a Cosmos," really is—at the end of *Song of Myself*, for example, when he declares "there is that in me—I do not know what it is—but I know it is in me," and similarly in "Our Old Feuillage," "O lands! all so dear to me—what you are, (whatever it is) I putting it at random in these songs, become a part of that, whatever it is," and also in "As I Ebb'd with the Ocean of Life," in which the apparent self-reconciliation of the end of the poem never fully clarifies the bafflement of the beginning: ". . . I have not once had the least idea who or what I am, / But that before all my arrogant poems the real Me stands yet untouch'd, untold, altogether unreach'd." And Whitman's heliotropic symbols of the self strongly imply incongruities between man and the sun with which they join him, for example in the overstatement of comic boasts: "Dazzling and tremendous how quick the sun-rise would kill me, / If I could not now and always send sun-rise out of me. / Who also ascend dazzling and tremendous as the sun," "Flaunt of the sunshine I need not your bask—lie over! / You light surfaces only, I force surfaces and depths also." Incongruity is implied also in the *sang-froid* of assuming the disinterested eminence of the sunrise that overlooks "the murder in cold blood of four hundred and twelve young men," an inhuman equanimity like that attributed by Santayana to Royce, and presumed also by Thoreau when in *Walden* he likens his conception of charity to the wholly autonomous radiance of the sun, and by Emerson in "Fate" when he views the "whole circle of animal life" from the sunlike "sufficient perspective" from which carnage appears "refined for higher use."[55]

In Hawthorne's and Melville's writings the phenomenology of experience is virtually explicit, which distinguishes them as more philosophically humanist than those of Emerson, Thoreau, and Whitman. Hawthorne's ironic modesty, for example, is a form of self-consciousness; he deprecates his failure to be inspired by the full light of day in "The Custom-House," but he implies in this passage and others, his fond depiction of Phoebe as symbolically an attenuated or domesticated ray of sunshine in *The House of the Seven Gables*, or his conversely satiric portrayal in the same novel of Jaffrey, whose countenance beams so brightly as to seem to make necessary an extra sprinkling of Concord's dusty streets, that to be equal to such prodigies of nature as the sun is to become less, not more, than human, as Santayana charges. But the deconstructive element of Hawthorne's writings lies not just, or at least not so remarkably, in exposing the monstrosity of man's presuming to become one with some presumably "objective" nature, embodied in a long list of uncompassionate idealists from Hooper through Aylmer to Hollingsworth, and not just in exposing the subjectivity of man's idealization of nature, such as that of Robin in "My Kinsman, Major Molineux" or of the Merrymount revelers, but in suggesting in some of the most basic structures of his major fiction that interpenetration between man and the world is the necessary and normal condition of consciousness.[56]

In Hawthorne's best-known work the semiosis of the scarlet letter is ubiquitous, extending past the thematics and symbolism to the composition of the novel, signifying not only specific meanings within discourse but the way in which discourse makes sense generally. There is no end to this process, no "ultimate signified" past which reference stops, not in the author's intention, nor in his inspiration, not even in his identity, which is to say that the scarlet letter can be taken as signifying signification. That *The Scarlet Letter* is derived from no experience of "objective" reality whatsoever "The Custom-House" is designed at length to demonstrate. Hawthorne's personal situation is shown redundantly, in all of its particulars, to be a lesser version of the personal situation that inspires him; he is forced, in part by loyalty to a friend and in part by circumstance (and in part also, if a campaign biography of a college classmate can be taken as a prostitution of Hawthorne's vocation, by an infidelity, a past, barely licit favor, the particulars of which are presumably never mentioned to his colleagues in the Custom-House and are definitely never mentioned in his description of his experience there) to reside no longer in his ideal chosen place, that used to be Brooke Farm, "an unredeemed, unchristianized, lawless region" not unlike that to which Dimmesdale imagines returning with Hester, but now among ordinary people whose humanity, and thus whose kinship with him, is only gradually realized, and who in turn gradually discount his original alienness and accept him as a nondisruptive member of the community. Hawthorne's situation as a political appointee in a nineteenth-century U.S. Custom-House is a comically reduced version of Hester's situation as an adulteress in seventeenth-century Boston, is the presence that indicates an absent and richer counterpart, is in short the signifier of the sign whose signified is Hester's ordeal.

The narrator of "The Custom-House" is not simply the creator and master of this semiosis, he is part of the semiosis, which is shown also and more obviously in the secondhand character of all the materials he uses to make his story. The letter is a piece of embroidery; the novel's background is supplied by another history, the chronicle of "Mr. Surveyor Pue," Hawthorne's ancient predecessor in the Custom-House, that is found in the attic; and the occasion that provides the final visionary experience that combines all of these signifiers into the composite, derivative one that will be the novel takes place away from the full light of day that Hawthorne confesses to be incapable of humanizing. It takes place in twilight, when the outlines of "objects" and hence their seeming objectivity are diminished, and in the parlor of the Old Manse, which is imbued not only with the personality of Hawthorne and his family (and thus is less a place than an extension of his self) but also with precisely the (lesser) weight of the same kind of interdependence and responsibility that keeps Hester in Boston. That the writer is so many stages removed from an "objective" reality constitutes no deficiency that can be repaired, no challenge that he might quest afterward to overcome, but rather an understatement of the absolute, irrecoverable nonentity of Hester or seventeenth-century Boston or hers and Dimmesdale's and Chillingworth's passion "as such."[57]

No wonder that the autobiographical discourse of *The Scarlet Letter* is a third as long as the fictional discourse, or that the letter A is so often, and so incongruously, inscribed on things and with things in the novel—on the sky, on a body, with cloth and thread and seaweed. *The Scarlet Letter* is written deconstructively about writing, a self-consciousness that will become increasingly pronounced in Hawthorne's writings, eventuating in the dizzying reflexiveness of *The Marble Faun*, with the hereditary, mythological, artistic determination of characters, the fatally repetitive events, the overwritten nature of the setting, Rome and Italy being the palimpsest of human culture, and the redundantly belated inspiration, thrice-removed from "life"—Hawthorne tracing the genesis of the novel to his viewing of a work of art, Kenyon's half-finished bust of Donatello, which is inspired by a prior viewing of another, precedent work of art, the Faun of Praxiteles, thus making *The Marble Faun* a work of art based on a work of art based on a work of art.[58]

A potentially deconstructive, metacritical meaning is most easily detected in the writings of Melville, and perhaps most easily in the superficially unlikely guise of Pip's madness. After being abandoned amid the "joyous, heartless, ever-juvenile eternities," one of which is the sun, "another lonely castaway, though the loftiest and the brightest," and therefore equal to the task of countenancing solitude, Pip is overwhelmed by what Thoreau and Whitman disguise with forced credulity and what Ahab holds at bay—the recognition of the possibility, even the certainty, that "there's nought beyond" the phenomenology of man's perception. Wholly disillusioned, Pip become the interpreter of interpretations, reading the declension of readings of the doubloon, from Ahab's down through Flask's, as nothing other than the declension of a verb—" 'I look, you look, he looks; we look, ye look, they look' "—nothing more than language, a judgment supported by the structure of the novel, which follows "The Doubloon" with "Leg and Arm: The Pequod Meets the Samuel Enderby of London," to show the power of perspective; from the epicurean point of view of the captain and the doctor of the Samuel Enderby, " 'what [Ahab takes] for the White Whale's malice is only his awkwardness.' " But if

Ahab's view is nothing more than interpretation, so is any other view. The second of these companion chapters does not supersede and cancel the first; the relationship between them is no simple irony. Rather, they coexist, the only inequality being measured by the different degree to which each corresponds to the pattern of discourse that *Moby-Dick* identifies as human. This suggests a broadening of standards according to which "what Ahab takes for the White Whale's malice" appears less the delusion of a monomaniac than the truth of mankind.[59]

Similarly, the skepticism embodied by Pip, although arguably becoming so dominant in Melville's later writings as to constitute an intimation of Melville's own eventual cynicism, can be seen phenomenologically to represent only the murmur of humanism becoming self-conscious. Pip comments on Queequeg's preparations for death, the provisioning of the coffin for an afterlife that is the strenuous continuation of Queequeg's present one, foresight that will of course provide for the survival of Ishmael, and also, of course, for the writing of a novel, " 'Queequeg dies game! . . . Pip, he died a coward.' " Queequeg is brave not only because of the dangers of the afterlife he anticipates and is eager to face; he is brave in his capacity to project, at what he presumes to be the hour of his death, any afterlife at all. At the verge of passing over to the "beyond," Queequeg refuses to concede that nothing is there. Pip is a coward not just because he cannot stand the rigors of the whaling life, nor the prospect of more struggle even after death, but because he cannot stand the rigors of belief. He is less a man than Queequeg, perhaps on the verge of no longer being man, perhaps already dead, as suggested by his shifting to past tense when contrasting himself with Queequeg, which is to say that Pip is close to man conscious of himself as no "thing" other than a signifier. That this consciousness is unhappy for Pip, and, ultimately, for Melville, only marks the relatively early, unself-conscious stage of humanism that both occupy. In "Bartleby," the scrivener's isolation makes him seem, like Pip, "a bit of wreck in the mid Atlantic," and his pathetic intransigence would seem to have been provoked by a disillusion like Pip's, the task while working at the Post Office of destroying all the dead letters sent in vain to dead people. And in the third chapter of *The Confidence-Man* "Old Black Guinea," one of the Confidence-Man's disguises, reacts opportunistically to the same kind of disillusion that makes Pip and Bartleby withdraw, trying to trick his victims into believing the disarming lie that he trusts in the sustenance of the same sun whose indifference drives Pip mad.[60]

This kind of bitterness is the first, purely negative reaction to romanticism, to which Melville himself seems not to have succumbed completely, at least not in *Moby-Dick*. The opening "Etymology" and "Extracts" are irreverent, not only toward prose fiction as a genre, in prefacing a novel so unconventionally, but also toward the "objectivity" of their topic, introducing the whale as the product less of nature than of discourse, a phenomenology that is qualified, however, by the satire of both having been compiled by Bartleby-like copyists: the "late consumptive usher to a grammar school" and the "sub-sub-librarian." Only later in the philosophizing of humanism does the probability that there is nothing beyond language and thought become trivial in comparison to the knowledge that everything, including the "land," remains potentially, in Heidegger's terminology, "ready-to-hand."[61]

Heidegger's calm phenomenological insight is beyond Melville, who approaches it only through a realization, explicated in *Pierre* and implicit throughout The *Confidence-Man*, even more terrifying than Ahab's suspicion, which is that the "nought" so maddening to Ahab and Pip and Bartleby may not be beyond but within: "Appalling is the soul of a man! Better one might be pushed off into the material spaces beyond the uttermost orbit of our sun, than once feel himself fairly afloat in himself," and, soon after in this same chapter from *Pierre*, which mixes the metaphor rhetorically so as to suggest the monstrous ubiquity of Man, and which begins to deconstruct the figure of Ahab as a pyramid in "Queen Mab" just as the former passage begins to deconstruct Pip's plight in "The Castaway," "by vast pains we mine into the pyramid; with joy we espy the sarcophagus; but we lift the lid—and no body is there!—appallingly vacant as vast is the soul of a man!"[62]

What Nick Carraway imagines to have beckoned to those Dutch explorers in the reverie with which Fitzgerald's *The Great Gatsby* famously concludes is no virgin. What beckons is rather that most familiar, best-known, most overused of attractions: "I became aware of the old island here that flowered once for Dutch sailors' eyes—a fresh green breast of the new world. Its vanished trees, the trees that had made way for Gatsby's house, had once pandered in whispers to the last and greatest of all human dreams; for a transitory enchanted moment man must have held his breath in the presence of this continent, compelled into an aesthetic contemplation he neither understood nor desired, face to face for the last time in history with something commensurate to his capacity for wonder."[63]

Less remarkable than that Fitzgerald's description would imply precolonial North America to be flirting with sixteenth-century Europe like a whore is that the implication, which contradicts the "objectivity" of the land, the uniqueness of the Dutch explorers' experience of the land, and, most important, Nick's regret over man's never again having the opportunity for such "wonder," is never made explicit. The "presence of this continent" exists nowhere else but in man's longing, and is nothing other than the specular image of this longing, which has a "breast," which "whispers" and "panders," which corresponds "aesthetically" to man's sense of beauty, and, finally, paradoxically, which is present only in Nick's lamenting an absence. The modern desire for presence, in the United States most often expressed in mysticisms of the "land," is strong enough in modern readings of this passage, including, apparently, Fitzgerald's, to make invisible the inherent deconstructive meaning. Before any machine is invented or civilization built, "the land" recedes absolutely, beyond any possibility of being recovered "as such." "America" is lost the instant "America" is noticed, and—what is simultaneous and synonymous—named. To realize the loss fully is not only "the end of the world," the title of Miller's last essay in *Errand Into the Wilderness,* from which the title of the last section of the last chapter of this reading semiotically differs. To realize the loss fully is also and more pertinently the end of "America," and of scholarship that, like Miller's, depends on "America" as the "object" of study and *raison d'être.* Perhaps eventually this scholarship will begin to suffer the fate of all successful discourses, exposure as what Bloom calls, in his most Blakean, prophetic style, the "Covering Cherub . . . [whose] baleful charm imprisons the present in the past, and reduces a world of differences into a grayness of uniformity." Perhaps modern American cultural historiography will some day get beyond that early stage of dependency that Bloom calls "tessera," the anxious pretension of completing that which is left undone by a predecessor, and move on toward the last stage, "apophrades," in which the difference of the predecessor can self-confidently and generously be admitted.[64]

In the meantime there is cause to long for the disappearance of "America" as avidly as Nietszche longs for nonentity, recalling Silenus's advice to Midas that the greatest boon is " 'not to have been born at all,' " the second greatest " 'to die soon,' " or as avidly as Foucault similarly longs for the disappearance of man: "if [humanism] were to disappear as [humanism] appeared, if some event of which we can at the moment do no more than sense the possibility—without knowing either what its form will be or what it promises—were to cause [humanism] to crumble, as the ground of Classical thought did, at the end of the eighteenth century, then one can confidently wager that man would be erased, like a face drawn in sand at the edge of the sea."[65]

NOTES

Chapter 1. The Phenomenon of Jonathan Edwards

1. Geoffrey Hartman, *Wordsworth's Poetry, 1787–1814* (New Haven: Yale Univ. Press, 1964); J. Hillis Miller, *Thomas Hardy, Distance and Desire* (Cambridge: Harvard Univ. Press, 1970); Shoshana Felman, "Turning the Screw of Interpretation," *Yale French Studies* 55/56 (Spain 1977): 102; John Carlos Rowe, *Henry Adams and Henry James* (Ithaca and London: Cornell Univ. Press, 1976), and *Through the Custom-House* (Baltimore and London: Johns Hopkins Univ. Press, 1982), and Paul B. Armstrong, *The Phenomenology of Henry James* (Chapel Hill and London: Univ. of North Carolina Press, 1983), which acknowledges the difficulty of introducing into American literary studies a "convergence between art and philosophy" since "in this country, the philosophical tradition behind [phenomenological analysis] is hardly known and rarely understood," *Preface*, p. vii; Lawrence Veysey, "Intellectual History and the New Social History," in *New Directions in American Intellectual History*, ed. John Higham and Paul K. Conklin (Baltimore: Johns Hopkins Univ. Press, 1979), p. 22; Martin Heidegger, *Being and Time*, trans. John Macquarrie and Edward Robinson, (1927; reprint, New York: Harper & Bros., 1962), p. 63; Jacques Derrida, "Implications," interview with Henri Ronse (1967), in *Positions*, trans. Alan Bass (1972; reprint, Chicago: Univ. of Chicago Press, 1981), pp. 6–7.

2. Jacques Derrida, *Of Grammatology*, trans. Gayatri Charavorty Spivak (1967; reprint, Baltimore: Johns Hopkins Univ. Press, 1974), p. 161; Michael Riffaterre, *Semiotics of Poetry* (Bloomington: Univ. of Indiana Press, 1978); Tzvetan Todorov, *Theories of the Symbol*, trans. Catherine Porter (1977; reprint, Ithaca: Cornell Univ. Press, 1982), p. 10; Northrop Frye, *Anatomy of Criticism* (Princeton: Princeton Univ. Press, 1957), p. 29.

3. Edmund Husserl, quoted in Herbert Spiegelberg, *The Phenomenological Movement* (The Hague: Martinus Nijhof, 1960), 1:90–91; Heidegger, *Being and Time*, p. 29.

4. The dualism of theist discourse conforms essentially to Kant's definition, according to which it amounts to "the certainty of the existence of objects of outer sense," as opposed to "idealism," with the provision that dualism is genuinely present only in theist discourse, whereas in humanist discourse it is only supposed, which provision makes the opposition between "dualism" and "idealism" in modern discourse a false or only apparent one, as Kant himself implies. Immanuel Kant, *Immanuel Kant's Critique of Pure Reason*, trans. Norman Kemp Smith (1929; reprint, New York: Macmillan, 1950), p. 344; Augustine, *The City of God*, trans. Marcus Dods (New York: Random House, 1950), p. 38.

5. *Misprision* is of course Harold Bloom's term in *The Anxiety of Influence* (New York: Oxford Univ. Press, 1973).

6. Husserl prefers the "terminologically unspent *Eidos*" to idea or ideal, both of which possess vague significations, and Heidegger fashions many terms from Greek roots, such as *hyletic* and *noematic*, to differentiate his meanings from common usage. Edmund Husserl, *Ideas: General Introduction to Pure Phenomenology*, trans. W. R. Boyce (1913; reprint, New York: MacMillan, 1931), p. 42; Martin Heidegger, *Being and Time*, introduction, esp. pp. 51–63. For a discussion of "degree zero," see Group μ (J. Dubois, F. Edeline, J. M. Klinkenberg, P. Minguet, F. Pire, H. Trinon), *A General Rhetoric*, trans. Paul Burrell and Edgar M. Slotkin (1970; reprint, Baltimore: Johns Hopkins Univ. Press, 1981), p. 30. Descartes is called a "mechanic theist" by John Ray in *The Wisdom of God Manifested in His Creation* (1691; 5th ed., London, 1709), pp. 43–

48, quoted by Wallace E. Anderson in the editor's introduction, *The Works of Jonathan Edwards,* vol. 6 of *Scientific and Philosophical Writings,* ed. Wallace E. Anderson (New Haven and London: Yale Univ. Press, 1980), 6:59, which is quoted, along with all other quotations from the Yale edition of Edwards's *Works,* with the permission of Yale University Press; Rousseau defines theism as natural religion in *Émile,* vol. 4, *Oeuvres Complètes,* ed. Bernard Gagnebin and Marcel Raymond (Paris: Gallimard, 1964), p. 303, quoted by Paul de Man in *Allegories of Reading* (New Haven and London: Yale Univ. Press, 1979), p. 221, and Kant identifies theism as a relatively affective and enthusiastic form of belief (in contrast, to add to the terminological confusion, to deism, which Kant defines as more cerebral and, implicitly, less completely human), in *Immanuel Kant's Critique of Pure Reason,* p. 525; the tendency to define theism as a relatively liberal form of belief remains current, as for example in Peter Gay's distinguishing between "fundamentalism" on the one hand and "rationalism, Unitarianism, simple Theism" on the other in the context of claiming that Newton's thought tends precociously toward the last. Peter Gay, *A Loss of Mastery* (Berkeley: Univ. of California Press, 1966), p. 114. *The Oxford English Dictionary* gives several examples of antonymous uses of *theism* from the seventeenth through the nineteenth century, according to which *theism* means "belief in one God as creator and supreme ruler of the universe, without denial of revelation: in this case distinguished from deism," *The Compact Edition of the Oxford English Dictionary* (Oxford: Oxford Univ. Press, 1971), s.v. *theism,* p. 3281. Perhaps the most famous example outside of religious diction of a word that is its own antonym is Freud's *heimlich,* among whose "different shades of meaning" there is "one which is identical with its opposite, *unheimlich,*" although *(un)heimlich* as Freud defines it is overdetermined in much the same way as some religious terms, being problematic precisely because its signification comes so close to deconstructing humanism. Sigmund Freud, "The 'Uncanny'" (1919), *On Creativity and the Unconscious: Papers on the Psychology of Art, Literature, Love, Religion,* ed. Benjamin Nelson, trans. under the supervision of Joan Riviere (New York: Harper and Row, 1958), p. 129. The advent of "the new theism" and of even newer theisms to come has recently been proclaimed by Germain Grisez in *Beyond the New Theism* (Notre Dame: Notre Dame Univ. Press, 1975), and a distinction between old and new theism has been drawn by Grisez, ibid., p. 3, and by Robert E. Whittemore, in "Jonathan Edwards and the Theology of the Sixth Way," *Church History* 35 (March 1966): 66, and this distinction is implied by H. P. Owen, whose definition of "Christian theism in its traditional form" as "belief in a morally perfect Creator who exists in the threefold form of Father, Son and Holy Spirit and who, in the person of the Son, became man in Christ for our salvation," can also be taken to represent current theological usage. H. P. Owen, "Morality and Christian Theism," *Religious Studies* 20, no. 1 (March 1984): 5.

    7. This is not to say that such generalizations will be acceptable to neopositivist historians, of which American academies have plenty, nor that they are immune to the uncomprehending application of criteria that it is the whole purpose of phenomenology to displace. See, for example, Lawrence Stone's reply to the late Michel Foucault's letter responding to Stone's "Madness" (*The New York Review of Books* [Dec. 16 1983]), in which Stone critically reviews Foucault's phenomenology of insanity: "A second problem is caused by the tenuous connection of structuralism to history. Even if they can be understood, the systematic structures of discourse that are alleged to underlie major intellectual changes cannot always be made to conform to the intractable realities of historical evolution as revealed in the records: the facts don't always support the theory." *The New York Review of Books* 30, no. 5 (March 31 1983): 42–43. It is sobering to read that any historian who has reached the eminence of a regular reviewer for *The New York Review of Books,* even given that journal's partisan delight in bashing a few "structuralist" heads every issue or two, can defer implicitly to "the intractable realities of historical evolution as revealed in the records." Such objections can be answered only by reference to the entire corpus of phenomenology or by silence. Foucault evidently chose the latter.

    8. Dissent against Perry Miller's depiction of intellectual movements, especially of Puritanism, is common and most often voiced on behalf of environmental "realities"—social,

cultural, economic—that Miller apparently fails to take into account; charges of this type, that whereas Miller naively supposes Puritanism to be monolithic it is in fact as diverse as the various environments that nurture it, have recently been compiled by Michael McGiffert in "American Puritan Studies in the 1960's," *William and Mary Quarterly*, 3d ser. 27 (1976): 40–41; that Miller is sensitive to this sort of criticism is apparent in many of the new introductions he writes for the essays collected in *Errand Into the Wilderness*, including the very first one, in which Miller concedes at the outset that in the interplay between errand and wilderness "a basic conditioning factor was the frontier—the wilderness," Perry Miller, *Errand Into the Wilderness* (Cambridge: Harvard Univ. Press, 1956), p. 1; and that Miller is sensitive to environmental influences throughout his scholarship was some time ago pointed out by David A. Hollinger in "Perry Miller and Philosophical History," *History and Theory* 7 (1960): 194–95. Sacvan Bercovitch is defensive throughout the preface to *The American Jeremiad* about the integrity of Puritanism as a movement and propitiating toward environmental approaches that would deny its existence, but he is surer of an American cultural "hegemony" having formed by the nineteenth century, so sure that he can discover by the end of the book adherence to the myth of the chosen status of the United States among nations in the least likely of texts, the writings of a "countercultural" historian of rock music. Sacvan Bercovitch, *The American Jeremiad* (Madison: Univ. of Wisconsin Press, 1978), pp. xi–xv, 158–59, 170, 204. Lowrie states both that a Puritan consensus exists and that Samuel Willard articulates it in Willards's *Complete Body of Divinity* (Boston, 1726), Ernest B. Lowrie, *The Shape of the Puritan Mind, The Thought of Samuel Willard* (New Haven and London: Yale Univ. Press, 1974), p. 7; Norman Fiering states that around the turn of the eighteenth century "it seems that nearly all the major intellectual figures [Montaigne, Bacon, Hobbes, Descartes, Gassendi, Leibniz, and Spinoza] were in some kind of contact," Norman Fiering, *Jonathan Edwards's Moral Thought and Its British Context* (Chapel Hill: Univ. of North Carolina Press, 1981), pp. 13–15; Davidson declares the link between Puritan New England and early Christian Asia Minor, also in his opening, and then says nothing more about it, James West Davidson, *The Logic of Millennial Thought* (New Haven and London: Yale Univ. Press, 1977), p. 12; and Coolidge reports on the current state of biblical scholarship, how it tends to reject assumptions of biblical inconsistency like the one held by Schneider (Herbert Wallace Schneider, *The Puritan Mind* [New York: Holt, 1930], p. 52), and how Puritanism might be taken as a continuation of biblical discourse, John S. Coolidge, *The Pauline Renaissance in England* (Oxford: Clarendon Press, 1970), pp. xiii–xiv, 141. Prefatory explanations of the *episteme*, also known as, simply, the "code," and, complexly, oxymoronically, the "positive unconscious of knowledge" are given by Michel Foucault in the foreword to the English edition of *The Order of Things* (New York: Vintage, 1970), p. xi; later in that book a less equivocal definition is given, stating that "in any given culture and at any given moment, there is always one *episteme* that defines the conditions of possibility of all knowledge, whether expressed in a theory or silently invested in practice," ibid., p. 168. Foucault's impact on American intellectual historians, especially that of his identifying discourse as the proper cynosure of intellectual historical research, is attested to by David A. Hollinger in "Historians and the Discourse of Intellectuals," *New Directions in American Intellectual History*, ed. John Higham and Paul K. Conklin, especially pp. 58–59. Samples of work appearing in the French historical journal *Annales* that exemplify the classification of the "*mentalité*" have recently been selected and translated in a series published by Johns Hopkins University Press, *Selections from the Annales*, ed. Robert Forster and Orest Ranum; trans. Elborg Forster and Patricia M. Ranum, 4 vols. (Baltimore and London: Johns Hopkins Univ. Press, 1978). The conception of the paradigm is central throughout T. S. Kuhn's *The Structure of Scientific Revolutions* (1962; reprint, Chicago: Univ. of Chicago Press, 1970); perhaps the best definition of it is the troubled one Kuhn adds as a postscript to a reprinting of the book in 1969, in which he regrets both the possible ambivalence of the term and some of the interdisciplinary uses to which the term is put, and even offers as an alternative *disciplinary matrix*, but all the while maintaining, even reinforcing, his original insistence that the paradigm, no matter what the paradigm is called, controls all scientific activity during the paradigm's ascendency, even to the extreme of determining the character of stimuli. Ibid., pp. 181, 195–96. About the conforming power of linguistic patterns, Derrida says that "within a certain historical epoch, there is a profound unity" among all kinds of discourse, and that "the writer writes *in* a language and *in* a logic whose proper system, laws, and life his discourse by definition cannot dominate absolutely." Derrida, *Of Grammatology*, pp. 79, 158. De Saussure's definition of the "state" of a language occurs in the context of his distinguishing between diachronic and synchronic linguistics, and of his preferring the latter as more revealing of the structures of languages and more receptive to what he identifies as scientific procedure. Ferdinand De Saussure, *Course in General Linguistics*, trans. Wade Baskin, ed. Charles Bally and Albert Sechehaye (New York: Philosophical Library, 1959), pp. 85–102. Curtius defines the *topos* as "something anonymous. It flows into the author's pen as a literary reminiscence. It has a temporal and spatial omnipresence like a scriptural motif. Typology . . . can advance the impersonal stylistic forms. In these impersonal stylistic elements we touch on a layer of historical life that is more deeply imbedded than that of individual invention." Ernst Robert Curtius, "Zur Literarästhetik des Mittelalters II" (1938), p. 139, translated and quoted by Alexander Gelley in "Ernst Robert Curtius: Typology and Critical Method," in *Velocities of Change*, ed. Richard Macksay (Baltimore: Johns Hopkins Univ. Press, 1974), p. 250. And Lucian Goldman's addition to the Freudian constituency of the mind appears in "Structure: Human Reality and Methodological Concept," in *The Languages of Criticism and the Sciences of Man*, ed. Richard Macksay and Eugenio Donato (Baltimore: Johns Hopkins Univ. Press, 1970), pp. 100–101. The structural integrity of theism, or of any other designation of a nonmodern discursive pattern, is not to be confused with the naïve and ignorant orthodoxy often ascribed to medieval tradition by a condescending modernism, as for example in Theodore Spencer's opening assertion in *Shakespeare and the Nature of Man* that "the first thing that impresses anyone living in the twentieth century who tries to put himself into Shakespeare's intellectual background is the remarkable unanimity with which all serious thinkers, at least on the popular level, express themselves about man's nature and his place in the world." *Shakespeare and the Nature of Man* (New York: Macmillan, 1949), p. 1.

9. After admonishing that there is no more a "real Edwards" than there is a *"res in facto posita*," James Carse continues to create a familiar modern one by "translating" Edwards's writings into an "idiom of an age strange to him," which is a more self-consciously modernist reading than is usually done, James Carse, *Jonathan Edwards and the Visibility of God* (New York: Scribners, 1967), p. 11.

10. Emerson's double-edged comments are from "Thoreau," *Selections from Ralph Waldo Emerson*, ed. Stephen Whicher, (Boston: Houghton Mifflin, 1957), p. 380.

11. A report of the efforts of early Edwardseans is given by Clyde A. Holbrook, *The Ethics of Jonathan Edwards* (Ann Arbor: Univ. of Michigan Press, 1973), chapters 7 and 8; Channing's approval of Edwards's latent mysticism is quoted by Perry Miller in *Jonathan Edwards* (1949; reprint, Cleveland: World Publishing Co., 1963), p. 292, and Channing's raptures over Edwards's personal narrative are quoted by Conrad Cherry in *Nature and Religious Imagination, From Edwards to Bushnell* (Philadelphia: Fortress Press, 1980), pp. 136–37, apparently from *Memoirs of William Ellery Channing*, ed. W. H. Channing (Boston, 1848), although Cherry's documentation here is vague; George Bancroft's well-known patronage of Edwards appears in his *History of The United States* (Boston: Little Brown, 1874), 3:398–99; and Harriet Beecher Stowe's appears in *Oldtown Folks*, ed. Henry F. May (1869; reprint, Cambridge: Harvard Univ. Press, 1966), p. 260.

12. The critic who is, understandably, tired by the argument over Edwards's modernity is Michael Colacurcio, in "The Example of Edwards: Idealist Imagination and the Metaphysics of Sovereignty," in *Puritan Influences in American Literature*, ed. Emory Elliott (Urbana: Univ. of Illinois Press, 1979), p. 55. Although Colacurcio begins by describing Edwards as consistently medieval epistemologically, he later describes him as stuck on the horns of a familiar dilemma, poised uncomfortably between a medieval theology of transcendent Deity and a modern one of immanent deity: "Edwards knows perfectly well that he is flirting with the edge of his own

metaphysical abyss, and he consciously pulls himself back." Ibid., p. 79; and in an earlier article, Colacurcio concludes simply that Edwards sires a family of American writers who emphasize the heart over the head, including Emerson, Hawthorne, Melville, William James, and Henry Adams. "The Dynamo and the Angelic Doctor," *American Quarterly* 17 (1965): 110–11.

13. For a brief history of "consensus historians" and their detractors, see John Higham's introduction to *New Directions in American Intellectual History*, pp. xi–xii; David A. Hollinger, "Historians and the Discourse of Intellectuals," ibid., p. 54; Daniel Howe, "Review Essay: Descendants of Perry Miller," *American Quarterly* 34, no. 1 (Spring 1982): 91; Alan Trachtenberg makes a point similar to Howe's in his review of Bercovitch's *The Puritan Origins of the American Self*, in which Trachtenberg's respect for the erudition of the book is qualified by the objection that after promising to analyze " 'the interaction of language, myth, and society,' " Bercovitch gives the third term "very short shrift." Alan Trachtenberg, "The Writer as America," *Partisan Review* 44 (1977): 472.

14. Michael McGiffert reports Morgan's praise for the modern scholarship of Puritanism and quotes a letter to him from Sidney Ahlstrom declaring that "Puritanism has become the area of American historical work where the greatest sophistication has been achieved." Michael McGiffert, "American Puritan Studies in the 1960's," p. 37; Emory Elliott, introduction to *Puritan Influences in American Literature*, ed. Emory Elliott (Urbana: Univ. of Illinois Press, 1979), p. xi.

15. The two representative works of contemporary American cultural historiography are Philip Greven, *The Protestant Temperament* (New York: Knopf, 1977), especially pp. 110–15, whose theoretical deficiencies include also the unadmitted or unself-conscious invention of a whole archive, that of early childhood and the family, which even Greven must on occasion confess or at least imply does not exist "as such" in the record of early American culture (see pp. 43, 156), and Norman Fiering, *Jonathan Edwards's Moral Thought and Its British Context*, especially pp. 15, 23–24, 87, 179, the most recent and comprehensive review of which follows what has become in reviews the customary qualification that Fiering's style leaves much to be desired, especially in comparison to Miller's (which may be after all an advantage in disguise given Miller's notorious presumed tendency to sacrifice scholarly care to rhetorical virtuosity) with the high praise that Fiering fosters "an increase in the sophistication of the sort of literary and cultural archaeology that has recurrently attracted critical interest, particularly since the publication in 1940 of Perry Miller's problematic and speculative essay, 'From Edwards to Emerson,' " and that Fiering achieves "the finest exposition of the character of Edwards' mind and thought that we have yet had" (David Laurence, Review Essay, "Moral Philosophy and New England Literary History: Reflections on Norman Fiering," *Early American Literature* 18, no. 2 [Fall 1983]: 187, 201).

16. That the real political power behind academic orientations present in France and necessary for the growth of deconstructive critiques like Barthes's and Derrida's might be absent in the United States is supposed by Evan Watkins in "Conflict and Consensus in the History of Recent Criticism," *New Literary History* 12, no. 2 (Winter 1981): 355.

17. Friedrich Nietzsche, *The Genealogy of Morals*, in *The Birth of Tragedy and the Genealogy of Morals*, Francis Golffing, (New York: Anchor, 1956), p. 149; Heidegger, *Being and Time*, p. 43; Adolph Reinach, quoted in Spiegelberg, *The Phenomenological Movement*, p. 202.

18. Kuhn, *The Structure of Scientific Revolutions*, pp. 136–38, John O. Lyons, *The Invention of the Self* (Carbondale: Southern Illinois Univ. Press, 1978), p. 198, Derrida, *Positions*, pp. 6–7, Todorov, *Theories of the Symbol*, pp. 188–89, de Man, *Allegories of Reading*, p. 136.

19. Kant, *Immanuel Kant's Critique of Pure Reason*, p. 539; G. W. F. Hegel, *The Phenomenology of Mind*, trans. J. B. Baillie, (1910; reprint, Evanston, Ill.: Harper and Row, 1967), p. 137, Husserl, "Philosophy as a Rigorous Science" (1910–11); *Phenomenology and the Crisis of Philosophy*, trans. Quentin Lauer, (New York: Harper and Row, 1965), p. 71.

20. For an interesting phenomenology of the Spanish explorations of North America, which contains, among other phenomenological revelations, the distinction that it is Whit-

man's Columbus who discovers "America," not Isabella's Columbus, who discovers something very different, see Edmundo O'Gorman, *The Invention of America* (Bloomington: Indiana Univ. Press, 1961).

21. Foerster's introduction is a rallying cry urging Americanist Ph.D.'s employed by departments of English to recognize their servitude and declare their independence: "The central fact is that American literature has had its own special conditions of development and its own special tendencies arising from these conditions. Among the literatures of the modern world, its case is unique." Norman Foerster, introduction, *The Reinterpretation of American Literature*, ed. Norman Foerster, (1928; reprint, New York: Russell & Russell, 1959), pp. xxii–xxiii; Matthiessen is so confident that the nationality of Emerson, Thoreau, Hawthorne, Melville, and Whitman is established that in *American Renaissance* he can defy Parrington's anticipated posthumous charge of "belletristic trifling" and concentrate just on the "foreground" of artistic achievement. F. O. Matthiessen, *American Renaissance* (New York: Oxford Univ. Press, 1941), introduction, p. ix; Parrington stresses not only the impact of imported ideals on American culture, but their liberalizing impact, without which, as is more than implicit in *Main Currents in American Thought*, American culture, especially in New England, would according to Parrington have remained a backwater of medievalism. V. L. Parrington, *The Colonial Mind, 1620–1800*, vol. 1, *Main Currents in American Thought* (New York: Harcourt, Brace, & World, 1927), especially pp. ix–x, 116, 122, 129, 152, 271, 328, 336, 388; Miller and Feidelson pair American writers with European ones—Jonathan Edwards with Kafka, Melville with Gide—so as to exalt both the stature and the modernity of the Americans. Perry Miller, *Jonathan Edwards*, p. 100, and Charles Feidelson, *Symbolism and American Literature* (Chicago: Univ. of Chicago Press, 1953), pp. 186–87, 190–91, 196–207; for an example of Mumford Jone's dissent, see Howard Mumford Jones, "The European Background," in *The Reinterpretation of American Literature*, ed. Foerster; William C. Spengemann, *The Adventurous Muse* (New Haven: Yale Univ. Press, 1977), and "Review Essay: Puritan Influences in American Literature, ed. Emory Elliott," *Early American Literature* 16, no. 2 (Fall 1982): 182; Norman Fiering, *Jonathan Edwards's Moral Thought and Its British Context* and *Moral Philosophy at Seventeenth-Century Harvard* (Chapel Hill: Univ. of North Carolina Press, 1982); John F. Lynen, *The Design of the Present* (New Haven: Yale Univ. Press, 1969), p. 26, and R. W. B. Lewis, "Literature and Things," review of Feidelson's *Symbolism and American Literature*, *The Hudson Review*, 7 (1954–55): 311–12, in which Lewis' point is that American literature is exposed by its susceptibility to "the big idea" as particularly lacking in masterpieces, which Lewis takes for granted are too rich to be comprehended by one.

22. Constance Rourke, *The Roots of American Culture and Other Essays*, ed. Van Wyck Brooks (New York: Harcourt, Brace, & Co., 1942), pp. 3–7.

23. Howard Mumford Jones makes a similar point, although, typically, only negatively, both to chastise the jingoism of modern American literary historians and to disparage theorizing in general: "The beginnings of American literary history rest, not in chauvinism, but in the diffusion of a theory of literary development enunciated by European writers." Howard Mumford Jones, *The Theory of American Literature* (Ithaca: Cornell Univ. Press, 1941), p. 71. The statement is correct not only in the anti-theoretical context of Mumford Jones's study but also in the alternately theoretical context of this reading.

24. A review of early American calls to produce American versions of Shakespeare's and Milton's works, although not this interpretation of them, is given by Russel Nye in *The Cultural Life of the New Nation* (New York: Harper, 1960), pp. 241–42.

25. Frederick Lewis Pattee, "A Call for a Literary Historian," *The American Mercury* (June 1924), reprinted in *The Reinterpretation of American Literature*, ed. Foerster, p. 18.

26. Frederick Jackson Turner, "The Significance of the Frontier" (1893), in *The Frontier in American History* (New York: Krieger, 1976), Walter Prescott Webb, *The Great Plains* (1931; reprint, New York: Grosse & Dunlop, 1976), and Henry Nash Smith, *Virgin Land* (Cambridge: Harvard Univ. Press, 1950). George Bancroft, *History of the United States*, 1:38, 4:135, Francis Parkman, *The Oregon Trail* (1849; reprint, New York: New American Library, 1970), especially

in claims that his exposure to the elements either improves his frail health or reconciles him with Indian stoicism to the inevitability of death, pp. 24–25, 159–60, and in descriptions of the Indian societies as so close to nature as to reincarnate the barbarous ancient Vandals and Teutons, pp. 71, 115; Webb's identification of the prairies as the most American of places occurs in *The Great Plains*, p. 29. Alexis de Tocqueville, *Democracy in America* (New York: Vintage, 1945), 1:21. Van Wyck Brooks, *The Writer in America* (New York: Dutton, 1953), pp. 3–4. For another recent statement of the conventional wisdom that Miller disregards environmental factors and overemphasizes intellectual ones, see James Hoopes, "Art as History: Perry Miller's *New England Mind*," *American Quarterly* 34, no. 1 (Spring 1982): 3–25; for estimations of Miller's historiography that recognize its environmentalist dimensions, see Hollinger, "Perry Miller and Philosophical History" and also Francis T. Butts, "The Myth of Perry Miller," *American Historical Review* 87, no. 3 (June 1982): 665–94; for an example of Miller's conception of the role of the environment in the formation of the American jeremiad, see both *The New England Mind*, vol. 2, *From Colony to Province*, pp. 31–32, and "Errand Into the Wilderness" (1952), in *Errand Into the Wilderness*, p. 12; and for Miller's conception of the ultimate dominance of the American environment in the formation of American Puritanism, see "Jonathan Edwards and the Great Awakening" (1949), ibid., p. 153; Matthiessen, *American Renaissance*, pp. 124, 236; Smith, *Virgin Land*, pp. 3–4.

27. Leo Marx, *The Machine in the Garden* (New York: Oxford Univ. Press, 1964), especially pp. 46–72. Floyd Stovall, *The Development of American Literary Criticism* (Chapel Hill: Univ. of North Carolina Press, 1955), pp. 3–4. Bercovitch, *The American Jeremiad*, pp. 39–40; Bercovitch earlier makes a similarly environmentalist point concerning the influences on Cotton Mather, whose "symbolic" style results, according to Bercovitch, from an unusual historical situation as a "casualty of change," Bercovitch, "Cotton Mather," in *Major Writers of Early American Literature*, ed. Everett Emerson (Madison: Univ. of Wisconsin Press, 1972), p. 98.

28. Leslie Fiedler, *Love and Death in the American Novel* (1960; reprint, New York: Dell, 1966), p. 31; Spengemann, *The Adventurous Muse*, p. 38; Laurence, "Moral Philosophy and New England History: Reflections on Norman Fiering," pp. 191, 200; Richard Slotkin, *Regeneration Through Violence* (Middletown: Weslyan Univ. Press, 1973), pp. 8, 22, 95, 144; D. H. Lawrence, *Studies in Classic American Literature* (1923; reprint, New York: Viking, 1966), especially pp. 7, 85. Annette Kolodny, *The Lay of the Land* (Chapel Hill: Univ. of North Carolina Press, 1975); John Seelye, *Prophetic Waters, The River in Early American Life and Literature* (New York: Oxford Univ. Press, 1977); David Scofield Wilson, *In the Presence of Nature* (Amherst: Univ. of Massachusetts Press, 1978); Cecelia Tichi, *New World, New Earth* (New Haven and London: Yale Univ. Press, 1979); Wayne F. Franklin, *Discoverers, Explorers, Settlers* (Chicago: Univ. of Chicago Press, 1979); Bernard Rosenthal, *The City of Nature* (Newark: Univ. of Delaware Press, 1980); Conrad Cherry, *Nature and Religious Imagination* (Philadelphia: Fortress Press, 1980).

29. Alexander Oleson, Introduction, *The Pursuit of Knowledge in the Early American Republic*, ed. Alexander Oleson and Sanborn C. Brown (Baltimore and London: Johns Hopkins Univ. Press, 1976), p. xvii; Wilson, *In the Presence of Nature*, p. 3; Franklin, *Discoverers, Explorers, Settlers*, p. 30 (Franklin is discussing Jefferson's description in the *Notes on the State of Virginia* of the "Natural Bridge"); Gay Wilson Allen, "How Emerson, Thoreau, and Whitman Viewed the 'Frontier,'" in *Toward a New American Literary History*, ed. Arlin Turner, Louis J. Budd, *et al.* (Durham: Duke University Press, 1980), p. 111; the compliment to Miller is paid by McGiffert in "American Puritan Studies in the 1960's," p. 39; and the Turnerian analysis of eighteenth-century Northampton is performed by Patricia J. Tracy in *Jonathan Edwards, Pastor* (New York: Hill and Wang, 1979), pp. 91–106.

30. Turner, "The Significance of the Frontier" in *The Frontier in American History*, p. 4, Slotkin, *Regeneration Through Violence*, p. 22. Parrington, *Main Currents in American Thought*, introduction, pp. ix–x; Kenneth Murdock, "The Colonial Experience in the Literature of the United States" (1956), in *Early American Literature*, ed. Gilmore, pp. 168–70; Marx, *The Machine in the Garden*, p. 47; Spengemann, *The Adventurous Muse*, p. 38; Patricia Caldwell, *The Puritan Conversion Narrative* (Cambridge: Cambridge Univ. Press, 1983), pp. 7, 26.

31. Hector Saint-John De Crèvecoeur, *Letters from an American Farmer,* (1782; reprint, New York: Dutton, 1957), Letter 1, pp. 1–12, Letter 2, pp. 38, 40–42.

32. Philip Freneau, *The Poems of Freneau,* ed. Harry Hayden Clark (New York: Hafner, 1960), p. 16; Thomas Jefferson, *Notes on the State of Virginia* (New York: Harper and Row, 1957), pp. 18, 22, 29–33, 80; William Bradford, *Of Plymouth Plantation,* ed. Samuel Eliot Morison (New York: Knopf, 1952), pp. 25–26, 61–63; John Winthrop, quoted in Robert C. Winthrop, *Life and Letters of John Winthrop* (1864; reprint, New York: Da Capo Press, 1971), 1:309–17, 376; Cotton Mather, *Magnalia Christi Americana, Books I and II,* ed. Kenneth B. Murdock (Cambridge: Harvard Univ. Press, 1977), bk. 1, chaps. 1 and 2; John R. Stilgoe, *Common Landscape of America, 1580 to 1845* (New Haven and London: Yale Univ. Press, 1982), pp. 8, 10. The quotation of Derrida is from "Structure, Sign, and Play in the Discourse of the Human Sciences," *The Languages of Criticism and the Sciences of Man,* ed. Macksey and Donato, p. 248.

33. The significance of romanticism in American culture has been noted frequently by literary critics, and as long ago as the 1920s, when Jay B. Hubbell says that romanticism provides the "tools" with which American writers could make something of the frontier. But in Hubbell's estimate, and in that of Norman Foerster in the essay that precedes Hubbell's in *The Reinterpretation of American Literature,* the frontier is clearly more substantively the contributor to American literature. Norman Foerster, "Factors in Literary History"; J. B. Hubbell, "The Frontier," *The Reinterpretation of American Literature,* ed. Foerster. Since then, Spengemann recognizes a special affinity between romanticism and American culture, but he agrees with Spiller and Brownson before him that the American variety is so distinct from European romanticism as to constitute a virtually separate genus. Spengemann, *The Adventurous Muse,* pp. 2–3. And there have been tendencies provincially to identify as peculiarly American literary attributes what can more generally be identified as modern ones, which are documents of the confusion between romanticism and American nationality, not analyses of it; see, for example, Lynen's opening contention that the duplication or multiplication of aspects of the self, including contradictory ones, is unique to American literature, when of course this is a common feature of modern discourse internationally. Lynen, *The Design of the Present,* pp. 1–3.

34. The neoromanticism of Matthiessen's position is strongly implied by his introductory comments to *American Renaissance,* preface, pp. vii–xvi.

35. The antagonism between Parrington and Miller is surprisingly heated, at least on Miller's part, for what seems initially to be simply an evidentiary dispute. Having the opportunity to make his disagreement with Parrington explicit, Miller, in his preface to the reprinting in *Errand Into the Wilderness* of his 1931 essay (which appears two years after Parrington's death in 1929) "Thomas Hooker and the Democracy of Connecticut," says that in claiming that the Connecticut River Valley Puritanism that Hooker comes to represent is more democratic than the Massachusetts Bay variety, "Parrington simply did not know what he was talking about." Miller, *Errand Into the Wilderness,* p. 17. Miller's point is less that Hooker is authoritarian than that the Mathers are equally democratic, or protodemocratic, and this point implies that more is at stake here than just the reputations of either Hooker or the Mathers. Miller's intent is to connect to modern American culture the mainstream of Puritanism, represented by the Mathers and Massachusetts Bay, not just a provincial tributary like that of the Connecticut River Valley. That Miller is successful and has for the most part superseded Parrington as a historian of Puritanism testifies not so much to the technical quality of his scholarship or the rhetorical quality of his style as to the utility of his conception of Puritanism to the modernist program of unifying American culture. The general difference between Parrington and Miller can perhaps best be seen by comparing Parrington's portrayal in *The Colonial Mind* of Puritanism as largely an anachronism with Miller's portrayal in *The Seventeenth Century* of Puritanism as contributing seminally to later developments in American culture.

36. For an example of Matthiessen's holistic conception of Western culture, see his likening of Melville to the English Renaissance rhetorician Sir Thomas Brown, *American Renaissance,* p. 124; for an example of Smith's syncretism, see his prologue to *Virgin Land,* especially his

promise to trace American environmentalism from its supposed beginnings in the early culture to the writings of Turner, *Virgin Land*, p. 4.

37. Carl Van Doren, *Benjamin Franklin* (New York: Viking, 1938), *Benjamin Franklin and Jonathan Edwards* (New York: Scribners, 1920), introduction, and Constance Rourke, *The Roots of American Culture and Other Essays*, ed. Van Wyck Brooks; Charles Feidelson, *Symbolism and American Literature*, especially p. 43, and Russel Nye, *The Cultural Life of the New Nation*, especially pp. 30–31; Daniel Boorstin, *The Lost World of Thomas Jefferson* (Boston: Beacon Press, 1960), pp. 4, 34–42, and Richard Chase, *The American Novel and Its Tradition* (Garden City, N.Y.: Doubleday, 1957), pp. 3–4; Alan Heimert, *Religion and the American Mind* (Cambridge: Harvard Univ. Press, 1966), pp. viii, 1–20, and Richard Poirier, *A World Elsewhere: The Place of Style in American Literature* (New York: Oxford Univ. Press, 1966), preface, pp. vii–xi, chap. 1, "Self and Environment."

38. The books by Cawelti and Drinnon are John Cawelti, *The Six-Gun Mystique* (Bowling Green, Ohio: Bowling Green University Press, 1970) and Richard Drinnon, *Facing West* (Minneapolis: Univ. of Minnesota Press, 1980).

39. Tocqueville says that "Puritanism was not merely a religious doctrine, but corresponds in many points with the most absolute democratic and republican theories." Tocqueville, *Democracy in America*, 1:33; Bancroft locates the seeds of the political organization that emerges from the Constitutional Convention in the organization of the Jewish tribes and in "other precursors." Bancroft, *History of the Formation of the Constitution of the United States* (New York: Appleton & Co., 1882), 2:322–23; Emerson's approval of Montaigne's essays is stated as an impression that he had written them himself "in some former life." Emerson, "Montaigne; Or, the Sceptic," *Works of Ralph Waldo Emerson in Five Volumes* (Boston: Houghton, Mifflin and Co., 1882), 2:133, and Thoreau practices a selective modernist reading in *A Week on the Concord and Merrimack Rivers*, "skipping the author's moral reflections, and the words 'Providence' and 'He' scattered along the page, to come at the profitable level of what he has to say." *A Week On the Concord and Merrimack Rivers* (New York: Apollo, 1961), p. 90.

40. Parrington describes Williams as a "transcendental mystic" and a "forerunner of Emerson and the Concord school, discovering an indwelling God of love in a world of material things," in *The Colonial Mind*, p. 62, Miller says that "what is persistent, from the covenant theology (and from the heretics against the covenant) to Edwards and to Emerson is the Puritan's effort to confront, face to face, the image of a blinding divinity in the physical universe" in the parenthetical introduction to the reprinting of "From Edwards to Emerson" in *Errand Into the Wilderness*, p. 185, he characterizes Solomon Stoddard's resistance against the blind following of the example set by the founders of Massachusetts Bay with the high praise that "William Ellery Channing could not be more precise, Emerson more self-reliant, Theodore Parker more resolute!" in *From Colony to Province* (Cambridge: Harvard Univ. Press, 1953), p. 286, and he endorses Whicher's linking of Puritanism to Transcendentalism in the conclusion of "From Edwards to Emerson," *Errand Into the Wilderness*, p. 202, and Spiller's program for the future study of early American literature appears in a Bicentennial Address selected as the introductory essay in *Toward a New American Literary History*, p. 3; Franklin, *Discoverers, Explorers, Settlers*, introduction, pp. xi–xii, Spengemann, *The Adventurous Muse*, pp. 2–3, Wilson, *In The Presence of Nature*, p. 19; Minter, *The Interpreted Design as a Structural Principle of American Prose* (New Haven: Yale Univ. Press, 1969), p. 36, Lynen, *The Design of the Present*, pp. 65–66, David Levin, *Cotton Mather* (Cambridge: Harvard Univ. Press, 1978), pp. 161, 251; Bercovitch, "The Puritan Errand Reassessed," in *Toward a New American Literary History*, p. 56 (and writ larger in the first chapter of *The American Jeremiad*, especially pp. 10–11), Lowance, *The Language of Canaan*, p. 210, Elliott, introduction, *Puritan Influences in American Literature*, p. xiv; Spengemann's litigious commentary appears in his "Review Essay: *Puritan Influences in American Literature*, ed. Emory Elliott," p. 176.

41. Parrington's championship of liberalism is evident throughout *Main Currents in American Thought*, and in this context especially so in *The Colonial Mind*, and Spengemann's discovery of a nascent intrepidness is evident especially in the second half of *The Adventurous*

Muse. The finding of a "court versus country" split is cited as one of the two most important developments of the recent study of early American culture by Michael Gilmore in his introduction to *Early American Literature*, ed. Michael T. Gilmore, pp. 4–5.

42. Lovejoy's contentions are that an implicit paradox of Plato's system is that the real is superior to the ideal as the necessary vehicle for the realization of the ideal, the shadow in the cave being implicitly superior to the invisible radiance without, that the implication of romantic monism inheres in the imperceptible gradations between levels of being in the "great chain," that the chain therefore is destined to collapse, and that the vantage of modern intellectual history is alone capable of appreciating these dialectical ironies. Arthur O. Lovejoy, *The Great Chain of Being* (1936; reprint, Cambridge: Harvard Univ. Press, 1950), pp. 52–53, 61, 245, and 288; Weber's dialectical analysis is evident in his painstaking description of the gradual ironic transformation of Protestant ethics from an ascetic to a worldly conduct of life, how "Christian asceticism, at first fleeing from the world into solitude," afterward "strode into the market-place of life, slammed the door on the monastery behind it, and undertook to penetrate just that daily routine of life with its methodicalness." Max Weber, *The Protestant Ethic and the Spirit of Capitalism,* trans. Talcott Parsons (1904–05; reprint, New York: Scribners, 1958), p. 104.

43. Schneider, *The Puritan Mind,* pp. 83, 52, 61; Ola Elizabeth Winslow, *Jonathan Edwards* (New York: Macmillan & Co., 1940), p. 98; Edwin Gaustad, *The Great Awakening in New England* (New York: Harper & Bros., 1957), p. 15; Edmund Morgan, *The Puritan Dilemma, The Story of John Winthrop* (Boston: Little, Brown, & Co., 1958), p. 8.

44. William Haller, *The Rise of Puritanism* (1938; reprint, New York: Harper & Row, 1958), p. 141, Haroutunian, *Piety Versus Moralism,* (1932; reprint, Hamden, Conn.: Anchor Books, 1964), Richard Niebuhr, *The Kingdom of God in America* (New York: Harper & Bros., 1937); Morgan, *Visible Saints* (New York: New York Univ. Press, 1963).

45. Gaustad, *The Great Awakening in New England,* pp. 81–82; Morgan, *Visible Saints,* p. 28; Heimert, *Religion and the American Mind,* p. 5, foreword, p. viii; the prevalence of dialectical interpretations in studies of American culture written in the 1950s and 1960s is noted in passing by Trachtenberg, "The Writer as America," pp. 467–68.

46. Miller, *The Seventeenth Century,* pp. 5–10, 21, 65–92, 148–54; "The Half-Way Covenant," *New England Quarterly* 6 (1933): 676–716; *Images or Shadows or Divine Things* (New Haven: Yale Univ. Press, 1948), introduction, p. 16; "Errand Into the Wilderness," in *Errand Into the Wilderness,* p. 15; "The Marrow of Puritan Divinity," ibid., pp. 53, 60–88; Hegel's analysis of the master-slave relationship appears in "Lordship and Bondage," *The Phenomenology of Mind,* especially pp. 238–39.

47. Clarence Faust, "The Decline of Puritanism," in *Transitions in American Literary History,* ed. Harry Hayden Clark (Durham: Duke Univ. Press, 1954), p. 36; the tension in Puritanism between immanence and transcendence is seen by Lynen in *The Design of the Present,* pp. 36–37, that between symbolic and nonsymbolic epistemologies is seen by Cherry in *Nature and Religious Imagination,* pp. 231–35, and that between "chronology" and "horology" is seen by Bercovitch, with deference to Melville's *Pierre,* in *The American Jeremiad* (Bercovitch in an earlier work shows himself to be nearly as clever, and equally as Hegelian, a dialectician as Miller in arguing that modern self-consciousness can grow organically out of Puritan self-abasement, in *The Puritan Origins of the American Self* [New Haven: Yale Univ. Press, 1975], p. 20.); that Miller's conception of Puritanism remains the dominant one at least through the 1960s is attested to by McGiffert in "American Puritan Studies in the 1960's," pp. 64–66, and that it is still powerful is implied by the fact that *American Quarterly* recently devoted an entire issue to discussions of Miller's historiography and by an article in that issue that says that Miller does not invent, but only somewhat overstresses, the modern aspects of Puritanism. James Hoopes, "Art as History: Perry Miller's *New England Mind,*" p. 8.

48. Mumford Jones criticizes those he considers Puritanism's apologists in "The European Background"; *The Reinterpretation of American Literature,* ed. Foerster, p. 63.

49. The example of a specialized study in conflict with its own findings is Lowrie's *The Shape at the Puritan Mind*, whose unexpected conclusion occurs on p. 234.

50. It should be clear by now that unitary theory is not here restricted to the so-called consensus intellectual history of the 1950s, nor to the so-called myth-and-symbol school of cultural and literary history. These movements are just single manifestations of a whole pattern of discourse that controls even those historicist interpretations that consider themselves to have supplanted consensus and myth-and-symbol theories. Thus the various environmentalist historicisms that deem themselves empirical correctives to loose cultural generalizing do not from this perspective challenge such generalizing fundamentally. For an old example of empiricist skepticism in the realm of literary history, see Van Wyck Brooks's insistence that "in reality books are bred by men, men by life, and life by books so that an element of social history can scarcely be dispensed with in any account of literary phenomena and forces." Van Wyck Brooks, *The Writer in America*, pp. 1–2; for a very new one, see Tracy's claim to disprove certain modernist misconceptions of Edwards through no more than a closer attention to the "facts," giving his writings a "real-life context" and a "social as well as intellectual matrix." Tracy, *Jonathan Edwards, Pastor* (1979), p. 6; for a review of the whole controversy between "consensus" historians and their rivals, see Higham's introduction to *New Directions in American Intellectual History*, pp. xi–xii. The closest to a genuine alternative to unitary theory at this point seems to be the so-called revisionist work of such American intellectual historians as Quentin Skinner, J. G. A. Pocock, and John Dunn. But in their polemic opposition to the establishment of great works and the timeless truths supposedly contained in great works Skinner *et al.* seem at least partly conditioned by the unitary theory they attempt to resist, opening themselves to the charge by historicist opponents of holding the ludicrous position that early discourse is to be valued for its irrelevance to the present. See, for a critical review of the "revisionist" intellectual history, Joseph N. Fermia, "An Historicist Critique of 'Revisionist' Methods for Studying the History of Ideas," *History and Theory* 20, no. 2 (1981): 113. Even if "revisionism" constitutes a potentially revolutionary departure in modern American intellectual historiography, the method has certainly not had any major influence on modern American literary historiography, which has yet to show anything like this sort of dissent. On the rare occasions when critical awareness of unitary theory appears in American literary studies, this awareness is voiced in contexts that neither call for nor imply theoretical revolt, as for instance in Spengemann's strong but brief condemnation of the monotonous nationalism of American Puritan scholarship in his review of *Puritan Influences in American Literature;* or in William L. Hedges's noting that "increasing degrees of romanticism or indigenousness" tend too much to be seen in the early literature, in service only to a preference for a more dialectically complex depiction of the early literature as evolving through contraries. William L. Hedges, "The Old World Yet: Writers and Writing in Post-Revolutionary America," *Early American Literature* 16, no. 1 (Spring 1981), 5; or in Mitchell Robert Breitwieser's objection to certain modernist interpretations of Cotton Mather's championship of innoculation, made in service only to joining Mather to another modernist party, that not of modern medicine but of homeopathy, to which belong also Hawthorne, Thoreau, Emerson, and Henry James. Mitchel Robert Breitwieser, "Cotton Mather's Pharmacy," ibid., pp. 42, 45.

51. Other than modern features are so prominent in Edwards's writings that all arguments for his modernity must show that modernism is present in them despite all appearances to the contrary, and the strength of these interpretations is directly related to the number of appearances they can acknowledge prior to advancing to the less apparent essences. Miller's disclaimer, that "in the strictly historical regard, then, there is no organic evolution from Edwards to Emerson," delivered in the parenthetical introduction to the reprinting in *Errand Into the Wilderness* of "From Edwards to Emerson," in which essay Miller continues to suggest a variety of less strictly historical and not quite organic links between Edwards and Emerson, can be taken as the model of this type of equivocation. Miller, *Errand Into the Wilderness*, p. 184. For later studies that follow Miller's example, see Shea's conceding repeatedly that Edwards's

typology explicitly resists confusing nature with spirit, prior to suggesting that this figuration does, after all, resemble the romantic symbolism of, say, Whitman, which does identify nature with spirit. Shea, "Jonathan Edwards," in *Major Writers of Early American Literature*, ed. Emerson, pp. 186–90; or James Carse's concluding torturously, after acknowledging the unmistakable pieties of Edwards's "God Glorified in Man's Dependence," that the sermon is, after all, a document not of divine sovereignty but of "divine sovereignty only so far as it magnifies the greatness of that which God has given us," and so becomes a "subtle but significant emendation of classical Calvinism." Carse, *Jonathan Edwards and The Visibility of God*, pp. 46–47; or Terence Erdt's similarly qualified presentation of Edwards's continual explicit discounting of the importance of the imagination in verifying election, that "but though firmly supporting the accepted standard and emphatically denying that visions contributed by the imagination can be the efficient cause of religious affection, Edwards nevertheless bespoke an important place for the faculty." Terence Erdt, *Jonathan Edwards and the Sense of the Heart* (Amherst: Univ. of Massachusetts Press, 1980), pp. 48–52; or Fiering's echo that although "Edwards did not generally think like a romantic, one who opposed unsullied nature to human feeling," Edwards does, intermittently, supposedly exhibit such a romantic or modern naturalism and in so doing only "fell short of a consistently modern philosophy of nature, but it may be surprising to some readers to see how close he came." Fiering, *Jonathan Edwards's Moral Thought and Its British Context*, pp. 85, 100. Even Parrington sees a theoretical possibility that Edwards's Calvinism might be outweighed or at least balanced by some intimation of liberality or "philosophical idealism"; Parrington concludes, however, that Edwards is "tragically" unable to free himself from dogma. Parrington, *The Colonial Mind*, pp. 156–65.

52. Probably the best-known example of a short refutation of an extended argument for Edwards's modernity is Vincent Tomas's attack on Miller, in which he charges that Edwards is a typically medieval thinker in placing himself "at the service of scripture, and was willing to take orders from it," and is therefore "a Puritan first, and a Newtonian or Lockean secondarily." Vincent Tomas, "The Modernity of Jonathan Edwards," *New England Quarterly* 25, no. 1 (March 1952): 70, 76. Similar opinions include Clarence Faust's, that Edwards's speculations on the ontology of spiritual entities is "ludicrously medieval." Clarence Faust, "Jonathan Edwards as a Scientist," *American Literature* 1 (January 1930): 393–404, reprinted in *Jonathan Edwards and the Enlightenment*, ed. John Opie (Lexington, Mass.: Heath, 1969), p. 43; Haroutunian's, that Edwards persists in medieval beliefs against the tide of cultural history, which is continually implied by pitting Edwards's piety against various heterodox moralisms in each chapter of *Piety Versus Moralism*; Clyde A. Holbrook's, that Edwards is an "antiquated bibliolator," in "Jonathan Edwards and his Detractors," *Theology Today* 30, no. 10 (October 1953): 389; Gaustad's, that Edwards is "less a harbinger of Channing than a reminiscence of Aquinas," in *The Great Awakening*, p. 83; Heimert's, that Edwards mimics the vocabulary of Lockean idealism and Newtonian physics without ever truly absorbing the conceptions of Locke or Newton, in Heimert, *Religion and the American Mind*, p. 41; Robert E. Whittemore's, that "Edwards is no modern," in support of Tomas's "devastating criticism of Miller's view," in "Jonathan Edwards and the Theology of the Sixth Way," p. 68; and Peter Gay's, that Edwards's sense of the past departs from "the modern world with its recognizable features and legible signposts for a fantastic landscape, alive with mysterious echoes from a distant past, and intelligible only—if it can be made intelligible at all—with the aid of outmoded, almost primitive maps. . . . Edwards's *History of the Work of Redemption* is a thoroughly traditional book, and the tradition is the tradition of Augustine," proving Edwards to be not "the first modern American" but "the last medieval American," in *A Loss of Mastery*, pp. 93–94, 116. More recent examples of the marginal scholarly opinion that Edwards does not anticipate modernity include Stephen Stein's surprisingly uninviting, almost perverse comment in the very opening of his "Editor's Introduction" to the latest volume of the Yale edition of Edwards's writings, declaring that publication of Edwards's manuscript commentaries on Revelation "does not promise to raise Edwards intellectual or religious stock." Stephen J. Stein, "Editor's Introduction," *The Works of Jonathan Edwards*, vol. 5, *Apocalyptic Writings*, ed.

Stephen J. Stein (New Haven and London: Yale Univ. Press, 1977), p. i, and several statements by Paul Helm—that "despite recent claims to the contrary . . . [Edwards] would hardly have recognized the post-Kantian world which most [not all?] Protestants live in today," that "it is strictly inappropriate to speak of habits of grace" according to Edwards's salvific theory, that Edwards is not a mystic, and that Miller's view of Edwards as having extended the covenantal relationship between man and God so radically as to make man responsible for his own salvation is incorrect—a commentary in a rather obscure volume collecting some of Edwards's writings on grace that represents perhaps the longest and most consistent refutation of the modernist interpretation in current scholarship. Paul Helm, "Editor's Note" and subsequent commentary, Jonathan Edwards, *Treatise on Grace and other Posthumously Published Writings*, ed. Paul Helm (Cambridge: James Clark & Co., 1971), pp. ix, 4, 8, 11, 15.

53. Leslie Stephen, "Jonathan Edwards" (1876), in *Critical Essays on Jonathan Edwards*, ed. William J. Scheick (Boston: G. K. Hall, 1980), p. 73. I. Woodbridge Riley, *American Philosophy: The Early Schools* (New York: Dodd, Mead, & Co., 1907), excerpted in Scheick, p. 97, and Clyde A. Holbrook, "Jonathan Edwards and His Detractors," pp. 388–91; Parrington, *The Colonial Mind*, p. 156, Van Doren, *Benjamin Franklin and Jonathan Edwards*, introduction, p. ix.

54. Miller, "From Edwards to Emerson," *Errand Into the Wilderness*, pp. 185–95; *Jonathan Edwards*, p. 292; Introduction, *Images or Shadows of Divine Things*, p. 18.

55. Frederick I. Carpenter, "The Radicalism of Jonathan Edwards," *New England Quarterly* 4 (October 1931): 631, Winslow, *Jonathan Edwards*, pp. 43, 149; Rufus Suter, "A Note on the Platonism of the Philosophy of Jonathan Edwards," *Harvard Theological Review* 52, no. 4 (1959): 283, Alfred Owen Aldridge, *Jonathan Edwards* (New York: Washington Square Press, 1964), pp. 41–42, 19–20 (Aldridge argues in an earlier article that Edwards is more of a benevolist than he knows, and that his criticisms of Hutcheson are unconscious praise. Alfred Owen Aldridge, "Edwards and Hutcheson, *Harvard Theological Review* 44 [1931]: 38); Sidney E. Ahlstrom, Introduction, *Theology in America*, ed. Sidney E. Ahlstrom (Indianapolis: Bobbs-Merrill, 1967), p. 37, Edward H. Davidson, *Jonathan Edwards, The Narrative of a Puritan Mind* (Cambridge: Harvard Univ. Press, 1960), pp. 53–54, 25; Peter Gay, *A Loss of Mastery*, p. 104, Richard L. Bushman, "Jonathan Edwards and Puritan Consciousness," *Journal for the Scientific Study of Religion*, 5 (1966): 383, Miller, *The Seventeenth Century*, p. 5, Daniel B. Shea, "Jonathan Edwards," in *Major Writers of Early American Literature*, ed. Emerson, pp. 186–88; Mason Lowance, *The Language of Canaan*, p. 252, Tracy, *Jonathan Edwards, Pastor*, p. 108, Miller, "The End of the World," in *Errand Into the Wilderness*, p. 234, Fiering, *Jonathan Edwards's Moral Thought and its British Context*, pp. 51, 148; William Scheick, Introduction, *Critical Essays on Jonathan Edwards*, Scheick, ed., p. xvi.

56. Miller, *Jonathan Edwards*, p. 48; Feidelson, *Symbolism and American Literature*, p. 49, Davidson, *Jonathan Edwards, The Narrative of a Puritan Mind*, p. 82, Shea, "Jonathan Edwards," in *Major Writers of Early American Literature*, ed. Emerson, p. 186, Roberty Daly, "Puritan Poetics," reprinted from *God's Altar: The World and the Flesh in Puritan Poetry* (Berkeley: Univ. of California Press, 1978), in *Early American Literature*, ed. Gilmore, p. 34, Lowance, *The Language of Canaan*, preface, p. ix, Cherry, *Nature and Religious Imagination*, p. 232; Todorov, *Theories of the Symbol*, p. 221.

57. "Out of Calvinistic Protestantism rose in that day four great teachers of four great nationalities, America, Great Britain, Germany, and France. Edwards, Reid, Kant, and Rousseau were all . . . expositors of the active powers of man." Bancroft, *History of the United States*, 9:501; "[The supposedly "subjective mood" of Puritan piety] blazed most clearly and most fiercely in the person of Jonathan Edwards, but Emerson was illuminated, though from afar, by its rays, and it smoldered in the recesses of Hawthorne's intuitions." Miller, *The Seventeenth Century*, p. 5. "Edwards, like any Shaftesburean, in his early writings accepted that natural euphoric transports alone could carry an appreciation of the harmony of the whole"; "It may not be altogether coincidence that Rousseau prepared his first draft of *The Social Contract* in 1755, the very year in which Edwards is believed to have written *True Virtue*"; "Thoreau's essential message was no different from Edwards's in *Religious Affections*." Fiering, *Jonathan*

Edwards's Moral Thought and Its British Context, pp. 86, 335, 350. Edwards's description of the Fall in *Original Sin* anticipates Cooper's in *The Last of the Mohicans*, and Edwards's supposed conception of the redemptive imagination in "A Divine and Supernatural Light" anticipates that of both Wordsworth and Cooper. Robert Milden, "*The Last of the Mohicans* and the New World Fall," *American Literature* 52, no. 3 (November 1980): 423. "The Coleridgean conception of mental activity is implicit in what Edwards says about what mental activity actually achieves—namely, an integrated perception of the singular meaning of a plurality of ideas taken as a whole." Sang Hyun Lee, "Mental Activity and the Perception of Beauty in Jonathan Edwards," *Harvard Theological Review* 69 (1976): 391–92. "Thus the spider [of Edwards's famous little essay] may serve present-day scholars as a provocative link between the seventeenth-century metaphysical, eighteenth-century rational, and nineteenth-century transcendental students of nature and 'nature's people'. . . . It was a vestige of such metaphysical inclination that led Whitman to identify with the dainty spider in 'The Noiseless Patient Spider.'" David Scofield Wilson, "The Flying Spider," *Journal of the History of Ideas* 32 (July 1971): 447–58, reprinted in *Critical Essays on Jonathan Edwards*, ed. Scheick, pp. 212–13. Fiering, *Jonathan Edwards's Moral Thought and Its British Context*, p. 254. Miller, *Jonathan Edwards*, pp. 159, 242. Carse, *Jonathan Edwards and the Visibility of God*, p. 97. Shea, "Jonathan Edwards," in *Major Writers of Early American Literature*, ed. Emerson, pp. 192, 194. Lee, "Mental Activity and the Perception of Beauty in Jonathan Edwards," p. 375. Roland André Delattre, *Beauty and Sensibility in the Thought of Jonathan Edwards* (New Haven and London: Yale Univ. Press, 1968), p. 94. Lynen, *The Design of the Present*, p. 114. Carse, *Jonathan Edwards and the Visibility of God*, p. 161. Shea, "Jonathan Edwards," in *Major Writers of Early American Literature*, ed. Emerson, p. 194. Wayne Lesser, "Textuality and the Language of Man," in *Critical Essays on Jonathan Edwards*, ed. Scheick, p. 292.

58. Miller says that William Ellery Channing "comes close" to the truth about Edwards "when he said that by making God the only active power in the universe, Edwards annihilated the creature, became in effect a 'pantheist,' and obliged men to ask whether any such thing as matter exists." Miller, *Jonathan Edwards*, p. 292; Douglass Elwood, *The Philosophical Theology of Jonathan Edwards* (New York: Columbia Univ. Press, 1960), "Introduction, Edwards and the Third Way," pp. 1–12, whose proposal of Edwards's "panentheism" is lately recalled with approval by Colacurcio in "The Example of Edwards: Idealist Imagination and the Metaphysics of Sovereignty," in *Puritan Influences in American Literature*, ed. Elliott, p. 72; Clarence Faust and Thomas Johnson, Introduction, *Jonathan Edwards*, ed. Clarence Faust and Thomas Johnson, (New York: Hill and Wang, 1962), p. liv; Delattre, *Beauty and Sensibility in the Thought of Jonathan Edwards*, p. 167; William Clebsch, *American Religious Thought* (Chicago: Univ. of Chicago Press, 1973), p. 18; Lowance, *The Language of Canaan*, p. 197.

59. That Edwards's "post-millennialism" anticipates at least modern historiography and maybe even modern utopianism is argued by virtually every modern critic who is interested in Edwards's "history of the work of redemption," including, since Miller and Heimert, C. C. Goen in "Jonathan Edwards: A New Departure in Eschatology," *Church History* 28 (March 1959): 25–40, reprinted in *Critical Essays on Jonathan Edwards*, ed. Scheick, p. 152; Lowance, both in an article, "Typology, Millennial Eschatology, and Jonathan Edwards," in *Literary Uses of Typology from the Late Middle Ages to the Present*, ed. Earl Miner (Princeton: Princeton Univ. Press, 1977), pp. 262–73, reprinted in *Critical Essays on Jonathan Edwards*, ed. Scheick, p. 189, and in the subsequent book, *The Language of Canaan*, Preface, p. ix; and Bercovitch, both in an article, "The Rites of Assent: Rhetoric, Ritual, and the Ideology of American Consensus," in *The American Self: Ideology and Popular Culture*, ed. Sam B. Girgus, (Albuquerque: Univ. of New Mexico Press, 1981), p. 12, and in *The American Jeremiad*, in which Bercovitch implies that apparently sanguine Puritan historiography, such as Edwards's is supposed to be, represents an early virulence of the nationalistic complacency and boosterism that would eventually plague modern American culture. See especially chapter 2, "The Blessings of Time and Eternity." The modernism of Edwards's church governance is praised by Miller, who interprets Edwards's conception of preparation as permitting grace to flow from natural causes, in "The

Rhetoric of Sensation," *Errand Into the Wilderness*, p. 183, and also, similarly, by Fiering, who holds that Edwards conceives of habit and will in ways sufficiently confused to allow the will to be conditioned by experience in *Jonathan Edwards's Moral Thought and Its British Context*, pp. 309–11, and by Karl Keller, who argues that in liberalizing the covenant Solomon Stoddard, and, implicitly, his grandson Jonathan Edwards after him, at least as long as Edwards follows Stoddardean practices in Northampton, "moved the predestinarian toward the democratic," in "The Loose Large Principles of Solomon Stoddard," *Early American Literature* 16, no. 1 (Spring 1981): 32; the less flattering portrait of Edwards as a satanic activist is implied by Tracy In *Jonathan Edwards, Pastor,* especially, p. 78. That Edwards's Calvinism can be seen as a predecessor of modern pessimism is probably first and most eloquently noted by Haroutunian, who begins *Piety Versus Moralism* with the encomium that "so long as men refuse to shut their eyes to the world, so long as they recognize their connection with and their dependence upon a world which supports them and often ignores their personal welfare, so long as they find happiness in self-denial and a love which grows out of wisdom, so long as their sense of the tragedy of life persists and can be transformed into victory over the world—there will be the essence of Calvinism." "Prelude," *Piety Versus Moralism*, pp. xxiv–xxv, a view echoed later by Randall Stewart, who contends that Calvinism has "a certain relevancy to the human condition at any time, and this relevancy is rediscovered from age to age." *American Literature and Christian Doctrine* (Baton Rouge: Louisiana State Univ. Press, 1958), p. 11; this position remains popular, perhaps because it permits a whole set of useful transformations, for example, of the low esteem in which Edwards holds the self *qua* creature into modern misanthropy, and of the damnation that Edwards assumes to be the result of sins against God into sadism and holocaust, which are of course sins against man, both of which transformations are performed by, among others, Carse, when likening Edwards's supposed sympathy for human victims with Picasso's in "Guernica." *Jonathan Edwards and the Visibility of God*, p. 161; by Lynen when likening Edwards to Eliot. *The Design of the Present*, pp. 346–47; by Harold Simonsin when likening the terror predicted in "Sinners in the Hands of an Angry God" to the terror anticipated in nuclear war. Introduction to *Selected Writings of Jonathan Edwards*, ed. Harold Simonsin, (New York: Ungar, 1970), p. 17; by Shea when likening Edwards's sense of "the terror of life" to that of Stephen Crane. "Jonathan Edwards," in *Major Writers of Early American Literature*, ed., Emerson, p. 192; and especially by Fiering, who on several occasions associates the modern interest in Edwards with the renewed gloom brought on by "the two great wars of the twentieth century and the Holocaust." Fiering, *Jonathan Edwards's Moral Thought and Its British Context*, p. 148, also pp. 222, 254. Finally, marriages between Edwards and modern phenomenologists are actually not so unusual, one having been arranged long ago by Miller when suggesting that Edwards is less interested in "things as such" than in perceptions of them. *Jonathan Edwards*, p. 64. And they are currently not uncommon, as for example in Carse's contention that because Edwards draws "no metaphysical distinction between the 'apparent' and the 'real,'" he may be considered akin to pragmatist or even existentialist theorists of behavior. *Jonathan Edwards and the Visibility of God*, pp. 42, 138, 143; in Lee's contention that Edwards is close to Pearce and other phenomenologists in seeming "to have drawn the conclusion that the present real-ness of the future events of a certain type can be explained only by the present real-ness of the general law, that is, the active tendency." "Mental Activity and the Perception of Beauty in Jonathan Edwards," p. 375; in Wallace E. Anderson's contention that Edwards is so "phenomenalistic" in his private notebooks that he finally, not surprisingly, "could hardly find language with which to express" his precocious insights. Editor's Introduction, Jonathan Edwards, *Scientific and Philosophical Writings*, p. 109; and in Lesser's that Edwards might be coupled with Saussure and Derrida in an alliance dedicated to the "radical upending of the Western metaphysical tradition." "Jonathan Edwards: Textuality and the Language of Man," *Critical Essays on Jonathan Edwards*, ed. Scheick, p. 292.

60. Robert E. Spiller, *et al.*, eds., *Literary History of the United States* (New York: Macmillan, 1957), p. 72.

61. Nietszche, *The Genealogy of Morals, The Birth of Tragedy and the Genealogy of Morals,* p. 228; Foucault, quoted by Alan Sheridan, *Michel Foucault, The Will to Truth* (New York and London: Tavistock, 1980), p. 196.

Chapter 2. Creation

1. Sereno Dwight, editorial comment, *The Writings of President Edwards with a Memoir of his Life* (New York, 1829–30), 1:54, and David Scofield Wilson, "The Flying Spider," *Critical Essays on Jonathan Edwards,* ed., Scheick, pp. 212–13. Newton writes in a letter to Richard Bentley "that Gravity should be innate, inherent and essential to Matter, so that one Body may act upon another at a Distance thro' a Vacuum, without the Mediation of anything else, by and through which their Action and Force may be conveyed from one to another, is to me so great an Absurdity, that I believe no man who has in philosophical Matters a competent Faculty of thinking, can ever fall into it. Gravity must be caused by an Agent acting constantly according to certain Laws." Sir Isaac Newton, Letters to Bentley, no. 4, *Isaac Newton's Papers and Letters on Natural Philosophy,* ed. I. B. Cohen, (Cambridge: Cambridge Univ. Press, 1958), pp. 302–3, quoted by Wallace B. Anderson in Editor's introduction, Edwards, *Scientific and Philosophical Writings,* ed. Anderson, p. 110; the "Agent acting constantly" that Newton cites as the necessary cause for gravity can only be that One whose schedule for the world Newton spends the end of his career trying to compute. The claim being made here that Edwards is not a scientist should be confused neither with Clarence Faust's old accusation that Edwards is deficient as an observor and thus does not deserve the title—insofar as both Newton and Locke are writing within the theist discursive pattern they are no more interested in nature for its own sake than Edwards and deserve the title no more than he, no matter how much greater their powers of thought or observation—nor with the recent disclaimers against Edwards's supposedly having been a scientific prodigy, which are based just on the recent, apparently conclusive textual evidence that the "Spider" essay is written while Edwards is a student at Yale and not while he is child in East Windsor. Clarence Faust, "Jonathan Edwards as a Scientist," *Jonathan Edwards and The Enlightenment,* ed. Opie, p. 42; Anderson, Editor's introduction, Edwards, *Scientific and Philosophical Writings,* ed. Anderson, p. 6.

2. Lovejoy, *The Great Chain of Being,* p. 14.

3. Perry Miller, "Jonathan Edwards on the Sense of the Heart," *Harvard Theological Review* 41 (1948): 123; that "competent scholars have regarded [Edwards's *Dissertation*] as his most important work" in an outdated consensus reported by Theodore Hornberger, "The Effect of the New Science on the Thought of Jonathan Edwards," *American Literature* 9 (November 1937): 196–207, reprinted in *Jonathan Edwards and the Enlightenment,* ed. Opie, p. 54.

4. *The Works of President Edwards in Eight Volumes* (London: Black & Son, 1817), 1:443, 445; hereafter cited as *Works*.

5. Edwards, *The Nature of True Virtue* (Ann Arbor: Univ. of Michigan Press, 1960), p. 64.

6. *Works,* 1:451.

7. *Ibid.,* p. 452; Elwood, *The Philosophical Theology of Jonathan Edwards,* p. 3.

8. Harvey G. Townsend, ed., *The Philosophy of Jonathan Edwards from His Private Notebooks* (Eugene: Univ. of Oregon Press, 1955), p. 174; hereafter cited as *Notebooks*.

9. Jonathan Edwards, *A Treatise concerning Religious Affections,* ed. John E. Smith (New Haven: Yale Univ. Press, 1959), p. 420.

10. *Ibid.,* p. 341; *Notebooks,* p. 166.

11. Augustine, *The City of God,* p. 31; Cotton Mather, *Magnalia Christi Americana, Ecclesiarum Clypei,* p. 337; Newton, *Principia,* General Scholium (1713 ed.), p. 483, quoted by Anderson in Editor's introduction, Edwards, *Scientific and Philosophical Writings,* ed. Anderson, p. 61.

12. Alexander Hamilton, "Federalist #1," *The Federalist Papers,* ed. Andrew Hacker, (1787–88; reprint, New York: Pocket Books, 1964), pp. 3–4, Jefferson, *Notes on the State of Virginia,*

p. 143; Emerson, Journal entry, October 1837, *Selections from Ralph Waldo Emerson*, ed. Stephen E. Whicher, (Boston: Houghton Mifflin, 1957), p. 81, "The Poet," *Works of Ralph Waldo Emerson in Five Volumes, Essays, Second Series,* 1:19, Carse, *Jonathan Edwards and the Visibility of God,* p. 60.

13. Edwards, *Religious Affections,* p. 96.

14. Ibid., p. 98; Introduction, ibid., p. 88. Concerning "deadful circumstances," one that happens to Edwards personally is an uncle succumbing to an urge to slit his throat during an awakening in Edwards's congregation in Northampton; Edwards may have been able to ease his distress over the state of his uncle's soul by recalling Augustine's citation of a possible excuse for suicide, but his career in Northampton may have been irreparably damaged by the incident, since the man's son, Edwards's cousin, later becomes a leader of the faction that strips Edwards of his ministry in Northampton in 1750. Winslow, *Jonathan Edwards,* p. 231. *Religious Affections,* pp. 288, 136.

15. Augustine, *The City of God,* p. 318, John Calvin, *Institutes of the Christian Religion,* trans. Henry Beveridge (Grand Rapids, Mich.: Eerdmans, 1957), 2:288–89.

16. Edwards, *Religious Affections,* p. 420.

17. Ibid., p. 100.

18. Newton, *Principia,* p. 483, quoted in Anderson, Editor's introduction, Edwards, *Scientific and Philosophical Writings,* ed. Anderson, p. 61.

19. Leon Howard, *"The Mind" of Jonathan Edwards: A Reconstructed Text* (Berkeley and Los Angeles: Univ. of California Press, 1963), entry #54, pp. 76, 77, hereafter cited as *Mind;* this passage from Edwards's notebooks is reprinted in Edwards, *Scientific and Philosophical Writings,* ed. Anderson, p. 370.

20. Paul Ramsey, introduction, Edwards, *Freedom of the Will* (New Haven and London: Yale Univ. Press, 1965), p. 66, *Original Sin,* ed. Clyde A. Holbrook (New Haven and London: Yale Univ. Press, 1970), p. 376.

21. *Freedom of the Will,* pp. 76, 211, *Notebooks,* p. 224; for a review of the Aristotelian and Thomist citation of the *in infinitum* regression, see Patterson Brown, "Infinite Causal Regression," in *Aquinas: A Collection of Critical Essays,* ed. Anthony Kenny (New York: Doubleday, 1969), pp. 214–36; that atheism represents not just a moral deficiency but a mental aberration is declared by Edwards also in his "Treatise on Grace," in which he characterizes it as a "strange disposition" (*Treatise on Grace and Other Posthumously Published Writings,* ed. Helm, p. 53), and that Edwards's opinion is widespread at least among Puritan theists is suggested by Samuel Willard's similarly diagnosing "practical atheism" as a sign of mental distraction in his *Complete Body of Divinity,* alluded to by Lowrie, *The Shape of the Puritan Mind,* p. 48.

22. Edwards, *The Nature of True Virtue,* p. 162; *Freedom of the Will,* p. 182; *Notebooks,* p. 87; *Mind,* entry #880, p. 87; Edward Taylor, the Preface, *God's Determinations Touching his elect . . . , The Poems of Edward Taylor,* ed. Donald E. Stanford (New Haven: Yale Univ. Press, 1960), vv. 3–4, p. 387.

23. Edwards, *Works,* 8:451, para. 61; Joseph Priestley, *Transactions of the American Philosophical Society* (Nov. 18, 1803), 6:120; Jefferson, *Writings,* Albert Ellery Berg, ed. (1907), 6:12; Lovejoy, *The Great Chain of Being,* pp. 149–51; Edgar Allan Poe, "Eureka," *Works,* ed. James A. Harrison (New York: AMS Press, 1965), 16:254; Heraclitus, quoted by Walter Wili, "The History of the Spirit in Antiquity," *Spirit and Nature,* Papers from the Eranos Notebooks, trans. Ralph Manheim, ed. Joseph Campbell (1937, 45, 46; reprint, Princeton: Princeton Univ. Press, 1954), p. 81; Poe, "The Conqueror Worm," *Works,* 7:87; "Letter to B.," *Works,* 7:xxxv.

24. That such theological use of linear causality is known as "occasionalist theory" is attested to by Fiering, *Jonathan Edwards's Moral Thought and Its British Context,* p. 95.

25. That Poe is a Neoplatonist and therefore sees nature to be ineluctably imperfectible, and that Poe subsequently denies the possibility of man's getting more than a glimpse of the radiance that shines outside the cave is recognized by Colcurcio, who also sees that this Neoplatonism connects Poe to Edwards; Colacurcio does not use this insight to comment upon the whole structure of American literature, nor does he seem to recognize the implica-

tion of the insight, which is that Poe is improperly considered a modern writer. Michael Colacurcio, "The Example of Edwards: Idealist Imagination and the Metaphysics of Sovereignty," in *Puritan Influences in American Literature*, ed. Elliott, p. 79.

26. Emerson, "Fate," *Works*, 3:34; Hegel, *The Phenomenology of Mind*, p. 124; Kant, *Immanuel Kant's Critique of Pure Reason*, pp. 223, 509; Husserl, *Ideas*, p. 176.

27. The quotation of Emerson is from "The Transcendentalist," *Works*, 5:269.

28. Miller, *Images or Shadows of Divine Things*, p. 27; Delattre, *Beauty and Sensibility in the Thought of Jonathan Edwards*, p. 50.

29. Edwards, *Notebooks*, entry no. 150, p. 183.

30. *The Nature of True Virtue*, pp. 40–41; a similar distinction between spiritual and natural beauties appears in Edwards's notebooks, printed in *Scientific and Philosophical Writings*, p. 380. That the original meaning of spirit, *Geist*, is breath or wind, an etymology that encourages the conflation of spirit and nature, may be a philological distortion practised by Grimm; Walter Wili suggests that the word more likely derives from motive or vital force, making it more consistent with the theist distinction between spirit and nature. Wili, "The History of the Spirit in Antiquity," in *Spirit and Nature*, trans. Manheim, ed. Campbell, p. 77. Aquinas, *Expositio super librum Boethii De Trinitate*, 11.2, quoted in George B. Klubertanz, S. J., *St. Thomas Aquinas on Analogy* (Chicago: Loyola Univ. Press, 1960), p. 47; Spencer, *Shakespeare and the Nature of Man*, p. 17.

31. Edwards, *Notebooks*, entry no. 42, p. 238.

32. Foucault, *The Order of Things*, p. 19.

33. Emerson, *Nature*, in *Works*, 5:34; Spiller, *et al.*, eds., *Literary History of the United States*, p. 72; Emerson, *Nature*, in *Works*, 5:55.

34. Thoreau, *A Week on the Concord and Merrimack Rivers*, p. 478; Herman Melville, *Moby-Dick* (Boston: Houghton Mifflin, 1956), p. 170; Carse, *Jonathan Edwards and the Visibility of God*, p. 60; Cherry, *Nature and Religious Imagination*, p. 8.

35. Edwards, *Notebooks*, entry no. 42, p. 258; *The Nature of True Virtue*, pp. 28–29, *Mind*, entry no. 1, p. 43, also printed in *Scientific and Philosophical Writings*, p. 335.

36. *Notebooks*, pp. 104, 262.

37. *Mind*, entry no. 1, p. 43; *Notebooks*, p. 183.

38. *Mind*, entry no. 61, pp. 34, 32, also printed in *Scientific and Philosophical Writings*, pp. 378, 380.

39. *Original Sin*, p. 404.

40. Ibid., pp. 401–2, 404.

41. *Treatise on Grace and Other Posthumously Published Writings*, ed. Helm, p. 34.

42. *Original Sin*, p. 404; Colacurcio recognizes the metaphysical consistency between linear causality and Edwards's proposing a continuous creation in *Original Sin*. "The Example of Edwards: Idealist Imagination and the Metaphysics of Sovereignty," *Puritan Influences in American Literature*, ed. Elliott, pp. 88–89.

43. Fiering identifies "occasionalist theory" as originating in patristic writings and as being widespread in the seventeenth and eighteenth centuries among Puritans and other Cartesians; Edwards, according to Fiering, may have absorbed it from a reading of Malebranche. Fiering, *Jonathan Edwards's Moral Thought and Its British Context*, p. 95; Willard's expression of "occasionalist theory" is alluded to by Lowrie, *The Shape of the Puritan Mind*, p. 70; Jefferson's comments on the wonderfulness of nature come in the course of discussing the natural anomaly, much puzzled over in the eighteenth century, of the discovery of (fossil) shells at high elevations. (Jefferson, *Notes on the State of Virginia*, pp. 32–33), and Hamilton's on the intrinsic formlessness of natural and political structures appear in "Federalist #15" and "Federalist #31," *The Federalist Papers*, pp. 43, 56–57. Kant's version of continuous creation is quoted in Stephen Toulman and Jane Goodfield, *The Discovery of Time* (New York: Harper and Row, 1966), p. 130, from Kant, *Allgemeine Naturgeschichte und Theorie des Himmels . . .* (1755), in *Werke in Zehn Bänden*, vol. 1 (Darmstadt: Wissenschaftliche Buchgesellschaft, 1968); Coleridge's version of the dialectic appears in *Aids to Reflection* (1825; reprint, London: George Bell

and Sons, 1904), p. 173, Emerson's in an 1841 journal entry, *Selections from Ralph Waldo Emerson*, ed. Whicher, p. 182, and Thoreau's in *Walden* (Boston: Houghton Mifflin, 1957), pp. 208–10 and in *Cape Cod* (New York: Thomas Y. Crowell, 1961), p. 81. Lynen links Edwards to Hegel in *The Design of the Present*, pp. 94–96; that Edwards's ontology is on the contrary not one of "becoming" is argued by Whittemore, who considers this an unfortunate medievalism. "Jonathan Edwards and the Theology of the Sixth Way," pp. 68, 71.

44. Aldridge, *Jonathan Edwards*, p. 5.

45. Edwards, *Works*, 1:462.

46. Ibid., pp. 452, 481; Lovejoy notes that Plato implies and Aristotle states the necessity of divine self-sufficiency. *The Great Chain of Being*, pp. 43–44.

47. Edwards, *Religious Affections*, p. 256.

48. *Notebooks*, entry no. 94, p. 253; *Freedom of the Will*, p. 182; Miller, *Images or Shadows of Divine Things*, entry no. 57, p. 61.

49. Edwards, *Works*, 1:480.

50. Augustine, *Confessions and Enchiridion*, trans. Albert C. Outler, (Philadelphia: Westminster Press, 1955), p. 348. Edwards, *Works*, 8:383–84; Melville's speculations on the timelessness of the whale in *Moby-Dick* can be taken as an irreverent misprision of Augustine's ingenious reconciliation of an eternal Creator and a finite Creation, Melville fancying in "The Fossil Whale" that since time begins with man and man is preceded in evolution by the whale, then the whale must be eternal, "having been before all time," a repositioning of divinity deeply within nature that is the primary goal not only of *Moby-Dick* but of all romantic discourse. Melville, *Moby-Dick*, p. 351.

51. Edwards, *Works*, 1:461; *Notebooks*, entry no. 553, pp. 136, 139.

52. *Works*, 1:459, 460; Lovejoy traces "emanationism" from Plato through Plotinus through medieval Christian writings such as those of Dante with the intention of showing that all of them contribute dialectically to the subversive weakening of the Great Chain. *The Great Chain of Being*, pp. 43–86.

53. Miller, *Jonathan Edwards*, pp. 186–87.

54. Edwards, *Works*, 1:529.

55. *Religious Affections*, pp. 326, 343; *Works*, 1:468; *Religious Affections*, p. 202.

56. Willard, *The Complete Body of Divinity*, p. 73, quoted in Lowrie, *The Shape of the Puritan Mind*, p. 59; Shea, "Jonathan Edwards," in *Major Writers of Early American Literature*, ed. Emerson, p. 125; Edwards, *Scientific and Philosophical Writings*, pp. 245–46; Colacurcio notes correctly that Edwards's natural metaphors do not necessarily imply that God can be "got to . . . through nature." "The Example of Edwards: Idealist Imagination and the Metaphysics of Sovereignty," in *Puritan Influences in American Literature*, ed. Elliott, p. 91.

57. Edwards, *Notebooks*, entry no. 880, p. 101, *The Nature of True Virtue*, p. 9; *Mind*, entry no. 64, p. 38; Alexander Pope, *An Essay On Man*, "Epistle I," vv. 29–32, in *The Poems of Alexander Pope*, ed. John Butt (New Haven: Yale Univ. Press, 1963), p. 505.

58. Edwards, *Works*, 1:529, Miller, *Jonathan Edwards*, p. 292.

59. Edwards, *Notebooks*, p. 184.

60. Anderson, Editor's introduction, Edwards, *Scientific and Philosophical Writings*, ed. Anderson, p. 6, and "Note on the 'Spider' Papers" in ibid., pp. 147–53; for the unlikelihood of Edwards's having read Locke early in his life see Anderson, Editor's introduction, in ibid., pp. 16–18, and Fiering, *Jonathan Edwards's Moral Thought and Its British Context*, pp. 13–24, 37, 125–26.

61. Anderson, Editor's introduction, Edwards, *Scientific and Philosophical Writings*, ed. Anderson, pp. 6, 44, 49, 109, 39.

62. Faust, "Jonathan Edwards as a Scientist," in *Jonathan Edwards and the Enlightenment*, ed. Opie, p. 43; Anderson, Editor's introduction, Edwards, *Scientific and Philosophical Writings*, ed. Anderson, pp. 48, 161, 168.

63. Emerson, *Nature*, in *Works*, 5:9; Jefferson, *Notes on the State of Virginia*, pp. 47, 53–54. The chain of being as Foucault interprets it in *The Order of Things* is ordained, not evolving, and

time is not a productive partner in the differentiation of species but an imperfection, either ontological in the speciation of the world or epistemological in the way man knows the world of species, which contributes only to a confusion among species that can be cleared up, imperfectly, only by taxonomies. The taxonomist tries to approximate the original diagram of Creation, which is spatial and timeless; he is the enemy of time, and time the enemy of his study: "There is not and cannot be even the suspicion of an evolutionism or transformism in classical thought; for time is never considered a principle of development for living beings in their internal organization; it is perceived only as the possible bearer of a revolution in the external space in which they live." Foucault, *The Order of Things*, p. 150.

64. Miller, *Images or Shadows of Divine Things*, entry no. 15, p. 46; Edwards, *Apocalyptic Writings*, pp. 185–87; Edwards, *Mind*, p. 140. David Pierce claims that Edwards's equation of God with space amounts to a declaration of immanent deity, "Jonathan Edwards and the New Sense of Glory," *New England Quarterly*, 41, no. 1 (March 1968), p. 89; Nicolas Cusanus, *De docta ignorantia* (1440), quoted in Lovejoy, *The Great Chain of Being*, p. 112; Giordano Bruno, *De la Causa*, in ibid., p. 120; Poe, "Eureka," *Works*, 16:204–5; Coleridge, *Aids to Reflection*, p. 154.

65. Miller, *Images or Shadows of Divine Things*, entry no. 777, p. 33.

66. Edwards, *Notebooks*, entry no. 54, pp. 250–51.

67. Ibid., entry no. 94, pp. 253, 254, 255; Edwards's discussion of the Trinity is more fully excerpted by Helm in Edwards, *Treatise on Grace and Other Posthumously Published Writings*, pp. 99–118.

68. Ibid., p. 77.

69. Oliver Wendell Holmes, *Pages from an Old Volume of Life*, *Works* (London: Riverside, 1891), 8:396, quoted in Helm, introduction, Edwards, *Treatise on Grace and Other Posthumously Published Writings*, ed. Helm, p. 43 (Helm disagrees with Holmes' surmise, concluding instead that the discussion of the Trinity remained in manuscript at Edwards's death simply because Edwards never got around to revising and publishing it.); Carse, *Jonathan Edwards and the Visibility of God*, pp. 87–88, 94; Hegel, *The Phenomenology of Mind*, pp. 81–83.

70. Edwards, *Notebooks*, entry no. 238, pp. 248, 258; Ludwig Feuerbach, *The Essence of Christianity*, trans. George Eliot (New York: Harper and Row, 1957), p. 12.

71. Miller, "From Edwards to Emerson," *Errand Into the Wilderness*, p. 195.

72. Lowrie's reading of Willard leads him to a similar and similarly emphatic conclusion about the Puritan ontology, even of the prelapsarian world: "by following this light [of nature] alone man never was, never is, and never will be capable of achieving communion with God, for that transcends nature's grasp. To be precise, even before Adam's fall, when there was not a trace of alienation between man and God, Adam in integrity still needed grace to effect the transition from the natural to the supernatural realm." Lowrie, *The Shape of the Puritan Mind*, p. 31.

Chapter 3. Providence

1. The letter to the Princeton trustees is quoted by Samuel Hopkins, *Life of Jonathan Edwards*, in Edwards, *Works*, 1:80–81.

2. Edwards, *Works*, 5:162; "God Glorified in Man's Dependence," in *Selected Sermons of Jonathan Edwards*, ed. Harry Norman Gardiner (New York: Macmillan & Co., 1904), p. 9; "Man's Natural Blindness in the Things of Religion," *Works*, 2:416; Willard, *The Complete Body of Divinity*, quoted by Clarence Faust in "The Decline of Puritanism," *Transitions in American Literary History*, p. 20; Edwards, *Works*, 5:333.

3. "God Glorified in Man's Dependence," *Selected Sermons*, p. 9; *Works*, 5:333; Ebenezer Turrell, *The Life and Character of the Reverend Benjamin Colman, Dd.* (Boston, n.d.), pp. 168–70.

4. The distinction between saintly laborers and saintly theologians appears in Edwards, *Notebooks*, p. 110.

5. *Original Sin*, p. 173; *Works*, 5:31, 42–43, 61, 71, 212. *The Great Awakening*, ed. C. C. Goen (New Haven and London: Yale Univ. Press, 1972), p. 144; *Original Sin*, p. 198.

6. *Works*, 5:30.

7. Ibid., p. 362; Edwards's fundamental distrust of appearances obliges him to note that miracles performed by Satan can look the same as ones performed by God: "[Satan] can not *exactly* imitate divine operations in their nature, though his counterfeits may be very much like them in external appearance; but he can exactly imitate their order." *Religious Affections*, p. 159. Edwards cites the example of Satan's miraculously sequestering his own chosen people, the Indians, in order to protect them from the Christian forces that are pervasive during the reign of Constantine. *Works*, 5:222. Edwards insists that no miracle gives sure evidence of its author, just as, in the *Dissertation*, he insists that no creature surely reveals the Creator; and his cautiousness over the evaluation of apparently wondrous happenings is of course identical to that of Cotton Mather, in deference to Increase Mather, who in turn defers to Lactantius, over "spectral evidence." Mather, *Magnalia*, Bks. 1 and 2, pp. 325–37.

8. Edwards, *Original Sin*, p. 171; Thomas Paine, quoted by Boorstin, *The Lost World of Thomas Jefferson*, p. 42.

9. Edwards, *Works*, 8:145, 244–45; Miller, *Images or Shadows of Divine Things*, p. 20; Mary Rowlandson, *The Sovereignty and Goodness of God, Together, with the Faithfulness of His Promises Delayed; Being the Narrative of the Captivity of Mary Rowlandson . . .* (1682), in *Puritans Among the Indians, Accounts of Captivity and Redemption, 1676–1724*, ed. Alden T. Vaughan and Edmund C. Clark (Cambridge, Mass. and London: Harvard Univ. Press, 1981), pp. 69–70.

10. Augustine, *The City of God*, pp. 361–62, 524, 38.

11. Edwards, *Works*, 5:355, 8:359, 5:354, 355. Edwards makes the point also in "God Glorified in Man's Dependence" that "God hath made man's emptiness and misery, his low, lost and ruined state into which he sunk by the fall, an occasion of the greater advancement of his own glory, as in other ways, so particularly in this, that there is much more universal and apparent dependence of man on God." *Selected Sermons*, p. 17.

12. Ibid., p. 25; *Works*, 8:141–42.

13. Ibid., 5:57, 90.

14. *Original Sin*, p. 184.

15. Ibid., pp. 187–88.

16. Ibid., pp. 197, 198.

17. Jefferson, *Notes on the State of Virginia*, pp. 8, 10.

18. Ibid., pp. 21–22, 17.

19. James Madison, "Federalist #37," *The Federalist Papers*, p. 89; Mather, *Magnalia*, pp. 117–18.

20. Edwards, *Works*, 5:23.

21. Ibid., p. 73. Bunyan distinguishes the less sophisticated divisions of human, animal, and material types in "Light For Them that Sit in Darkness" (1675), quoted by Donald E. Stanford, "Edward Taylor," in *Major Writers of Early American Literature*, ed. Emerson, p. 73.

22. Edwards, *Selected Sermons*, pp. 45, 63.

23. *Works*, 5:96.

24. Ibid., p. 101.

25. Ibid., p. 91.

26. Ibid., p. 173.

27. Ibid., p. 350.

28. Ibid., pp. 144, 145.

29. Ibid., p. 332; Willard, *The Complete Body of Divinity*, pp. 290–95, quoted in Lowrie, *The Shape of the Puritan Mind*, p. 216.

30. Edwards, *Works*, 8:436.

31. Ibid., 5:150.

32. Quoted by Van Doren, *Benjamin Franklin and Jonathan Edwards*, p. 360; Edwards, *Works*, 5:348.

33. Edwards, *Apocalyptic Writings*, p. 150.

34. *Selected Sermons*, pp. 36–37; Carse, *Jonathan Edwards and the Visibility of God*, pp. 103–4.

35. Edwards, *Freedom of the Will*, p. 291.

36. *Works*, 8:334; *Religious Affections*, p. 405.

37. *Selected Sermons*, pp. 81, 82; *Works*, 5:290. Edwards repeats this point in the sermon "True Grace Distinguished from the Experience of Devils": "Not that wicked men in this world have any more holiness or true virtue than the damned, or have wicked men, when they leave this world, any principle of wickedness infused into them; but when men are sent into hell, God perfectly takes away his Spirit from them, so as to all its merciful common influences, and entirely withdraws all restraints of his Spirit of good providence." *Works*, 8:99.

38. *Original Sin*, pp. 141–42; *Selected Sermons*, pp. 75–76, 86.

39. *Religious Affections*, introduction, p. 88.

40. *Apocalyptic Writings*, pp. 322, 369–70, 374; Davidson, *The Logic of Millennial Thought*, pp. 151–59.

41. "The population of this world is a conditional population; not the best, but the best that could live now." Emerson, "Fate," *The Conduct of Life*, in *Works*, 3:19. This kind of sorrow also appears in "Experience," in which Emerson concedes both that he will not live to experience the apotheosis of man and that his writing is not sufficiently revolutionary to constitute genuine prophecy. "Experience," *Essays, Second Series*, in *Works*, 1:66–67. But despair is continually a potential of Emerson's humanism, in his earlier writings as well as in his later and supposedly less confident ones, for example in "The Poet," where he regrets "looking in vain" for an actual poet who corresponds to the ideal poet he invokes (ibid., p. 36), or even in a relatively topical essay like "Wealth," in which he laments that he has "never seen a rich man." *The Conduct of Life*, *Works*, 3:79. What has been misnamed the "Neoplatonism" peculiar to certain of Emerson's writings, or to certain strains of modern writing in general, is better classified as nothing genuinely Platonic at all, which is to say, nothing theistic, but as a uniquely modern potential of Emerson's whole discourse, which states an identity between human being and perfection and at the same time paradoxically implies the failures of men, whether Transcendentalists or Philosophers or New England Reformers or Representative Men, actually to perfect themselves, and a unique potential, moreover, of all humanist discourse, which exposes man to the risk of failing to live up to himself the instant it invents for him a self worthy of living up to. Analyzed with this particular radical distinction between theism and humanism in mind, the sympathetic interest of modern scholars in millennial discourse appears to be not-very-well-sublimated self-pity.

42. Augustine, *The City of God*, p. 308; Edwards, *Notebooks*, pp. 235–36.

43. *Apocalyptic Writings*, p. 375; *Religious Affections*, p. 115.

44. The inquisitorial Stoddard is portrayed by Davidson, *Jonathan Edwards: The Narrative of Puritan Mind*, p. 41, and Cotton distinguishes goats from pigs in *The New Covenant . . .* (London, 1654), quoted in Coolidge, *The Pauline Renaissance in England*, pp. 92–93.

45. Edwards, *Notebooks*, p. 198; *Works*, 8:306. This definition of the subordinate function of civil authority can also be found in Augustine, who allows that the City of God "avails itself of the peace on earth, and, so far as it can without injuring faith and godliness, desires and maintains a common agreement among men regarding the acquisition of the necessaries of life, and makes the earthly peace bear upon the peace of heaven," (*The City of God*, p. 97) and can be found also in the Bible, in such injunctions as God's promise to the Jews that He will make the Gentiles to be of service to them, and to Him, indirectly as "nursing fathers" to the Church (Isaiah 49: 23). That such separation between church and state is universally accepted by all seventeenth- century Separatists and Congregationalists in England is attested to by Coolidge, *The Pauline Renaissance in England*, pp. 68–69.

46. Edwards, *Original Sin*, p. 50; *The Nature of True Virtue*, pp. 76, 94; *Original Sin*, pp. 383–83; for a definition of "*storgé*" and a review of its prevalence in seventeenth- and eighteenth-century moral treatises, see Fiering, *Jonathan Edwards's Moral Thought and Its British Context*, p. 158; Madison, "Federalist #10," *The Federalist Papers*, p. 17.

47. Edwards, *Selected Sermons*, pp. 100–101, 106; Tracy implies that events master Edwards throughout his pastorate in Northampton, especially after the Great Awakening and disaster-

ously after Edwards decides to tighten Stoddard's requirements for church membership. *Jonathan Edwards, Pastor,* pp. 169–82; Carse concludes similarly, if a bit more charitably, that Edwards is too much an intellectual and a dreamer to be an effective pastor. *Jonathan Edwards and the Visibility of God,* p. 181; Winthrop, quoted in Parrington, *The Colonial Mind,* p. 46; John Adams, *Discourses on Davila,* in *Works,* ed. Charles Francis Adams, (Boston: Charles C. Little and James Brown, 1851), 6:242; Paine, "Common Sense," ed. Isaac Kramnick (London: Pelican, 1976), p. 65, and, later in "Common Sense," Paine warns that "he that will promote discord under a government so equally formed as [is a republican one] would join Lucifer in his revolt," p. 96; Paine's nonsatirical use of Biblical imagery is noted by Bercovitch, although in the other context of Bercovitch's argument that such anomalies expose the pervasive, undeliberate nationalism of the "American jeremiad" even when it seems most critical of American culture. *The American Jeremiad,* p. 121.

48. Edwards, *Notebooks,* p. 246; *Selected Sermons,* pp. 32–33, Holbrook, *The Ethics of Jonathan Edwards,* p. 19.

49. Edwards, *Apocalyptic Writings,* p. 353; *Works,* 8:356, 291, 239–40.

50. "In private, he may have decided that the regenerate and unregenerate were chosen before the creation of the world, but he certainly concealed the doctrine at Enfield." Aldridge, *Jonathan Edwards,* p. 30.

51. Hawthorne, *The Scarlet Letter* (Boston: Houghton Mifflin, 1960), p. 164; *The Marble Faun* (New York: New American Library, 1961), pp. 121–22; William Wordsworth, *The Prelude,* bk. 6 vv. 557–778, in *Poetical Works,* ed. Thomas Hutchinson, revised by Ernest De Selincourt (1904; reprint, London: Oxford Univ. Press, 1971), pp. 535–37; James Fenimore Cooper, *The Last of the Mohicans* (New York: AMSCO School Publications, n.d.), pp. 39–45; Thoreau, *A Week on the Concord and Merrimack Rivers,* pp. 366–67; Tracy, *Jonathan Edwards, Pastor,* p. 134; Carse, *Jonathan Edwards and the Visibility of God,* p. 20.

52. Edwards, *Selected Sermons,* pp. 125, 127.

53. *Religious Affections,* p. 441; *Works,* 8:107.

54. Ibid., 5:263.

55. Thomas Shepard, *The Journal,* in *God's Plot, The Paradoxes of Puritan Piety,* ed. Michael McGiffert (Amherst: Univ. of Massachusetts Press, 1972), p. 150.

56. Edwards, *Works,* 5:130, Mather, *Magnalia,* Bks. 1 and 2, p. 94; Edwards, *Works,* 2:506.

57. *Works,* 5:175.

58. Ibid., 8:181.

59. Ibid., 1:513; *Selected Sermons,* p. 175.

60. Coleridge, *Aids to Reflection,* preface, p. xvii; Bancroft, *History of the United States,* 3:398–99. Davidson is sensitive to the irregularities of the structure of Providence articulated in theist discourse, which he terms the "afflictive model of progress." *The Logic of Millennial Thought,* pp. 129–41; although attributively a more accurate representation of the theist discourse of Providence than is usually achieved by modern scholarship, Davidson's is still unselfconsciously humanist to the degree that "afflictive progress" is an oxymoron that, according to modern usage, tends paradoxically to combine the opposites it contains, in this case fusing affliction and progress so as dialectically to bring the latter out of the former. A more ingeniously modernist interpretation of the irregularities of the theist discourse of Providence is managed by Lynen, who accounts them precocious intimations of the experimental deviations from narrative sequence that characterize some contemporary fiction. *The Design of the Present,* p. 59.

61. Edwards, *Works,* 5:275, 276.

62. Bancroft, *History of the United States,* 3:398–99.

63. Miller, *Images or Shadows of Divine Things,* p. 7; Heimert, *Religion and the American Mind,* pp. 68, 65; C. C. Goen, "Jonathan Edwards: A New Departure in Eschatology," in *Critical Essays on Jonathan Edwards,* ed. Scheick, p. 158; Ursula Brumm, *American Thought and Religious Typology,* trans. John Hoaglund (New Brunswick: Rutgers Univ. Press, 1970), excerpted as "Jonathan Edwards and Typology" in *Early American Literature,* ed. Gilmore, p. 74; Scheick,

"The Grand Design: Jonathan Edwards's *History of the Work of Redemption,*" *Eighteenth-Century Studies* (Spring 1975), pp. 300–314, reprinted in *Critical Essays on Jonathan Edwards,* ed. Scheick, p. 177; Lowance, "Typology, Millennial Eschatology, and Jonathan Edwards," in Scheik, ed., *Critical Essays,* p. 189; Stein, Editor's introduction, Edwards, *Apocalyptic Writings,* ed. Stein, pp. 15, 45; Davidson, *The Logic of Millennial Thought,* p. 78; Bercovitch, "The Rites of Assent: Rhetoric, Ritual, and the Ideology of American Consensus," in *The American Self: Myth, Ideology, and Popular Culture,* ed. Girgus, p. 12; Bercovitch, *The American Jeremiad,* p. 98; Gay, *A Loss of Mastery,* pp. 93–94.

64. Edwards, *Apocalyptic Writings,* p. 120. When Edwards uses *gradual* in the modern sense, such as for example in discussing the imperceptibly slow preparation for and consolidation of the experience of grace, which experience itself is, on the contrary, instantaneous, he distinguishes *gradual* as denoting only natural, and hence to him inferior, process. *Treatise on Grace and Other Posthumously Published Writings,* ed. Helm, pp. 37–38.

65. John Locke, *Some Thoughts Concerning Education* (1692), para. 184, and Daniel Defoe, *The Family Instructor,* 1:i (1741), p. 21, both quoted in *The Compact Edition of the Oxford English Dictionary,* svv. "gradual" and "gradually," p. 1185. Examples of pleonastic specifications of the meaning of *gradual* are: "Saving faith . . . is not only Gradually, but Specifically distinct from all common faith." *Le Blanc's World surveyed of famous voyages and travailes,* trans. Francis Brook (1660), a iv, and "Human Reason doth not only Gradually, but Specifically, differ, from the Phantasticke Reason of Brutes." Nehemiah Grew, *Cosmologia Sacra: or a discourse of the universe, as it is the creature and kingdom of God* (1701), 2:vii, p. 83, "gradually," *OED* (compact ed.), p. 1185.

66. John Milton, *Paradise Lost, Complete Poems and Prose,* bk. 5 vv. 482–84, ed. Merritt Y. Hughes (New York: Merrill, 1957), p. 313; Increase Mather, *Dissertation Wherein the Strange Doctrine . . .* (Boston, 1708), pp. 92–93, quoted in Davidson, *The Logic of Millennial Thought,* p. 77; Joel Barlowe, *The Columbiad* bk. 3, vv. 1–2, *The Works of Joel Barlow* (Gainesville, Fla.: Scholars' Facsimiles & Reprints, 1970), 2:485; John Woolman, *The Journal of John Woolman* (Secaucus, N.J.: Citadel, 1975), p. 167. Freneau concocts a teratological structure in "The Millennium" grafting the suddenly miraculous onto the gradually progressive in an explanation of the Day of Judgment as being brought to pass by a slight eccentricity in the orbit of the earth, a tiny but nonetheless unnatural repeal of natural law generating a process so long in fruition as to resemble the fulfillment of natural law. "The Millennium," in *Poems of Freneau,* ed. Clark, p. 148.

67. Edwards, *Works,* 8:281.

68. *Notebooks,* p. 189; *Works,* 8:173, 5:207–8; *Apocalyptic Writings,* p. 357; *Works,* 5:253, 257; Augustine, *The City of God,* pp. 722, 23; Moses Lowman, *A Paraphrase and Note on the Revelation of St. John* (London, 1737), alluded to by Stein, Editor's introduction, Edwards, *Apocalyptic Writings,* ed. Stein, p. 57.

69. Origen responds critically to chiliasm as expressed by the early Church Father Irenaeus, and argues against giving canonical status to Revelation. Quoted in Stein, Editor's introduction, Edwards, *Apocalyptic Writings,* ed. Stein, p. 2. Edwards's diurnal metaphor for the advent of the Millennium is excerpted from his notebooks by Stein, ibid., pp. 212–13.

Chapter 4. Grace

1. Edwards, *Works,* 8:542–43.

2. That innateness is implied by Locke's discourse is emphasized, for example, by Anderson in his Editor's introduction, Edwards, *Scientific and Philosophical Writings,* ed. Anderson, pp. 120–21.

3. John Locke, *An Essay Concerning Human Understanding* (London and New York: J. M. Dent & Sons, 1965), 1:90–91.

4. Edwards, *Notebooks,* pp. 223, 64, 89.

5. *Religious Affections*, pp. 93, 94, 160, 268; "Personal Narrative," in David Levin, *Jonathan Edwards: A Profile* (New York: Hill and Wang, 1969), p. 29. Levin provides a reliable text of the document that has come to be called the "personal narrative," the first published version of which appears in Samuel Hopkins's *The Life and Character of the Late Reverend Mr. Jonathan Edwards* (Boston, 1765).

6. Edwards, *Religious Affections*, p. 286; *Works*, 3:535–36, *Notebooks*, p. 245.

7. *Religious Affections*, p. 291; Emerson, *Nature, Works*, 5:48; Willard, *The Complete Body of Divinity*, p. 120, quoted in Lowrie, *The Shape of the Puritan Mind*, p. 78; Hamilton, "Federalist #31," *The Federalist Papers*, p. 59; Erdt, *Jonathan Edwards and the Sense of the Heart*, p. 52. Wolfgang Iser summarizes the distinction between the classical definition of imagination as a passive, image-retaining capacity of the mind and the romantic, modern definition of the imagination as the active, creative power virtually indistinguishable from the entire mind when the mind is acting at its highest potential, which brings nonexistent phenomena into being in epitomes of the creative process as redefined by Hegel and other romantic writers. Iser, *The Act of Reading, A Theory of Aesthetic Response* (Baltimore: Johns Hopkins Univ. Press, 1978), pp. 136–37.

8. Edwards, *Notebooks*, p. 127; *Works*, 8:405.

9. *Original Sin*, p. 381; *Works*, 8:6; *Religious Affections*, p. 161.

10. Ibid., p. 205; *Notebooks*, p. 123; *Selected Sermons*, p. 9.

11. *Mind*, p. 102, reprinted in *Scientific and Philosophical Writings*, ed. Anderson, p. 346; *Religious Affections*, p. 303; Poe, *Marginalia, Works*, 16:89.

12. Miller, *Jonathan Edwards*, pp. 275–76; Edwards, *Mind*, p. 26.

13. Erdt, *Jonathan Edwards and the Sense of the Heart*, p. 20; Fiering, *Jonathan Edwards's Moral Thought and Its British Context*, pp. 125–26; Kant, *Immanuel Kant's Critique of Pure Reason*, p. 309; Hegel, *The Phenomenology of Mind*, pp. 152–69; Emerson, *Nature, Works*, 5:52; John Marsh, Preliminary Essay, Coleridge, *Aids to Reflection*, p. xxxii; Coleridge, ibid., p. 104.

14. Edwards, *Notebooks*, p. 249; *Works*, 8:122; *Religious Affections*, pp. 382–83.

15. Delattre, *Beauty and Sensibility in the Thought of Jonathan Edwards*, pp. 146, 4, 133; Lee, "Mental Activity and the Perception of Beauty in Jonathan Edwards," p. 390; Fiering, *Jonathan Edwards's Moral Thought and Its British Context*, p. 110.

16. Edwards, *The Nature of True Virtue*, p. 1.

17. Ibid., p. 31; *Mind*, p. 35; *The Nature of True Virtue*, p. 103.

18. "Personal Narrative," Levin, *Jonathan Edwards: A Profile*, p. 30; Edwards, *Freedom of the Will*, p. 376.

19. *Original Sin*, p. 142, "Personal Narrative," Levin, *Jonathan Edwards: A Profile*, p. 27.

20. Edwards, *Works*, 1:526; Isaiah 40:18: "To whom then will you liken God, or what likeness compare with him?"; Edwards, *Mind*, p. 114.

21. *Notebooks*, p. 209.

22. *Works*, 8:500; *The Nature of True Virtue*, pp. 98, 99.

23. Ibid., p. 12; *Notebooks*, p. 244.

24. Hugh Henry Brackenridge, *Modern Chivalry*, ed. Lewis Leary, (New Haven: College and University Press, 1965), p. 83.

25. Kant, *Immanuel Kant's Critique of Pure Reason*, "I, Transcendental Doctrine of Elements"; Laurence notes the difference between Edwards's and Kant's aesthetics, that "there is resistance, decisive in Edwards . . . to the organization of the human subject developing from Cambridge Platonism to Kant, in which autonomy (not dependence), creativity (not createdness), and especially imagination (in its familiar, to us, Coleridgean sense), emerge as the leading concepts," but for the very different purpose of showing Edwards and whatever tradition he represents to be merely sterile and even treacherous in being un-Kantian, representing "a tradition recurrently given to dead ends and led up a series of box canyons." Laurence, "Moral Philosophy and New England Literary History: Reflections on Norman Fiering," pp. 196–97, 200.

26. Edwards, *Works*, 5:20, 32.

27. *Religious Affections*, pp. 416, 140; *Works*, 8:425–26.

28. *Religious Affections*, p. 324.

29. Ibid., p. 304; *Selected Sermons*, p. 75; *The Great Awakening*, p. 147.

30. *Selected Sermons*, p. 75.

31. *Works*, 3:131.

32. Ibid., pp. 123, 543–44, 553.

33. Ibid., pp. 310–11, 309–10; the Separatist practice is reported by Samuel Eliot Morison in his introduction to Bradford's *Of Plymouth Plantation*, p. xviii.

34. Edwards, *The Great Awakening*, pp. 191, 192, 195, 197, 198.

35. Ibid., pp. 199, 202, 200; Colacurcio recognizes the consistency between Edwards's emphasizing the otherworldliness of Phoebe's conversion and Edwards's metaphysics. "The Example of Edwards: Idealist Imagination and the Metaphysics of Sovereignty," *Puritan Influences in American Literature*, ed. Elliott, pp. 64–65.

36. Aldridge, *Jonathan Edwards*, p. 19; Davidson, *Jonathan Edwards, The Narrative of a Puritan Mind*, pp. 25–26; the love note to Sarah is reproduced in Aldridge, *Jonathan Edwards*, p. 20.

37. Stephen J. Stein, "Jonathan Edwards and the Rainbow: Biblical Exegesis and Poetic Imagination," *New England Quarterly* 47 (Spring 1974): 440–56.

38. Ibid., p. 449; Edwards, *Scientific and Philosophical Writings*, ed. Anderson, pp. 289–301; Stein, "Jonathan Edwards and the Rainbow," pp. 450, 452.

39. Miller, "The Rhetoric of Sensation," *Errand Into the Wilderness*, p. 183; "Jonathan Edwards and the Awakening," ibid., p. 163; Delattre, *Beauty and Sensibility in the Thought of Jonathan Edwards*, p. 36; Tracy, *Jonathan Edwards, Pastor*, p. 109, Miller, *Jonathan Edwards*, pp. 186–87 and "The Rhetoric of Sensation," *Errand Into the Wilderness*, p. 181; Carse, *Jonathan Edwards and the Visibility of God*, p. 143; Fiering, *Jonathan Edwards's Moral Thought and Its British Context*, pp. 285, 299, 309–11; Edwards, *Treatise on Grace and Other Posthumously Published Writings*, ed. Helm, pp. 74, 96; Helm mentions correctly in the Editor's Note to this collection that in reference to Edwards's writings, "it is strictly inappropriate to speak of habits of grace." p. 8.

40. Edwards, "Personal Narrative" in Levin, *Jonathan Edwards: A Profile*, p. 25. Portions of this discussion of Edwards's personal narrative appeared an article, R. C. De Prospo, "The 'New Simple Idea' of Edwards's Personal Narrative," *Early American Literature* 14 (Fall 1979): 193–204, and are quoted with the permission of *Early American Literature*.

41. Edwards, "Personal Narrative," in Levin, *Jonathan Edwards: A Profile*, p. 25.

42. Ibid., p. 27; Shepard, *The Journal*, in *God's Plot*, p. 166.

43. Edwards, "Personal Narrative," in Levin, *Jonathan Edwards: A Profile*, p. 27; Edwards, *Notebooks*, p. 173.

44. "Personal Narrative," Levin, *Jonathan Edwards: A Profile*, pp. 27–28, Edwards, *The Great Awakening*, pp. 194, 151; Poe, *Marginalia*, *Works*, 16:88; *Eureka*, ibid., p. 200; Shea's clever term for Edwards's inarticulateness is "reverent plagiarism." "The Art and Instruction of Edwards' *Personal Narrative*," *Critical Essays on Jonathan Edwards*, ed. Scheick, p. 271.

45. Edwards, "Personal Narrative," in Levin, *Jonathan Edwards: A Profile*, p. 28; Melville, *Moby-Dick*, p. 382.

46. Edwards, "Personal Narrative," in Levin, *Jonathan Edwards: A Profile*, p. 37; "The whole of [Edwards's] life—including his foolish days of intoxication and his barren days of organized religious enterprise . . . takes shape within the *Personal Narrative* as a single, crowded yet coherently patterned moment meaningfully related to the whole of God's redemptive activity." Minter, *The Interpreted Design*, p. 76.

47. Edwards, "Personal Narrative," in Levin, *Jonathan Edwards: A Profile*, pp. 35–36.

48. Daniel B. Shea, *Spiritual Autobiography in Early America* (Princeton: Princeton Univ. Press, 1968), p. 201; Laurence, "Moral Philosophy and New England Literary History: Reflections on Norman Fiering," pp. 212–13; Emerson, "The Lord's Supper," *Selected Writings of Ralph Waldo Emerson* (New York: Random House, 1940), p. 115; Thoreau, *Walden*, chap. 9, "Ponds"; Edwards, "Personal Narrative," in Levin, *Jonathan Edwards: A Profile*, p. 38.

49. Lyons, *The Invention of the Self*, p. 11; Poe, "Ligeia," *Works*, 2:248–68; William Bartram,

The *Travels of William Bartram*, p. 336; Franklin, *The Autobiography*, ed. Russel Nye, (Boston: Houghton Mifflin, 1958), for whose conformity to Edwards's analysis of the will, see chapter 5.

Chapter 5. Theism and Humanism

1. Rowe, *Through the Custom-House*, preface, xi.

2. Holmes, "Jonathan Edwards," in *Critical Essays on Jonathan Edwards*, ed. Scheick, p. 217; Opie, Introduction, *Jonathan Edwards and the Enlightenment*, p. v; the arguments by Aldridge, Heimert, and Smith linking Frankin and Edwards are collected and summarized by Fiering, *Jonathan Edwards's Moral Thought and Its British Context*, pp. 346–47, and Minter's appears in *The Interpreted Design*, p. 4; Van Doren, *Benjamin Franklin and Jonathan Edwards*, Introduction, pp. ix, xxxiii; Fiering, "Benjamin Franklin and the Way to Virtue," *American Quarterly* 30 (1978): 207; Fiering, *Jonathan Edwards's Moral Thought and Its British Context*, pp. 346–47; Lynen, *The Design of the Present*, p. 124; Bercovitch, "The Ritual of American Autobiography: Edwards, Franklin, Thoreau," *Révue Française d'Études Américaines* 14 (May 1982): 141, 143.

3. Aldridge, *Jonathan Edwards*, p. 2.

4. Quoted in Van Doren, *Benjamin Franklin*, p. 171.

5. Benjamin Franklin, *Autobiography and Other Writings*, p. 1.

6. Ibid., p. 3.

7. Ibid., p. 5.

8. Foucault, *The Order of Things*, p. 75.

9. Franklin, *Autobiography*, pp. 10–16, 29. Franklin notes a similarly practical value in his literacy in its having "improved" him to the extent that he is better company for the gentry of New Jersey than is his master, Keimer, during their stay in Burlington to print currency; ibid., p. 51.

10. Ibid., pp. 7–9, 18, 91, 51, 62–63, 47, 93, 136–37.

11. Marcus Aurelius, *Meditations* (New York: Penguin, 1964), pp– 36–40.

12. Robert F. Sayre, *The Examined Self: Benjamin Franklin, Henry Adams, Henry James* (Princeton: Princeton Univ. Press, 1964), excerpted as "The *Autobiography* of Benjamin Franklin," in *Early American Literature*, ed. Gilmore, pp. 87–89, 91. On the subject of Franklin's schemes for self-improvement in the memoirs, Fiering says that "habit was comparable to a disposition or inclination of the psyche that leads a person to behave in a particular way," implying that in modifying behavior Franklin modifies the will. *Jonathan Edwards's Moral Thought and Its British Context*, pp. 309–10; this is to confuse the habitual according to modern definition, which does not distinguish radically between behavior and inclination, and the habitual according to theist definition, which allows behavior to be consistent, even over a lifetime, without ever evidencing the will, and which permits behavior to be altered, according to such prudential techniques as those recommended by Franklin in the memoirs, without ever implying that such modification alters or even touches the will.

13. Franklin, *Autobiography*, p. 52.

14. Ibid., pp. 22, 52, 74, 90–91, 96–100.

15. The quotation from "Poor Richard" is in Franklin, *Works*, ed. Jared Sparks (Boston: Hilliard, Gray, & Co., 1836), 2:97.

16. Franklin, "A Dissertation on Liberty and Necessity, Pleasure and Pain" (1725; reprint: New York, Facsimile Text Society, 1930), p. 4; Lynen, in his attempt to link Franklin and Edwards, notes that Franklin deduces rationally in the "Dissertation" that the will cannot be free. *The Design of the Present*, p. 128.

17. Franklin, *Works*, 2:1–3, Edwards, *Mind*, entry no. 880, p. 87; Gay, *A Loss of Mastery*, p. 92; Franklin, "Speech to the Constitutional Convention," quoted in Van Doren, *Benjamin Franklin*, p. 748.

18. Miller, "From Edwards to Emerson," *Errand Into the Wilderness*, pp. 185, 202–3.

19. The original and subsequent mottos for *Nature* are both given in *Selections from Ralph Waldo Emerson*, ed. Whicher, p. 21; *"Alle Guten, alle Bösen / folgen ihrer Rosenspur. / Küsse gab sie uns und Reben, / einen Freund, geprüsst im Tod. / Wollust ward dem Wurm gegeben, / und der Cherub steht vor Gott,"* (Johann Christoph Friedrich von Schiller, "An die Freude," 27–32, *Schillers Werke:* 1 (Weimar: Herman Böhlaus Nachfolger, 1943), p. 170; similar transformations of the great chain can be found throughout the best-known European romantic writings, in Shelley's *Queen Mab,* for example, where "The passions, prejudices, interests, / That sway the meanest being, the weak touch / That moves the finest nerve, / And in one human brain / Causes the faintest thought, becomes a link / In the great chain of nature," Percy Bysshe Shelley, *Queen Mab,* 2:103–8, *The Complete Works of Percy Bysshe Shelley* (New York: Gordian, 1965): 1, 78; Edwards, *The Nature of True Virtue,* p. 9.

20. Emerson, *Nature, Works,* 5:15–18.

21. Emerson, "Fate," *The Conduct of Life, Works,* 3:34; Emerson expresses the same confidence in perceiving the ideal emerge from even the meanest and most vicious of realities in the motto-poem to "Wealth": "What oldest star the fame can save / Of races perishing to pave / The planet with a floor of lime? / Dust is their pyramid and mole: / Who saw what ferns and palms were pressed / Under the tumbling mountain's breast, / In the safe herbal of the coal? / But when the quarried means were piled, / All is waste and worthless, till / Arrives the wise selecting will, / And, out of slime and chaos, Wit / Draws the threads of fair and fit." Emerson, "Wealth," ibid., 3:69–70. Augustine, *The City of God,* p. 383; Adams, *Discourses on Davila,* pp. 394–95; Jefferson, *Notes on the State of Virginia,* pp. 80–81; Hegel, *The Phenomenology of Mind,* p. 207; Thoreau, *A Week on the Concord and Merrimack Rivers,* pp. 277–78.

22. Emerson, *Nature, Works,* 5:15–18; Edwards, *Notebooks,* entry no. 42, p. 238.

23. Emerson, "Divinity School Address," *Works,* 5:108–9.

24. Ibid., p. 109; "The Last Supper," *The Complete Essays and Other Writings of Ralph Waldo Emerson* (New York: Modern Library, 1940), p. 115.

25. Heidegger, *Being and Time,* pp. 400–401.

26. Emerson, *Nature, Works,* 5:42; "The Poet," *Essays, Second Series, Works,* 1:21; "History," *Essays, First Series, Works,* 1:11–12.

27. "Experience," *Essays, Second Series, Works,* 1:62; "Works and Days," *Society and Solitude, Works,* 2:145; "History," *Essays, First Series, Works,* 1:11–12.

28. Feidelson, *Symbolism and American Literature,* p. 78.

29. Emerson, *Nature, Works,* 5:22–23; "Self-Reliance," *Essays, Second Series, Works,* 1:53–56.

30. "Circles," *Essays, Second Series, Works,* 1:241–45; "Fate," *The Conduct of Life, Works,* 3:11–12, 25, 34.

31. "The Poet," *Essays, Second Series, Works,* 1:19, "History," *Essays, First Series,* 1:16; *Nature, Works,* 5:17; Whitman, *Leaves of Grass* (New York: Norton, 1973), *Song of Myself,* st. 41, vs. 1049.

32. Emerson, "The American Scholar," *Works,* 5:74, 75; "The Poet," *Essays, Second Series, Works,* 1:19.

33. "Experience," ibid., 1:47–48; "Divinity School Address," *Works,* 5:111, 105.

34. "Self-Reliance," *Essays, First Series, Works,* 1:56–57; "Circles," ibid., 1:240; "The American Scholar," ibid., 5:91; "The Poet," *Essays, Second Series,* ibid., 1:28; "Experience," ibid., 1:59–60; "Fate," *The Conduct of Life,* ibid., 3:32; "Character," *The Complete Essays and Other Writings,* p. 366.

35. Hawthorne, *The Blithedale Romance* (New York: Norton, 1958), p. 247; *The Marble Faun,* pp. 48–50; Melville, *Pierre, or the Ambiguities* (Evanston and Chicago: Northwestern Univ. Press, 1971), p. 6.

36. Emerson, "Experience," *Essays, Second Series, Works,* 1:66, 73.

37. Henri Peyre, *What is Romanticism?* (Birmingham: Univ. of Alabama Press, 1977), introduction, p. ix; Bloom, *The Anxiety of Influence,* p. 125; Todorov, *Theories of the Symbol,* p. 167; Henri Bergson, quoted in Peyre, *What is Romanticism?,* p. 4; Derrida, "The Law of Genre," *Critical Inquiry* 7, no. 1 (Autumn 1980): 61–62; Hans Eichner, "The Rise of Modern Science and the Genesis of Romanticism," *PMLA* 97, no. 1 (January 1982): 8; de Man, "Sign and Symbol in

Hegel's *Aesthetics*," *Critical Inquiry* 8, no. 4 (Summer 1982): 763; de Man, *Allegories of Reading*, p. 82.

38. Kuhn, *The Structure of Scientific Revolutions*, p. 150; Foucault, *The Order of Things*, introduction, p. xii; *The Archaeology of Knowledge*, introduction, pp. 4–5; *The Order of Things*, preface, pp. xxii, xxiii; Todorov, *Theories of the Symbol*, pp. 10, 285–92; Lyons, *The Invention of the Self*, p. 6; James Engell, *The Creative Imagination* (Cambridge: Harvard Univ. Press, 1981), p. 6; D. W. Robertson, Jr., "Some Observations on Method in Literary Studies," in *New Directions in Literary History*, ed. Cohen, p. 73; Joel Conarroe, "Editor's Column," *PMLA* 95, no. 1 (January 1980): 3–4; Daniel Stempel, "Blake, Foucault, and the Classical Episteme," *PMLA* 96, no. 3 (1981): 403.

39. Husserl, *Ideas*, p. 81; "Author's Preface to the English Edition," *Ideas*, pp. 12, 48, 149.

40. Heidegger, *Being and Time*, pp. 251–52; Jacques Lacan, *The Language of the Self*, trans. Anthony Wilden (1956; reprint, Baltimore: Johns Hopkins Univ. Press, 1968), pp. 34–35; de Man, *Allegories of Reading*, pp. 50, 298–300; Michael Fried, "Painter into Painting: On Courbet's *After Dinner at Ornans* and *Stonebreakers*," *Critical Inquiry* 8, no. 4 (Summer 1982): 619–34, 641–42.

41. Derrida, "Semiology and Grammatology," Interview with Julia Kristeva, *Positions*, pp. 26–29.

42. Todorov, *Theories of the Symbol*, pp. 155–56; Jonathan Culler, *In Pursuit of Signs* (Ithaca: Cornell Univ. Press, 1981), p. 192; Todorov, *Theories of the Symbol*, p. 61; Derrida, "Semiology and Grammatology," *Positions*, pp. 19–20; Lacan, *The Language of the Self*, p. 30.

43. Nietszche, *The Birth of Tragedy*, *The Birth of Tragedy and the Genealogy of Morals*, p. 4; Nicolai Hartman, quoted in Spiegelberg, *The Phenomenological Movement*, p. 369; Heidegger, *Being and Time*, p. 363; René Girard, "Tiresias and the Critic," *The Languages of Criticism and the Sciences of Man*, ed. Macksey and Donato, p. 19; Eugenio Donato, "The Two Languages of Criticism," ibid., p. 46; Lyons, *The Invention of the Self*, p. 18; Derrida, "Positions," Interview with Jean-Louis Houdebine and Guy Scarpetta (1971), *Positions*, pp. 63–64; "Structure, Sign, and Play in the Discourse of the Human Sciences," *The Languages of Criticism and the Sciences of Man*, ed. Macksey and Donato, pp. 250–52.

44. De Man, "Sign and Symbol in Hegel's *Aesthetics*," pp. 767–70; Geoffrey Hartman, "History-Writing as Answerable Style," *New Directions in Literary History*, ed. Cohen, p. 97; Hawthorne, *The House of the Seven Gables* (New York: Signet, 1961), pp. 101, 102, 225; *The Marble Faun*, pp. 242–43, 318–19; *Our Old Home*, *The Centenary Edition of the Works of Nathaniel Hawthorne*, (Ohio State Univ. Press, 1970), 5:91; Husserl, *Ideas*, pp. 167, 189; Heidegger, *Being and Time*, pp. 71, 370; Fish, "With the Compliments of the Author: Reflections on Austin and Derrida," *Critical Inquiry* 8, no. 4 (Summer 1982): 701.

45. Foucault, *The Order of Things*, pp. 341–42.

46. Claude Lévi-Strauss, *Tristes Tropiques*, trans. John Russell, (1955; reprint, New York: Athenaeum, 1972), p. 397; Melville, *Pierre*, p. 119; Emily Dickinson, Poem #122, "After great pain, a formal feeling comes—," *Final Harvest* (Boston: Little, Brown, 1961), p. 73.

47. Foucault, *The Order of Things*, "Foreword to the English Edition," p. xii; Lacan, "Of Structure as an Inmixing of Otherness Prerequisite to Any Subject Whatever," in *The Languages of Criticism and the Sciences of Man*, ed. Macksey and Donato, p. 190, Kuhn, *The Structure of Scientific Revolutions*, pp. 152–59.

48. De Saussure, *Course in General Linguistics*, p. 87; Lyons, *The Invention of the Self*, pp. 26–27; Foucault, *The Archaeology of Knowledge*, p. 174.

49. Lévi-Strauss, quoted in Culler, *In Pursuit of Signs*, p. 27; Roman Jacobsen, quoted by Victor Erlich, *Russian Formalism* (The Hague: Mouton, 1955), p. 269; Roland Barthes, quoted by Todorov, *Theories of the Symbol*, p. 244; Barthes, "The Two Criticisms," (1963), in *Velocities of Change*, ed. Macksey, p. 68; Culler, *In Pursuit of Signs*, p. 103; Julia Kristeva, *La Révolution du langage poétique* (Paris, 1974); Bloom, *The Anxiety of Influence*, p. 96; Riffaterre, *Semiotics of Poetry*, p. 137: "The Stylistic Approach to Literary History," in *New Directions in Literary History*, ed. Cohen, pp. 147–50.

50. Derrida, *Of Grammatology*, p. 87.

51. Derrida, "Semiology and Grammatology," *Positions*, p. 24.

52. Rowe, *Through the Custom-House*, p. 6; Miller, "The End of the World" (1951), *Errand Into the Wilderness*, pp. 238–39; "Religion and Society in the Early Literature of Virginia" (1949), ibid., p. 99; "Errand Into the Wilderness," (1952), ibid., p. 12.; "Jonathan Edwards and the Great Awakening" (1949), ibid., p. 153; "Nature and the National Ego" (1955), ibid., pp. 209–10. The motivated backwardness of the criticism of American literature as it is practiced in the United States is immediately apparent to anyone who reads American literature and American literary criticism from the vantage of contemporary literary theory, to Rowe, for example, who comments in the conclusion of *Through the Custom-House* that "the obsessive concern with literary nationalism in American studies disguises a fundamentally poetic and linguistic problem (such as the 'anxiety of influence') as the particular issues of a unique culture, history, and literature. . . . American literary study has remained notably untheoretical (despite a wealth of theories of American literature) and often stubbornly unphilosophical. . . ," p. 193.

53. There are several versions in print of this comment by Faulkner. One appears in the transcript of the class conferences Faulkner holds in 1957–58 at the University of Virginia: "No, it was not my intention to write the pageant of a country, I simply was using the quickest tool I had. I was using what I knew best, which was the locale where I was born and had lived most of my life. That was just like the carpenter building the fence—he uses the nearest hammer," *Faulkner in the University*, ed. Frederick L. Gwynne and Joseph Blotner (New York: Vintage, 1959), p. 3.

54. George Santayana, *Character and Opinion in the United States* (New York: Norton, 1967), pp. 114, 126.

55. Thoreau, *Walden*, p. 218; Whitman, *Leaves of Grass, Song of Myself*, § 24, vs. 497, § 50, vs. 1309; "Our Old Feuillage," vs. 68; "As I Ebb'd With the Ocean of Life," § 2, vv. 27–28; *Song of Myself*, § 25, vs. 560; ibid., § 40, vv. 987–88; ibid., § 34, vs. 875; Thoreau, *Walden*, p. 53; Emerson, "Fate," *The Conduct of Life, Works*, 3 : 34.

56. Hawthorne, "The Custom-House," *The Scarlet Letter*, p. 40; *The House of the Seven Gables*, pp. 76, 118–19.

57. "The Custom-House," *The Scarlet Letter*, pp. 38–39.

58. *The Marble Faun*, pp. 274–75. That nature must be transformed into a system of signs as the condition of becoming intelligible is implied also by Thoreau, with almost the self-consciousness, though not at all the ennui, of Hawthorne's semiotics; in the climactic "Spring" chapter of *Walden* the famous passage portraying the thawing of the hillside as identical to the original Creation presents an evolutionary metamorphosis both of nature and, simultaneously, of language, suggesting, if not the priority of language, at least coordination between linguistic and another, "natural," form of signification. *Walden*, p. 209; similar passages occur in *A Week on the Concord and Merrimack Rivers*, one likening the holes inscribed by rocks spun by the current in the river bed to natural autographs, another asserting that nature is as legible and primitively meaningful as a "papyrus." *A Week on the Concord and Merrimack Rivers*, pp. 310, 395; the whole structure of *A Week* freely combines literary and "natural" hermeneutics, interspersing readings of books with readings of the landscape to imply, as does the "Reading" chapter of *Walden*, that there is no more than a graphical difference between the signification of words and the signification of "things." And that the "land" is lost as an "objective" reality the instant "nature" occupies a central place in romantic discourse in the United States is implied also by the consistently elegiac presentation of the forests and the culture of the forests, for example in originally depicting the prototypical American frontiersman as nearing his dotage and railing against the incursions of the "settlements" and in recalling even the mid-eighteenth century American wilderness with continual premonitions of its eventual disappearance, by the earliest major American romantic writer, James Fenimore Cooper, in *The Pioneers* (1823; reprint, New York: Holt, Rinehart and Winston, 1959), pp. 1–15, and *The Last of the Mohicans*, pp. 1–2.

59. Melville, *Moby-Dick*, pp. 139, 335, 340.

60. Ibid., p. 367; "Bartleby," *Billy Budd and the Piazza Tales* (Garden City, New York: Anchor, 1973), pp. 138, 153; *The Confidence-Man* (New York: Norton, 1972), p. 7; Melville's "Benito Cereno" can be seen in this light to contain both consequences of this disillusion, the submissiveness of Cereno and the malignity of Babo. The interpretation of Pip's meta-interpretation of the doubloon takes a bit further Rowe's discussion of this passage: "[the doubloon] becomes a symbolic representation of the process of symbolization, itself." *Henry Adams and Henry James*, p. 23.

61. Heidegger, *Being and Time*, especially § 16, pp. 102–7.

62. Melville, *Pierre*, pp. 284–85.

63. Fitzgerald, *The Great Gatsby* (New York: Scribners, 1953), p. 121; for typically humanist interpretations of this passage, evaluating it as "an elegy for the lapsed American dream of innocent success" or as "a mere salute to the memory of a vanished America," see Fiedler, *Love and Death in the American Novel*, pp. 315–16, and Marx, *The Machine in the Garden*, pp. 356–64; and for another semiotic interpretation of the inverse relationship between the presence of signifiers and the absence of the "things" they signify in American discourse of the land generally, see Stilgoe's *Common Landscape of America, 1580 to 1845*, which notes that the wilderness is scarce on the colonial New England frontier and abundant in colonial New England towns, New England frontiersmen scarcely mentioning the wilderness while civilized Boston clergymen "preached sermon upon sermon about the wilderness a few miles west," p. 51.

64. Bloom, *The Anxiety of Influence*, p. 39.

65. Nietszche, *The Birth of Tragedy, The Birth of Tragedy and the Genealogy of Morals*, p. 29; Foucault, *The Order of Things*, pp. 386–87.

BIBLIOGRAPHY

Adams, John. *Discourses on Davila*. Edited by Charles Francis Adams. Boston: Charles C. Little and James Brown, 1851. Vol. 6.

Ahlstrom, Sidney. *Theology in America*. Indianapolis: Bobbs-Merrill, 1967.

Aldridge, Alfred Owen. "Edwards and Hutcheson." *The Harvard Theological Review*, No. 44 (1931): 35–53.

————. *Jonathan Edwards*. New York: Washington Square Press, 1964.

Anderson, Wallace E. Editor's introduction. Jonathan Edwards. *Scientific Writings*, edited by Wallace E. Anderson. Vol. 6 of *The Works of Jonathan Edwards*, John E. Smith, General Editor. New Haven and London: Yale Univ. Press, 1980.

Armstrong, Paul B. *The Phenomenology of Henry James*. Chapel Hill and London: Univ. of North Carolina Press, 1983.

Augustine. *The City of God*. Translated by Marcus Dods. New York: Random House, 1950.

————. *Confessions and Enchiridion*. Translated by Alfred C. Outler. Philadelphia: Westminster Press, 1955.

Aurelius, Marcus. *Meditations*. New York: Penguin, 1964.

Bancroft, George. *History of the Formation of the Constitution of the United States*. New York: Appleton & Co., 1882.

————. *History of the United States*. 10 vols. Boston: Little Brown, 1874.

Barlow, Joel. *The Works of Joel Barlow*. Introduced by William K. Bottorff and Arthur L. Ford. Gainesville, Fla.: Scholars' Facsimiles & Reprints, 1970. Vol. 2.

Barthes, Roland. "The Two Criticisms." In *Velocities of Change*, edited by Richard Macksey. Baltimore and London: Johns Hopkins Univ. Press, 1974.

Bartram, William. *The Travels of William Bartram*. Edited by Russel Nye. Boston: Houghton Mifflin, 1958.

Bercovitch, Sacvan. *The American Jeremiad*. Madison: Univ. of Wisconsin Press, 1978.

————. "Cotton Mather." In *Major Writers of Early American Literature*, edited by Everett Emerson. Madison: Univ. of Wisconsin Press, 1972.

————. "The Puritan Errand Reassessed." In *Toward a New American Literary History*, edited by Arlin Turner and Louis J. Budd. Durham: Duke Univ. Press, 1980.

————. *The Puritan Origins of the American Self*. New Haven: Yale Univ. Press, 1975.

————. "The Rites of Assent: Rhetoric, Ritual, and the Ideology of American Consensus." In *The American Self: Ideology and Popular Culture*, edited by Sam B. Girgus. Albuquerque: Univ. of New Mexico Press, 1981.

———. "The Ritual of American Autobiography: Edwards, Franklin, Thoreau." *Révue Française d'Études Américaines*, no. 14 (May 1982): 139–50.

Bloom, Harold. *The Anxiety of Influence*. New York: Oxford Univ. Press, 1973.

———, ed. *Deconstruction and Criticism*. New York: The Seabury Press, 1979.

Boorstin, Daniel. *The Lost World of Thomas Jefferson*. Boston: Beacon Press, 1960.

Brackenridge, Hugh Henry. *Modern Chivalry*. Edited by Lewis Leary. New Haven: College and University Press, 1965.

Bradford, William. *Of Plymouth Plantation*. Edited by Samuel Eliot Morison. New York: Knopf, 1952.

Breitwieser, Mitchell Robert. "Cotton Mather's Pharmacy." *Early American Literature* 16, no. 1 (Spring 1981): 22–49.

Brooks, Van Wyck. *The Writer in America*. New York: Sutton, 1953.

Brown, Patterson. "Infinite Causal Regression." In *Aquinas: A Collection of Critical Essays*, edited by Anthony Kenny. Garden City, N.Y.: Doubleday, 1969.

Brumm, Ursula. *American Thought and Religious Typology*. Translated by John Hoaglund. New Brunswick: Rutgers Univ. Press, 1970. Excerpted as "Jonathan Edwards and Typology." In *Early American Literature*, edited by Michael T. Gilmore. *Twentieth Century Views Series*. Series Editor Maynard Mack. Englewood Cliffs, N.J.: Prentice-Hall, 1980.

Bushman, Richard L. "Jonathan Edwards and Puritan Consciousness." *Journal for the Scientific Study of Religion* 5 (1966): 383–96.

Butts, Francis T. "The Myth of Perry Miller." *American Historical Review* 87, no. 3 (June 1982): 665–94.

Caldwell, Patricia. *The Puritan Conversion Narrative*. Cambridge: Cambridge Univ. Press, 1983.

Calvin, John. *Institutes of the Christian Religion*. Translated by Henry Beveridge. Grand Rapids, Mich.: Eerdmans, 1957.

Campbell, Joseph, ed. *Spirit and Nature*. Papers from the Eranos Notebooks. 1937, 1945, 1946; reprint, Princeton: Princeton Univ. Press, 1954.

Carpenter, Frederick I. "The Radicalism of Jonathan Edwards." *New England Quarterly*, no. 4 (October 1931): 631–33.

Carse, James. *Jonathan Edwards and the Visibility of God*. New York: Scribners, 1967.

Cawelti, John. *The Six-Gun Mystique*. Bowling Green, Ohio: Bowling Green Univ. Press, 1970.

Channing, William Ellery. *Memoirs of William Ellery Channing*. Edited by William H. Channing. Boston, 1848.

Chase, Richard. *The American Novel and Its Tradition*. Garden City, N.Y.: Doubleday, 1957.

Cherry, Conrad. *Nature and Religious Imagination, From Edwards to Bushnell*. Philadelphia: Fortress Press, 1980.

Clark, Harry Hayden, ed. *Transitions in American Literary History*. Durham: Duke Univ. Press, 1954.

Clebsch, William. *American Religious Thought*. Chicago: Univ. of Chicago Press, 1973.

Cohen, Ralph, ed. *New Directions in Literary History*. Baltimore and London: Johns Hopkins Univ. Press, 1974.

Colacurcio, Michael. "The Dynamo and the Angelic Doctor." *American Quarterly* 17 (1965): 696–712.

——. "The Example of Edwards: Idealist Imagination and the Metaphysics of Sovereignty." In *Puritan Influences in American Literature,* edited by Emory Elliott. Urbana: Univ. of Illinois Press, 1979.

Coleridge, Samuel Taylor. *Aids to Reflection.* 1825; reprint, London: George Bell & Sons, 1904.

Conarroe, Joel. "Editor's Column." *PMLA* 95, no. 1 (January 1980): 3–4.

Coolidge, John S. *The Pauline Renaissance in England.* Oxford: Clarendon Press, 1970.

Cooper, James Fenimore. *The Last of the Mohicans.* New York: AMSCO School Pubs., n.d.

——. *The Pioneers.* New York: Holt, Rinehardt, and Winston, 1959.

Cotton, John. *The New Covenant. . . .* London, 1654.

Crèvecoeur, Hector Saint-John, de. *Letters from an American Farmer.* New York: Dutton, 1957.

Culler, Jonathan. *In Pursuit of Signs.* Ithaca: Cornell Univ. Press, 1981.

Curtius, Ernst Robert. *Zur Literarästhetik des Mittelalters.* Germany, 1938.

Daly, Robert. *God's Altar: The World and the Flesh in Puritan Poetry.* Berkeley: Univ. of California Press, 1978. Excerpted as "Puritan Poetics." In *Early American Literature,* edited by Michael T. Gilmore. Englewood Cliffs, N.J.: Prentice-Hall, 1980.

Davidson, Edward H. *Jonathan Edwards, The Narrative of a Puritan Mind.* Cambridge: Harvard Univ. Press, 1960.

Davidson, James West. *The Logic of Millennial Thought.* New Haven and London: Yale Univ. Press, 1977.

Delattre, Roland André. *Beauty and Sensibility in the Thought of Jonathan Edwards.* New Haven and London: Yale Univ. Press, 1968.

De Man, Paul. *Allegories of Reading.* New Haven and London: Yale Univ. Press, 1979.

——. "Sign and Symbol in Hegel's Aesthetics." *Critical Inquiry* 8, no. 4 (Summer 1982): 761–75.

De Prospo, R. C. "The 'New Simple Idea' of Edwards's Personal Narrative." *Early American Literature* 14 (Fall 1979): 193–204.

Derrida, Jacques. "The Law of Genre." *Critical Inquiry* 7, no. 1 (Autumn 1980): 55–82.

——. *Of Grammatology.* Translated by Gayatri Chakravorty Spivak. Baltimore: Johns Hopkins Univ. Press, 1974.

——. *Positions.* Translated by Alan Bass. Chicago: Univ. of Chicago Press, 1981.

——. "Structure, Sign, and Play in the Discourse of the Human Sciences." In *The Languages of Criticism and the Sciences of Man,* edited by Richard Macksey and Eugenio Donato. Baltimore and London: Johns Hopkins Univ. Press, 1970.

De Saussure, Ferdinand. *Course in General Linguistics.* Translated by Wade Baskin. Edited by Charles Bally and Albert Sechehaye. New York: Philosophical Library, 1959.

Dickinson, Emily. *Final Harvest.* Boston: Little Brown, 1961.

Donato, Eugenio. "The Two Languages of Criticism." In *The Languages of Criticism and the Sciences of Man,* edited by Richard Macksey and Eugenio Donato. Baltimore and London: Johns Hopkins Univ. Press, 1970.

Drinnon, Richard. *Facing West.* Minneapolis: Univ. of Minnesota Press, 1980.

Dwight, Sereno, ed. *The Writings of President Edwards with a Memoir of his Life.* New York, 1829–30.

Edwards, Jonathan. *Apocalyptic Writings.* Edited by Stephen J. Stein. Vol. 5 of *The Works of Jonathan Edwards.* General Editor John E. Smith. New Haven and London: Yale Univ. Press, 1977.

———. *Freedom of the Will.* Edited by Paul Ramsey. Vol. 1 of *The Works of Jonathan Edwards.* General Editor John E. Smith. New Haven and London: Yale Univ. Press, 1957.

———. *The Great Awakening.* Edited by C. C. Goen. Vol. 4 of *The Works of Jonathan Edwards.* General Editor John E. Smith. New Haven and London: Yale Univ. Press, 1972.

———. *Images or Shadows of Divine Things.* Edited by Perry Miller. New Haven: Yale Univ. Press, 1948.

———. *The Mind of Jonathan Edwards: A Reconstructed Text.* Edited by Leon Howard. Berkeley and Los Angeles: Univ. of California Press, 1963.

———. *Original Sin.* Edited by Clyde A. Holbrook. Vol. 3 of *The Works of Jonathan Edwards.* General Editor John E. Smith. New Haven and London: Yale Univ. Press, 1970.

———. *The Nature of True Virtue.* Ann Arbor: Univ. of Michigan Press, 1960.

———. *The Philosophy of Jonathan Edwards from His Private Notebooks.* Edited by Harvey Townsend. Eugene: Univ. of Oregon Press, 1955.

———. *Scientific and Philosophical Writings.* Edited by Wallace E. Anderson. Vol. 6 of *The Works of Jonathan Edwards.* General Editor John E. Smith. New Haven and London: Yale Univ. Press, 1980.

———. *Selected Sermons.* Edited by Harry Norman Gardiner. New York: Macmillan & Co., 1904.

———. *A Treatise Concerning Religious Affections.* Edited by John E. Smith. Vol. 2 of *The Works of Jonathan Edwards.* General Editor John E. Smith. New Haven and London: Yale Univ. Press, 1959.

———. *Treatise on Grace and Other Posthumously Published Writings.* Edited by Paul Helm. Cambridge: James Clark & Co., 1971.

———. *The Works of President Edwards in Eight Volumes.* London: Black & Son, 1817.

Eichner, Hans. "The Rise of Modern Science and the Genesis of Romanticism." *PMLA* 97, no. 1 (January 1982): 8–30.

Elliott, Emory, ed. *Puritan Influences in American Literature.* Urbana: Univ. of Illinois Press, 1979.

Elwood, Douglass. *The Philosophical Theology of Jonathan Edwards.* New York: Columbia Univ. Press, 1960.

Emerson, Everett, ed. *Major Writers of Early American Literature.* Madison: Univ. of Wisconsin Press, 1972.

Emerson, Ralph Waldo. *The Complete Essays and Other Writings of Ralph Waldo Emerson.* New York: Modern Library, 1940.

———. *Selected Writings of Ralph Waldo Emerson.* New York: Random House, 1940.

———. *Selections from Ralph Waldo Emerson.* Edited by Stephen E. Whicher. Boston: Houghton Mifflin, 1957.

———. *The Works of Ralph Waldo Emerson in Five Volumes.* Boston: Houghton Mifflin & Co., 1882.

Engell, James. *The Creative Imagination.* Cambridge: Harvard Univ. Press, 1981.

Erdt, Terence, *Jonathan Edwards and the Sense of the Heart.* Amherst: Univ. of Massachusetts Press, 1980.

Erlich, Victor. *Russian Formalism.* The Hague: Mouton, 1955.

Faulkner, William. *Faulkner in the University.* Edited by Frederick L. Gwynne and Joseph Blotner. New York: Vintage, 1959.

Faust, Clarence. "The Decline of Puritanism." In *Transitions in American Literary History,* edited by Harry Hayden Clark. Durham: Duke Univ. Press, 1954.

———, and Thomas Johnson. Introduction. In *Jonathan Edwards,* edited by Clarence Faust and Thomas Johnson. New York: Hill and Wang, 1962.

———. "Jonathan Edwards as a Scientist." *American Literature* 1 (January 1930): 393–404. Reprinted in *Jonathan Edwards and the Enlightenment.* Edited by John Opie. Lexington, Mass.: Heath, 1969.

Feidelson, Charles. *Symbolism and American Literature.* Chicago: Univ. of Chicago Press, 1953.

Felman, Shoshana. "Turning the Screw of Interpretation." *Yale French Studies* 55/56 (Spain 1977): 94–207.

Fermia, Joseph N. "An Historicist Critique of 'Revisionist' Methods for Studying the History of Ideas." *History and Theory* 30, no. 2 (1981): 113–34.

Feuerbach, Ludwig. *The Essence of Christianity.* Translated by George Eliot. New York: Harper and Row, 1957.

Fiedler, Leslie. *Love and Death in the American Novel.* 1960, reprint, New York: Dell, 1966.

Fiering, Norman. "Benjamin Franklin and the Way to Virtue." *American Quarterly* 30 (1978): 199–223.

———. *Jonathan Edwards's Moral Thought and Its British Context.* Chapel Hill: Univ. of North Carolina Press, 1981.

———. *Moral Philosophy at Seventeenth-Century Harvard.* Chapel Hill: Univ. of North Carolina Press, 1982.

Fish, Stanley. "With the Compliments of the Author: Reflections on Austin and Derrida." *Critical Inquiry* 8 no. 4 (Summer 1982): 693–721.

Fitzgerald, F. Scott. *The Great Gatsby.* New York: Scribners, 1953.

Foerster, Norman, ed. *The Reinterpretation of American Literature.* 1928; reprint, New York: Russell & Russell, 1959.

Forster, Robert, and Orest Ranum, eds. *Selections from the* Annales. Translated by Elborg Forster and Patricia M. Ranum. Baltimore and London: Johns Hopkins Univ. Press, 1978.

Foucault, Michel. *The Archaeology of Knowledge.* Translated by A. M. Sheridan Smith. New York: Pantheon, 1972.

———. *The Order of Things.* New York: Vintage, 1970.

Franklin, Benjamin, *Autobiography and Other Writings.* Edited by Russel B. Nye. Boston: Houghton Mifflin, 1958.

———. "A Dissertation on Liberty and Neccessity, Pleasure and Pain." New York: Facsimile Text Society, 1930.

————. *Works.* Edited by Jared Sparks. Boston: Hilliard, Gray, & Co., 1836. Vol. 2.

Franklin, Wayne F. *Discoverers, Explorers, Settlers.* Chicago: Univ. of Chicago Press, 1979.

Freneau, Philip. *The Poems of Freneau.* Edited by Harry Hayden Clark, New York: Hafner, 1960.

Freud, Sigmund. "The 'Uncanny.'" *On Creativity and the Unconscious: Papers on the Psychology of Art, Literature, Love, Religion.* Edited by Benjamin Nelson. Translated under the supervision of Joan Rivier. New York: Harper and Rowe, 1958.

Fried, Michael. "Painter into Painting: On Courbet's *After Dinner at Ornans* and *Stonebreakers.*" *Critical Inquiry* 8, no. 4 (Summer 1982): 619–49.

Frye, Northrop, *Anatomy of Criticism.* Princeton: Princeton Univ. Press, 1957.

Gaustad, Edwin. *The Great Awakening in New England.* New York: Harper & Bros., 1957.

Gay, Peter. *A Loss of Mastery.* Berkeley: Univ. of California Press, 1966.

Gelley, Alexander. "Ernst Robert Curtius: Typology and Critical Method." In *Velocities of Change,* edited by Richard Macksey. Baltimore and London: Johns Hopkins Univ. Press, 1974.

Gilmore, Michael T., ed. *Early American Literature, A Collection of Critical Essays. Twentieth Century Views Series.* Series Editor Maynard Mack. Englewood Cliffs, N.J.: Prentice-Hall, 1980.

Girard, René. "Tiresias and the Critic." In *The Languages of Criticism and the Sciences of Man,* edited by Richard Macksey and Eugenio Donato. Baltimore and London: Johns Hopkins Univ. Press, 1970.

Goen, C. C. "Jonathan Edwards: A New Departure in Eschatology." *Church History* 28 (March 1959): 25–40. Reprinted in *Critical Essays on Jonathan Edwards.* Edited by William J. Scheick. Boston: G. K. Hall, 1980.

Goldman, Lucien. "Structure: Human Reality and Methodological Concept." In *The Languages of Criticism and the Sciences of Man,* edited by Richard Macksey and Eugenio Donato. Baltimore and London: Johns Hopkins Univ. Press, 1970.

Greven, Philip. *The Protestant Temperament.* New York: Knopf, 1977.

Grisez, Germain. *Beyond the New Theism.* Notre Dame: Notre Dame Univ. Press, 1975.

Group μ [J. Dubois, F. Edeline, J. M. Klinkenberg, P. Minguet, F. Pire, H. Trinon]. *A General Rhetoric.* Translated by Paul Barrell and Edgar M. Slotkin. Baltimore and London: Johns Hopkins Univ. Press, 1981.

Haller, William. *The Rise of Puritanism.* 1938; reprint, New York: Harper and Row, 1958.

Hamilton, Alexander; John Jay; and James Madison. *The Federalist Papers.* Edited by Andrew Hacker. New York: Pocket Books, 1964.

Haroutunian, Joseph. *Piety Versus Moralism.* 1929; reprint, Hamden, Conn.: Anchor, 1964.

Hartman, Geoffrey. "History-Writing as Answerable Style." In *New Directions in Literary History,* edited by Ralph Cohen. Baltimore and London: Johns Hopkins Univ. Press, 1974.

————. *Wordsworth's Poetry, 1787–1814.* New Haven and London: Yale Univ. Press, 1964.

Hawthorne, Nathaniel. *The Blithedale Romance.* New York: Norton, 1958.

———. *The House of the Seven Gables.* New York: Signet, 1961.

———. *The Marble Faun.* New York: New American Library, 1961.

———. *Our Old Home. The Centenary Edition of the Works of Nathaniel Hawthorne.* N.p.: Ohio State Univ. Press, 1970. Vol. 5.

———. *The Scarlet Letter.* Boston: Houghton Mifflin, 1966.

Hedges, William L. "The Old World Yet: Writers and Writing in Post-Revolutionary America." *Early American Literature* 16, no. 1 (Spring 1981): 3–19.

Hegel, G. W. F. *The Phenomenology of Mind.* Translated by J. B. Baillie, 1910; reprint, Evanston, Ill.: Harper and Row, 1967.

Heidegger, Martin. *Being and Time.* Translated by John Macquarrie and Edward Robinson. New York: Harper & Bros., 1962.

Heimert, Alan. *Religion and the American Mind.* Cambridge: Harvard Univ. Press, 1966.

Helm, Paul. Editor's Note. Jonathan Edwards. *Treatise on Grace and Other Posthumously Published Writings.* Edited by Paul Helm. Cambridge: James Clark & Co., 1971.

Higham, John, and Paul K. Conklin, eds. *New Directions in American Intellectual History.* Baltimore and London: Johns Hopkins Univ. Press, 1977.

Holbrook, Clyde A. *The Ethics of Jonathan Edwards.* Ann Arbor: Univ. of Michigan Press, 1973.

———. "Jonathan Edwards and his Detractors." *Theology Today* 10 (October 1953): 384–96.

Hollinger, David A. "Perry Miller and Philosophical History." *History and Theory* 7 (1960): 189–207.

Holmes, Oliver Wendell, *Pages from an Old Volume of Life.* London: Riverside, 1891.

Hoopes, James. "Art as History: Perry Miller's *New England Mind.*" *American Quarterly* 34, no. 1 (Spring 1982): 3–25.

Hornberger, Theodore, "The Effect of the New Science on the Thought of Jonathan Edwards." *American Literature* 9 (November 1937): 196–207. Reprinted in *Jonathan Edwards and the Enlightenment,* Edited by John Opie. Lexington, Mass.: Heath, 1969.

Howard, Leon. *"The Mind" of Jonathan Edwards: A Reconstructed Text.* Berkeley and Los Angeles: Univ. of California Press, 1963.

Howe, Daniel. "Review Essay: Descendents of Perry Miller." *American Quarterly* 34, no. 1 (Spring 1982): 88–94.

Hubbell, J. B. "The Frontier." In *The Reinterpretation of American Literature,* edited by Norman Foerster. 1928; reprint, New York: Russell & Russell, 1959.

Husserl, Edmund. *Ideas: General Introduction to Pure Phenomenology.* Translated by W. R. Boyce. New York: Macmillan, 1931.

———. *Phenomenology and the Crisis of Philosophy.* Translated by Quentin Lauer. New York: Harper & Row, 1965.

Iser, Wolfgang. *The Act of Reading, A Theory of Aesthetic Response.* Baltimore and London: Johns Hopkins Univ. Press, 1978.

Jefferson, Thomas. *Notes on the State of Virginia.* New York: Harper & Row, 1957.

————. *Writings.* Edited by Albert Ellery Berg. Washington, D.C.: Issued under the Auspices of the Thomas Jefferson memorial association of the United States, 1903–04. Vol. 6.

Jones, Howard Mumford. "The European Background." In *The Reinterpretation of American Literature,* edited by Norman Foerster. 1928; reprint, New York: Russell & Russell, 1959.

————. *The Theory of American Literature.* Ithaca: Cornell Univ. Press, 1941.

Kant, Immanuel. *Allgemeine Naturgeschichte und Theorie des Himmels . . . . Werke In Zehn Bänden.* Darmstadt: Wissenschaftliche Buchgesellschaft, 1968. Vol. 1.

————. *Immanuel Kant's Critique of Pure Reason.* Translated by Norman Kemp Smith. 1929; reprint, New York: Macmillan, 1950.

Keller, Karl. "The Loose, Large Principles of Solomon Stoddard." *Early American Literature* 16, no. 1 (Spring 1981): 27–42.

Kenny, Anthony, ed. *Aquinas: A Collection of Critical Essays.* Garden City, N.Y.: Doubleday, 1969.

Klubertanz, George P., S. J. *St. Thomas Aquinas on Analogy.* Chicago: Loyola Univ. Press, 1960.

Kolodny, Annette. *The Lay of the Land,* Chapel Hill: Univ. of North Carolina Press, 1975.

Kristeva, Julia. *La Révolution du langage poétique.* Paris, 1974.

Kuhn, T. S. *The Structure of Scientific Revolutions.* 1962; reprint, Chicago: Univ. of Chicago Press, 1970.

Lacan, Jacques. *The Language of the Self.* Translated by Anthony Wilden. Baltimore and London: Johns Hopkins Univ. Press, 1968.

————. "Of Structure as an Inmixing of Otherness Prerequisite to Any Subject Whatever." In *The Languages of Criticism and the Sciences of Man,* edited by Richard Macksey and Eugenio Donato. Baltimore and London: Johns Hopkins Univ. Press, 1970.

Lawrence, D. H. *Studies in Classic American Literature.* 1923; reprint, New York: Viking, 1966.

Lee, Sang Hyun. "Mental Activity and the Perception of Beauty in Jonathan Edwards." *The Harvard Theological Review* 69 (1976): 364–96.

Lesser, Wayne. "Textuality and the Language of Man." In *Critical Essays on Jonathan Edwards,* edited by William J. Scheick. Boston: G. K. Hall, 1980.

Levin, David. *Cotton Mather.* Cambridge: Harvard Univ. Press, 1978.

————. *Jonathan Edwards: A Profile.* New York: Hill and Wang, 1969.

Levi-Strauss, Claude. *Tristes Tropiques.* Translated by John Russell. New York: Athaneum, 1972.

Lewis, R. W. B. *The American Adam.* Chicago and London: University of Chicago Press, 1955.

————. "Literature and Things." Review of Charles Feidelson's *Symbolism and American Literature. The Hudson Review* 7 (1954–55): 308–14.

Locke, John. *An Essay Concerning Human Understanding.* London and New York: J. M. Dent & Sons, 1965.

Lovejoy, Arthur O. *The Great Chain of Being.* 1936; reprint, Cambridge: Harvard Univ. Press, 1950.

Lowance, Mason I., Jr. *The Language of Canaan.* Cambridge: Harvard Univ. Press, 1980.

———. "Typology, Millennial Eschatology, and Jonathan Edwards." In *Literary Uses of Typology from the Middle Ages to the Present,* edited by Earl Miner. Princeton: Princeton Univ. Press, 1977. Reprinted in *Critical Essays on Jonathan Edwards.* Edited by William J. Scheick. Boston: G. K. Hall, 1980.

Lowman, Moses. *A Paraphrase and Note on the Revelation of St. John.* London, 1737.

Lowrie, Ernest B. *The Shape of the Puritan Mind, The Thought of Samuel Willard.* New Haven and London: Yale Univ. Press, 1974.

Lynen, John T. *The Design of the Present.* New Haven and London. Yale Univ. Press, 1969.

Lyons, John O. *The Invention of the Self.* Carbondale: Southern Illinois Univ. Press, 1978.

McGiffert, Michael. "American Puritan Studies in the 1960's." *William and Mary Quarterly,* 3d ser., 27 (1976): 36–67.

Macksey, Richard and Eugenio Donato, eds. *The Languages of Criticism and the Sciences of Man.* Baltimore and London: Johns Hopkins Univ. Press, 1970.

———, ed. *Velocities of Change.* Baltimore and London: Johns Hopkins Univ. Press, 1974.

Marsh, John. "Preliminary Essay." Samuel Taylor Coleridge. *Aids to Reflection.* 1825; reprint, London: George Bell & Sons, 1904.

Marx, Leo. *The Machine in the Garden.* New York: Oxford Univ. Press, 1964.

Mather, Cotton. *Magnalia Christi Americana.* Edited by Kenneth B. Murdock. Cambridge: Harvard Univ. Press, 1977. Vols. 1 and 2.

Mather, Increase. *Dissertation Wherein the Strange Doctrine . . . .* Boston, 1708.

Matthiessen, F. O. *American Renaissance.* New York: Oxford Univ. Press, 1941.

Melville, Herman. *Billy Budd and the Piazza Tales.* Garden City, N.Y.: Anchor, 1973.

———. *The Confidence-Man.* New York: Norton, 1972.

———. *Moby-Dick.* Boston: Houghton Mifflin, 1956.

———. *Pierre, or the Ambiguities.* Evanston and Chicago: Northwestern Univ. Press, 1971.

Milden, Robert. "*The Last of the Mohicans* and the New World Fall." *American Literature* 52, no. 3 (November 1980): 407–29.

Miller, J. Hillis. *Thomas Hardy, Distance and Desire.* Cambridge: Harvard Univ. Press, 1970.

Miller, Perry. *Errand Into the Wilderness.* Cambridge: Harvard Univ. Press, 1956.

———. *From Colony to Province.* Vol. 3 of *The New England Mind.* Cambridge: Harvard Univ. Press, 1953.

———. "The Half-Way Covenant." *New England Quarterly* 6 (1933): 676–716.

———. Introduction. *Images or Shadows of Divine Things.* Edited by Perry Miller. New Haven: Yale Univ. Press, 1948.

———. *Jonathan Edwards.* 1949; reprint, Cleveland: World Publishing Co., 1963.

———. "Jonathan Edwards on the Sense of the Heart." *The Harvard Theological Review* 41 (1948): 123–45.

————. *Orthodoxy in Massachusetts*. Vol. 1 of *The New England Mind*. 1933; reprint, Gloucester, Mass.: Peter Smith, 1965.

————. *The Seventeenth Century*. Vol. 2 of *The New England Mind*. Cambridge: Harvard Univ. Press, 1939.

Milton, John. *Complete Poems and Prose*. Edited by Merritt Y. Hughes. New York: Merrill, 1957.

Minter, David. *The Interpreted Design, Design as a Structural Principle in American Prose*. New Haven and London: Yale Univ. Press, 1969.

Morgan, Edmund. *The Puritan Dilemma, The Story of John Winthrop*. Boston: Little, Brown, & Co., 1958.

————. *Visible Saints*. New York: New York Univ. Press, 1963.

Murdock, Kenneth. "The Colonial Experience in the Literature of the United States." In *Early American Literature*, edited by Michael T. Gilmore. Englewood Cliffs, N.J.: Prentice-Hall, 1980.

Newton, Isaac. *Isaac Newton's Papers and Letters on Natural Philosophy*. Edited by T. B. Coles. Cambridge, 1958.

————. *Principia*. General Scholium. London, 1713.

Niebuhr, Richard. *The Kingdom of God in America*. New York: Harper & Bros., 1937.

Nietszche, Friedrich. *The Birth of Tragedy and the Genealogy of Morals*. Translated by Francis Golffing. New York: Anchor, 1956.

Nye, Russel. *The Cultural Life of the New Nation*. New York: Harper, 1960.

O'Gorman, Edmundo. *The Invention of America*. Bloomington: Indiana Univ. Press, 1961.

Oleson, Alexander, ed. *The Pursuit of Knowledge in the Early American Republic*. Baltimore and London: Johns Hopkins Univ. Press, 1976.

Opie, John, ed. *Jonathan Edwards and the Enlightenment*. Lexington, Mass.: Heath, 1969.

Owen, H. P. "Morality and Christian Theism." *Religious Studies* 20, no. 1 (March 1984): 5–17.

The Compact Edition of the Oxford English Dictionary. Oxford: Oxford Univ. Press, 1971.

Paine, Thomas. "Common Sense." Edited by Isaac Kramnick. London: Pelican, 1976.

Parkman, Francis. *The Oregon Trail*. New York: New American Library, 1970.

Parrington, V. L. *The Colonial Mind*. Vol. 1 of *Main Currents in American Thought*. New York: Harcourt, Brace, & World, 1927.

Pattee, Frederick Lewis. "A Call for a Literary Historian." In *The Reinterpretation of American Literature*, edited by Norman Foerster. 1925; reprint, New York: Russell & Russell, 1959.

Peyre, Henri. *What is Romanticism?* Birmingham: Univ. of Alabama Press, 1977.

Pierce, David C. "Jonathan Edwards and the 'New Sense' of Glory." *New England Quarterly* 41, no. 1 (March 1968): 82–95.

Poe, Edgar Allan. *Works*. Edited by James A. Harrison. New York: AMS Press, 1965.

Poirier, Richard. *A World Elsewhere: The Place of Style in American Literature*. New York: Oxford Univ. Press, 1966.

Pope, Alexander. *The Poems of Alexander Pope.* Edited by John Butt. New Haven: Yale Univ. Press, 1963.

Priestley, Joseph. *Transactions of the American Philosophical Society* 6 (November 1803).

Ray, John. *The Wisdom of God Manifested in His Creation.* 1691; reprint, 5th ed., London, 1709.

Riffaterre, Michael. *Semiotics of Poetry.* Bloomington: Univ. of Indiana Press, 1978.

————. "The Stylistic Approach to Literary History." In *New Directions in Literary History,* edited by Ralph Cohen. Baltimore and London: Johns Hopkins Univ. Press, 1974.

Riley, I. Woodbridge. *American Philosophy: The Early Schools.* New York: Dodd, Mead, & Co., 1907. Excerpted in *Critical Essays on Jonathan Edwards.* Edited by William J. Scheick. Boston: G. K. Hall, 1980.

Robertson, D. W. "Some Observations on Method in Literary Studies." In *New Literary History,* edited by Ralph Cohen. Baltimore and London: Johns Hopkins Univ. Press, 1974.

Rosenthal, Bernard. *The City of Nature.* Newark: Univ. of Delaware Press, 1980.

Rourke, Constance. *The Roots of American Culture and Other Essays.* Edited by Van Wyck Brooks. New York: Harcourt, Brace & Co., 1942.

Rousseau. Jean Jacques. *Émile. Oeuvres Complètes.* Edited by Bernard Gagnebin and Marcel Raymond. Paris: Gallimard, 1964. Vol. 4.

Rowe, John Carlos. *Henry Adams and Henry James.* Ithaca: Cornell Univ. Press, 1976.

————. *Through the Custom-House.* Baltimore and London: Johns Hopkins Univ. Press, 1982.

Rowlandson, Mary. *Narrative of the Captivity of Mary Rowlandson. Accounts of Captivity and Redemption, 1676–1724.* Edited by Alden T. Vaughan and Edmund C. Clark. Cambridge: Harvard Univ. Press, 1981.

Santayana, George. *Character and Opinion in the United States.* New York: Norton, 1967.

Sayre. Robert E. *The Examined Self: Benjamin Franklin, Henry Adams, Henry James.* Princeton: Princeton Univ. Press, 1974. Excerpted as "The *Autobiography* of Benjamin Franklin" in *Early American Literature.* Edited by Michael T. Gilmore. *Twentieth Century Views Series.* Series Editor Maynard Mack. Englewood Cliffs, N.J.: Prentice-Hall, 1980.

Scheick, William J., ed. *Critical Essays on Jonathan Edwards.* Boston: G. K. Hall, 1980.

————. "The Grand Design: Jonathan Edwards' *History of the Work of Redemption.*" *Eighteenth-Century Studies* (Spring 1975): 300–314. Reprinted in *Critical Essays on Jonathan Edwards.* Edited by William J. Scheick. Boston: G. K. Hall, 1980.

Schiller, Johann Christophe Friedrich von. *Schillers Werke.* Weimar: Harman Böhlans Nachfolger, 1943.

Schneider, Herbert Wallace. *The Puritan Mind.* New York: Holt, 1930.

Seelye, John. *Prophetic Waters, The River in Early American Life and Literature.* New York: Oxford University Press, 1977.

Shea, Daniel B. "The Art and Instruction of Jonathan Edwards's *Personal Narrative.*" *American Literature* 36 (March 1965): 17–32. Reprinted in *Critical Essays on Jonathan Edwards.* Edited by William J. Scheick. Boston: G. K. Hall, 1980.

————. *Spiritual Narrative in Early America.* Princeton: Princeton Univ. Press, 1968.

Shelley, Percy Bysshe. *The Complete Works of Percy Bysshe Shelley.* New York: Gordian, 1965.

Shepard, Thomas. *The Journal. God's Plot, the Paradoxes of Puritan Piety.* Edited by Michael McGiffert. Amherst: Univ. of Massachusetts Press, 1972.

Sheridan, Alan. *Michel Foucault, The Will to Truth.* New York and London: Tavistock, 1980.

Simonsin, Harold. Introduction. In *Selected Writings of Jonathan Edwards,* edited by Harold Simonsin. New York: Ungar, 1970.

Slotkin, Richard. *Regeneration Through Violence.* Middletown: Wesleyan Univ. Press, 1973.

Smith, Henry Nash. *Virgin Land.* Cambridge: Harvard Univ. Press, 1950.

Spencer, Theodore. *Shakespeare and the Nature of Man.* 1942; reprint, New York: Macmillan, 1949.

Spengemann, William C. *The Adventurous Muse.* New Haven and London: Yale Univ. Press, 1977.

———. "Review Essay: Puritan Influences in American Literature, Emory Elliott, ed." *Early American Literature* 16, no. 2 (Fall 1982): 176–86.

Spiegelberg, Herbert. *The Phenomenological Movement.* 2 vols. The Hague: Martinus Nijhof, 1960.

Spiller, Robert. Introduction. In *Toward a New American Literary History,* edited by Arlin Turner and Louis J. Budd. Durham: Duke Univ. Press, 1980.

———, et al., eds. *Literary History of the United States.* New York: MacMillan, 1957.

Stein, Stephen J. Editor's Introduction. In *Jonathan Edwards, Apocalyptic Writings,* edited by Stephen J. Stein. New Haven and London: Yale Univ. Press, 1977.

———. "Jonathan Edwards and the Rainbow: Biblical Exegesis and Poetic Imagination." *New England Quarterly* 47 (Spring 1974): 440–56.

Stempel, Daniel. "Blake, Foucault, and the Classical Episteme." *PMLA* 95, no. 1 (January 1980): 388–407.

Stephen, Leslie. "Jonathan Edwards." In *Critical Essays on Jonathan Edwards,* edited by William J. Scheick. Boston: G. K. Hall, 1980.

Stewart, Randall. *American Literature and Christian Doctrine.* Baton Rouge: Louisiana State Univ. Press, 1958.

Stilgoe, John R. *Common Landscape of America, 1580 to 1845.* New Haven and London: Yale Univ. Press, 1982.

Stone, Lawrence. "Reply" to Michel Foucault. *The New York Review of Books* 30, no. 5 (March 31, 1983): 42–43.

Stovall, Floyd. *The Development of American Literary Criticism.* Chapel Hill: Univ. of North Carolina Press, 1955.

Stowe, Harriet Beecher. *Oldtown Folks.* Edited by Henry F. May. Cambridge: Harvard Univ. Press, 1966.

Suter, Rufus. "A Note on the Neoplatonism of the Philosophy of Jonathan Edwards." *The Harvard Theological Review* 52, no. 4 (1959): 283–84.

Taylor, Edward. *The Poems of Edward Taylor.* Edited by Donald E. Stanford. New Haven: Yale Univ. Press, 1966.

Thoreau, Henry David. *Cape Cod.* New York: Thomas Y. Crowell, 1961.

———. *Walden.* Boston: Houghton Mifflin, 1957.

———. *A Week on the Concord and Merrimack Rivers.* New York: Apollo, 1961.

Tichi. Cecilia. *New World, New Earth.* New Haven and London: Yale Univ. Press, 1979.

Todorov. Tzvetan. *Theories of the Symbol.* Translated by Catherine Porter. Ithaca: Cornell Univ. Press, 1982.

Tomas, Vincent. "The Modernity of Jonathan Edwards." *New England Quarterly* 25, no. 1 (March 1952): 60–85.

Toulman, Stephen, and Jane Goodfellow. *The Discovery of Time.* New York: Harper and Row, 1966.

Trachtenberg, Alan. "The Writer as America." *Partisan Review* 44 (1977): 466–75.

Tracy, Patricia J. *Jonathan Edwards, Pastor.* New York: Hill and Wang, 1979.

Turner, Arlin, and Louis J. Budd, *et al.*, eds. *Toward a New American Literary History.* Durham: Duke Univ. Press, 1980.

Turner, Frederick Jackson. *The Frontier in American History.* New York: Krieger, 1976.

Turrell, Ebenezer. *The Life and Character of the Reverend Benjamin Coleman, Dd.* Boston, n.d.

Van Doren, Carl, *Benjamin Franklin.* New York: Viking, 1935.

———. *Benjamin Franklin and Jonathan Edwards.* New York: Scribners, 1920.

Veysey, Lawrence. "Intellectual History and the New Social History." *New Directions in American Intellectual History.* Ed. John Higham and Paul K. Conklin. Baltimore: Johns Hopkins Univ. Press, 1979.

Watkins, Evan. "Conflict and Consensus in the History of Recent Criticism." *New Literary History* 12, no. 2 (Winter 1981): 348–65.

Webb, Walter Prescott. *The Great Plains.* 1931, reprint, New York: Grosset & Dunlop, 1976.

Weber, Max. *The Protestant Ethic and the Spirit of Capitalism.* Translated by Talcott Parsons. New York: Scribners, 1958.

Whittemore, Robert E. "Jonathan Edwards and the Theology of the Sixth Way." *Church History* 35 (March 1966): 60–75.

Wili, Walter. "The History of the Spirit in Antiquity." In *Spirit and Nature,* edited by Joseph Campbell. 1937, 1945, 1946; reprint, Princeton: Princeton Univ. Press, 1954.

Willard, Samuel. *Complete Body of Divinity.* Boston, 1726.

Wilson, David Scofield. "The Flying Spider." *Journal of the History of Ideas* 32 (July 1971): 44–58. Reprinted in *Critical Essays on Jonathan Edwards.* Edited by William J. Scheick. Boston: G. K. Hall, 1980.

———. *In the Presence of Nature.* Amherst: Univ. of Massachusetts Press, 1978.

Winslow, Ola Elizabeth. *Jonathan Edwards, 1703–1758.* New York: MacMillan & Co., 1940.

Winthrop, Robert C., ed. *Life and Letters of John Winthrop.* 1864, reprint, New York: Da Capo Press, 1971.

Woolman, John. *The Journal of John Woolman.* Secaucus, N.J.: Citadel, 1975.

Wordsworth, William. *Poetical Works.* Edited by Thomas Hutchinson and revised by Ernest De Selincourt. 1904; reprint, London: Oxford Univ. Press, 1971.

INDEX